THE POLITICS AND CIVICS
OF NATIONAL SERVICE

THE POLITICS AND CIVICS
OF NATIONAL SERVICE

LESSONS FROM THE CIVILIAN CONSERVATION CORPS, VISTA, AND AMERICORPS

MELISSA BASS

BROOKINGS INSTITUTION PRESS
Washington, D.C.

Copyright © 2013
THE BROOKINGS INSTITUTION
1775 Massachusetts Avenue, N.W., Washington, D.C. 20036
www.brookings.edu

Library of Congress Cataloging-in-Publication data

Bass, Melissa.
    The politics and civics of national service : lessons from the Civilian Conservation Corps, Vista, and AmeriCorps / Melissa Bass.
        pages   cm
    Includes bibliographical references and index.
    ISBN 978-0-8157-2380-6 (hardcover : alk. paper)
    1. National service—United States. 2. Voluntarism—United States. 3. Civilian Conservation Corps (U.S.) 4. AmeriCorps (U.S.) 5. AmeriCorps*VISTA. I. Title.
    HD4870.U6B37 2013
    361.6—dc23   2012045776

10 9 8 7 6 5 4 3 2 1

Printed on acid-free paper

Typeset in Adobe Garamond

Composition by Cynthia Stock
Silver Spring, Maryland

Printed by R. R. Donnelley
Harrisonburg, Virginia

For Eden, always.

Contents

Preface

"The Political Scientist as Democrat" are the words that open David Adamany's introduction to E. E. Schattschneider's *The Semi-Sovereign People*.[1] In his essay, Adamany writes of "Schattschneider's insistence that scholarship aid Americans in self-government by addressing itself to the theory and practice of democracy."[2] In his commitment to a discipline serving large public purposes Schattschneider was not alone. James Ceaser argues that liberal democracy needs political scientists "willing to engage in a constructive enterprise on [its] behalf"; Harvey Mansfield asks political scientists to decide "whether they have done justice to the American Constitution"; and Raymond Seidelman argues that "until political scientists realize that their democratic politics cannot be realized through a barren professionalism, intellectual life will remain cleaved from the genuine if heretofore subterranean dreams of American citizens."[3]

While these scholars, among others, have different understandings of just what political scientists should be committed to—the Constitution in particular, liberal democracy in general, or American democracy however defined and debated—they believe that political scientists should have normative commitments. This conviction differentiates them from the many who aspire, in Bernard Crick's words, "to take politics out of politics . . . to be neutral, scientifically objective, and 'value-free.'"[4] And importantly, even atypically, they ground their work in real political systems. According to Ceaser, this "normative commitment grounded in reality" is part of what defines traditional political science. From my perspective, this commitment is exactly what defines citizenship. I come to this project with a basic belief that we don't stop being citizens when we start doing political science.

For introducing me to this transformative understanding of citizenship, I owe a debt of gratitude to Harry Boyte, a debt I can only hope to repay through a future full of public work. I am equally indebted to Carmen Sirianni and Steven Teles, who have been exemplary teachers, colleagues, and friends. If I had had the opportunity to work with only one of these professors, I would have thought myself lucky, and I would have been right. Through our many years of shared work, Carmen has never failed to remind me of what is important, each and every time I forget. Steve had even harder tasks: he shepherded me through graduate school and convinced me that I could write a book, and then showed me how. To say that he went above and beyond the call of duty does not even come close; he deserves an award simply for the number of e-mails he answered.

I also must thank the faculty and staff at the Center for Information and Research on Civic Learning and Engagement (CIRCLE) at Tufts University for generously funding my research and writing, and for giving me a collegial refuge on multiple occasions. In particular, Peter Levine offered critical support at this book's start and at its finish. Thanks also to Dan Kryder and Marc Landy for their helpful contributions as members of my dissertation committee and to the Gordon Foundation and the Department of Politics at Brandeis University for supporting my graduate studies that led to this work. The College of Liberal Arts at the University of Mississippi gave me further financial support, and my colleagues in the university's Department of Public Policy Leadership—Dawn Bullion, Robert Haws, Michael Metcalf, David Rutherford, Eric Weber, and especially Christian Sellar—provided the structure and encouragement I needed that enabled me to finish this project after so many years.

For their indispensable inspiration and distraction throughout this project, I must thank my friends, especially Lisa Ferrari, Jan Leuchtenburger, Shirley Schultz, Dianne White, Susan Schantz, Amy Agigian, and Gar Culbert. Thanks also to my teachers—formal and informal—in particular Lew Friedland, Barbara Nelson, Jim Farr, and Stan and Nancy Johnson.

Most of all, I thank my family. My grandparents lived the entire history that I study, and what I learned from them cannot be found in any archive. My sister, who does more public work than anyone else I know, shows me how the principles I study can be put into practice and gives me a model to aspire to. My parents have provided support and encouragement forever: they always let me follow my own path, even when they didn't know where it would lead, and neither did I. That this path led me to work I love is a blessing. That it led me to my daughter is a miracle. Thank you, Eden, for making everything mean so much more.

THE POLITICS AND CIVICS
OF NATIONAL SERVICE

1

Introduction:
National Service as Public Policy for Democracy

In the weeks following the terrorist attacks of September 11, 2001, President George W. Bush encouraged Americans to go shopping and to visit Disneyland. At a time when the president enjoyed near-universal support for his handling of the crisis, this bully pulpit directive fell conspicuously flat. It turned out that Americans wanted their president to ask more of them. Several months later, Bush changed his appeal: he stopped telling Americans to shop and started asking them to serve.

The president's call for Americans to engage in service to their communities and country, echoed by presidents who came before and after him, builds on the nation's long and cherished traditions of local volunteering and citizen service in the military. However, the call for citizens to participate in programs such as the Peace Corps and AmeriCorps is both relatively new and repeatedly contested. The American experience with civilian national service—with federal programs that engage participants in work, at home or abroad, that fills a public need, typically done by young adults paid subsistence wages for a year or two—dates back only to the New Deal and has had a rocky, but instructive, history.[1]

In 1933 President Roosevelt created America's first, largest, and most highly esteemed domestic national service program: the Civilian Conservation Corps. Through the CCC, nearly three million unemployed men worked to rehabilitate, protect, and build the nation's natural resources by planting trees, building dams, forging trails, fighting fires, preventing floods, and more. At the same time, the CCC's enrollees benefited from the program's social environment, job training, and educational opportunities, and contributed to the support of their families. By giving citizens publicly valued and valuable work, the CCC showed what citizens and government could accomplish together. Yet the CCC was America's shortest-lived national service program. Despite its widespread popularity, strong arguments for its continued relevance, and valiant presidential efforts, Congress ended it in 1942. With so much in its favor, why did the program die?

A generation later, President Johnson created America's longest-running domestic national service program: Volunteers in Service to America, or VISTA. Since 1965 and continuing to this day, more than 170,000 VISTA volunteers have fought in the War on Poverty, helping to improve job opportunities, education, health, housing, and more in low-income communities while gaining an in-depth understanding of these communities' needs and capacities. VISTA recruited service- and advocacy-oriented citizens to show what citizens, communities, and government could accomplish together, even in some of our nation's most impoverished areas. Yet VISTA was America's smallest and, historically, least well known and most politically contentious program; in fact, presidents Nixon and Reagan tried to kill it. Lacking many of the CCC's advantages in policy design and development (see box 1-1), how did VISTA survive? And given its hard-won survival, why did it not grow and flourish?

Another generation later, President Clinton created America's current and most wide-ranging domestic national service program: AmeriCorps. AmeriCorps incorporated two preexisting programs—VISTA and the smaller National Civilian Community Corps (NCCC)—and created a large new program—AmeriCorps*State and National—to vastly expand Americans' national service opportunities. Since 1994, more than 775,000 AmeriCorps members have worked to meet the nation's pressing educational, public safety, health, and environmental needs, while learning from the experience and earning money for their higher education. AmeriCorps recruits service-oriented members and instills a sense of service-oriented citizenship to show what citizens, communities, and government can accomplish together. It differs in design (see box 1-1) and history from its predecessors, including incorporating but not significantly expanding two previous programs. Like VISTA, AmeriCorps was threatened by Republican opponents for much of its first decade and beyond. Yet unlike VISTA or the CCC, AmeriCorps lived to be supported and expanded by future presidents, including a Republican, George W. Bush. So although it started in a much less advantageous political position than did the CCC or VISTA, AmeriCorps has done far better. How

Box 1-1. *Domestic Civilian National Service in the U.S.*

	CCC	VISTA	AmeriCorps[a]
Dates	1933–42	1964–93 (joined AmeriCorps)	1993–present
Top enrollment	~500,000/year	~6,000/year	88,000/year[b]
Target participants	Unemployed, needy young men and veterans	College students and graduates; residents of poor communities	Groups mixed by race, class, etc.
Service work	Environmental conservation	Anti-poverty; direct service, capacity building, and community organizing	Education, health, economic opportunity, the environment, and veterans; direct service and local volunteer support
Living arrangements	Residential camps	Poverty communities, at economic level of residents	Independent living (except NCCC)
Structure	Strongly national	National-local partnership	Strongly federated
Remuneration	Room, board, medical care, $30/month (for family)	Poverty-level living allowance, health insurance, modest end-of-service award	Minimum-wage-level living allowance, health insurance, $5,350/year education award
Main understanding of citizenship	Public work (lesser: constitutional, patriotic, service)	Service and advocacy (lesser: constitutional)	Service (lesser: constitutional, patriotic, public work)
Key debates	Permanence: Will we always need national service?	Volunteers' work: Is national service doing what it should?	Validity: Should there be national service? Size: How big should national service become?

a. AmeriCorps comprises VISTA, the National Civilian Community Corps, and AmeriCorps State and National programs. Information current as of July 2012.

b. Some 75,000 members funded through regular appropriations and 13,000 one-time positions funded through the American Recovery and Reinvestment Act of 2009 (stimulus funds).

did it grow in size and support? Further, given this success, why is national service still less available as an option for Americans today than it was at its start, when Roosevelt established the CCC?

This book is an effort to answer these questions—to understand the politics of national service—and to capture these programs' lessons as "public policy for democracy"—to understand the civics of national service.[2] I attempt to explain why, after nearly eighty years, domestic civilian national service has yet to be deeply institutionalized in the United States, and what this means for future national service policymaking. Sociologists typically understand an institution to be a stable, structured pattern of behavior broadly accepted as part of a culture.[3] Both army enlistment and "attending college" are commonly recognized institutions, and national service could be a similar institution if it became widely recognized and supported—by government and society—as a feasible, long-term policy option for addressing the nation's needs and a practical life option for large numbers of young adults.[4] For political scientists, institutions have an influence "on social actors—on who they are, on what they want, on how and with whom they organize . . . such that they change the way these actors engage in politics."[5] Just as the military and higher education act as institutions in these ways, so could national service. Broadly speaking, advocates want national service to become an institution in both senses, and this is in large part what its critics fear.[6]

I also attempt to explain how national service has acted as public policy for democracy—that can "empower, enlighten, and engage citizens in the process of self-government"—and how this process has changed over time.[7] Although national service can serve multiple goals, fostering an ethic of active, responsible citizenship is generally high on the list, particularly given the widespread concern over the state of civic engagement in the United States.[8] Coupled with concern about the country's other pressing needs, this goal has led many to call for expanding and reforming national service.[9] Advocates, however, often *assume* that national service will foster citizenship, paying insufficient attention to different understandings of what citizenship means and how policy designs advance or undermine different conceptions or characteristics of citizenship.

I seek to explain the politics and civics of national service with several ends in mind. First, this work serves to remedy the regrettable lack of even basic documented policy history for VISTA and AmeriCorps beyond their first years and of any documented history for national service as a whole. Second, it furthers our understanding of twentieth-century American political development by comparing programs founded during three distinct political eras—the New

Deal, the Great Society, and the early Clinton years—and tracing the programs over time. To a remarkable extent given their relatively small size, the CCC, VISTA, and AmeriCorps reflect the policymaking ethos and political controversies of their eras, illuminating principles that hold well beyond the field of national service. At the same time, the "start and stop, start over, and start over again" feature of national service program building is atypical and deserves explanation in its own right. Third, this work furthers our understanding of policies' didactic functions, especially as they relate to citizenship and also in ways that extend beyond national service. Finally, it draws lessons from this history and analysis with the goal of informing future policymaking. What ideas should policymakers keep in mind as they seek to make national service an even more effective means of civic engagement and renewal?

When studying national service it is reasonable to ask, why domestic civilian programs and not the military or the Peace Corps? Although the military and the Peace Corps encourage responsible, engaged citizenship, I focus on domestic civilian national service because of its unique political dynamic. No one questions whether national defense is properly a federal government responsibility; many question whether civilian service is. Further, unlike the Peace Corps, domestic national service directly affects domestic political interests. So while military and international service have political ends, domestic national service raises greater concerns about politicization—about who is served, how, and to what end. That said, given that both the military and the Peace Corps significantly influence debate and decisionmaking on domestic civilian national service, I do address them, treating them as "shadow cases."

Within the universe of domestic national service programs, why choose the CCC, VISTA, and AmeriCorps? First, when discussing national service in the United States, journalists, scholars, and advocates focus on these three programs; they are our largest and most recognized. Second, they all enroll large numbers of young people, a demographic group whose qualities of citizenship and levels of civic engagement are of particularly acute concern. Finally, these programs can be easily compared across time.

The book's chapters analyze the programs' policy designs—their causes and consequences—by examining policy debates, the legislative process, administrative decisionmaking, program evaluations, and the content of the policies themselves. In doing so, this work draws mainly upon archival and other documentary research, supplemented by interviews in the VISTA and AmeriCorps cases. This work might be thought of as a large puzzle. For some programs (especially the CCC), in some time periods (such as VISTA's early years and AmeriCorps's founding) and for some issues (such as VISTA's and

AmeriCorps's civic impacts), definitive research already exists: other scholars contribute these pieces, and I gratefully fit them into this larger work. But many pieces remained to be found through original research, including some hidden in boxes not opened in the thirty years since they had been sealed. Thus, this is a work of integration and discovery; its value comes in part from new knowledge and understanding of the individual programs and even more so from the comparisons that multiple cases traced over the span of nearly eight decades allow and the questions that only such temporal sweep allows us to answer.

So, contrary to other types of research, this work is not designed to test hypotheses, although I hope it suggests fruitful avenues for future scholarship of this kind. Neither is it typical policy analysis, measuring the economic costs and benefits of various programs. Instead, it assesses political and civic costs and benefits, and it is my hope that this kind of analysis becomes as standard to policy analysis as economic assessment is. Finally, it draws upon but is not in itself an evaluation of the impacts of different national service programs on participants, communities, and areas of work. Certainly, identifying best civic practices—and further refining how we measure civic outcomes and determine best practices—is critical in designing future policy. However, so is understanding that these practices will be put into action— sanctioned, implemented, and supported over time—only within a political environment that must be accommodated, even if it is to be transformed. Therefore, this work relies on arguments that are not only empirical but also normative and political.

My analysis and explanations principally draw on and contribute to the literature on policy feedback, how policies influence future politics and policymaking. As University of California (Berkeley) political scientist Paul Pierson explains in his seminal article "When Effect Becomes Cause: Policy Feedback and Political Change," policy feedback can operate on multiple levels, in different directions, and through a variety of mechanisms—or may be absent altogether.[10] Pierson differentiates between feedback effects on mass publics and on governing elites, and identifies two major feedback mechanisms— resource and incentive effects, and information and meaning (or interpretive) effects. To give a simple example, through its education program the CCC taught thousands of young men to read, and with this skill these men were better able and more likely to vote. This created a *resource* feedback effect: the program provided a resource (classes that led to literacy) that increased participants' voting rates, which contributed to electoral outcomes and thus to future policy decisions. The CCC's policy of giving its participants time off to vote also promoted voting, creating an *incentive* feedback effect leading to the same outcome. That the CCC treated its participants well led them to believe that government was responsive to citizens' needs. This created an *interpretive* feedback effect: responsive government is worth participating in. Feedback effects are not limited to voting; they include all types of political engagement. They are not always positive: they include making people less likely to become involved and spurring opposition. They are not focused solely on a program's beneficiaries; they can affect a broader public and a narrower group of policy elites. The types of policy feedback effects Pierson identifies are all relevant for untangling the politics and civics of national service, and I draw on them directly and through the scholars who prompted and have furthered his line of inquiry. When assessing how policy can affect politics at the level of mass publics—what I label the "civics" of national service, including both the general public and national service participants—I draw most centrally on works by public policy scholars Anne Larason Schneider and Helen Ingram, and Suzanne Mettler. In *Policy Design for Democracy*, Schneider and Ingram identify core elements found in virtually all policies and discuss how their design can support or undermine citizenship; I use this work to both organize and inform my program analyses.[11] I also draw on Mettler's model for how policies can affect civic engagement, through resource and interpretive effects on citizens' civic capacity and dispositions—in short, citizens' ability and willingness to engage in politics and public life.[12] In my work, I often label this the "teaching" or "lessons" of national service. Mettler uses her model to explain the positive long-term civic impact of the GI Bill on World War II veterans, elaborated on in her award-winning book *Soldiers to Citizens: The GI Bill and the Making of the Greatest Generation*.[13] Although our works differ in method and scope, they share a complementary focus on the civic effects of national service policy in the context of twentieth-century American political development.

Policy can also affect politics and future policymaking at the elite level by influencing elected officials, administrators, and interest groups, as well as the larger institutions in which they work. In seeking to explain the fate of national service programs, I draw on Pierson's general policy feedback work and on the specific policy feedback concept of path dependence.[14] Path dependence is evident when the costs of reversing an established policy grow over time, making major policy redesign increasingly difficult—even in cases where the established policy is suboptimal, or even dysfunctional. That said, redesigns do happen, and a critical question is, what happens then? This is what the University of Virginia's Eric M. Patashnik investigates in *Reforms at*

Risk: What Happens after Major Policy Changes Are Enacted.[15] Patashnik develops a policy feedback model for understanding the outcome of major reforms based on different levels of investment and changes in group identities and affiliation. Although the politics of new programs and of modest reforms to them—the dynamics I study here—differ from the politics of major reforms, the variables and range of outcomes he identifies are highly instructive.

Policy feedback certainly cannot account for all of the nearly eighty-year history of national service policymaking. Both within and across programs, political influences not generated by the policies themselves (or policy more generally) as well as larger changes in modes of governance and political culture play a role, and sometimes take the lead. I explore and explain these dynamics, especially those that highlight changes in norms of policy and policymaking over time. That said, policy feedback dynamics loom large, and one cannot make sense of national service policy history in their absence.

To gain a better understanding of the choices that policymakers have in crafting national service policy, in chapter 2 I explore their options with regard to the role for government, the purpose of national service, the work supported, educational opportunities offered, participants recruited, and requirements and inducements mandated and provided, paying particular attention to their civic and political implications. I also present five aspects of citizenship—constitutional citizenship; critical citizenship; and citizenship as patriotism, as service, and as work. While neither exhaustive nor mutually exclusive, these approaches suggest different goals and designs for national service. It is important to note that I do not offer or use a set definition of *citizenship* when assessing programs. Instead, I have tried to uncover how policymakers, administrators, and others understood citizenship in their times and its relationship to their programs, and to assess the programs against these understandings.

Chapter 2 provides the conceptual background for the empirical case study chapters that follow, on the Civilian Conservation Corps (chapters 3–5), VISTA (chapters 6–8), and AmeriCorps (chapters 9–11). In the first chapter on each program, I explain the program's philosophical and programmatic antecedents and discuss how they fit in (or failed to fit in) with contemporary definitions of national service. In the following two chapters, I explain the program's policy design, how it changed over time, and with what civic and political consequences. In each program's second chapter, I focus on the program's purpose and government role, and in the third on the program's remaining policy elements—more broadly, its "tools, rules, and targets."[16] With this understanding of the programs' histories and development, in the final chapter I explain the paradoxes of national service policymaking and draw lessons for future policymaking.

Regarding the politics of national service, why have programs been so difficult to create and institutionalize, and why have they not built upon one another? Conversely, how do we explain and what can we learn from the hard-won survival of VISTA and AmeriCorps? Answering these questions requires that we look at factors that consistently influenced national service policymaking over time and the larger political dynamics that changed over time. Factors that influenced national service policymaking time and again include national service's centrist appeal and lack of deep, broad-based support; the strong association between specific programs and their founding presidents and parties; and the changing definition of national service itself. These factors typically complicated program creation and growth, and worked against continuity between programs. Larger political factors that influenced national service policymaking include changes in the size and scope of government action, the nature of federalism, the civic experience of government and community organizations, the organization of interest groups, and the meaning and influence of liberal and conservative ideologies. Combined with time-bound events, these factors account for the CCC's demise and the other programs' survival, and AmeriCorps's relative success. Building on these strengths, as well as improving the match between members and their service placements and increasing AmeriCorps's visibility would aid its institutionalization. Expanding the program so that every young adult is able and encouraged to enroll would also accomplish this, but only in the context of forsaking a national service mandate. Paradoxically, the best way to encourage national service and make it an option for all who want it is to abjure the goal of making it a requirement for everyone.

Regarding the civics of national service, why has the connection between national service and citizenship been so variable and frequently so tenuous? And what can we learn from the programs' civic lessons? Changes in civic norms and program priorities largely account for variability, while inattention to the civic, policy, and political lessons of participants' program involvement and service helps account for the programs' weaknesses as civic education. As the CCC and AmeriCorps cases show, national service can make its participants' civic development a priority; they also reveal the limits of making it a priority in add-on fashion. Connecting AmeriCorps's civic education to members' actual service work, emphasizing the many ways people can work to address public problems and thus act as citizens, and more strongly identifying the program with the government that created and funds it can all help AmeriCorps better fulfill its citizenship mission. At the same time, it is critical to recognize the limits of fostering political participation through the program itself, for instance by allowing members to register voters or engage in policy advocacy, given what supporting this type of work would be likely to cost the program in political endorsement. Any effort to improve AmeriCorps as a civic program should not jeopardize the civic lessons it now teaches, by making its survival and growth less likely. In sum, the book concludes with a discussion of the possibilities for, and limits of, crafting a civilian national service policy that strongly supports participants' civic development and is itself strongly endorsed by politicians and the public.

2

Citizenship and the Elements of Policy Design

In the United States the idea of national service has long been contested, always the exception rather than the rule.[1] But there have been exceptions: members of the military service, some conscripted, have ably defended the nation. To channel martial energy into peaceful pursuits, the philosopher William James advocated waging a "moral equivalent of war." Years later President Franklin Delano Roosevelt created a "tree army" through the Civilian Conservation Corps (CCC). President Kennedy's famous words—"Ask not what your country can do for you; ask what you can do for your country"—inspired thousands to join his Peace Corps and later President Johnson's "domestic Peace Corps": Volunteers in Service to America (VISTA). Inspired by these models, President Clinton created AmeriCorps to vastly expand national service opportunities; President George W. Bush expanded both AmeriCorps and the Peace Corps; and President Obama expanded them even further.

In keeping with American tradition, however, the future of U.S. national service remains in flux. It is too early to know whether the historical exceptions will become the future rule on a large scale, especially because even they have come under fire. AmeriCorps faced the threat of significant cuts as recently as 2011, echoing the even more dire threats in 2003, 1999, 1995, and, in fact, for much of the 1990s. VISTA faced similar threats in 1971, 1976, and 1981, and throughout most of the 1970s and 1980s. Even the broadly popular CCC faced large cuts in 1936 and 1941, and by mid-1942, the program suffered the most significant cut possible: it was ended.

None of America's main domestic civilian national service programs—AmeriCorps, VISTA, or the Civilian Conservation Corps—has (yet) been firmly institutionalized, nor have they built upon one another. One goal of this project is to explain why neither of these things has happened. Another goal is to explain the programs' civic missions and impacts. In doing both, understanding policymakers' choices is essential. In *Policy Design for Democracy*, Anne Larason Schneider and Helen Ingram identify six common elements of policy design: goals, agents and implementation structures, target populations, rules, tools, and rationales. In the context of national service, these elements are the role of government (rationales, and agents and implementation structures); purpose of the program (goals); service work supported and educational opportunities provided (tools); participants (target populations); and obligations and inducements (tools and rules).[2] Schneider and Ingram focus on explaining the possible civic feedback effects that policymakers' various choices have on these elements; in my discussion of the specific policy design options available for national service, I will include their possible political feedback effects.

As explained by Paul Pierson and elaborated on by Suzanne Mettler, these policy elements can provide resources and incentives as well as information and meaning (interpretations) that can influence individuals' and groups' capacities and predispositions.[3] Politically, the question is, how do a program's elements positively or negatively affect the ability (capacity) and willingness (predisposition) of elected officials, administrators, and interest groups to support the program? In his work on reform, Eric Patashnik specifically examines the extent to which policies lead to investments and changes in group identities and affiliations to explain their fate, ideas that are helpful in understanding programs' development more generally.[4]

Civically, the question is how do a program's elements positively or negatively affect its participants' and the broader public's ability and willingness to act as citizens? On this latter question, we must recognize that citizenship is a multifaceted and contested concept: it means different things to different people and in different contexts. So, before exploring the potential political and civic feedback effects of different national service policy design options, I explore five views of citizenship, drawn from America's national service programs themselves and expanded upon with reference to contemporary political theory—constitutional citizenship; critical citizenship; citizenship as patriotism; citizenship as service; and citizenship as work. I discuss how national service might support any of these perspectives, in complementary and, sometimes, contradictory ways.

Conceptualizing Citizenship

The very existence and specific content of national service support particular understandings of citizenship; however, decisionmakers rarely explicitly identify them, let alone choose among them. Advocates focus on the ideas behind a policy and typically emphasize those that will unite supporters, not divide them into factions. Policymakers tend to focus on feasibility and efficiency, not abstract theories. Clarity is important precisely because these actors' choices promote and preclude certain understandings largely by default. While national service can support multiple perspectives on citizenship simultaneously, and indeed they overlap in some areas, no program can support all equally. And choices matter: although many believe democracy's success to be inevitable, citizens enable it to function. Therefore, how the United States prepares and engages its citizens as citizens—as rights-bearing, contributing, and committed members of the polity—should be a permanent priority. What qualities are deemed necessary, however, depends on one's perspective—both on what citizenship means and how it is fostered.

Constitutional Citizenship

Citizen usually describes a constitutional legal status: people born or naturalized in the United States are American citizens. Citizenship from this perspective is state-centered and involves legal rights and obligations. Generally, citizens must follow the law and actively support the institutions of our constitutional democracy: representation fails if people do not vote; crisis looms when people demand more from government than they pay for in taxes. However, these principles are not necessarily democratic themselves. As the civic education scholars Joel Westheimer and Joseph Kahne argue, totalitarian leaders also need citizens to obey the law and pay taxes; therefore, these actions "are not about democratic citizenship."[5] Others note that although such habits are not sufficient to sustain a democracy, they are necessary for it.[6] This point is particularly relevant to national service: nothing is inherently democratic about it or its lessons, and totalitarian governments have supported it. But whether national service can encourage democratic citizenship, and whether it must be democratic itself to do so, are important questions.

Complicating things further, not all citizens have their full complement of rights and obligations, especially young citizens.[7] Youth are typically thought to lack a certain knowledge and maturity, so they must wait for full citizenship. These civic disadvantages, however, do not instantly disappear at age

18; and as civic and political studies show, they affect young adults' ability both to exercise their rights and to meet their obligations.[8] Young people need continuing opportunities to develop their civic skills and attitudes, with national service being one possibility. With respect to voting, for instance, through national service participants could be directly taught how to register to vote (or even be required to register) and why voting is important—thereby increasing both their civic capacity and predisposition. Or perhaps simply through their national service experience they might indirectly gain a greater knowledge of and appreciation for what government does, and then want to assert their influence through the ballot. Whether directly or indirectly, through resource or interpretive effects, national service might contribute to constitutional citizenship, although certainly not without question.

Critical Citizenship: Advocacy and Resistance

Although youth overall are less politically engaged than their elders, this is not to say that all youth are politically uninvolved or quiescent: throughout history young people have engaged in political activity that no totalitarian leader would tolerate and few democratic leaders appreciate. Constitutional democracy, however, requires critical as well as compliant citizens. In essence, young activists use their rights—of free speech, assembly, and petitioning—to fight for political change. Change is commonly associated with the left and the goal of expanding government services, but it is also pressed by many on the right, who want to alter or limit government's scope.

National service might support critical citizenship from either perspective. By giving participants an in-depth, close-up experience with government, it could alert participants to shortcomings or limitations they may wish to oppose. Exposing participants to diverse socioeconomic conditions might sensitize them to social injustice or demonstrate that social problems are individual in nature. National service might also directly support advocacy, with participants challenging government policies through their service. Whether directly or indirectly, through resource or interpretive effects, national service could encourage critical citizenship. But whether national service should do this is controversial. Is national service simply an example of a democratic government using its resources to increase democratic participation? Or is it a government program advocating ideologically based criticism of government policy and government itself? This debate raises further questions about the meaning and purpose of national service and citizenship.

Citizenship as Patriotism

A third way of understanding citizenship is as patriotism: feeling a special identification with and affection for one's country, as well as being concerned about and willing to sacrifice for its well-being.[9] National service, particularly military service, is often viewed as a sacrifice citizens should be willing to make for their country. However, by bringing citizens together to protect or improve the country, national service of all kinds can reflect and instill affection, identification, and concern. The emphasis here is on national service's interpretive effects. But whether national service *should* inspire patriotism is just as controversial as whether it should encourage political activism.[10] Patriotism can range from a proper regard for one's homeland to a malevolent disregard for others', from a commitment to helping one's country live up to its ideals to a rationale for excusing its worst failings.[11] Further, given the global, interdependent nature of many problems, others argue that national patriotism is counterproductive and so they stress global citizenship.[12] However, there is even less consensus on the meaning or appropriateness of global citizenship than on citizenship in general.[13] These, too, are reasons that the idea of national service for citizenship is contested.

Citizenship as Service

Fourth, citizenship can be understood as service, overlapping with the patriotic and, through the draft, the legal obligations of citizenship. In the view of military sociologist Charles Moskos, "There is no more basic form of national service than military service," and for much of the twentieth century, the two were largely synonymous.[14] However, since the draft ended, not many young Americans have experienced it. Today fewer than 10 percent of American adults under age 65 have served.[15] Clearly this is one traditional means of nurturing citizenship that has lost its general socializing function.

On the other hand, a sizeable number of young people engage in community service, drawing on a tradition as old and as deep as—and even broader than—military service. Survey results vary, but anywhere from 20 to 36 percent of young Americans report having volunteered in the past year.[16] Community service comprises a range of activities, from volunteering in hospitals and homeless shelters to cleaning up riverbeds and tutoring younger children, to name just a few. Young people are serving through their schools, churches, youth clubs, and groups specifically founded for service. This work is further supported by national organizations such as the Points of Light Foundation, America's Promise, and the Corporation for National and Community Service. To a large extent, national service in the United States has come to mean community service.

From this perspective, citizenship is defined in communitarian terms: by helping those in need and their community as a whole, citizens fulfill their civic responsibilities.[17] This is citizenship located in civil society, not government—complicating discussions of national service, which by definition is connected in some way to the state. Its advocates argue that constitutional, government-centered citizenship is too "thin," leaving citizens with no fulfilling role.[18] Others argue that Americans are learning this lesson too well, disavowing politics as a necessary part of citizenship in favor of charity.[19] However, activist and author Paul Rogat Loeb finds that service can be a "way in" to politics and other forms of civic engagement: students "want to help. They don't want to deal with complicated issues and factions, or the messy contention of politics. Instead, they've revived approaches to involvement that focus on individual service. . . . Yet these same approaches often then lead them back toward larger social change."[20]

Whether service is defined as citizenship in itself, whether it should lead to other forms of engagement, or whether it is related to citizenship at all are contested topics, especially relevant for national service policymakers. If service is citizenship, then participating in national service is not only being a citizen at the time but, through resource or interpretive effects, may be expected to lead to increased service-citizenship in the future. If service is not citizenship but rather a precursor to it, then its resource and interpretive effects should lead to other acts of citizenship, whether voting, advocacy, or the like. What the relationship should be and how to establish it make even this perspective on the relationship between national service and citizenship open to debate.

Citizenship as Work

Finally, there is the work approach to citizenship, which encompasses both individual job-holding and collective public work. The job-holding, or earning, citizenship connection centers on the principles of independence and self-government, the idea that true American citizens support themselves.[21] This is citizenship grounded in the market and has been largely accepted throughout American history. But it has also been justifiably challenged because millions of Americans—including slaves, women, and immigrants—have been denied the opportunity to become self-supporting, have been denied outright the right to work for pay, have faced a lack of available jobs, or had their unpaid labor disregarded. Some effort has been made to sever the connection between citizenship and earning for these (and other) reasons, but typically efforts have sought to open the avenues to paid work to those who have been excluded. National service can and has played this role through both its resource and interpretive effects, providing work to those in need and preparing participants for future employment, although, as always, not without controversy.

National service has also supported a public work understanding of citizenship. The definition of *public work*, as offered by theorists Harry C. Boyte and James Farr, is worth quoting at length. Public work is

> the expenditure of visible efforts by ordinary citizens whose collective labor produces things or creates processes of lasting civic value. . . . It solves common problems and creates common things. It may be paid or voluntary, done in communities, or as part of one's regular job. Public work takes place with an eye to general, other-regarding consequences. It is also work done "in" public—places that are visible and open to inspection. And it is cooperative work of "a" public: a mix of people whose interests, backgrounds, and resources may be quite different.[22]

From the public work perspective, citizens are understood as "co-creators of the public world."[23] As such, public work locates citizenship in all three sectors: the state, the market, and civil society. What matters is not where the work is done but what work is done, how, and with what consequences, in terms of both civic skill development and creation of public goods. In *Building America*, Boyte and Nancy N. Kari argue that voluntary associations, schools, the professions, and government have a largely forgotten history of engaging citizens in public work and that its loss has weakened the ties between everyday life, public life, and politics, and between local communities and the nation.[24] The consequence is that today's Americans have an impoverished sense of democratic citizenship, a sense that national service might be able to strengthen by engaging participants in significant public work.

Citizenship and its relationship to national service are multifaceted and contested. Beyond the tensions described above, national service can be a way for young people to earn their citizenship, to learn citizenship, or to be citizens. While most theorists combine these three elements, what they emphasize affects program design and its lessons. For example, the late conservative intellectual William F. Buckley Jr. principally saw national service as the first, as

Box 2-1. *Different Perspectives on Citizenship*

Constitutional citizenship	Legal status, rights, and obligations
	Connection to national service: service could become an obligation; participants could learn about the workings of government through service
Critical citizenship	Advocacy and resistance
	Connection to national service: service could sensitize participants to injustice or otherwise show need for political change; participants could engage in advocacy though service
Patriotism	Commitment and loyalty to one's country and fellow citizens
	Connection to national service: service could help develop and reinforce patriotism
Service	Fulfilling one's civic responsibilities through helping the community and those in need
	Connection to national service: can directly engage participants in these efforts
Work	Earning/job-holding: fulfilling one's civic responsibilities by supporting oneself and one's family
	Connection to national service: participants may support themselves and their families through service; may learn job skills
	Public work: collective efforts to solve problems or create things of lasting public value, may or may not be paid
	Connection to national service: can directly engage participants in these efforts

"qualifying [youth] for fully active and fully rewarded citizenship."[25] He also saw national service as pedagogy, as "inculcating" citizenship.[26] In both ideas, citizenship is a future state reached through national service. Political theorist Benjamin R. Barber emphasizes service's pedagogical purpose even more strongly, stating that its "primary goal" is "to teach social responsibility and citizenship."[27] However, he also understands service as an act of citizenship, as a "responsibilit[y] of citizens."[28] For him, citizenship is both a present and a future state. Boyte and Kari, while concurring on national service's educative possibilities, even more strongly emphasize its potential to allow youth to be present-day citizens. To the extent that participants are engaged in "visible effort on common tasks of importance to the community or nation" they are doing citizens' work.[29]

In spite of the challenges, there are important reasons to not abandon the idea of citizenship but to strengthen our understanding and use of the concept of citizenship, in this specific policy debate and more broadly. As the signers of the 1994 Civic Declaration argue, "Citizenship offers a unifying creed for a nation struggling to build a strong multiethnic and cross-generational democracy amidst incredible diversity. . . . We draw shared values . . . in the common ground of our shared tasks and obligations."[30]

Any of the citizenship perspectives discussed above can act as this "unifying creed" and can be used to argue in favor of national service. Nonetheless, I believe that the public work perspective, with its emphasis on learning and being a citizen through work, offers a particularly powerful framework for understanding the possible contributions of national service to American democracy. So although I discuss how different policy designs support or undermine citizenship from multiple perspectives, I pay particular attention to its impact on citizenship understood as public work.

Policy Elements

While policymakers rarely define the relationship between service and citizenship explicitly, their implicit assumptions influence their policy decisions and ultimately shape their programs. As Schneider and Ingram explain in *Policy Design and Democracy*, policymakers have a number of decisions to make as they craft a policy, from specifying its role to stating its purpose and the means to accomplish it. Policymakers rarely delineate the full range of options or their potential civic and political implications. Incentives often cause them to blur lines of conflict, but the conflicts always remain; they can be downplayed and deferred but not avoided altogether.

Government's Role

The first question to ask when designing national service policy is what role government should play: the answer can range from total state control to no state involvement whatsoever. Throughout U.S. history, the answer "none" has often prevailed and has remained influential even when there has been support for a civilian national service program, which is one reason that programs have been few and, the CCC aside, small. National service advocates obviously see a role for government but still must decide what form it should take and make the case that it will strengthen and not, as opponents argue, weaken citizenship.

Any Role for Government?

Opponents charge that in national service programs—as in all federal programs—pork barreling, inefficiency, and poor performance predominate. But they also levy charges specific to national service: that it not only fails to strengthen citizenship and communities' capacity but actively undermines them by reducing civic capacity and predisposition. The strength of service in their view is directly related to its distance from government, especially at the national level.

These opponents base their argument on a quintessential American trait, first identified by Alexis de Tocqueville, that here citizens take the initiative to solve public problems. They share Tocqueville's conviction that the more government insinuates itself into civil society, the more citizens' efforts will be displaced, dampening the civic spirit that such efforts nourish and depend upon. They believe America has been trapped for over a hundred years in this vicious circle, and that national service exacerbates it exponentially. Just as bad, opponents say, national service corrupts the very meaning of service. They believe that citizenship, like morality, cannot be legislated and that "a monster-sized new federal program cannot provide people with a desire to serve."[31]

National service advocates obviously answer the question differently, believing that the federal government can play a constructive role. First, they argue that genuine self-government does not require citizens to shun government institutions. Citizens can engage with their government and, if necessary, reorient it to public purposes. Therefore, they say, "civic national service can be an important tool for re-stating the role of government and re-honoring public life."[32] Second, they marshal evidence against the claim that "if government does, citizens won't." For example, in an extensive study, Harvard social scientist Theda Skocpol finds that "for most of U.S. history, politics and government encouraged rather than stifled civil society."[33] Instead of seeing a zero-sum game, in which any increase in government is offset by a decrease in civil society, national service proponents believe that there simply can be more or less public activity. Certainly, people might choose less, concluding that public life is not worth their effort or that it is best left to professionals. These views would legitimately undermine self-government, but advocates believe that national service acts more as an antidote to such views than an accelerant. Even if government organizes the service, citizens still do the work.

Finally, supporters address opponents' most critical charge, that government corrupts the very meaning of service and citizenship. Advocates argue that while neither requires government support, neither precludes it. Government may not be able to legislate civic engagement or instill a desire to serve directly, but, they believe, it can and should provide opportunities, encouragement, and for some, requirements. They cite the fact that government encourages, and has required, military service and mandates jury service.[34] Granted, these activities make unique demands upon participants: neither military nor jury service is an equivalent of civilian national service. Nonetheless, supporters believe that in these cases the language of "service" is still appropriately employed.

What Kind of Role for Government?

Beyond making the case that government has a legitimate role to play in national service, advocates must also set the terms of that role. Will it be large or small, concentrated at the national, state, or local level? A large federal government role will invite strong opposition from national service's critics. However, the nature of the work and other factors might make a centralized program more efficient while also promoting its participants' sense of national citizenship and, if the program is done well, generating public goodwill toward the federal government—a pro or a con, depending on one's view. On the other hand, a state- or locally controlled program will be closer to citizens and could be more responsive while also giving more politicians a stake in its success. Alternatively it may lead to uneven quality, obscure accountability, and reduce the program's coherence and visibility. Thus the potential civic and political policy feedback dynamics vary; they do not point to a "right answer" but to a range of possibilities.

The same holds true for setting the relationship between government and civil society. Concern for administrative ease might lead policymakers to favor a large government role at any level, or more authority might be vested in community organizations, blurring somewhat the lines between the public and nonprofit sectors. Again, this may be a good thing, combining the two sectors' strengths, or it might exacerbate their weaknesses while undermining democratic accountability.

Next, supporters need to place the program within the federal government. Will it be independent or part of a larger agency? Independence can reinforce the importance of national service *as* national service, but independence may also make the program an appealing political target for opponents. If the program is part of a larger agency, will it be housed with programs that do similar work—conservation, poverty relief, education, and so on—or grouped with other service and volunteer programs? The former could help integrate citizen service into agencies' everyday work but also might bury the idea and practice of national service so deep within the bureaucracy as to hide it from view. Grouping different service programs together could reinforce the connections between various types of service—full time and part time, paid and unpaid, by young people and senior citizens—or lead to nonproductive debates over what constitutes true "service."

Finally, the administration must choose its leaders. Will they be recognized national service experts? Will they have extensive government experience? Will they be able to build supportive coalitions within government, between interest groups, and with the public? Political scientists Jameson Doig and Erwin Hargrove find in their study of "entrepreneurs in government" that the most successful agency and program leaders "search for and identify new opportunities for social action, allocate funds and talent to pursue these novel paths, and in time set firmly in place new programs and new strategies."[35] These leaders have the skills and personalities to take advantage of opportunities—and create opportunities—to solidly institutionalize their programs, within government and within society. One way they do this is through framing, and reframing, their program's purpose.

The Purpose of National Service

Providing needed services. Mixing races and classes. Teaching skills and instilling values. Saving alienated, impoverished youth. Saving selfish, overprivileged youth. That national service might accomplish these goals and more is why it has been called "the Veg-o-Matic of domestic policy."[36] Advocates generally support all of these objectives: they want servers to do good and be better for the experience. When pressed to set priorities, however, supporters are often caught in a bind: clarity of purpose is important, but it is also problematic.

Knowing a program's overriding goal is helpful, if not necessary, for answering detailed policy design questions—what work to support, whom to recruit, and so on. It is necessary for evaluation and accountability. No program can do everything, particularly because some goals are likely to be mutually exclusive. Clarity lets administrators identify which of all the things they could do, they must do. Finally, how advocates describe purposes educates participants, staff, and the public, answering questions such as "Why are we doing this?" and "What is national service about?" Which purposes advocates emphasize, and how clearly and consistently they do so, critically affects the "teaching," in this case the interpretive effects, of national service.

Organizing purposes according to priority is not easy. Purposes can be hard to untangle; doing valuable work and gaining skills, for example, are mutually dependent. Even when they are separable, advocates can disagree on their relative value. What is most important: providing opportunities for disadvantaged youth, sensitizing privileged youth, or assembling a diverse group? Given inevitable disagreements, advocates and legislators typically dissemble for the sake of coalition building: approving a program often depends on multiple, unclear purposes, giving lawmakers with different interests different reasons to support it.[37] Nonetheless, programs must be justified, however expansively.

A typical but ultimately immaterial distinction is whether the overriding goal is to benefit the servers or those served. One problem is that it can be difficult to identify who is served.[38] Who benefits when participants plant trees, preserve historical documents, or supervise volunteers building a playground? Another problem arises when those served are identifiable. National service gives young people who are too often seen as deficient and in need of services themselves an opportunity to prove their worth. Often, however, it simply turns participants into service providers and the elderly, children, or those less fortunate into clients. While national service calls on its participants to act as citizens, its broader goal is to encourage citizenship generally. As Barber explains, "The idea is not that one is ennobling those who serve or rescuing those who are served but one that is empowering both."[39] Framing the distinction as one of "server" and "served" undermines this effort.

A common alternative is to draw a distinction between servers and the society they help.[40] However, just as specific goals can be hard to disaggregate, so can benefits. Obviously society benefits when necessary work is being done; clearly servers benefit from what they learn. But who benefits when participants develop a commitment to civic engagement? The servers may live fuller lives, but the nation benefits from their ongoing contributions. Who benefits when servers learn to work across lines of race and class? Participants may be gaining a marketable skill, but the nation benefits from more productive race relations. In short, who benefits when servers become more committed, effective citizens? Participants benefit, but the nation needs citizens at least as much as individuals need to be citizens.

A more useful approach is to ask whether national service should be justified by the work accomplished or by other outcomes, such as citizenship. Moskos argues that "the focus . . . must always be on the services provided," with all other benefits flowing from this.[41] Anything less is wasteful "make-work" that only engenders a false sense of participants' civic self-worth. Others disagree. Barber, for one, argues that the "focus on 'outcomes' and effectiveness

. . . may be politically useful, [but] it diverts attention from the primary goal: to teach social responsibility and citizenship."[42] Similarly, Buckley argues that "the guiding purpose here is the spiritual animation of the giver, not the alms he dispenses."[43]

All of these authors believe that national service can inculcate or express citizenship; the differences lie in how they see the relationship, with implications for everything from program accountability to broad public lessons. They also provide direction for the second-tier questions of policy design, beginning with what work to support.

National Service Work

In deciding what work to support, national service advocates must determine both what is needed and what is acceptable. In arguing for a large-scale program, proponents cite studies documenting widespread unmet social needs, generally defined as publicly valuable tasks that the market finds unprofitable and conventionally staffed government and nonprofit agencies find unaffordable. In their influential 1986 study, Richard Danzig and Peter Szanton identify fifty tasks and settings that could use national service assistance; they estimate that the work could support nearly 3.5 million full-time participants.[44] However, as these authors acknowledge, the whole concept of "unmet social needs" is open to challenge, given that "neither the marketplace nor our political processes have so far found [them] more pressing than other claims. . . . In the absence of evidence of [market and political] failure . . . the net benefit of meeting any such unmet need . . . is presumptively negative."[45] National service proponents counter that the extent and severity of social needs provide ample evidence of failure and that because national service is created through the political process, it is in itself a means by which our politics can signal the priority of these unmet needs.

Even if unmet social needs are worth addressing, a question remains: which are appropriate for national service? Anti–national service libertarians argue none—that if we need, for example, nurses' aides, "we should raise pay, pursue labor-saving technology, [and] allow more legal immigration."[46] Proponents obviously see a role for national service; however, even they acknowledge some work to be untenable. A major concern is that participants might displace permanent workers: national service is supposed to ameliorate social problems, not add to them by increasing unemployment. Unions have strongly criticized national service on these grounds, however. Simply protecting existing jobs is often insufficient to placate labor interests. The unions' interest in staffing the service sector means that they care about future jobs as well—jobs that might be created in the absence of national service.[47] Labor's pull within the Democratic Party—the party most likely to support large-scale national service—ensures that job protection will strongly influence policy design. The downside is that unions will have the most leverage to protect "real" jobs, those that offer the most highly valued work. Making this work off-limits to national service participants has the potential to turn national service into exactly what its critics call it: "make-work" of little public value.

A second concern is that national service work will privilege a particular party or ideology, which raises the question of just what should count as service. Child care is always high on proponents' to-do list. But should participants be allowed to work in church-run centers? Or read Bible stories to children? These questions pique liberals' concern about separation of church and state. Is tutoring immigrants to take the U.S. citizenship exam an impartial service? What about registering new citizens to vote? Republicans in particular may be concerned that participants will encourage people to register for a specific party (presumably the Democrats), that immigrant or poor citizens might be predisposed to one party (again, presumably the Democrats), or that those not willing to register on their own should not be voting at all. Feeding the homeless is the quintessential service activity, but should participants help homeless families apply for food stamps? Teaching schoolchildren to use computers seems wholly unobjectionable. But should participants write grant applications to the Department of Education for a computer lab? Or help students lobby their school board for new computers? Is helping others engage in advocacy considered service? Is advocacy itself service?

Conservative critics argue that the two are inconsistent, that the essence of service is the one-on-one act of care. Radical critics, conversely, argue that advocacy is the only appropriate service, that without an explicit focus on social justice, service merely makes injustice more socially conscionable. Deciding what tasks to permit involves principled questions about service and pragmatic considerations of what Congress and organized interests will accept. In so deciding, policymakers determine not just what work national service will accomplish but what lessons it will teach.

Education through National Service

Asking what participants should learn through their service explicitly raises the question of policy feedback; the answer will influence what work they do and how it is organized, and any formal training they receive. Perhaps participants should learn marketable job skills. If so, their service should directly relate to a regular job, and they should work with skilled supervisors who can ensure they do their service well and prepare them for post-service employment. This is a tall order. Many social needs go unmet precisely because they call for performing low-skill, "dead end" tasks. Limiting national service tasks to those on a career ladder would preclude a great deal of necessary work. Further, work that is too closely related to an existing job is likely to run afoul of union interests, and skilled supervisor-trainers are expensive. Philosophical concerns also enter the picture: Too much focus on job training risks encouraging participants to view service from a "what's in it for me" perspective and undermining the emphasis on participants' contributing, not just receiving, services. So policymakers must weigh the trade-offs in lessons and the costs of teaching them.

Should participants learn leadership and decisionmaking skills? If so, they should help design projects and determine their own tasks. John Beilenson argues: "Asking young people . . . to plan out their work each day, to take turns serving as a site leader, and to spend time investigating the impact [of] their service . . . distinguishes the service experience from entry-level jobs."[48] Such responsibility, however, has a price: by introducing extra uncertainty and "messiness" to the process, it can create headline-grabbing mishaps.

Should participants learn teamwork? If so, participants' service should be group based—conservation or playground building, for example—and not individual, such as home health assistance. The downside is that individual, one-on-one service work might answer a greater need. Promoting cross-cultural understanding also requires group work, and a diverse membership. A residential program giving participants experience living with people different from themselves would also help. To promote multicultural learning across communities and the country, participants might serve far from their familiar territory—westerners serving in the South, urban youth in Appalachia, as well as the more typical suburbanites in central cities. Participants would also have to work with neighborhood residents directly, as opposed to providing "indirect service" in social service offices dominated by a more uniform bureaucratic culture. All of these choices have trade-offs. Sending participants across country or providing housing dramatically increases costs. Exposing participants to unfamiliar cultures and locales comes at the expense of increasing their commitment to their home communities. Requiring direct service limits participants' chances to learn to navigate the myriad organizations, institutions, and systems that increasingly affect individuals' and communities' well-being. It also reduces participants' leverage: in the time it takes to tutor one child, a participant might recruit and schedule community volunteers to tutor half a dozen.

In addition to teaching these lessons through experience, national service can offer diverse formal learning opportunities. They all strive to enhance the national service experience, but they can distract from it, too, leaving policymakers to weigh their civic and political costs and benefits.

High school completion and college prep classes might be offered or required, especially in programs geared toward disadvantaged youth. Although not specifically civic, given that education level correlates positively with civic and political participation, the classes would serve civic ends.[49] In that sense, they lend a civic dimension to the post-service education awards that national service programs may offer: if the awards allow participants who otherwise could not afford college to pursue higher education, through resource effects the awards increase the likelihood of their recipients' future civic engagement. Further, if the dynamic that Mettler found with the original GI Bill still holds today, the awards may increase civic engagement through interpretive effects as well.

Policymakers also might offer specific citizenship-related education and training, with various approaches reflecting different understandings of what citizenship requires and how it is best fostered. One option is the civics approach, through which participants learn about the structure and function of government. National service can provide a concrete context: participants could study how the program moved from idea to bill to law, learn how it is administered, and examine its support. "Current issues" is another approach. Participants could learn about domestic and international problems, discuss political and policy debates, and learn how to access and evaluate information. Again, these lessons could be placed in the context of the participants' service. Those working with the homeless could learn about the problem's causes and extent; those serving in schools could attend school board meetings; and so on.

One criticism of service as civic education is that service by itself does not increase participants' likelihood of becoming politically active.[50] Civics and current issues programs might increase participants' political knowledge and interest and could act as a bridge between their service experiences and the realm of government, public policy, and politics. At the same time, civics courses are often criticized for teaching an unreflective acceptance of America's political institutions, and neither civics nor current issues programs typically focus on helping participants develop civic and political skills.

A third option is to offer exactly this. No one is born knowing how to write letters to public officials, chair meetings, speak in public, or organize fundraisers, yet those who can are more likely to be involved in politics and public life.[51] Learning these skills in conjunction with national service could increase participants' effectiveness and their future civic and political engagement. However, this kind of skills training has its own critics because "placing technique at the center of service trainings weakens a potentially powerful opportunity to engage people in . . . civic ideas and concepts."[52] More on this shortly, but first to the most common approaches for connecting learning with service—diversity training and reflection activities.

Breaking down racial and class barriers is a key goal for many national service advocates, and many a service participant has navigated ropes courses, engaged in trust-building exercises, and attended cultural sensitivity sessions. Given America's social relations, it is hard to take issue with efforts to break down these barriers. Nonetheless, their effectiveness and appropriateness are open to question. For example, former White House national service staffer Robert Gordon describes "the shoe game," a "sensitivity-building exercise" in which participants "don someone else's footwear and discuss what it felt like." Gordon came away believing that "limited federal funds shouldn't be spent on the shoe game."[53]

Reflection activities are often part of diversity training but are also used more broadly. Through journal writing or discussion, they invite participants to think about their service. What have they found difficult, surprising, or inspiring? What are they contributing and learning? Reflection is designed to make service's implicit lessons explicit. In Buckley's book *Gratitude*, a fictional character, Robert Ely, serves for a year in a nursing home. Years later, when asked how his service changed him, Ely doesn't have an answer.[54] Reflection proponents think that service participants should be able to do much better. Critics, on the other hand, question the value of discussing service as opposed to just performing it or, if they support discussing, of doing so in highly personalized terms. The latter support conceptual and political training and discussion.

What might this look like? Civic scholar Scott J. Peters suggests discussing the meaning of citizenship, democracy, and politics, and "teach[ing] a repertoire of concepts that are useful in helping people 'map' and negotiate their political environments," including power and interests.[55] Political theorist Eric Gorham offers an explicit critique of Buckley's Robert Ely, asking, "Did he learn citizenship? Did he learn how to reason? . . . Did he learn *anything* about the politics, economics, and issues surrounding service?"[56] Had Ely served in a Gorham-designed program, he would have participated in discussion groups emphasizing "countersocialization and countereducation, the development of reflective skepticism, and the inculcation of casuistic reasoning."[57] This approach is a long way from Moskos's admonition that "the focus of national service must always be on the services provided," with citizenship flowing from the performance of civic duty, and critics abound among both supporters and opponents of national service.

Who Participates?

National service's work and education goals depend in part on who is serving, and one heated debate concerns who should participate. Supporters typically advocate national service for young adults, those who have not yet started careers or incurred family obligations that would be disrupted and who are typically capable of physical labor that equally unencumbered senior citizens might not be. Further, supporters emphasize a pedagogical rationale, with national service conceived of as a "rite of passage" with staying power: when youth and young adults engage in service, they are more likely to continue.[58] Conversely, if people do not serve when they are young, they are less likely to do so later in life.[59] Critics, however, argue that a focus on young adults penalizes those least capable of political resistance; excuses elders from addressing problems their generation created; and demonstrates hostility toward youth, who would "become slaves for several years doing the dirty work of society."[60] These charges notwithstanding, efforts to increase older adults' participation have had more to do with spreading service opportunities than displacing youth.

Even with a focus on youth, *which* youth remains a question. Should national service target the privileged, the disadvantaged, or all classes? In his 1910 essay "A Moral Equivalent of War," James argues for conscripting the "gilded youth." While the less privileged will do hard work regardless, without national service the wealthy might live their entire lives in "unmanly ease."[61] Three generations later, Moskos echoes this sentiment, asking, "What kind of society excuses its privileged from serving?"[62] Critics, however, see national service as a benefit squandered on the well-off (if it is voluntary and offers rewards) or a waste of the time and talents of the nation's best-educated (if it is mandatory).

Others favor the poor, arguing that they have the most to gain, not only financially but also through "the value of the experience itself and the sense of attachment to the community."[63] They also believe that compared with traditional anti-poverty programs national service is more effective. Moskos argues (referring to military service, but he generalizes to national service overall) that "whatever success the military has had as a remedial organization for deprived youth derives largely from its association with nonmarket values, such as national defense" and precisely because it is not a welfare agency.[64] What supporters see as effective, beneficial, and "infinitely more progressive than the status quo," critics see as an attempt to "force low-income kids to build roads and empty bedpans."[65] If service is mandatory, the force is direct; if it is the only way for low-income youth to pay for college, the force is indirect, but it is still force.

Finally, many supporters favor a mix of participants. Moskos observes, however, that "civilian service has persistently suffered from class polarization," with programs targeted toward the elite and others toward the poor, with little for those in between.[66] One way to ensure a mix of participants is to make national service mandatory; barring that, skillful use of incentives is required. But, like everything else, these policy elements are contested.

Obligations and Inducements

No single issue inflames national service opponents more than the thought that it might become obligatory. At best, they believe it to be a contradiction in terms—"forced volunteerism"; at worst, a form of slavery.[67] Thus, critics oppose not only compulsion but voluntary programs that they fear may lead to compulsion. As a result, Moskos argues that "if the fears about mandatory service could be assuaged, the opposition to comprehensive voluntary programs would surely diminish."[68] Consequently, most national service supporters propose voluntary programs and distance themselves from mandatory designs. But while some—most notably Buckley—truly do not aspire to compulsion, others merely find it impolitic, and others, such as Barber, fail to heed Moskos's admonition altogether.[69] In fact, Barber believes that optional programs will leave those who are most in need of service's pedagogical benefits relegated to second-class citizenship because they "are, in fact, least likely to volunteer."[70] For Barber, inducements are insufficient. For other supporters, they are key, and for opponents, they are just one more error.

Inducements can be positive or negative, although the lines between them, and between strong inducements and compulsion, are fuzzy. Negative inducements could range from a tax surcharge or the loss of student loan eligibility to suspension of young adults' favorite, their driver's license. Positive inducements run a similar range, from living stipends and student loan forgiveness to vouchers for a down payment on a house. Inducements are typically seen as necessary to attract especially middle-class or wealthy participants to a voluntary program, and living stipends and paid expenses are needed to enroll disadvantaged youth.

Opponents believe that inducements, just like requirements, are inconsistent with service, that material gain (or threat) negates its altruistic, character-building effect. "Indeed," Bruce Chapman of the Discovery Institute argues, "when coercion or inducements are provided . . . the spirit of service is to that degree corrupted."[71] "Paid volunteerism" is another favorite contradiction in terms. But even those who value rewards have to determine their kind and level. Gorham, for example, supports paying servers a "decent wage" (otherwise they are simply exploited workers) but does not believe they should get special privileges, which would undermine their integrity.[72] Others believe that service requires sacrifice, that at minimum participants should forgo more than they receive. An Ivy League graduate who passes up a Wall Street job to join a national service program would be making such a sacrifice. But what about the high school graduate who could not find other work? The two participants might provide exactly the same service, but only one has sacrificed to do so.[73] Others hold that service's tangible benefits to society should outweigh servers' benefits.[74] Thus, participants' compensation should be less than their labor's value. For others, the key is reciprocity, that participants and the public should benefit from one another. Moskos concludes *A Call to Civic Service* on this note, arguing that "national service conceives a . . . balanced approach to citizenship. 'Ask what your country can do for you,' " he urges, " '*and* what you can do for your country.' "[75] The choices are many, and they matter, not least of all for the lessons they teach.

Policy Combinations

Policymakers have many policy design choices, but often these choices hinge upon one another or, conversely, are incompatible. To a degree policy elements cluster together, forming distinct models. One model can be viewed as national service done in communities; another as community service supported by the national government. A mandatory, residential program run directly by the federal government that brings together diverse participants who work in teams and wear uniforms will be most strongly national, although its work will still be done in local communities. Conversely, a locally administered program run through existing nonprofits that recruits area participants and fully integrates them into the organization's ongoing work will be most strongly community based, although still supported by the federal government. Each of these models can be followed more or less faithfully and,

Box 2-2. *National Service Policy Elements*

Government's role	Should government be involved at all?
	If yes, should government's role be large or small, concentrated at the national, state, or local level?
	What role should nongovernmental organizations play?
	Where should the program be housed within government, and who should lead it?
Purposes	Is the priority for servers to benefit or those being served/society?
	Should the priority be work or other outcomes?
Work	Should servers engage in direct service, indirect service (leveraging, capacity building), advocacy, or a combination?
	Issues include displacement of regular workers, and potential for work to privilege a party or ideology
Education	Should participants learn job skills, leadership and decisionmaking, teamwork, or cross-cultural understanding, or a combination?
	Should academic courses be offered?
	Should citizenship education be offered, and if so, should it emphasize civics, current issues, technical civic skills, diversity training, reflection, conceptual training, or a combination?
Participants	How youth-focused should the program be?
	Should recruitment emphasize the disadvantaged, privileged, or middle class?
	Should race and class mixing be a goal?
Obligations and inducements	Should service be mandatory?
	What, if any, inducements should be offered? Penalties for not serving or benefits for serving, or both?
	Should the program emphasize sacrifice or reciprocity?

when supplemented by other policy elements, create unique programs with equally unique political and civic feedback effects.

Over time the United States has chosen various designs for national service, and sometimes has chosen not to have national service at all. We have pursued different models; supported different purposes, kinds of work, and educational goals; recruited different kinds of participants; and offered different rewards. The following chapters describe the choices that policymakers made at three points in time, during the 1930s, the 1960s, and the 1990s, when they created the Civilian Conservation Corps, VISTA, and AmeriCorps, respectively. These chapters also explore the civic and political consequences of policymakers' choices as they played out over time, interacted with larger political forces, and set the stage—or not—for future policymaking.

The Civilian Conservation Corps

D rive through almost any American state or national park and most likely you will find a marker commemorating the work of the Civilian Conservation Corps. For nine years—from 1933 to 1942—the CCC put over three million unemployed men to work rehabilitating, protecting, and building America's natural resources; their work remains of environmental consequence today. The CCC also had important civic and political consequences. Although not considered so at the time, it was America's first, and largest, civilian national service program; understanding its lessons as public policy for democracy and its development and demise is central to assessing the possibilities and limits of national service more broadly.

Civically, the CCC influenced how its participants and the public understood their relationship to government and the meaning of citizenship. The principles of reciprocity and collaboration between government and citizens were central. The CCC emphasized a work-based approach to citizenship but also incorporated constitutional, patriotic, and service understandings. Sometimes it viewed CCC enrollees as present-day citizens, sometimes as citizens in training. This conceptual diversity reflects the contested nature of American citizenship and prevailing cultural norms. Most striking, however, was the sheer pervasiveness of the language and idea of citizenship. The CCC had an explicit, formative, civic mission: to create citizens. In no other national service program, past or present, has citizenship been such a driving, central concern.

Politically, the CCC was never deeply institutionalized, nor was it used as a model for future national service policymaking. Well recognized and strongly supported, the CCC certainly had institutional potential. Its support, however, was largely contingent on the Great Depression; it was conceived as a short-term measure and, despite attempts by the Roosevelt administration, never achieved the permanence that institutionalization requires. Its influence on future policymaking was thus limited: it is hard to build upon a program that no longer exists. The intimate connections between the CCC and President Roosevelt, the Democratic Party, and the New Deal era also limited its future influence and foreshadowed a pattern that over time has facilitated and constrained the creation and development of America's national service programs.

3

The CCC's Roots and Relationships

In his first inaugural address, President Roosevelt declared that the "nation asks for action, and action now. Our greatest primary task is to put people to work."[1] Within a month and a day, the promise of action yielded the Emergency Conservation Work program, better known as the Civilian Conservation Corps. Three months later nearly 275,000 men were working in the nation's forests.[2] That government might work with such speed, and on this scale, is extraordinary; that it occurred through the cooperation of four federal government departments—Labor, War, Agriculture, and Interior—all coordinated by an independent agency nearly devoid of staff is a near-miracle. What was this program that inspired such feats, and where did it come from?

The CCC's Roots

The premise of the CCC was simple: take unemployed young men and older veterans from families on or in need of relief—what we call welfare—and have them do "simple work . . . forestry, the prevention of soil erosion, flood control, and similar projects."[3] Enrollees lived in forest camps and, in exchange for their labor, received room, board, and $30 a month—nearly $500 a month in 2010 dollars—most of which they sent home to their families. The Department of Labor selected the enrollees, Interior and Agriculture planned and supervised the work, and the Army was in charge of the camps.[4]

Identifying the inspiration for the program is harder. Despite the fact that several European countries had work programs, national service scholars

Kenneth Holland and Frank Hill argue that they had negligible influence on the creation of the CCC; domestic influences, including practical small-scale programs and a broadly amenable culture, were determinative.[5] Before 1933 a number of U.S. cities and states had developed camps and forest work programs. As governor of New York, Roosevelt gave 10,000 men temporary employment planting trees as part of the state's reforestation program.[6] California had a program that foreshadowed the CCC even more closely: in 1932 it was running thirty camps for indigent men, who worked in state forests and on highways.[7] These efforts hinted at what might be done, but still, no one had experience running a program that would recruit younger participants, assist their families, transport many of them across the country, and operate on a scale that from its start was almost one hundred times larger than California's program ever was.

What the CCC could draw on for inspiration was America's experience as a settler nation and its cultural proclivity to mythologize work, particularly in the outdoors. As the previous chapter explained, work in America has strong civic dimensions. In arguing for work programs over cash relief, Roosevelt said that "the overwhelming majority of unemployed Americans . . . would infinitely prefer to work."[8] For him and others, the statement was nearly tautological: Americans want to work because working makes them American. Further, beyond valorizing work, Americans valorized work in the country. As Holland and Hill explain, "Living in and working from temporary shelters and pioneer battling with the wilderness were . . . in the American blood."[9] Drawing on this legacy, the CCC offered something of the pioneer experience to its modern, twentieth-century youth, an experience widely believed to be physically, morally, and civically fortifying. In Hill's assessment, "the whole earth-and-work association was a constructive thing" and conducive to building public support.[10]

Beyond shaping popular culture, these beliefs influenced America's philosophers: William James certainly drew on them when advocating a universal conscription of young men into an "army enlisted against nature."[11] If James's idea had any bearing on the CCC's founding, however, it would have been through Franklin Roosevelt—the individual most responsible for its genesis. And although Roosevelt had known James in college, his inspiration for the CCC was personal, not academic: as CCC historian John A. Salmond characterized it, "Roosevelt's love of the land was both passionate and total."[12] As a state senator, vice presidential candidate, and governor, Roosevelt consistently pressed for conservation measures, becoming a national environmental leader. It is no surprise that his first effort at work relief as president was the CCC and that "of all the New Deal agencies, [the CCC] was his personal creation."[13] Presidential leadership here was critical, just as it has been with subsequent national service programs. FDR's commitment helped ensure overwhelming passage in Congress and helped the program garner public attention. Presidential leadership, however, had both limits and drawbacks then just as it has in later programs. Over time, factors aside from the president's role accounted for congressional and public support or lack of support for the CCC, and in the end, no amount of presidential devotion could save it.

The CCC as National Service

In retrospect, the national service elements of the CCC are clear. It was a federal program that engaged its participants, mostly young adults, in full-time, short-term, subsistence-wage work that filled a public need. During its lifetime, however, the CCC was not seen as national service, a fact that contributed to its demise. Because it was created foremost to address mass unemployment, policymakers and the public categorized it principally as a relief measure. Further, it did not fit the prevailing military and Jamesian definitions of national service; observers readily perceived it as a relief effort but not as national service. Finally, its supporters had reasons for keeping it that way. A national service framing might have enabled the CCC to survive past its ninth year, but it also might have killed it at conception.

The CCC and the Military

To the extent that national service fit the American context, it was closely associated with military service. Given the Army's large role in running the CCC, the Corps might eventually have been seen as national service by association. However, despite the CCC's being called a forest army or tree army complete with "soil soldiers," the *civilian* in its name was there for a reason. The CCC was not regarded as national service in this military context,[14] and the military and the Roosevelt administration wanted to keep it that way. The only reason the Army ran the camps was that it knew how to manage men and materiel on a mass scale and on short notice. Drafted into CCC service, the Army leadership on the whole considered it a distraction.[15] There were exceptions: most officers on CCC duty quickly warmed to the task, finding it "far more interesting and challenging than routine peacetime duties."[16] Others advocated military training for enrollees to strengthen the Reserves. The former found strong support within the administration; the latter were promptly silenced. Roosevelt's appreciation for the Army's enthusiasm went only so far.

Given FDR's insistence on Army involvement, why the ambivalence? The Army's role was controversial not only within the War Department but among Americans. The administration anticipated opposition from "a public largely pacifistic at heart" and faced it from liberals, pacifists, and union leaders.[17] As a result, when the CCC's director, Robert Fechner, promoted the program, he rarely failed to issue a variant of this disclaimer: "The CCC is not a military organization. . . . There is no drill nor target practice; there is no heel-clicking nor saluting. . . . [CCC] men are trained not to be soldiers but to be good citizens."[18] This message became so ingrained within the CCC that even when the nation was in dire need of soldiers, the program held fast to its civilian identity, limiting any chance that its role would be understood as, or as including, military service. Ironically, emphasizing the CCC's nonmilitary nature, to counter the immediate-term negative policy feedback of organized opposition to the Army, eventually created a longer-term negative policy feedback effect: the policy meaning that administrators took from the effort undermined their capacity to ensure its continuation in changing circumstances.

Still, people made connections that could have helped to reframe the CCC. Contemporaries certainly hinted at the CCC's national service dimensions: they spoke of the two million who had "served their country" by 1937 and of current enrollees rendering "a real service to the Nation."[19] Second, many saw CCC service as solid preparation for military service. In 1941, for example, James McEntee, who succeeded Fechner as CCC director, wrote that "had it not been for the . . . CCC program, a great segment of the man power now equipped for effective national service would have been wasted."[20] Third, some thought that the CCC could become a national service program as part of an even larger comprehensive national service plan. In 1940 Representative Jerry Voorhis (D-Calif.) introduced a National Service Act that would have required all young men to serve a year in the military or a civilian agency; the CCC would be among their options.[21] These efforts notwithstanding, the CCC still never acquired a national service identity from its intimate, but strictly bounded, relationship to the military. However, this was not the only option. The CCC also could have drawn on the national service legacy of William James.

The CCC and William James

Although he was not responsible for the CCC, James introduced America to the idea of civilian national service. Because of this close association, the fact that the CCC diverged from James's model actually made it harder to recognize it as national service. And although a few innovators attempted to move the CCC closer to James's ideal, in general policymakers were content, or even determined, to keep their distance.

The CCC was a Jamesian "army enlisted against nature," but James's compulsory, universal ideal and rhetorical emphasis on conscripting "gilded youth" were untenable as CCC policy. Given the Great Depression, the program had to be targeted to the needy; further, any hint of compulsion would have confirmed union fears of "labor regimentation" and encouraged charges of communism, fascism, or both.[22] These ideological concerns highlight another reason that CCC supporters typically eschewed the national service label: European governments, most notably Hitler's Germany, had national service; the United States did not.[23] At the same time, the need for transatlantic ideological contrast led supporters to stress the CCC's democratic purposes—communicating a larger vision for the program.

Certainly some supporters connected the CCC and James, either seeing it as "a practical fulfillment of James's idea" or wanting it to be.[24] In fact, in 1941 a group of college-educated youth, advised by a sociologist who helped set up the early work camps of the Weimar Republic, organized an experimental CCC camp based on James's philosophy.[25] Their goal was to create a non-Army-run, self-governing "leadership training" camp with participants from all classes, whose work would be determined jointly with the local community. With solid support from the president and the Department of Agriculture, Camp William James opened but immediately floundered because of internal conflicts and external political challenges. The sum of the critiques was that the camp was a "starry-eyed and impractical" experiment that was run by a presumed fascist and allowed the "pampered sons of rich families" to "usurp . . . relief meant only for the nation's underprivileged."[26] The experiment lasted less than two months. And while it neither appreciably contributed to the CCC's demise nor dimmed broader prospects for civilian national service, it did nothing to aid either cause. To this day it serves to highlight the difficulty of fully integrating participatory democratic principles into national service.

How administrators and participants, elites and the broader public framed the CCC—in relationship to American history, culture, and philosophy, and as national service or otherwise—influenced its effectiveness as public policy for democracy and its place in policy history. The CCC's framework proved necessary for its creation and allowed it great success for a time, but it was insufficient for the larger task of institutionalization. Its framework, however, was not solely responsible for this shortfall; its programmatic elements followed the same pattern.

4

The CCC's Purpose and Government's Role

A program such as the CCC comprises multiple, overlapping elements that influence its political support and viability and communicate lessons to participants and the public, in large part through policy feedback dynamics. In short, these elements shape the politics and civics of the program, which in turn influence future policy development. Drawing on Anne Larason Schneider and Helen Ingram's framework, these elements include the program's purpose (goals) and the role it gives to government, including how government's role is organized and supported (rationales, and agents and implementation structures).[1] These elements are the focus of this chapter; the program's "tools, rules, and targets"—the service work it supports, its educational goals and content, the type of participants it recruits, and its obligations and inducements—are covered in the next chapter.

Politically, the CCC's design generated much support, but efforts to translate this support into long-term viability faltered. The CCC was not originally designed for institutionalization, and modifying the program to achieve it sometimes backfired, and always fell short. Civically, the CCC stressed the principles of reciprocity and collaboration—most strongly early on—while emphasizing citizenship in its work and other variations strongly throughout its history. Indeed, citizenship was a central justification for the program, beginning with its purpose.

The Purpose of the CCC

Over the CCC's nine-year history, its purpose expanded and its emphasis changed, with new goals layered atop previous ones. The CCC began with the twin purposes of work relief and conservation, evolved into a youth training program, and finally tried to be a program for national defense. Policymakers made these shifts mainly by recasting what the CCC had always done, so as to minimize the risks associated with changing a popular program. Their efforts, however, yielded weak results. In the language of policy feedback, over time the CCC's purposes failed to create sufficiently strong, positive, political meaning effects: what the program meant to citizens and policymakers did not change enough to fit radically changing circumstances. Civically the record is more mixed, but ultimately the shift away from the national service framing implicit in the work relief–conservation focus and the move away from seeing enrollees as working citizens lessened the program's civic impact. Both of these developments, the political and the civic, contributed to the CCC's eventual demise.

Work Relief and Conservation

However the CCC is described—by Congress's awkwardly titled "Act for the Relief of Unemployment through the Performance of Useful Public Works and for Other Purposes"; in FDR's words "conserving not only our natural resources but our human resources"; or by its own label of its work as "reforestation and relief"—it embodied twin purposes from the start.[2] To a remarkable extent these purposes dovetailed; although not equally important, they were seen as largely interrelated and complementary. This harmony led to a high level of programmatic coherence that supported the principles of reciprocity and collaboration and communicated a sense of citizenship, particularly a present-oriented, work-based understanding.

Equal billing aside, unemployment relief—not environmental conservation—was the CCC's sine qua non. Again, FDR's "greatest, primary task [was] to put people to work." The civic rationale was clear: citizens (men at least) worked and earned, and without jobs, millions might lose—or never gain—their standing as wage-earning citizens. Furthermore, work could, and should, create things of value to the country: citizens also did *public* work. Scott Leavitt of the U.S. Forest Service explained the connection in 1937: Through the CCC, "the threatened resources of America's youth . . . were sent to the rescue of the devastated and endangered resources of the forest. . . . And it came to pass that in applying the remedies of regeneration to the land, the young men themselves have correspondingly and likewise benefited."[3] Such sentiments echoed throughout the CCC, often manifesting as protest against the charge that the CCC did "make-work." Speaking on its fourth anniversary, CCC Director Fechner argued that "the jobs needed the men as badly as the men needed the jobs. We did not engage in any 'made work,' but we do feel that in thousands of instances we made men."[4] By working at needed and valuable jobs, CCC enrollees were understood to be doing the work of citizens.

The benefits to the participants and society were seen as similarly intertwined. Obviously the enrollees benefited from the economic and educational opportunities the CCC provided, and the public and posterity reaped the environmental benefits of their work. Workers supported their families, communities near the camps profited, and the country benefited from a generation of young citizens "saved." This sense of reciprocity was coupled with a strong belief in collaboration, that together participants and the government could address the nation's severe challenges. As described by enrollee Allen Cook, the CCC "was not only a chance to help support my family but to do something bigger—to help on to success this part of the president's daring new plan to down Old Man Depression."[5] In both respects, participants were doing public work. Moreover, at a time when the Depression created a crisis of confidence as severe as the crises afflicting the economy and environment, this attitude conveyed a deep sense of hope and possibility for change that also became a shared, public good. In FDR's words, the CCC's "moral and spiritual value [accrued] not only to those . . . who [were] taking part but to the rest of the country as well."[6]

From this perspective, the Great Depression combined with the CCC's stated purpose to provide a larger context for enrollees to contribute to the country—to perform national service. In short, the combination created powerful, meaning-based civic feedback effects. As an unemployment relief program, the CCC was not simply about giving poor young men jobs. As an environmental conservation program, it was not just about planting trees. In both respects it was about changing how people thought about the Depression and the country's future, and what they believed they and their government could do to make things better. That was its larger lesson in national service.

Work Training

But if this focus taught profoundly positive civic lessons, it also confronted both civic and political limits, particularly for those not content with the CCC as an emergency relief agency. The CCC was open to two main critiques. The first was inherent in the logic of unemployment relief itself. The argument went like this: Sure, the CCC could give temporary jobs to young men; but if they were no more likely to find regular employment at the end of their enrollment, how much better off were they, really? The CCC's overriding purpose should be preparing young men for the future, not just seeing them through the present.[7] The justification for this view was civic and pre-cedented on a wage-earning, future-oriented, work-based definition of citizen-ship. As one CCC education adviser explained, "When Johnny Q. Enrollee is discharged from CCC camp . . . he cannot be a very good citizen unless he has the opportunity to get a job and the ability to hold it."[8] This critique stresses a weakness in policy feedback effects: in the view of critics, the CCC's purpose and design should have created greater job-training resource and interpretive effects, leading to the positive civic (and other) outcomes that come with higher levels of employment.

The second critique was the product of programmatic ambition. There was little in the CCC's original purpose or design to allow it to expand beyond helping the poor or to justify its existence in good times. This critique also stresses a weakness in policy feedback effects: because of its design, the CCC failed to provide the resource, incentive, and meaning effects that would allow policymakers and others to successfully advocate for its institutionalization. Thus, critics in this camp were less focused on young men's prospects for permanent employment than their own prospects for creating a permanent CCC. The critiques were distinct, but they converged to support a shift in the CCC's mission toward job training.

Although Congress failed to make the CCC permanent (the details dis-cussed shortly), in 1937 Congress did codify the program's altered raison d'etre: "The CCC as a monetary relief and job-giving agency [was] replaced by the CCC as a work-training agency."[9] This change mattered but should not be overstated. From the start, the president (among others) held that enrollees would leave the CCC "ready for a reentrance into the ranks of industry, bet-ter equipped than before"; within its first year, the CCC had an organized education program.[10] Nonetheless, training did not fit as well with the goal of conservation as work relief had and attenuated the CCC's critical, if implicit, national service mission.

Actually, the conflict was between those who believed that conservation and training themselves were in tension, and those who did not, which mani-fested as a debate over work hours and the pedagogical value of work.[11] Those who saw work and training as basically compatible—most importantly the president and the CCC director—pressed to keep the forty-hour CCC work week, emphasized on-the-job training, and supported formal instruction only after hours. They believed that learning to do "an honest day's work" well was the most important job training, and resulted in immediate returns through more and better conservation work.[12] Furthermore, if there were a conflict, this group knew its priorities: in Labor Secretary Frances Perkins's words, the CCC should "encourage the development of [enrollee] capacities to a maximum extent *consistent with the interests of the work program* [emphasis added]."[13] This view guaranteed that both participants and the public would benefit. Those on the other side believed that a work-training trade-off was in play and thus advocated reducing the work hours to allow more training.[14] Even with regard to on-the-job training, their motto might have been (as it was for one work supervisor) "Don't let the job interfere with the men."[15] Here the participants would gain, but the benefits to the public would come in the future, as enrollees later found work and became productive citizens. The CCC's director won the fight over work hours but not on keeping the CCC's original mission.

By arguing that the need for youth training (and environmental conservation) was not confined to hard times, advocates hoped to make the CCC a permanent option for young Americans. Their plan would have gone a long way in institutionalizing the CCC, but at some cost to the CCC as national service. By severing the connection between the CCC and work relief, advocates undercut an often overlooked but important goal of national service—the example that enrollees and the CCC set for the country. The change can be seen in the president's words: in recommending that Congress make the CCC permanent, FDR spoke of the "moral and spiritual [improvement] of our citizens who have been enrolled in the Corps and of their families."[16] Gone was his reference to the moral and spiritual value of the CCC to the nation. The sense that the CCC was helping the nation "[gain] control over its collective destiny" required the national service ethic that the Depression implicitly brought to it.[17] To sustain this sense of purpose in the absence of crisis, the CCC would have needed to adopt an explicit national service framing, stating that the CCC's goal was to create needed public goods (such as healthy forests) and in the process create and inspire good citizens (or conversely, to create good citizens by having them create needed public goods) regardless of the economy. It did not.

National Defense

Where did this leave the CCC on the eve of World War II? It had not been made permanent, so it had to justify and fight for its existence in a profoundly altered context. However, its leaders had taken every opportunity since its founding to disavow all military connotations, which made a rhetorical or programmatic about-face all the more difficult. Its training focus had undercut its broadest, albeit implicit, national service ethic and created a gap that made it difficult to argue that the CCC could always address emergencies, first the Great Depression and next the coming war. Furthermore, the training focus had done this without dislodging from the public mind the connection between the CCC and unemployment relief—a disadvantageous association when young men's labor was suddenly in high demand.[18]

All of these factors converged to make it all but impossible to square the CCC's identity as a national defense program with its identity and development up to that point. Not that its leaders did not try valiantly. In addition to highlighting its success in graduating "two and a half million young men of military age, physically more able and eager to defend the country," they stressed what it had to offer as a going concern: improving domestic military bases, training men for noncombat military jobs, giving men who were too young or physically unfit the preparation they needed for future military service, and making America "more worth protecting and defending" through its conservation work.[19] But the dissonance was too great. A strictly military definition of national service prevailed, and the CCC was unable to sufficiently sell itself as a vital complement. In short, the CCC's purpose failed to provide the meaning effects that might have allowed supporters to secure its future. In the language of the times, the CCC was given an "honorable discharge" in 1942, thanked for services effectively rendered but no longer needed.[20]

Government's Role

In 1933 the CCC *was* needed, and its services were well organized by the federal government. Given the economic crisis and the voters' rejection of President Hoover's perceived laissez-faire response to it, there was no question that the new president would amply employ federal power. The CCC was a prime example. Run almost exclusively by the federal government, it was the quintessential national program. Nonetheless, the CCC leadership still had to work with other levels of government and with communities, as well as organize and support the program within the federal government. How this worked influenced the CCC's effectiveness, its political standing, and its civic lessons.

A National Program

Upon his inauguration, Roosevelt likened the Depression to war, requiring a strong and speedy national government response.[21] The CCC was one result: it could be run by the "existing machinery" of government and enroll 250,000 men within a matter of months.[22] And although the CCC's work did not require national administration, it facilitated it: in the West, most forestland was federally owned, and in the East, the Interior and Agriculture departments had a history of cooperation with state-level forest officials. [23]

The civic impact of this arrangement was not lost on the CCC's leadership. One month after the program's creation, Director Fechner told Americans that "the president believes that one of his major responsibilities is to . . . instill in [citizens] a greater faith in our government and in its sincere efforts to end the Depression."[24] This was a national program with an explicit goal of engendering faith in the national government. It was also national in scope, with a presence in every state. In *This New America*, two CCC chaplains wrote that "the meeting of East and West in the camps should bring a new appreciation of democracy," "a new baptism of patriotism, and an increased consciousness of national unity."[25] Finally, it was also federated, which allowed enrollees to see "reciprocal relationship[s] built up between the governmental bureaus, state agencies, and their fellow men."[26] In these respects the CCC communicated civic lessons, but they could prove positive only if the relationships were well managed.

Managing Outside Relationships

By all accounts the CCC was well known and widely popular. In fact, by 1936 it "had become the most highly regarded of all New Deal agencies" and enjoyed support not only from Democrats but also 67 percent of Republicans and their party's presidential nominee.[27] Beyond general public support, the CCC developed positive relationships with states and localities, largely based on economics. In exchange for allowing CCC camps on their lands, states reaped the benefits of CCC work projects free of charge. More important, the CCC released them from a not inconsequential portion of their relief burden, providing jobs to enrollees and allotments to their families. So although lower-level officials had little say over the program, they still had a stake in its success and incentives to provide political support: they received substantial benefits for their citizens at no cost to themselves.

In addition to these benefits, which accrued more or less nationwide, the CCC provided a boost to the communities near its camps, which built up local support for the program. In particular, the hiring of thousands of "local experienced men"—typically older, unemployed woodsmen—as supervisors was critical to avoiding charges that "outsiders" were stealing local forestry jobs, and buying supplies locally endeared the CCC to business owners.[28] These factors largely account for the "exceptional popularity" that researcher Michael Sherraden found at the local level.[29] Specifically, he found that 85 percent of letters to the CCC from citizens and community groups were positive, with 22 percent of these asking that a camp remain open and nearly 42 percent asking for a new camp.[30] Clearly, the CCC's challenge was not generating political support; its policy design created ample incentives for that. The challenge was managing demand.

Its popularity may be one reason that its leadership actively and successfully discouraged the creation of a CCC association, despite support from enrollees, alumni, and other advocates.[31] Fechner justified his opposition by stating, "There [is] no need for enrollees or ex-enrollees organizing. Nearly all efforts stressed teaching patriotism and Americanism—very altruistic. [But] if any nation is overorganized for this purpose it is the United States."[32] Given that teaching patriotism was a very public CCC goal, his argument is not terribly convincing. More likely the CCC leaders saw no advantage and significant drawbacks: an association might make demands on pay, benefits, working conditions, and camp programming—all things that the CCC was able to negotiate, although not always easily, from within. What it lost was a very large, powerful ally, with members in every congressional district, that could have lobbied for permanence and the program's continuation. Interest groups were scarce at that time compared with later periods, but those that existed were typically large, nationally federated organizations, with local chapters that combined "social or ritual activities with community service, mutual aid, and involvement in national affairs."[33] Through these associations, average citizen members were able to learn about, debate, and vote on policy priorities; the results then were communicated to policymakers by the organization's elected leadership, who might well represent more people than members of the U.S. House had constituents.[34] The CCC's policy design provided resource and incentive effects for this type of interest group creation, but these can be—and in this case were—overridden. A decision to strengthen the CCC's autonomy over the short run weakened its very survival over the long run.

Managing Inside Relationships: CCC Leadership

President Roosevelt played a critical role in designing the CCC and remained involved, "sketch[ing] broad policy lines" and having "the final word on important policy matters" throughout its duration.[35] However, as director, Fechner was most responsible for the CCC's remarkable successes and its limitations.[36] He faced a novel challenge: "to cooperate with [four Cabinet] departments [Labor, War, Agriculture, and Interior] for the creation of an entirely new agency."[37] Yet Fechner was not chosen because of his government management skills, or even his conservation or relief experience. He did not have either. He was chosen because he was vice president of the American

Federation of Labor (AFL), a man who could allay the fears of a concentrated interest that was deeply concerned about and sharply critical of the proposed CCC.[38] Selecting him would not be the last time that important national service policy decisions were made to placate labor; managing labor-service tension is a recurrent challenge, and one the CCC addressed well.

How Fechner's background helped him to direct the CCC is more equivocal. As John Salmond recounts, "Fechner had not been trained to innovate, but to conciliate; not to lead, but to suggest."[39] He excelled at managing relations among the departments' representatives, which was critical because the actual work of the CCC—virtually everything it did from the moment a young man inquired about joining to the moment of his discharge, from the day a camp was sited to the day it was dismantled—was carried out by other departments, each with its own modus operandi. However, when directing the CCC demanded innovation and leadership, Fechner fell short. A common critique was that he "lacked sufficient vision" to see beyond "the simple provision" of work and conservation.[40] In Fechner's own words, he had "a little hesitation to agreeing to any substantial change . . . in nature of an experiment."[41]

These limitations made Fechner an atypical New Dealer, "a potato bug amongst dragonflies" in his own words.[42] As an uneducated southern conservative, he did not want to draw nor could he have drawn the New Deal's best and brightest to the CCC: the agency's intellectual inhospitableness, limited authority, and impermanence made it decidedly unattractive for anyone with talent and ambition. The lack of inventive thinkers also may have contributed to the CCC's limitations: at least after 1937, Fechner's approach very likely hindered the CCC's prospects.[43] But what alternative vision might have prevailed? Given a choice between Fechner's narrow focus and others' broader but less civic job-training vision, Fechner's conservatism may not have been a true social loss.

Managing Inside Relationships: The CCC's Status

This same ambiguity applied to the CCC's status within the federal government. Its emergency establishment, its erratic funding, its lack of permanence, and its institutional structure and location all affected its ability to fulfill its purposes, both narrowly and broadly understood.

EMERGENCY ESTABLISHMENT. In Kenneth Holland and Frank Hill's assessment, "For better or worse, and probably for both, the CCC [had] borne from birth the characteristics of an organization doing an emergency job with resources . . . already on hand."[44] These characteristics included a broad grant of policymaking authority to the executive branch and rushed policymaking by the executive branch. First, Congress gave the president "permissive authority": the original CCC authorization was a mere six paragraphs long, and as temporary, emergency legislation it was not "compelling and controlling, as it should be if it were urging a permanent policy."[45] In short, Congress deferred.

The result was decisionmaking in reaction to immediate needs and events. For example, the Department of Agriculture was originally assigned to run the camps; the Army took over only when speed superseded planning as a priority. However, the precedent stuck: the Army never left. What if planning had prevailed over expedience? The USDA had a long history of "bureaucratic autonomy"—the ability to shape policy with little political interference—that allowed for substantial innovation and institutionalization.[46] It is likely that under USDA management the CCC would have had stronger intellectual leadership, more experimentation, and an increased chance for permanence. Expedience similarly limited enrollment to young, unmarried men, even as exceptions for veterans and Native Americans proved that the CCC could accommodate older, married enrollees. What if the CCC had not been so youth-oriented? To the extent that job training is largely considered the province of the young, the CCC's job-training focus may have proved a less viable mission. On the other hand, to the extent that national service is also associated with the young, this focus too may have been less viable.

FUNDING. Short-term decisionmaking prevailed as well on CCC funding and enrollments. FDR set an initial target of 250,000 enrollees, to be financed through "the use of unobligated funds, [previously] appropriated for public works."[47] This decision raised the ire of labor unions, but it solved a number of problems with Congress. Given the rush, no one knew just how much the program would cost and therefore what to request; what was known is that work relief would be expensive. (The program eventually consumed approximately 4 percent of the entire federal budget.) Bypassing an initial funding request helped limit debate and bought the program several, essentially cost-free, months in which to prove itself.

Later, competing interests collided. In early 1935 FDR's philosophical commitment to work relief, continued mass unemployment, and the end of the CCC's two-year authorization converged: the president not only called for the CCC's continuation but proposed a massive expansion.[48] Congress overwhelmingly concurred, believing it both good policy and smart politics. In most districts, the CCC was popular enough to make a vote against it electorally risky, and CCC expansion held electoral promise, bringing new camps to every state and hundreds of districts, and increased patronage opportunities.[49] CCC enrollment went from nearly 242,000 to almost 506,000 within five months.[50]

Unbeknownst to Congress or the CCC leadership, the president intended much of this increase to be temporary. FDR had his own political calculus: 1936 was an election year, and he intended to run on a balanced-budget platform. To demonstrate a measure of economy, he ordered enrollment reduced to 300,000 by July 1936. However, to further aid his election prospects and to quell the expected public discontent over camp closings, he intended to campaign on making the CCC permanent at this level. From his perspective, fiscal responsibility (at least in the short term) and a CCC institutionalized for the long term would allow him to realize both his electoral and programmatic ambitions. He failed to consider that members of Congress had their own needs and ambitions, which led to a revolt against the downsizing and then against CCC institutionalization.[51]

A majority of House Democrats organized to thwart the downsizing and threatened to block the president's entire relief appropriation unless he agreed to an enrollment of 400,000.[52] Roosevelt capitulated. However, he moved forward on CCC permanence, confident that the same dynamic that had frustrated one goal all but guaranteed success of the other.

PUSHING FOR PERMANENCE. Permanence within the federal government is somewhat overstated: even "permanent" agencies are subject to annual appropriations (which can be zero) and legislative overhaul (which can include repeal). Nonetheless, the presumption and practical reality of permanent status was something CCC supporters wanted and worked for. Their failure shows the power of both precedence and circumstances.

In committee hearings, advocates and opponents debated the practical and symbolic consequences of permanence. On the practical side, advocates argued that they "need[ed] permanency . . . [for] the long-range planning of projects and to obtain the best type of personnel."[53] As it stood, the CCC could undertake only projects it could finish by the end of its authorization, and its personnel were not covered by civil service provisions. More broadly, they stressed the ongoing need for conservation and the expectation of continued high youth unemployment.[54] Opponents countered that most CCC projects did not require years to complete, that civil service protection merely propagated bureaucracy, and that the CCC's cost-effectiveness was questionable.[55] They also challenged the program's fundamental youth development precepts, specifically that work should take precedence over education (in 1937) and that military training would detract from both work and education (in 1939). Opponents wanted these and other issues to be studied, debated, and potentially changed.[56] Essentially they wanted a program that had been designed in a matter of weeks and had operated substantially unchanged—and well—for years to be rationalized and possibly redesigned. It was not a surprise that no one stepped up to the plate.

But given that opponents of permanence still supported continuing the CCC and proponents conceded that the program would always depend on ongoing congressional support, substance was less important to the debate than symbolism. First, the CCC would gain a presumption of permanence. As supporters hoped, opponents feared, and one member simply acknowledged, "Once we establish one of these new agencies permanently, it is extremely difficult to dispense with it."[57] As Eric Patashnik found in his study of policy reforms, policy actors make investments, or not, based in part on the expectation that a policy will continue, investments that would make reversing or eroding the policy unattractive.[58] As a temporary emergency program, the CCC could never create that expectation. Second, permanence would make a moral statement. For supporters, that statement was that the nation was forever committed to attending to its human and natural resource needs: young men would always need work and training, and worthwhile work would always be available for them to do. In one USDA representative's opinion, "It would be very bad business to do anything that in any way would retard this program. . . . Would it not be unpatriotic, immoral, and decidedly indiscreet?"[59] From opponents' perspective, the message was that the nation was forever going to be in a slump. One member of Congress asked, "How would it affect the morale of our people, especially the youth of America, to say that the Civilian Conservation Corps is going to be a permanent organization, . . . that it affords the future they will have to look toward?"[60]

In the end, neither the practicalities nor possible meanings determined the permanence bills' fate; the institutional needs and habits of Congress did. In 1937, after years of executive branch aggrandizement and following close on the heels of Roosevelt's much-maligned attempt to increase the size of the Supreme Court and "pack" it with justices who would support his policies, the Democratic House of Representatives declared congressional independence: it voted by an overwhelming 389-7 to reauthorize the president's "pet baby" but not do his bidding by making it permanent, and stood firm against the more compliant Senate.[61] By 1939 a precedent was set. Despite administration claims that permanence would increase CCC effectiveness, a large majority of Congress was happy with the CCC as it was, enjoyed the electoral benefits that came with ongoing positive reauthorization votes, and was ill-disposed to investing the time needed to address the CCC's long-term possibilities. Again in 1939, reauthorization was never in question, yet the permanence provision did not even make it out of committee.

INSTITUTIONAL STRUCTURE AND LOCATION. One of the CCC's most distinctive features was its institutional structure: the programmatic cooperation between departments was "a unique and significant experiment" with policy and political consequences.[62] Fechner long held that the CCC policy benefited and the program itself demonstrated laudable bureaucratic restraint by drawing on existing departmental expertise.[63] These factors contributed, albeit slightly, to Congress's approval. That this structure gave individuals in various departments a vested interest in the Corps was of greater consequence: it spread support for the CCC throughout the executive branch but failed to concentrate it. As a result, the CCC had a broader base of support than it needed when the program was deemed necessary but insufficient support to successfully defend itself when it was threatened. None of the cooperating departments could claim full credit for the program's many successes, and none would fold with its demise; the incentives it provided for department staff to work on its behalf were limited. Only the CCC's small coordinating office was fully at stake.

But small as it was, employing a scant fifty people, the CCC office was the program's public face in the capital.[64] And importantly, for most of its history it was independent; Fechner reported directly to the president. However, by 1939 FDR decided to organize his alphabet soup of independent agencies. At first, the CCC was to be housed in a new Department of Public Works. Fechner objected, explaining that "unless such a department took over all [of the] agencies that have an important part in the work of the CCC, it would not be practicable."[65] Moving from the frying pan into the fire, the president ultimately placed the CCC in the new Federal Security Agency—a forerunner of today's Department of Health and Human Services. Its placement there revealed, in Salmond's assessment, "that in Washington at least it was now considered that the CCC had more-sophisticated functions—tasks concerned with the welfare and training of youth—than simply work relief."[66] Fechner passionately disagreed, arguing that if the CCC had to be put into a larger department it should be in a works—not a welfare—department.[67] That he was overruled shows how little regard Washington had for his intellectual leadership; that he quit in protest shows how seriously he took the matter; that the president refused his resignation shows how valued was his administrative skill. However, FDR's insistence that Fechner stay on mattered only briefly. Fechner died a mere six months later.

The CCC survived for several more years, and neither Fechner's death nor the move to the FSA determined its eventual demise. But it had lost its most prominent work advocate just when its institutional location further downplayed the importance of enrollees' contributions. To the extent that Charles Moskos is correct, that national service should be justified based on the work that servers perform as opposed to the good done the servers, these changes diminished the CCC as national service.[68] The conservation aspects of the CCC were never the totality of the program, nor were they ever totally lost, but they were important and unfortunately became less so.

5

The CCC's Tools, Rules, and Targets

Like its purpose and role for government, the CCC's tools, rules, and targets—the service work it supported, its educational goals and content, the type of participants it recruited, and its obligations and inducements— influenced its political support and viability and communicated lessons to participants and the public, in large part through policy feedback dynamics. In short, these lower-level policy elements further shaped the politics and civics of the program, which in turn influenced future policy development. As the previous chapter explained, the CCC's design details generated much political support but were unable to overcome obstacles to long-term viability. Indeed, in some cases they contributed to the program's end. Civically, these details reinforced the principles of reciprocity and collaboration—most strongly early on—while always emphasizing citizenship in its many variations, especially citizenship understood as work.

Work and the CCC

The work of the CCC provided not only environmental benefits but also civic and political benefits. Civically, the work program allowed enrollees to contribute their labor to publicly valued projects, giving them an experience of citizenship. In doing so they set an example, showing the public that even downtrodden youth could be capable citizens. Their work also demonstrated that even in the midst of the Great Depression, citizens and government could fulfill public purposes. Politically, the CCC's work helped build broad support: the work program's design and justification minimized controversy, and the necessity, visibility, and quantity of the work itself maximized public and official goodwill.

The focus on conservation certainly fit the president's interest, but it also helped counter concerns about costs and competition. Regarding the CCC's high price tag, Roosevelt stressed that "this type of work is of definite, practical value, not only through the prevention of great present financial loss, but also as a means of creating future national wealth [that] will pay dividends."[1] It was a sound investment because the nation would get more than its money's worth. Unlike today, economic development and environmental protection on public lands were not in conflict; they were seen to go hand in hand. In part this accord was due to the nation's specific environmental crises: when South Carolinians could see Kansas soil in the sky, the consequences were as much economic as ecological. But in part it was due to the time's, and thus the CCC's, expansive understanding of conservation work. The CCC not only planted trees, it built bridges and dams, laid telephone lines, and created recreation areas—all of which facilitated economic development. As a result, the CCC's conservation focus was remarkably uncontroversial, even with business.

Furthermore, the CCC could work on a massive scale because the nation's forests and fields could absorb the labor of hundreds of thousands of workers while "not," as the president frequently noted, "interfering with normal employment."[2] The CCC did not compete with private industry, nor did it replace professional foresters or local woodsmen. In fact, given the need for skilled, experienced supervisors, the CCC was something of a full forestry employment program. Finally, having the Interior and Agriculture departments—not the Army—run the work program appeased labor's concerns about "regimentation."

The CCC's work also generated widespread public support. For a public newly waking to environmental concerns—the era saw the Dust Bowl's devastation and the founding and growth of major environmental organizations—the kind and quantity of the CCC's work mattered.[3] No discussion—no speech, article, or report—was complete without a list of accomplished work. For example, in 1937 CCC enrollees planted 365,233,500 trees, built 1,081,931 check dams, and laid more than 9,960 miles of telephone lines, and these were just three major types of work among more than 150.[4] With up to half a million young men working at any one time, it would have been a very poor program indeed that did not produce significant work. Nevertheless, the quantities were impressive and were designed to impress, as were statements that the CCC had furthered state and national forest development by ten to twenty years in just its first two years.[5] Also impressive was the CCC's emergency response work, which officials specifically highlighted. Beyond their everyday work of clearing brush and building dams to prevent forest fires and floods, enrollees were on call when these disasters struck nonetheless, earning the gratitude of citizens living in destruction's path and bolstering the program's public esteem.

The CCC also benefited from its work being visible and concrete. Average citizens could visit a state park, walk the new trails, rest on new benches, all courtesy of the CCC. Even if most Americans never made such a trip, never had their home saved from fire or their farm saved from erosion, and never saw enrollees planting trees, they knew about these accomplishments through newspaper reports, movie newsreels, letters that enrollees sent home, and word of mouth. They could picture this work and understand its value. The CCC shared this characteristic with the New Deal's other work relief program, the Works Progress Administration, but it benefited more.[6] For while the CCC's work was visible to members of the public, even residents living nearby often had to go out of their way to see it. The CCC, and its reputation, was protected by the trees. CCC headquarters received few complaints about enrollee laziness, in part because the Corps as a whole was genuinely productive and in part because few outsiders ever saw what slacking there was. In addition, given the small number of complaints the Corps received, its officials were able to promptly follow up on them, which further promoted the public's perception of its industriousness. WPA workers, based in cities, rarely had the luxury of keeping their missteps out of sight.

The CCC also benefited from the dearth of conservation work done previously. Before the WPA began, buildings and roads were regularly being constructed; its significant contribution during the Depression was allowing this work to continue. Important as that was, it was not something special.[7] The CCC, on the other hand, performed work that had not and would not have been done in its absence, even in good times. Although some forest work had been done earlier, the CCC simply overwhelmed it in scale. It was doing something new and bold—and at the same time, old and familiar. As Michael Sherraden wrote, "The simple, hard, communal work and country living of the CCC represented a return to [a more] pristine era."[8] This combination of novelty and nostalgia proved a potent recipe for the program's legitimacy, one that future programs would try to emulate but with far less success.

These factors—quantity, necessity, visibility, and connection to both past and future—had an enormous impact on the CCC enrollees themselves. In 1935 Frank Hill wrote: "The impact of actual work seen is startling. . . .

Many a World War [I] veteran may . . . wonder if he actually helped make the world safe for Democracy. But no enrollee can doubt the contribution of his peacetime army has been tangible."[9] Later the praise deepened. A high school counselor wrote, "The CCC enrollees feel a part-ownership as citizens in the forest that they have seen improve through the labor of their hands."[10] Finally, the enrollees had their own stories, summed up simply and powerfully by former enrollee Harry Dallas: "There was pride in the work. We built something, and I knew I helped, and saw the result. It was something you could take pride in, and there wasn't a lot of pride available in those days."[11] In the language of policy feedback, the CCC's design had powerful civic meaning effects.

The CCC's inability to translate the admiration for its work program into permanence shows how highly contingent the support for civilian national service was, and continues to be. Despite its voluminous accomplishments, in 1942 much work remained. Clearly, the need for conservation continued, but policymakers considered that need an insufficient rationale for preserving the Corps. In the absence of additional justification, such as mass youth unemployment, they decided that the CCC was no longer essential. Its work and the lessons it taught to enrollees and the public came to an end.

Education for and through the CCC

A central point of this book is that all policy design elements have potential civic and political feedback effects. Civically, these elements act as pedagogy, teaching participants and the public about their relationship to government and the meaning of citizenship. The CCC's design emphasized reciprocity, collaboration, and a largely work-based understanding of citizenship. In addition, however, the CCC had an explicit three-part enrollee education program: on-the-job training, camp living, and classes. These activities made up most of the enrollees' daily experience and gave the CCC its reputation as "a great school. . . . [Enrollees] can be taught much, about work, about the government . . . and about the lives they want to live."[12]

The education program's main goal was to foster employability and citizenship, which led to its strong emphasis on work-based citizenship. Constitutional, patriotic, and service meanings were also part of the program, and administrators used them to counter any serious (or for that matter trivial) enrollee predisposition toward critical citizenship. The CCC was not particularly concerned that enrollees would be insufficiently engaged politically or civically. It was concerned, however, that they might be inappropriately engaged, possibly joining mass movements that could topple America's constitutional democracy, as young people had done in other countries. This concern also led to a general future orientation, the idea that enrollees would take on their civic responsibilities as they grew older and wiser—and lost any radicalism they may have contemplated in their youth. These perspectives conflicted somewhat with the idea that enrollees were already doing the work of citizens. The Army's role of overseeing camp living and classes exacerbated these tensions: any government authority would be likely to have eschewed teaching critical citizenship, but the Army, given its authoritarian culture, often went so far as to undermine constitutional principles.

More so than other parts of the Corps's program, the education component varied by place and time and caused some conflict throughout its history. Critics found the education and work training inadequate, lamenting Army control and too little central support. CCC scholar John Saalberg's assessment is worth quoting at length:

> Objective evaluation of the CCC educational program is extremely difficult. Not that its shortcomings were hard to perceive, but that they were so numerous. The program always lacked specific direction. Funds were always inadequate. Insufficient time was allocated for instruction. Classes were held at the wrong time. . . . Most instruction was poor. . . . Yet, despite this, the CCC as a whole was remarkably successful as a training agency. . . . It developed [enrollees'] habits of orderliness, their approved behavior, and respect for authority; it aided in their acquisition of new skills and knowledge; it developed desirable attitudes toward work. . . . [And] it operated mainly for the benefit of a unique youth group—one which was not fertile ground for formal education.[13]

Saalberg then asks whether the CCC would have done better had it focused more on education and less on work. He concludes: "Certainly Roosevelt and Fechner did not believe so."[14] Their belief in work's pedagogical value is worth remembering, as are the strengths and weaknesses of the supplementary education program they created, somewhat reluctantly, to complement it.

Training on the Job

In the CCC, on-the-job training served a dual purpose—to train enrollees for their CCC work and to prepare them for future employment—through dual means—teaching them good work habits and specific job skills. Robert Fechner gave the former top priority. In particular, he believed that "the knowledge that he can do a [full] day's work helps make a man of a callow youth."[15] It not only makes him more employable, "it makes him more democratic."[16]

In addition, through their work, enrollees learned specific skills—"to operate heavy machinery, to use a wide variety of tools, . . . to build roads and bridges, to construct lodges . . . as well as practical forestry and soil erosion prevention methods."[17] For the CCC to accomplish its public work mission, enrollees had to learn to do their assigned tasks well; in the process, many of them gained practical skills.

Fechner and others believed, however, that "merely to get work—and good work—done was only part of [the] problem."[18] They aspired to provide a broader context. Thus, supervisors should "explain why a job was done a certain way and . . . how a specific job tied in with a whole group of other jobs."[19] As the training program advanced, it included rotating work assignments—giving enrollees experience with a variety of jobs and showing them why a project was needed, how it would proceed, and what benefits it would produce.[20] Consequently, "few of the young men who have taken an understanding part in [the CCC's work] . . . have done so without gaining a clearer conception of the dignity of useful labor."[21]

On-the-job training had its limits, though. Nearly half of enrollees were from urban areas where conservation-related job skills were in little demand. Furthermore, the average enrollee spent only ten months in the program, not long enough to be trained fully as a skilled worker. In addition, not all enrollees were exposed to a variety of tasks or took an "understanding part" in their projects.[22] Many work supervisors, not trained as teachers, were unwilling or unable to meet these larger training requirements.[23] Still, Holland and Hill found that on the whole enrollees gained sufficient skills and habits to produce high-quality work while they served in the CCC and to become sought-after employees outside of it.[24] Thus "the training carried on during the day by superintendents, technicians, and foremen [was] clearly of the greatest importance in the development of enrollees from raw youth to useful workers and responsible citizens."[25]

Camp Living

Fechner's insistence on a forty-hour work week still left 128 hours to fill, week after week, in camp. For the enrollees, the camps largely defined their CCC experience. In turn, Army administration and diverse enrollee backgrounds largely defined the camps. These elements—the importance of the camps, Army administration, and enrollee diversity—combined to create a powerful civic experience for many enrollees, but one with clear limits.

The CCC's founders fully intended camp life to be formative. FDR firmly believed that outdoor living was good for mind, body, and spirit. Others put greater stock in the camps' social—as opposed to natural—environment. In Hill's view, each camp "put two hundred young men into a self-sustaining settlement where they would learn to cooperate in the routine of a common life."[26] Fechner's goal was even more explicitly civic: for camp "life and activities . . . to strengthen and improve the individual as a citizen in a democracy."[27] In short, the camps were to be "civic laboratories."[28]

The laboratories' raw materials were the enrollees—most of them young and inexperienced, many disadvantaged even by Great Depression standards. The CCC provided a basic living unknown to some and held them to expectations often equally unfamiliar. From an enrollee's testimony that he "discovered for the first time the value of an ordered existence" and the assistant director's assertion that "the emphasis placed on cleanliness [and] good order . . . helps to make better citizens" to an academic assessment that "good appearance and respect for officials were demanded," encouraging virtuous personal habits clearly was considered well within the program's proper sphere.[29]

Even more important, the CCC introduced many enrollees to the wider world. Decades later, this simple fact still stands out in bold relief:

> Ask a CCC veteran what he got out of the experience, and invariably his first response is that he learned to "get along with other people." But this doesn't mean an appreciation of ethnic or cultural diversity; it means something much simpler: this was often . . . their first exposure to life beyond home, farm, [and] village.[30]
>
> Farm boys, city boys, mountain boys, all worked together. I was a farm kid. I didn't know how other people lived or what other people thought about the world. In the CCC we didn't have a choice, we had to work together and get to know each other.[31]

As explained below, what strikes a twenty-first-century observer is often deplorable homogeneity and isolation: enrollees were chosen by sex and class, segregated by race and age, and housed in camps largely cut off from the world. With radio reception even hard to get, Holland and Hill concluded that the typical enrollee "tends to think less and hear less about public affairs than he did before."[32] Still, the diversity within these insular camps often defined enrollees' experience, with civic implications. In Fechner's estimation, "Change of environment and association with other enrollees . . . have broadened the vision of the lads and have stimulated . . . the upbuilding of a national culture."[33]

Getting along in the camps was facilitated—and constrained—by Army administration. As part of their overall welfare function, the Army's camp leaders encouraged clubs and teams—the "constructive recreational activities" portion of the CCC's "program of citizenship improvement."[34] Enrollees, many with no Boy Scout, 4-H, or similar experience, became "joiners" and, ultimately, members of what Harvard political scientist Robert Putnam identifies as America's "civic generation."[35] Because youth involvement helps predict adult activity and group activity contributes to democracy, the CCC's recreation program may have been as civically significant as intended.[36]

Beyond clubs, "the greatest opportunities for training in democracy" were seen to "lie in the numerous opportunities for group thinking on camp problems," albeit "within the limitations of Army regulations."[37] Camps varied on this score. As Ray Hoyt described in 1935, "Some camps are conducted on a self-government plan. Others are ruled by two-fisted Army officers who go to the limit," but both of these examples were outliers.[38] All camps had enrollee leaders (chosen by camp administrators); many had "safety sentinels," recreation committees, and discussion groups; and some had camp advisory councils.[39] Usually, however, enrollee input found little room to flourish. In 1935 Hill found that camp commanders tended to "discourage frank discussion" out of "an almost panicky fear of 'agitators' "; seven years later, he came across one who had enthusiastically established an enrollee council, only to abolish it when enrollees proposed "changing camp regulations to permit two recreational trips to town a week instead of one."[40]

Camp commanders were generally more comfortable promoting citizenship with requisite twice-daily flag tributes and at camp assemblies where they reminded enrollees of their future civic responsibilities.[41] The stress on what Holland and Hill label "conforming citizenship," exemplified in one camp commander's vision of the ideal enrollee, may have been typical:

> If I Were an Enrollee: I would faithfully carry out all orders and instructions. . . . I would not hesitate to devote extra time . . . to any undertaking for the benefit . . . of my camp. . . . I would eat the mess provided for me without griping. . . . I would under all circumstances be loyal to my superiors. . . . I would not be unduly influenced by others. . . . I would strive to conduct my life [so] as to make my parents and my company commander proud.[42]

Holland and Hill advocated engaging enrollees more fully in camp governance, to encourage "contributing citizenship."[43] The experimental Camp William James, mentioned earlier, went even further with respect to democratic governance. However, neither idea fit the standard vision of how a government program should operate: in the words of CCC official James McEntee, "If the government foots the bill, it should control the camps."[44]

Camp living promoted elements of the public work, patriotic, constitutional, and service approaches to citizenship while downplaying participation in and disavowing critical citizenship. Holland and Hill, focusing on the camps' civic limits, concluded that enrollees "will not usually have acquired from camp living or camp education a deeper understanding of American democracy."[45] They overly discounted or simply missed the civic benefits of the program as it was, but they did identify its problems. And as they suggest, its limitations extended to formal education.

Formal Classes

Saalberg's comments on the shortcomings of CCC education focused on formal class work. Unlike the camps, class work was not part of the CCC's initial design and, unlike on-the-job training, was harder to add. Furthermore, it was not a priority for either the president or the CCC director. As a result, the education program was given short shrift, particularly early on. Yet the lack of top-level attention on education had certain benefits. Ironically, some of them would be lost as education advocates gained ground.

One indication of education's low priority was the deference given to Army leaders over educators. The U.S. Office of Education proposed hiring camp "educational advisors" (combination teacher–guidance counselors), but the Army objected to any camp authority figure outside the military chain of command. It relented only after it was given supervisory power over the advisers and the right to limit the civic and other lessons they could teach.[46] Another indication was the program's budget: the CCC allotted only about 35 cents a year per enrollee for educational supplies.[47] The result was libraries, schoolrooms, workshops, and courses cobbled together from whatever could be found. The tight budget was obviously a weakness, but it led to some surprising benefits. For example, when Fechner prohibited using CCC funds for constructing schoolrooms, camps built them on their own; and as Hill observed, "There is something about a schoolhouse built by boys who want it that makes advisors and officers throw their bodies protectively before its crude walls."[48]

The lack of internally allocated resources also forced educational advisers to look outward, to the surrounding community, for book donations, volunteer teachers, and access to buildings and equipment. Their efforts strengthened community-camp relations. As one camp adviser saw it: "The camp and the community should exchange benefits. . . . If we have the use of high school buildings, we open our first aid and swimming classes to . . . [local] students."[49] The reciprocity that characterized enrollees' relationship to the

CCC then operated between the CCC and local communities. The education program's dependence on "splendid cooperation . . . from colleges, correspondence schools, local communities and states, as well as public and private organizations" allowed it a good measure of success despite low funding.[50]

Following the CCC's 1937 congressional reauthorization, the CCC's statute recognized formal education and training as fundamental goals that would from then on receive increased attention and funding. Fechner still balked, choosing to interpret the statutory language "that at least ten hours each week may be devoted to general education and vocational training" as including training on the job and otherwise limited to after-hours.[51] The education program changed much more significantly in other ways, although with equivocal results.

Before 1937 the education program was largely voluntary and decentralized. Participation of enrollees was generally optional, on paper and in practice; approximately 60 percent took classes in 1935,[52] and courses varied from camp to camp. In 1934 educational advisers were told, "The activities you carry on must grow out of the needs and wishes of the men. There is no program planned outside the camp and imposed from above."[53] The results were wide-ranging: academic classes for everyone from illiterates to college students; vocational courses in everything from auto mechanics to baking and typing; and special-interest courses galore. Post-1937, however, participation became more centralized, and encouragement to take courses was replaced by a requirement that enrollees with three or fewer years of schooling attend classes and an expectation that all others take first aid and at least one other class.[54] Fewer courses were offered. Those that were focused on basic academic and vocational instruction (and less so on "hobbies"), using more standardized, formal curricula developed by the Office of Education.[55]

One might think that educators would have supported a universal program geared toward academic and job-relevant subjects. Many educators, however, lamented the changes as counterproductive: many enrollees flourished in the CCC precisely because it was unlike their school experience, and their being allowed to choose whether to participate and what courses to take—two hallmarks of "adult education"—communicated that CCC education was different.[56] At the same time, the official curricula also appeared to violate adult education standards by employing language—including admonitions such as "Follow the rules!" and "Be on time for everything!"—that Eric Gorham has described as infantile.[57]

The CCC's civics lessons—which focused predominantly on constitutional citizenship but included patriotic, service, and work themes—generally suffered from the same infantile presentation and the constraints of military control. Ned Dearborn's *Once in a Lifetime: A Guide to the CCC Camp,* written for CCC enrollees and staff, presented a strongly populist view of government and citizenship, but it was overly simplistic and directive: "Don't kid yourself into thinking you are not important. Everyone is important in a democracy."[58] "You who have been given such a break by the government, which is sincerely interested in your well-being, ought especially to feel civic-minded."[59] These abbreviated lessons, typically taught in lectures by camp commanders, were the most common form of formal civic education, and even the full-fledged courses, Holland and Hill concluded, "were seldom so organized as to cover [the] field competently and interestingly."[60] Group discussions suffered similarly, with many enrollees "severely limited in speech when discussions of social and political matters developed," depending on the views of the camp commander.[61] Overall, Holland and Hill believed, "the most important fact . . . was that they were attempting to teach the principles of democracy within an authoritarian atmosphere."[62]

Given these factors, the formal class work component's major civic contribution probably came through its general education courses. One educational adviser believed that "training for citizenship includes . . . the elimination of illiteracy, instruction in the fundamental school subjects, and the continuance of high school and college work for enrollees whose training was interrupted."[63] By 1939 approximately 75,000 illiterate enrollees had learned to read and another 700,000 enrollees had furthered their education.[64] Given the strong connection between education and civic engagement, the civic benefits of the academic program were far from insignificant.[65] As Suzanne Mettler found in her study, a good part of the GI Bill's civic outcomes derived from the resource effects it produced; the CCC did the same on a more basic and less intense level.[66] Its direct attempts at teaching civics, something the GI Bill never aspired to, were much less effective. Enrollees' overall experience, including on-the-job training and camp living, as well as their work and their interaction with government, taught them more about citizenship than any "civics class" ever could.

The education program's political impact was equally ambiguous. Although the general public did not oppose it, they did not appear to value it as highly as many members of Congress or educators did. After all, they were already paying for public schools. At the same time, in the eyes of education advocates the CCC always fell short, even in its clearest responsibility of job training. None of these disconnects decisively contributed to the CCC's termination, but they made it more difficult to convincingly justify the CCC's existence as a successful training program, ultimately vital for national defense.

The CCC's Enrollees

The CCC's most obvious civic impacts were on its participants; in turn, who these participants were and how they were chosen had a profound impact on the CCC. Adhering to legislative mandates and CCC requirements, state and local relief agencies selected enrollees, overseen by the Department of Labor. Civically, the Corps's composition and organization shaped enrollees' experience in camp, and the enrollment process influenced their view of government. At the same time, Congress, the Department of Labor, and CCC administrators determined the CCC's policies largely by what they perceived as their political consequences.

As well as deciding who the CCC's participants would be, these agencies had to figure out what they would be. "Armies have 'privates,' factories 'hands' . . . schools 'pupils' or 'students.' . . . [These labels] did not seem to fit. . . . One thing was sure: they were enrolling for service. This act conferred upon them a title . . . 'enrollees.' "[67] Compared with future programs' designations, particularly VISTA's "volunteers," the "enrollee" label was politically uncontroversial, if not exactly inspiring. And if *enrollee* did not stress the contributions participants were to make, as *worker* might, neither did it highlight that they were receiving services, as *beneficiary* or *client* would have. In this instance, the CCC's principle of reciprocity was probably best served through neutral language.

Sex and Age

So who would the CCC's enrollees be? Given the Corps's makeup, it is notable that nothing in its original authorization limited or even targeted enrollment to young men; however, with little discussion and less controversy, they became the CCC's principal constituency. Given the CCC's proposed work and contemporary gender role expectations, the idea that women could profitably contribute and benefit went unexplored. When women were mentioned at all, comments like those made by the governor of Idaho—who hoped CCC enrollees would "remain here, marry our girls, and raise Idaho potatoes"—were more common than a 1935 editorial writer's closing charge: "And let us have a CCC for women!"[68]

The CCC's work and the Depression's disproportionate impact on youth led to a focus on young men. In 1933 more than a third of America's nearly 15 million unemployed were younger than 25.[69] The specter of a "generation lost" loomed. Further, the work envisioned—labor in often remote locales—demanded a physically capable, unencumbered workforce. So, with the exception of Native Americans (who could be married but who also worked in their home communities) and veterans (who were older and often married but whose powerful political claim and organization overrode typical policy-making considerations), enrollment was limited to young single men.

What constituted "young" changed over the CCC's life. When the Corps was established, the age range for "junior" (nonveteran) enrollees was 18 to 25; later the upper limit was extended to 28 and subsequently lowered to 23, and the minimum age was reduced to 17.[70] As job opportunities began increasing for 20-somethings, the average age of enrollees quickly became lower than the eligibility requirements suggest: by late 1935 well over half of junior enrollees were 17 or 18 years old. Their young age was one reason for the CCC's emphasis on education and training.[71] Youth had the need and capacity for the work, and they could benefit most from the program.[72]

Class

Given the Depression's devastation, unquestionably the CCC had to recruit from the unemployed and needy. (It also limited enrollment to citizens, providing a concrete lesson in the benefits of this official status.) The CCC changed its means test over time, but it always enrolled the poor. This policy ensured a great deal of economic homogeneity among enrollees, but the Depression's depths also led to a degree of social diversity unexpected in a means-tested program.

At its founding, the CCC required that enrollee families be "on or in need of relief," as determined by their local relief agency, with state quotas set by population.[73] In 1935, however, when the president aspired to increase enrollment to 600,000, he also decided to limit enrollment to men from families that were on relief, to better target resources to the neediest people and better alleviate local relief burdens.[74] Although the overwhelming majority of enrollees had always been on relief, this new policy created problems. First, it caused resentment in local communities because some needy youth were excluded for what they perceived as inflexible, bureaucratic reasons and because families that were struggling to stay off relief (and hoping their sons' enrollment would help) were forced to go on relief to qualify for enrollment.[75] Second, it caused resentment at the state level because states that could not fill their quotas with relief candidates lost their slots.[76] Third, it caused resentment in camp communities because more than 400 proposed camps had to be abandoned when enrollment under the new requirement fell short.[77] Combined with an improving economy and the shift in mission, the relief requirement was short-lived. When job training replaced "work and relief" in 1937, Congress limited CCC enrollment to "youthful citizens" who were "unemployed and in needy circumstances," standards somewhat more liberal than even the original policy had set.[78]

All three standards shared a focus on the disadvantaged, but as the CCC's head of selection wrote, "Aside from the more-than-ordinary economic distress . . . the enrollees . . . represent a fairly good cross section of the millions of families that make up the country."[79] Given the CCC's work and living conditions, it is not surprising that the Corps drew disproportionately from rural areas and small towns as opposed to cities, but the discrepancy was not large.[80] Former enrollee Al Hammer's memory of "farm boys, city boys, and mountain boys" all working together is largely accurate. In addition, geographic diversity was supplemented by a degree of social diversity. The Depression not only exacerbated existing poverty, it introduced many to it. In his guide to CCC camp life, Dearborn included sample enrollee life stories, and although they are not statistically representative, they are instructive: the small-town, middle-class boy whose father lost his job, the poor city youth with struggling immigrant parents, the rich suburbanite whose father's brokerage firm had failed, the young "man of the house" who supported his mother and siblings.[81]

As described earlier, this diversity significantly contributed to the camp experience. It also influenced the enrollment experience. The Depression's broad impact reduced the stigma of need; as Fechner often said, these were young men "idle through no fault of their own."[82] Consequently, local selection agents typically were helpful—and most enrollees who were asked said, "They treated me fine."[83] This courtesy provided enrollees with another positive, real-life civics lesson, one that Suzanne Mettler found repeated in her study of GI Bill recipients a decade later and that contrasts with political scientist Joe Soss's finding regarding welfare recipients in more recent times.[84] Furthermore, enrollees themselves understood that they were not at fault, which—along with the fact that they earned their keep—lessened the stigma of participating in a program for the poor.

Race

Although most CCC qualification requirements went largely uncontested, its policies on race did not. By law, racial discrimination was prohibited.[85] How this played out in practice was more equivocal. Overall, the CCC proved much more effective in helping enrollees within the boundaries of prevailing racial norms than in challenging the norms.[86] Most often it did not even try to challenge them. African Americans had the right to expect better, but typically they had been subjected to worse. In this, the CCC represented a small step forward.

Aside from Native Americans, who had their own separate CCC program, CCC selection was by law required to be color-blind. When it came to enrolling African Americans, however, many state and local relief offices had no intention of following the law.[87] The relief director in Georgia, whose population was 36 percent African American, refused to enroll any blacks at all until the national head of selection threatened to stop the state's enrollment entirely; Arkansas's relief director was quite proud and satisfied to have enrolled three African Americans.[88] Outside the South blacks were enrolled, but black organizations often had to press for equitable inclusion.[89] Nationally, the CCC never enrolled blacks in proportion to their need but did eventually enroll them in proportion to population, at 10 percent.[90]

Segregation was standard practice and soon official policy. Before 1935 a few camps were integrated. But separate camps for blacks and whites were the rule in the South and common elsewhere, and in mixed-race camps, barracks and work groups were often segregated.[91] After 1935, in an effort to impose uniformity and in keeping with his unenlightened racial views, Fechner mandated separate camps nationwide.[92]

Siting camps for blacks posed its own problems. Local communities, usually so eager for a camp, often objected, a sentiment held equally—and sometimes more forcefully—outside the South as in it.[93] In an effort to ease the placement of African Americans, Fechner decided to keep all black enrollees in their home states, let governors choose the camp sites, and staff all military positions in these camps with white officers—all of which did more to offend African Americans than placate local whites.[94]

Eventually black officers were allowed to hold leadership positions in African American camps, as were enrollees; in integrated camps, these positions would most likely have remained closed to them.[95] While not justifying "separate but equal," consensus holds that black enrollees were as well served by the CCC as whites.[96] Further, given their more limited opportunities outside the CCC, black enrollees on average stayed longer, which increased both their contributions to the program and their benefits from it.[97]

Character

The above requirements did not exhaust the CCC's selection criteria. As Fechner explained, "There is one other requirement—and that is *character*. We want to give these jobs to men who are clean-cut, purposeful, and ambitious—the finest young men that can be found."[98] Policies barred young men convicted of a serious crime, or on probation or parole.[99] Clearly, CCC administrators had every incentive, from easing supervision on-site to national public relations, to keep the number of known troublemakers to a minimum. Local selection agents had the opposite interest, and many "clung rather stubbornly to the idea that a CCC camp was a dumping ground for local youth problems."[100] Overall, CCC values prevailed. In interviews of aging former enrollees, author Donald Dale Jackson found them "obedient, patriotic . . . resilient, [and] grateful for the chance."[101] The most important character requirement, however, was a desire to be there. While enrollees had any number of obligations, their participation was not among them.

Obligations and Inducements

Without question, voluntarism—that CCC enrollees participated by choice— was considered crucial to its success. Fechner emphasized that "no one will be 'drafted' or even urged to enroll. . . . Only those who are *anxious* to have a part . . . are wanted."[102] This policy made the CCC's job easier, but more important, it was necessary for gaining union and public support. The drawback was that it all but precluded a national service framing: both the contemporary military and Jamesian approaches were conscription based. Given that the CCC would not have existed if it were mandatory, and that a national service framing might not have stuck (or allowed the CCC to survive) even if it had been, voluntarism was much more a blessing than a curse.

Optional participation, however, did not preclude other requirements. First, enrollees were expected to serve for six months, with the option to reenlist.[103] Enforcement, however, depended almost solely on moral suasion. In keeping with voluntary enlistment, enrollees who "went over the hill" were subject to no penalty beyond losing the privilege to reenroll. Combined with the Army's lax orientation, the result was an approximately 18 percent desertion rate; most who left did so within hours to a few weeks.[104] Desertion was a recognized problem, but not everyone who left early caused concern—those who left for private employment had the CCC's blessing. The CCC proudly announced their numbers almost as frequently as its work accomplishments, for they suggested that the CCC's training program was working, that enrollees were achieving "wage-earning citizenship" and opening slots for others to take their places, and that the economy was recovering.[105] The departures also sent the message that for individual enrollees, any private sector work was more important than their CCC work. This idea distinguishes the CCC from later national service programs, in which service is seen as a break from normal employment but not at all inferior to it.

Enrollees' second obligation, to remit most of their pay to their families (typically $25 of their $30 in monthly earnings), was strongly enforced, for sound economic, political, and civic reasons.[106] Macro-level, this policy created an economic stimulus. Because enrollees did not have to pay for their basic necessities, their alternative would have been to save, which, however personally responsible, would have done nothing to foster a demand for goods. Micro-level, it had an obviously beneficial economic impact on families, which in turn generated significant political support. By exponentially spreading the CCC's benefits, the remission policy deepened public backing. The policy also had a civic impact on enrollees. "Providing a major part of the family income has developed a sense of responsibility within these young men, most of whom have never . . . [been] able to contribute to the support of their families."[107] By making enrollees, in the words of one, "useful to our families," it introduced them to an important aspect of adult citizenship.[108]

Enrollees' third obligation was to follow the rules. Upon enlistment, they pledged to "obey those in authority and observe all the rules and regulations thereof to the best of my ability."[109] Here the CCC could rely on more than moral suasion, yet camp officers—military men though they were—did not have full military authority. The most severe punishment was expulsion—the equivalent of an employer's power to fire—with docking of pay, suspension of privileges, and assignment of extra duties the lesser options.[110] In Hoyt's estimation, as a result officers had to "display leadership and ability to command in excess of that normally required [of those] with more 'power.'"[111] Granted, this leadership fell rather short: in its first four years, about 7 percent of enrollees were discharged for disciplinary reasons.[112] Combined with high levels of desertion and "honorable" employment discharges, the result was significant turnover, which was contrary to the interests of the conservation program. Nonetheless, the CCC's disciplinary policies simultaneously succeeded in ensuring the order necessary for camp living while not abridging the civil rights of enrollees who were, after all, voluntarily enrolled in a nonmilitary program.

Enrollees' obligation to work was their final and most fundamental duty. It embodied half of the CCC's principle of reciprocity, the idea that enrollees should create, as well as receive, benefits. That they did so strongly influenced their experience. One enrollee recalled first entering the mess hall: "I could not restrain myself from comparing this to the notoriously famous soup line. But what a contrast; there were no downcast faces here."[113] Another summed it up well: "I feel I have given value for dollars received, and that I am again of use to the country."[114]

The value of enrollees' receiving their "keep" and more—that substantial inducements were provided—also cannot be overstated. Even during the economic recovery, more than 77 percent of enrollees cited wanting to help their families as a reason, and most often the chief reason, for enrolling, and none could have participated if their living expenses were not covered.[115] Through the CCC, enrollees experienced a standard of living that many had never had or no longer had. The civic implications were apparent, even to the enrollees themselves. In the words of one, "When a man looks under his cot and sees two good pairs of shoes, procures three wholesome meals a day, and can go down to the doctor every time he has a stomachache, it's pretty hard to make himself believe that they are going to junk the Statue of Liberty."[116]

Writing in the 1980s, sociologist Morris Janowitz held that the CCC "was a form of civic education because it joined together rights and obligations"— the right to a job during a depression and the obligation to perform conservation work.[117] The language of rights was not prevalent in contemporary writing, but one instance is telling. In 1935 enrollee James Kidwell wrote: "As a citizen I am transformed. Government is a hateful thing to a bum. In his misshapen vision, it is a hateful monster that denies his inherent rights. But, behold, the government has remembered me. It has given me a job, a world of comforts and many luxuries. . . . My old radical tendencies are being replaced by the stirrings of . . . good citizenship."[118] "Transforming" enrollees as citizens was not accomplished in every case; Holland and Hill estimate that for about 30 percent of enrollees, the CCC had had little impact, at least short term.[119] Still, the very fact of their participation in a program designed like the CCC, as opposed to one designed differently or none at all, had an impact— on the enrollees and the broader public, civically and politically.

Conclusion: The Politics and Civics of the CCC

The Civilian Conservation Corps was the first, largest, most highly esteemed, and most explicitly civic of America's civilian national service programs. It was also the shortest-lived and surprisingly not well understood. These facts make teasing out its civic and political lessons all the more important. Answers to three questions are key. First, how did the CCC act as national service and public policy for democracy? Second, why did Congress end the CCC in 1942, thwarting its institutionalization? Third, why was the CCC's influence on future national service policymaking so limited?

Box 5-1. *The CCC at a Glance*

Dates	1933–42
Enrollment	250,000 at founding, ~500,000/year at peak
	More than 3 million total
Purposes	Work relief and conservation
	Work training (1937 on)
	National defense (post–Pearl Harbor)
Government role: Administration	Run by the national government
	Implemented by the Army and Departments of Labor, Interior, and Agriculture
	Small coordinating office, first independent, later in the Federal Security Agency
Government role: Outside relationships	Publicly and locally well known and supported
	No organized supportive interest groups
Government role: Status within government	Established and continued on an emergency basis
	Never made permanent
	Ended by Congress, over FDR's objections
Work	Environmental conservation and infrastructure development
	Natural disaster response
	Quantity, visibility, and necessity of work contributed to its support

National Service and Citizenship in the CCC

In retrospect, the CCC was national service: it was a federal program that engaged mainly young enrollees in full-time, short-term, subsistence-wage work that filled a public need. However, because it was nonmilitary, voluntary, and means-tested, few recognized it as national service at the time. This lack of recognition contributed to its demise, as an entire generation of young men was called to military national service. It also contributed to the CCC's failure to influence the next generation of national service policymaking.

Participants	Needy men ages 17–28, with family to support
	Typically separate camps for whites and blacks
	Separate programs for needy veterans and Native Americans
Education	On-the-job training
	Camp living
	Formal classes
Obligations and inducements	Voluntary six-month term of service, no time limits
	Remit $25 of $30 monthly pay to family
	Received pay, room and board, and health care
Main civic points	Based on reciprocity and citizen-government partnership
	"Creating citizens" was a key goal, civic language was pervasive
	Emphasized work, as well as patriotic, constitutional, and service perspectives; both present and future orientation
Main political points	Ended because of lack of organized institutional and interest group support, lack of permanent status, insufficient program leadership, and WWII
	Failed to influence future programs because of dismantling; its close tie to FDR, Democratic Party, and New Deal era; lack of national service framing

Although policymakers came to recognize voluntary, civilian service programs as national service, they did not see that a means-tested work and training program could also qualify, for several reasons.

First, the importance of reciprocity weakened. During the CCC's lifetime, policymakers who valued training over conservation—who assigned a higher priority to enrollees' receipt of services than to their work—gained influence. A generation later, job-training programs would reflect this priority even more strongly, while national service programs went in the opposite direction. Second, the CCC's civic mission was *formative*. No one joined the CCC because of an intense commitment to conservation or a deep patriotic desire to serve; men joined because they were poor and needed work. Lack of initial civic motivation was partly to blame for obscuring the CCC's national service identity in future decades. National service advocates neglected the fact that many enrollees acquired an appreciation for conservation and a belief that they were performing important national service. The CCC developed enrollees' sense of citizenship. Certainly in no other program was the language and idea of citizenship, covering multiple perspectives, so pervasive. Belief that creating citizens was precisely what a national service program should do, however, weakened among national service policymakers and advocates.

Third, the connection between work and citizenship also weakened. If working and citizenship are wholly unrelated, then a job-training program will not be seen as serving civic ends, as national service must. This view was held largely by future policymakers, and it was wholly at odds with thought at the time.[120] In addition, if demonstrating citizenship through public work is unrecognized, the same loss results. Only by completely discounting the civic and educative nature of enrollees' conservation work could Holland and Hill argue that the CCC failed to develop enrollees' "contributing" citizenship skills. Enrollees were learning to be contributing citizens by *being* contributing citizens.

Finally, although the CCC's other civic lessons were not all beneficial, their total effect was also positive. The Corps's textbook civics lessons were weak, but the enrollees' continued education had civic benefits. Camps were not model democracies, but enrollees learned to live and work with others much different from themselves. Many camp commanders believed that allowing space for critical citizenship would undermine patriotism by definition, and in so believing undermined First Amendment constitutional citizenship lessons as well. However, enrollees' experience with government—local, state, and federal—was a civics lesson in itself, all the more powerful because it was real.[121] And although the CCC leaned toward teaching an unreflective patriotism, it also led many enrollees to see the value in democratic government. Overall, the CCC's ultimate civic success was giving enrollees the sense that they were valued and valuable citizens, with the program contributing, along with others such as the GI Bill, to the creation of America's "civic generation."[122]

The Politics of National Service in the CCC

How well the CCC fit or did not fit the changing definitions of national service and citizenship is not the only reason that Congress ended it or that policymakers did not use it later as a national service model. Political reasons—some unique to the times, others due to the changing nature of the times, and still others consistent across time—also played a role.

The reasons for the CCC's lack of institutionalization were mostly unique to the times. One was the belief that it had succeeded (or for some, failed) and so was no longer needed. This argument could prevail because of the limited power of New Deal–era organized interests. Within government, the CCC was not well enough organized to defend itself: it had few dedicated personnel, none well respected for their vision.[123] Further, none of the cooperating departments had a sufficient incentive to fight for continuation: the CCC's demise would not threaten their existence. Outside government, labor and business groups had been brought along, but none had reason to fight for it. Most critical, there was no organized group of CCC supporters—enrollees, alumni, local foresters, community leaders, and others—willing and able to press Congress for its continuation.

The CCC's lack of permanent status and ultimate demise also demonstrate the power of external events, which threaten national service programs repeatedly. If not for Roosevelt's attempted Supreme Court packing plan, the CCC most likely would have become permanent. Allowing it to become a recognized, ongoing program as opposed to a temporary relief measure may not have guaranteed its continuation but surely would have made the possibility more likely. The other external event was the war itself.

Given the CCC's acclaim and the unique reasons for its end, it is not surprising that it inspired policy entrepreneurs in the years and decades following its demise. What is more surprising is the limited scale of their success, both in terms of creating other youth conservation programs and of these programs serving as the basis for new national service policy. It took fifteen years for an offshoot of the CCC to take root, and when it did, its differences were as notable as its similarities: the Student Conservation Association, founded in 1957 by Elizabeth Cushman and Martha Hayne, was a tiny nonprofit summer program for college students, who worked in the national parks. As small as the CCC had been big, it helped inspire the federal government's Youth Conservation Corps, founded in 1971. At its peak, the YCC enrolled 32,000 young people a year in summer conservation work. The federal government returned to supporting year-round conservation work in 1978, when it created the Young Adult Conservation Corps, but that program and the YCC were short-lived: Congress defunded them in 1981. Both before and after the federal defunding, a number of state governments created their own youth conservation programs, but it would be more than another decade before the federal government provided them with funds and then created its own 1,000-member National Community Conservation Corps.[124] And although these efforts became part of the country's new national service program, AmeriCorps, neither they nor the CCC were used as models for AmeriCorps.

Time-bound reasons and consistent factors limited the CCC's influence over future national service policymaking, even before AmeriCorps. The main time-bound factor is simply that the program ended. In 1942 the CCC's administrative infrastructure was dismantled, leaving little to build on, and by the 1960s most personnel involved in the CCC had retired, limiting the supply of practical expertise and institutional memory.

The consistent factors center on the connections that the CCC—and all domestic civilian national service programs—have with their founding presidents, parties, and eras. The CCC was intimately tied to FDR when Harry Truman assumed the presidency and strongly associated with the Democrats when Dwight Eisenhower took office. In addition, the CCC's approach to national service and its failure to identify itself as national service were products of the era and thus hard to reclaim and continue into the post–World War II social and political environment. This lack of a national service identity obscured its value as a model for national service during the Kennedy and Johnson years. By the time Bill Clinton took office, the CCC's national service legacy had been claimed by supporters but was honored only as a noble experiment of the past—not used as the basis for building national service into the future.

Part

II

Volunteers in Service to America

Since 1965 more than 170,000 Americans have served in the Volunteers in Service to America (VISTA), working to combat poverty in the United States. VISTA is the nation's longest-running domestic civilian national service program; it continues today as part of AmeriCorps. As a result, understanding VISTA's history (in this part, its pre-AmeriCorps history) and its lessons as public policy for democracy is the next step in assessing the possibilities and limits of national service.

Like the CCC, VISTA influenced how its participants and the public—particularly members of VISTA's communities—understood their relationship to government and the meaning of citizenship. However, VISTA's approach emphasized the principle of sacrifice as opposed to reciprocity, and the idea of government as catalyst as opposed to partner. Sacrifice meant that volunteers were to give more than they gained; government as catalyst, that they were to accomplish more with less, addressing the plight of millions by engaging only several thousand volunteers. Citizenship was implicit in VISTA's approach; but the program mainly emphasized service and advocacy, along with certain constitutional and work perspectives. Most notable, however, is that VISTA intended to recruit people who already had a strong sense of citizenship; political theorist Eric Gorham is correct when he writes that VISTA did not "make pretensions to training [volunteers] for citizenship."[1] However, it is wrong to conclude that as a result VISTA did "not promote citizenship or educate [volunteers] politically."[2] VISTA did not make nurturing citizenship an explicit goal, but VISTA service influenced its participants' civic inclinations, often in politically controversial ways.

Politically, VISTA was never ended, but like the CCC, it was never deeply institutionalized or used as a model for subsequent policymaking. VISTA was not publicly or politically well recognized, accepted, or strongly supported as a feasible policy option for addressing the nation's needs or considered a practical life-option for large numbers of young adults. VISTA reached its peak pre-AmeriCorps enrollment of 5,000 in 1968 and spent much of the next twenty years fighting for its life. That VISTA survived is a testament to its ideological and programmatic flexibility and to defenses afforded by the post–New Deal political system, which allowed it to overcome more resistance than the CCC ever faced. Still, surviving is not thriving: VISTA remained small and beleaguered. As a result, policy entrepreneurs interested in creating an American national service institution quickly looked elsewhere for ideas and inspiration.

6

VISTA's Roots and Relationships

"Ask not what your country can do for you—ask what you can do for your country." With these words President John F. Kennedy called America to national service. And while Kennedy's national service legacy is tied to the Peace Corps, he also laid the groundwork for what became, under Lyndon Johnson, Volunteers in Service to America. VISTA was established by the Economic Opportunity Act of 1964, which launched Johnson's War on Poverty initiative.

Through VISTA an average of 4,000 people a year, mostly young adults, lived and worked in impoverished communities for one to two years, "helping people help themselves." In exchange, volunteers received a minimal living stipend, health insurance, and a small, monetary end-of-service award.[3] VISTA's administration reflected the complexity of America's federal system, with national, state, and local governments sharing power among themselves and with institutions of civil society. Projects were proposed by local government and nonprofits, approved by the national office, and subject to state governors' vetoes. Volunteers were typically selected and assigned by the national office, sponsored and supervised by local organizations, and trained by both.

VISTA's Roots

Compared with its structure, VISTA's lineage is straightforward. For our purposes, it is important to note the CCC's absence from its family tree. Since the CCC's demise, there had been several attempts to establish new conservation and national service programs. In tracing the CCC's influence, most striking is that what the CCC explicitly joined—the idea that participants should both receive and create benefits—the ultimate Kennedy proposals (and later Johnson programs) explicitly divorced. Kennedy initiated both a Youth Employment program (that included a Youth Conservation Corps), which became the Job Corps, and a National Service Corps (NSC), which became VISTA, warning that the two "should not be confused." "The Youth Employment program is designed for those young people who are in need of help. . . . The National Service Corps, . . . for those . . . who wish to be of help."[4] The CCC's work training advocates never wholly eradicated the CCC's national service ethic, but they effectively erased it from the minds of the next generation's policymakers. National service advocates would challenge this stark distinction—and the CCC's marginalization—within several years, yet another generation would pass before they received strong political support. In the meantime, domestic civilian national service would be framed as a counterpart to the Peace Corps.

To many, the logic of a domestic Peace Corps was self-evident. Sargent Shriver, the Peace Corps's founding director and head of VISTA's first parent agency, the Office of Economic Opportunity (OEO), believed that "it was bound to happen. After the first surge of Peace Corps volunteers served and came back, America's idealists began asking, 'If we're going to serve the poor abroad, why not also serve them at home?'"[5] The need was there, and so was the interest, especially among those wishing to heed the president's call but unable to go overseas.[6] Beyond supply and demand was politics: at the time, the Peace Corps was, in the late Senator Daniel Patrick Moynihan's estimation, "perhaps *the* great success of the Kennedy administration."[7] By creating a domestic counterpart, officials hoped to build upon and broaden the Peace Corps's support.

Given that VISTA's founders explicitly worked from the Peace Corps model, it is not surprising that they saw the latter as "the only precedent that existed."[8] But they soon realized that moving from an international context to a domestic one was not simply a matter of dispensing with a passport. First, the problem of poverty is different in a land of plenty from what it is in a country with little. As Moynihan explained, America's challenges were more social than technological.[9] Second, different problems require different strategies. Accordingly, "VISTA [had] far more in common with . . . social work than with the Peace Corps," including connecting people to available services, challenging the powers that be, and serving as a symbol "of mobility."[10] Finally, the politics were different. America's governors and mayors, activists and professionals, and citizens all had influence over VISTA in ways that their counterparts in Peace Corps host countries did not. Certainly, some of these stakeholders supported VISTA, but others were offended by the idea of America needing assistance like some "backward African state" and concerned with VISTA's many domestic political implications.[11]

These differences notwithstanding, the Peace Corps analogy proved irresistible, not only to policymakers but to future national service advocates hoping to build on the Peace Corps mystique, and to journalists looking for a readily comprehensible, shorthand descriptor for civilian national service programs of all stripes. The analogy was not entirely off the mark. At their core, both programs drew on America's history of voluntarism.

As the President's Study Group on a National Service Program acknowledged, "The citizen volunteer is a tradition of our democratic society. . . . There is no doubt about the desire of the American to give his brother a hand."[12] The problem with relying solely on existing volunteer efforts was twofold: many more volunteers were needed, and many potential volunteers "lack[ed] a guide" to help them get involved.[13] National service volunteers could be these guides. Small but powerful—growing only to "an optimum of 5,000"—the national service program would be a "fuse" that "when lit [would] explode the latent desire of the American citizen to help out his countryman."[14]

Beyond tradition, national service planners also built on recent community action efforts. Starting with the Ford Foundation's Grey Areas projects and New York City's Mobilization for Youth, these efforts emphasized community rather than individual change and engaging the disadvantaged in social change efforts.[15] Looking to give substance to President Kennedy's equivalent of FDR's New Deal—called the New Frontier—Kennedy administration officials introduced these ideas first to the President's Committee on Juvenile Delinquency and Youth Crime and then to the President's Study Group on a National Service Program. Further, the Ford Foundation and the juvenile delinquency committee strongly influenced Johnson's War on Poverty initiative, which included VISTA.[16] In short, VISTA was influenced by community action from multiple sources. As a result, in addition to inspiring Americans who were not in need to aid those who were, VISTA was committed to engaging the poor in collective self-help and action.

Conceived in the spirit of Kennedy's New Frontier Peace Corps and made real as part of Johnson's Great Society War on Poverty, VISTA bore the imprint of both and was intimately associated with neither. The lack of close ties worked to VISTA's disadvantage early on but allowed it greater flexibility over time. At the same time, its dual heritage set the stage for a decades-long battle to identify and reclaim VISTA's "true" intent. This was a fight over the means and ends of anti-poverty efforts, and simultaneously the means and ends of national service.

VISTA as National Service, or Not

Much more so than the CCC, VISTA was intended to be national service, and was: it was a federal program that engaged its participants, mostly young adults, in full-time, short-term, subsistence-wage work that filled a public need. In fact, it was originally called the National Service Corps. However, with its name change, national service disappeared from VISTA's vocabulary. More important, even though civilian service had become recognized as national service, traditional military and Jamesian definitions of national service prevailed. To the extent that VISTA deviated from these, it soon was not seen as national service but, at best, a small step in the right direction. Over time, the benchmark for what counted as national service shifted, making it (for supporters) less an existing program than a desired goal.

VISTA and the Military

In the 1960s, as in the 1930s, national service was still principally associated with the military. VISTA did not change this view. Although VISTA volunteers fought in the "War" on Poverty and were sometimes called "poverty warriors," VISTA was never seen as a variant of military national service nor did it ever become a civilian equivalent. Some national service supporters—military and civilian—challenged this disconnect, but for most it was a political reality to be accommodated, not contested.

First, War on Poverty language aside, VISTA's planners wanted to avoid the appearance of the program as domestic militarization, just as CCC planners wanted to disassociate the Corps from any such label. So, for example, in deciding upon a new name for the National Service Corps (which had the drawbacks of being closely associated with Kennedy and, worse, having failed to win congressional approval), the Johnson administration rejected several with the word *brigade* because of its "martial connotations."[17]

Second, planners did not want to offend pro-military sensibilities (not that they succeeded). Two Kennedy-era decisions will illustrate. First, Kennedy planned to nominate William Anderson, America's well-known and highly respected first nuclear-submarine commander, to head the NSC. Anderson's laurels were expected to help the program gain support in Congress. They did not. At least one senator "wanted to know what qualified a submarine captain to operate a social welfare program."[18] Even when the program was called the National Service Corps, its national service framing was contested: it is much harder to imagine a senator asking what qualified Anderson to run a *national service program*, albeit a *civilian* national service program. Further, the senator's question shows the complete military-civilian disconnect. Military (Army) expertise had been essential for the CCC's success; for the Corps's national service successor, it was considered irrelevant. Association would not make VISTA the military's civilian equivalent.

"Separate but equal" was another possibility, but a second decision precluded this option. Under the Kennedy plan (and Johnson program), service corps volunteers could apply for draft deferments, but they would not be exempt or deferred automatically.[19] Although opponents still characterized VISTA as a haven for draft dodgers, military service kept its pride of place, with civilian service not treated, as many hoped, as its "moral equivalent."[20]

VISTA and William James

Johnson's War on Poverty is frequently cited as "the" example of William James's "moral equivalent of war"—a marshaling of leadership, public commitment, and resources to battle to improve, not destroy, people's lives. Because VISTA provided the War on Poverty's "troops," one might assume that it grew out of James's national service vision. It did not; it grew out of the much differently designed Peace Corps. Although some national service advocates hoped to build upon VISTA to reach James's goal, policymakers steered clear of most of James's key elements.

Certainly, there were similarities: VISTA was originally designed to recruit well-educated, upper-middle-class youth to live and work among the poor at their standard of living. This is as close to James's vision of "gilded youth" experiencing "toil and pain" as one is likely to find. But the differences are more striking. VISTA was in no way a "conscription of the whole youthful population": it was entirely voluntary and recruited only a minute fraction of that population. This was done on principle and as a matter of cost: drafting and supporting millions was not seen as feasible, politically or economically. Further, not all of VISTA's participants were young—all ages were welcome—and even the young were expected to be "mature." For VISTA volunteers would not be washing dishes or working on fishing fleets, as James envisioned; they would be working with children and others who could be hurt, in communities that could be offended. "Knocking the childishness" out of volunteers was not in VISTA's job description.[21]

In practice, VISTA moved civilian national service further away from James's vision than had the CCC. Yet, in theory, James's ideas resonated with an even larger group of national service advocates. For this group, James's model, minus its pacifism, defined true national service.

VISTA and National Service Writ Large

Since California Democratic Representative Jerry Voorhis's National Service Act of 1940, most national service advocates sought to combine military and civilian service into a comprehensive system. In essence, advocates adopted James's model for mass participation without replacing military service with civilian: individuals would serve in one or the other. So advocates supported military service but supported universal service just as strongly, and were disturbed by the draft's inequities.[22] The armed forces did not need everyone; civil society arguably had the capacity to fill the gap. This effort gathered steam just years after VISTA's creation. That VISTA played such a small role shows both its limited influence and how the definition of national service kept changing.

Comprehensive national service gained an institutional identity and elite support with creation of the National Service Secretariat in 1966.[23] At the same time, the idea received broader public attention when Secretary of Defense Robert McNamara called for "every young person in the United States to give two years of service to his country," either in a military or civilian capacity.[24] In 1969 a surprising 79 percent of Americans supported a one-year requirement for men.[25] They were not, however, asked what they would be willing to pay for such a program: one estimate put the figure at $3 billion a year.[26] Infrastructure was another issue. In 1966 reporter Marion Sanders noted that "the plain fact is that there are no existing service groups which could effectively absorb [such] large numbers. . . . A new framework will have to be invented."[27] Sanders's new framework would include VISTA, increased to "at least double" its size. However, even a doubled VISTA would have accommodated only 6,000 out of a proposed corps of 500,000.

VISTA's marginal status can also be measured in pages. In one nearly 600-page National Service Secretariat report, VISTA merits a scant five pages; in Sanders's six-page *New York Times* article, fewer than three sentences.[28] Further, in making "The Case for a National Service Corps," Sanders, among others, disregarded the fact that Kennedy's National Service Corps had been enacted, as VISTA, just two years earlier.

Even VISTA's own staff could fail to see it as national service. In 1971, after President Nixon announced the planned merger of the Peace Corps and VISTA into the ACTION agency, VISTA's staff wrote that ACTION's founding "clearly suggest[s] the possibility of *some form of national service in the future* [emphasis added]."[29] President Carter's ACTION director, Sam Brown, argued against VISTA's national service framing another way, explaining that "ACTION is the one agency in Washington that should think of the nation, *not in terms of the nation* [emphasis added], but in terms of . . . communities and neighborhoods."[30] This was one rare point of agreement between the Carter and Reagan administrations.

Throughout VISTA's existence and beyond, what qualified as "real" national service—as well as its desirability—changed. Nonetheless, unlike advocates' dreams of a comprehensive national service program, and despite the efforts of opponents to end both their dreams and VISTA itself, VISTA actually existed and was the country's principal civilian national service program for the next three decades.

As with the CCC, how VISTA administrators and participants, elites and the broader public framed VISTA influenced its effectiveness as public policy for democracy and its place in policy history. VISTA's framework proved resilient enough for the program to survive changing administrations and governing ideologies but insufficient for it to reach the larger goal of deep institutionalization. VISTA's framework was not solely responsible for its resilience or lack of institutionalization; the programmatic elements that undergirded the program contributed as well.

7

VISTA's Purpose and Government's Role

A program such as VISTA comprises multiple, overlapping elements that influence its political support and viability and communicate lessons to participants and the public, in large part through policy feedback dynamics. In short, these elements shape the politics and civics of the program, which in turn influence future policy development. Drawing again on Anne Larason Schneider and Helen Ingram's framework, these elements include the program's purpose and the role the program gives to government, as well as how government's role is organized and supported. This chapter focuses on these elements; the next chapter, on the program's "tools, rules, and targets"—the service work it supports, its educational goals and content, the type of participants it recruits, and its obligations and inducements.

Politically, VISTA's policy design generated great controversy that worked against deep institutionalization: administrations typically responded by scaling it back or attempting to end it. Civically, VISTA embodied the principles of sacrifice and government-as-catalyst; one source of controversy was whether the volunteers and the program lived up to these ideals. Another was VISTA's association with critical—and not just service-oriented—citizenship. VISTA suffered both politically and civically from the resulting clash of views, as well as its neglect of citizenship as an explicit goal.

The Purpose of VISTA

Given its long, contested history, VISTA's overarching purpose remained remarkably consistent. As proposed under President Kennedy, created by the 1964 Economic Opportunity Act, and reauthorized by the 1973 Domestic Volunteer Act, VISTA was to provide full-time, yearlong volunteers who would serve in local agencies to help eliminate poverty. However, statutory consistency masks significant conflict over the source of and solution to poverty. From the CCC's perspective, the answers were straightforward and widely accepted: unemployment was the source, and work the solution. With unemployment below 5 percent at VISTA's founding and never nearing Great Depression levels in its history, VISTA's answers were never either this simple or widely accepted. Was the goal to bring the poor into the mainstream of a basically just society? Or was it to change a fundamentally *unjust* society? In VISTA scholar David Pass's language, the former reflects a combined compensatory-service ideology that sees the poor as needing services to overcome their deficiencies and deprivation. The latter reflects a community-advocacy ideology that says, "The poor must organize themselves . . . to redress an imbalance of power in society."[1] He argues that from its conception VISTA had strong strands of both, which generated ongoing tension.

Ideological conflict ensued almost immediately, with the massive political changes of the 1960s, and then intensified with partisan changes in administration. In general, the Republicans identified with Kennedy's early plan; President Carter's Democrats, with VISTA's early practice. Each group charged the other with subverting VISTA's true purpose and promised a return to its original intent. These efforts resulted in policy change but never as much as new administrations sought: local organizations, civil servants, and Congress served as moderating influences, and any changes yielded weak results. Further, as Eric Patashnik's work on reform would suggest, by not requiring significant investments by stakeholders or altering stakeholders' identities or affiliations, these changes were prone to reversal with each new administration. Politically, the fact and substance of the changes worked against institutionalization, creating escalating cycles of policy conflict instead of settled acceptance and downsizing instead of growth. Civically, the ideological tug-of-war translated into a dual focus on service-oriented citizenship (associated with the compensatory-service ideology) and critical citizenship (associated with the community-advocacy ideology). As dominant ideologies shifted, so did VISTA's civic focus. However, the most important civic impact resulted from what was missing, namely, an explicit civic mission for volunteers. This shortcoming reduced its potential as civic education and made the lessons it did teach less positive. Overall, stumbling blocks to VISTA's success as national service were set into its very purpose.

The Kennedy Plan: Quietly Serving the Poor, Maybe

Kennedy's National Service Corps had four goals: to provide full-time volunteers to work with the needy; for volunteers to motivate others to serve;
to dramatize human needs; and to draw people into helping professions.[2] By
achieving them, the program would have impact beyond its meager numbers: it would "act as a catalyst to greater citizen effort."[3] These goals helped
determine the program's policy design, as this chapter explains later. For now,
it is important to note that they supported particular views of citizenship.
For instance, the goal of bringing people into helping professions communicated that citizens' paid work was of public value, a key public work principle.
But even more so, the plan stressed citizenship through service: that good
citizens volunteered to help the less fortunate. Thus corps volunteers would
provide "personal service to human problems."[4] Examples of proposed projects included teaching Native Americans construction skills, helping released
psychiatric patients, and mentoring urban youth.[5]

Politically, the Kennedy plan is notable for what it would not do. For
example, it would not interfere with state and local prerogatives; send volunteers to projects without local invitation or without a plan for eventual
withdrawal; compete with or substitute for existing projects, volunteers, or
workers; administer projects from Washington; or recruit needy, unskilled
young people as volunteers.[6] This list is in striking contrast with the CCC's,
which specifically put needy, unskilled young people to work in Washington-
designed and -administered projects with little local involvement. One important similarity was its approach to race: when pressed, officials disavowed the
goal of combating segregation.[7] Finally, volunteers would be covered by the
Hatch Act, which prohibited partisan activity. The National Service Corps
was to be "truly a nonpolitical program," grounded firmly in compensatory-
service ideology.[8]

These assurances aside, some legislators were concerned about the program's potential to veer off into community-advocacy territory, fearing that
volunteers "will provoke; they will agitate"; they "will feel perfectly free to
disregard local social structures."[9] That the administration opposed giving
governors veto power over volunteers' assignments (Congress later added a
provision giving them veto power) exacerbated their fears.[10] However, judging
from all the administration presented on the proposed program, Kennedy's
officials intended for volunteers to quietly, unobtrusively provide services to
help the poor enter the American mainstream.

Johnson's Cacophony

Before Kennedy's assassination, Congress tabled the National Service Corps bill. Soon thereafter, Johnson renamed and revived it as part of the Economic Opportunity Act. It was essentially ignored in debate. Having failed earlier, administration officials wanted it that way, burying it in a mere paragraph. Further, it was minuscule—just a fraction of 1 percent of the bill's requested funds—so easy to ignore. Finally, Congress did not ask questions because, like it or not, they knew what it was.[11] After passage, it was not ignored for long.

President Johnson expressed what many hoped when he explained that VISTA volunteers' job was "to guide the young . . . to encourage the down-trodden, to teach the skills which may lead to a more satisfying and rewarding life."[12] Robert Kennedy, now a senator representing New York, expressed what more than a few feared when less than a year later he said their job was "to make the people dissatisfied with landlords and politicians—dissatisfied even with this United States senator."[13] These statements illustrate VISTA's dual ideological underpinnings but misrepresent their relationship. Even as LBJ was promoting the compensatory-service frame, he embraced elements of the community-advocacy approach. As one adviser explained: "You can send [them] in to teach. . . . But inevitably the VISTA people are going to see that . . . people . . . have to vote . . . or get on the local board of education or what have you. Johnson fully knew that."[14] But there were limits. In Moynihan's view, LBJ "had no sympathy whatever for financing a conflict of the Democratic poor against the [nation's] Democratic mayors."[15] He wanted the poor to vote (for Democrats). He did not want disruption, nor did members of Congress (Kennedy apparently excepted). As administration official Joseph Califano noted, as a result Johnson "got a lot of complaints from the Hill about the VISTA kids, that they were organizing political actions against incumbent mayors, incumbent school board members. We put out I don't know how many directives . . . to stop that."[16]

If Johnson's perspective shows the precarious ideological balancing act he wanted VISTA to perform, Kennedy's shows just how far and fast the ideological terrain had shifted. As his brother's attorney general, Kennedy oversaw development of the National Service Corps; its plans never mention the poor's relationship to politicians, let alone argue for agitation—and Kennedy himself disavowed such purposes. By 1966 Kennedy's political calculus had changed, but even more, the definition of *liberal* had changed. Once firmly grounded in compensatory-service ideology, it was now aligned with community-advocacy.

Within VISTA both approaches coexisted in tension and ambiguity (as they would have within the NSC), but the program's bias had shifted from service under the early plan to advocacy under VISTA.

These factors were amply evident internally. For example, in 1968 VISTA administrators were concerned that "too many projects [had] degenerated into custodial day care" when they should be "ambitious, bold, and creative"—projects that would "[make] VISTA the most significant force and moral voice in the war against poverty."[17] At the same time, VISTA volunteers charged these same administrators with preventing exactly this. One complained, "We thought—out of ignorance—that we would actually be allowed to create change."[18] Others—dismissed for organizing a restaurant workers' strike—said, "We were terminated . . . for doing our job too effectively and thereby rocking the boat."[19] VISTA's director, William Crook, responded: "The choice [we] faced was simple: either get rid of the volunteers or sacrifice the entire program" in the community.[20] But the choices were not simple. With decentralized training and weak supervision, administrators had few ways to communicate the boundaries of acceptable action; they had a hard time determining them. One sponsor saw a "lack of clarity" from Washington: he could not tell whether volunteers were supposed to be "change agents" or "helpers and technicians." But he also noted that "political realities [may well] preclude any clear, sharp definition."[21] Another political reality was that ambiguity left VISTA open to critiques from all sides.

Nixon's Charge: Lower the Noise Level

Although VISTA was a tiny program, it so offended Richard Nixon that in his presidential bid he campaigned against it specifically, and against the Office of Economic Opportunity (OEO) more generally.[22] This case of negative policy feedback led Nixon to question whether VISTA could serve any purpose. During his tenure as president, his administration covertly tried to end it and, failing that, reoriented it toward direct service, in keeping with Nixon's goal of "enlisting millions of citizen volunteers to attack the nation's social ills."[23] Nixon's theme could have come straight from Kennedy's National Service Corps's plans, and in 1973 Nixon appointed Michael Balzano, who wrote a dissertation arguing that VISTA had illegitimately repudiated its NSC past, as director of VISTA's new parent agency, ACTION.[24] Shifting VISTA's purpose, however, did not reduce the ideological conflict. If anything, it inflamed it further.

In 1970 a VISTA evaluator struck a familiar note, arguing that "if it ever knew what it was, [VISTA] is now philosophically unglued."[25] VISTA needed a coherent mission, and its leaders had one. As acting Director C. Robert Lane explained, "VISTA is no longer going to be this place where you can do your own thing. . . . [We] are striving for a new type of volunteer who will work within the system and lower the noise level."[26] Lane's boss, Office of Economic Opportunity Director Donald Rumsfeld, was blunter, arguing: "It's simple. The governors have got absolute veto power over the program. So it's a waste of time to train someone who doesn't want to be a VISTA and would rather be a Weatherman."[27] Some ambiguity remained—Rumsfeld supported groups that challenged "wrongful or illegal" city practices, for example – but the shift was decisive.[28]

To this end the program banished "community organization" from its official vocabulary and aimed to significantly decrease these types of projects.[29] More important, the administration moved VISTA out of the anti-poverty-focused OEO to a new agency—ACTION—which focused on voluntarism. ACTION brought VISTA, the Peace Corps, the small-business-focused Active Corps of Executives (ACE) and Service Corps of Retired Executives (SCORE), and the senior citizen–focused Foster Grandparents and Retired Senior Volunteer Program (RSVP) together based on a "philosophy which says that those of us who are more fortunate than others should take the time to help others to help themselves."[30] Volunteer opposition to the move—both institutional and ideological—led nearly half of current and former volunteers to join the National VISTA Alliance. Among other actions, the NVA (unsuccessfully) sued VISTA officials in U.S. District Court for imposing "arbitrary and selective cutbacks" as part of a conspiracy to change VISTA into a "service-oriented, Red Cross-type program."[31] For Nixon's VISTA appointees, this was exactly the point.

Under Carter, a Louder Voice for the Poor

When Jimmy Carter became president in 1977, he appointed two well-known former anti-war activists, Sam Brown and Marjory Tabankin, to head ACTION and VISTA, respectively. The type of people Nixon had tried to keep from becoming VISTA volunteers were now running the program. Brown's personal retrospective is worth quoting at length. Writing in 1980, he explained:

> In 1965, when I first heard about VISTA, I was beginning to be a little suspicious of everything the federal government was doing. . . . The War on Poverty seemed a cruel hoax. . . . I didn't see how VISTA volunteers committed to one year of service would be of much help. I wasn't impressed. . . .

In 1969, I was in Washington and went around to see friends at the National Welfare Rights Organization. There I met my first VISTA volunteer. . . . Finding one VISTA volunteer working for an organization like National Welfare Rights was interesting; finding a lot of them was surprising. Clearly, I didn't know much about VISTA. . . .

I wasn't sure [VISTA] would ever be understood or ever be popular. . . . By 1969, VISTA volunteers had a reputation of being the shock troops of the War on Poverty. . . . [And] VISTAs were shocking some people. . . . I wondered if VISTA would survive. . . .

When I became director of ACTION in 1977, I discovered just how close VISTA had come to not surviving; there was no request in the federal budget for money for the next year and some of the volunteers, all talented people, were being restricted more and more to administrative jobs in social service agencies. Gone was the emphasis on citizen participation. Gone was the idea of poor people helping themselves. VISTA, one of the government's most unusual programs, was on its way to becoming quite ordinary.[32]

To rescue VISTA from Republican banality, Brown reclaimed and reinforced its focus on community-advocacy. Under Nixon, "the focus of VISTA moved steadily toward one-on-one service delivery," turning volunteers into "low-paid social workers"; Carter's volunteers would be community organizers, setting up women's crisis centers, assisting co-ops, researching issues.[33] True, Brown identified a few worthy Nixon-era project "exceptions" and also continued some "one-on-one" projects, such as legal aid and drug counseling.[34] Still, the shift was unmistakable. Under Nixon, volunteers were not to be "true believers of Saul Alinsky," the famed radical populist; under Carter, Alinsky quotations graced VISTA's recruitment brochure and the Alinsky-inspired Midwest Academy received VISTA funding.[35] Nixon's people wanted VISTA to "lower the noise level"; Carter's wanted VISTA to be "a louder voice for the nation's poor."[36]

VISTA attracted attention. In 1978 Congress investigated charges that volunteers were engaged in "inappropriate, unproductive, and sometimes illegal activities."[37] Ultimately VISTA reined in its most politically charged practices. Still, with Congress and the presidency in Democratic hands, Carter officials' understanding of VISTA's purpose was generally accepted; most of VISTA's left-leaning practices were deemed in-bounds, and the program enjoyed solid support. It was only after their tenure that the Carterites' commitment to community-advocacy nearly proved fatal.

Reagan's Goal: Silence

From the Reagan administration's perspective, "the intent of the legislation establishing VISTA was to create a program to help the disadvantaged better cope with poverty-related problems."[38] Arguably, this view goes beyond Balzano's argument that VISTA had wrongly denied its NSC mandate and puts the most conservative spin possible on that mandate. Thus, under Carter, "VISTA [had] become a home for . . . social revolutionaries who [saw] the program not as a people-to-people attempt to assist the poor and disadvantaged, but as a vehicle for social and political upheaval."[39] However, VISTA's problems went beyond violating its statutory mandate: because, according to Reagan and members of his administration, "paid volunteers" are not "genuine volunteers," VISTA—and the very idea of domestic civilian national service—were fundamentally misconceived.[40] So they would end it. What Nixon's people attempted only privately, Reagan's wholeheartedly embraced. Reagan's first VISTA director, James Burnley, "work[ed] as hard as [he could] to be the last VISTA director."[41] Only when he and his many successors were thwarted by Congress did they embrace Nixon's strategy, focusing VISTA on compensatory-service projects such as illiteracy, hunger, and homelessness.[42] In attempting to end VISTA and reorient it, politics—specifically, the Reagan administration's ideology—drove policy, but the reverse was also true: VISTA's earlier policies provided incentives and meanings that contributed to the conservative counterreaction.

Politically, Reagan officials' belief that the program served no good purpose was rejected. Friends of VISTA (started by Carter officials) and VISTA's congressional champions prevailed. But one reason VISTA prevailed was its ideological flexibility, something built into its policy design. It did not need to engage in community-advocacy; it could be grounded in more conservative-friendly compensatory-service. Both its congressional supporters and the opposing administration knew this, making the former less likely to consent to termination and the latter less willing to fight to the death.

Under Bush: Quietly Serving the Poor, Twenty-Five Years Later

George H. W. Bush was the first president to take office pleased with VISTA, and the first Republican not to work for its demise. He was also the only president to inherit the program from a president of his own party (Ford's brief tenure aside), so he did not have to fight a preexisting ideological slant contrary to his interests. However, Bush not only identified with the compensatory-service ideology and projects that Reagan's appointees had instituted, as a "kinder, gentler" Republican, he embraced the program itself. Speaking at a White House ceremony in honor of VISTA's twenty-fifth anniversary, Bush explained that "you don't often notice [VISTA volunteers] at work, because theirs is a quiet mission. But . . . when I talk of the 'thousand points of light,' please know that no light is more dazzling, brighter, than the VISTA volunteers."[43] None of his Republican predecessors would have held such a ceremony, or said anything close.

To a large extent the program had come full circle, with Bush's "points of light" fulfilling the need that Kennedy's planners saw for communities that lacked "a guide, a light, a person whose example they can . . . respect."[44] On the other hand, VISTA also bore the marks of all of the years in between: surviving multiple near-death experiences had left it smaller, less well known, and less politically and civically consequential than Kennedy had envisioned and, arguably, Johnson had achieved decades earlier.

Government's Role

Divergent ideologies also drove administrations' views of government's proper role in VISTA, as elsewhere. Nonetheless, VISTA was consistently presented, and largely run, as a local program supported by the national government. As such, VISTA's leadership had to manage its relationships with other levels of government and with communities, as well as organize and support the program within the federal government itself. How this worked influenced VISTA's effectiveness, its political standing, and its civic lessons.

A "Local" National Program

Just as Roosevelt had to justify the extraordinary federal foray into unemployment relief when he proposed the CCC, so Kennedy and Johnson had to justify an unprecedented federal role in volunteer service when pushing for the NSC and VISTA. Traditionally, local voluntarism was seen as a bulwark against national government power, not a cause for its extension. However, while FDR embraced a strong national government role nonetheless, these later presidents simultaneously extended and denied federal power.

On the one hand, VISTA extended the national government's reach by placing thousands of volunteers it chose into communities and projects it also chose. On the other, the program disguised this power under a cloak of local control: volunteers would be placed only in "locally planned and initiated projects, at the invitation of community institutions, and under local supervision."[45]

Moynihan argues that "the need for outside intervention to appear locally initiated was always in view. That there was an element of deception in this posture—that it was altogether deception—should not be doubted."[46]

Why the need for deception? First was the program's purpose: its goal was to build the capacity of the community to address its own needs. For the federal government to determine those needs could appear counterproductive, even hypocritical. Even more important, downplaying federal power was the only way to secure passage. Unlike the CCC, which operated mainly on federal lands at a time of few organized environmental interests, VISTA would work in communities over which the national government had little authority, that were full of contending interests. Foresters in the CCC, given their leading role, could rest assured that the program would not cause them trouble. And no matter what the CCC did, the trees could not start making demands. Not so with VISTA: local elites could not assume that the program would respect their views or that it could control all of the reactions, especially of the poor, that it expected to "catalyze." In policy feedback language, they were concerned that VISTA would provide resources and incentives, information and meanings that would lead to political activity against their interests. As it was, Kennedy's National Service Corps was not passed, largely because of concerns about federal overreach; to pass VISTA, Johnson had to grant governors a veto over projects. The result was a federal program that had ambivalence toward federal power written into its very structure.

From an early-twenty-first-century perspective, one might expect Democratic presidents to embrace a federal role, however limited, in voluntary service. What is surprising is that two of three Republican presidents held similar views. In fact, Nixon argued that in this area "the role of government has been confirmed."[47] Only Reagan rejected this view. Politically, an administration's acceptance of VISTA's federal-local approach was necessary but not sufficient for securing its support. Nixon still tried to eliminate it, but Reagan tried much harder.

Civically, VISTA's governmental approach held promise and peril. It had the potential to strengthen citizenship in VISTA's volunteers by connecting them to two key sites of citizenship—the nation and local communities—and in local citizens by emphasizing their civic responsibilities. But it also had the potential to so obscure accountability that not only might these lessons go unrealized but the whole program might falter. Like the CCC's outcomes, these would turn on how well VISTA's administrators managed inter- and intragovernmental relationships, a task infinitely more complex for VISTA.

Managing Outside Relationships

Given VISTA's purpose and structure, it is not surprising that its external relations—with the public, communities, interest groups, and its volunteers— were a challenge. Nor is it surprising, given its long history, that these relationships changed over time. What is surprising is that these relationships proved strong enough to allow VISTA to have a long history.

THE GENERAL PUBLIC. Compared with the CCC, VISTA was at a disadvantage in building external support. Viewed nationally, the program was hard to see: it had only several thousand volunteers, spread across the country, integrated (however imperfectly) into local organizations and communities. Early on, the *New York Times* noted, "VISTA is almost a household word, although not in the most flattering sense. 'You know, the reaction I've gotten several times,' said [one volunteer]. 'It's a floor wax.'"[48] Twenty years later the paper struck a similar note: "The public perception is that VISTA is either dead or a credit card."[49] This is not to say that VISTA was always an unknown victim of mistaken identity. In 1966 the vast majority (90 percent) of college students knew of it, and 53 percent expressed interest in joining.[50] But the program had to work to raise its public profile by advertising, recruiting on campuses, even producing a documentary. It could not rely, as the CCC largely had, on the natural publicity of personal experience and word of mouth.

LOCAL COMMUNITIES. Locally, VISTA's benefits were also often hard to see, and not always seen *as* benefits. "For those already in power, those who resisted change, VISTA was nothing short of subsidized anarchy."[51] As a result, in its first decade it was "a rare instance when a mayor or a county commissioner [came] to the defense of VISTA volunteers."[52] A 1970 review found that 23 percent of VISTA projects had engendered conflict with local decisionmakers or controversy within the community or both—enough to account for some official concern but far from the majority of it.[53] Projects that sparked battles, however, received more attention than those that were well accepted, or even acclaimed. For example, the Texarkana (Arkansas) City Council's efforts to fire local VISTA volunteers for not "understand[ing] the South and its need to move slowly" (read: for upsetting the racial hierarchy) generated much more press than the decision of several poor West Virginia counties to buy cars for their VISTA volunteers to support their much appreciated work.[54]

Equally important, VISTA's self-help philosophy worked against highlighting any VISTA role. As one volunteer stated: "I want [the community people] to do it. When a program works, I want them to feel that it's their success, not mine."[55] Another explained: "We did a self-help housing project in one county. Except for the first few families that came in, they wouldn't know VISTA from shmista. . . . That's the only way to do this job."[56] This reluctance to draw public attention stands in stark contrast to the CCC's practice of placing markers at its work sites. To this day many of these plaques remain across the country. In short, the programs' different approaches to on-the-ground publicity contributed to different policy feedback effects, one lending itself to public knowledge and support, the other not.

It would be inaccurate to say that VISTA never generated local support, but often a crisis is what brought it to the fore. VISTA's first funding emergency, when congressional budgetary inaction cost volunteers their stipends in fall 1967, is instructive. Volunteers who had come to help poor communities had to turn to these communities for help themselves. Churches took up collections, stores provided groceries, chambers of commerce set up loan funds, and twenty-five New York City corporations pledged support for their city's volunteers—all of these efforts drew positive press coverage.[57] "Eventually, Congress acted and the funds were restored, but not until VISTA had learned that it had friends that it never knew existed"—friends it would need in the years to come.[58]

INTEREST GROUPS. If elements of VISTA made it harder to generate broad support, its organization and timing allowed it to develop narrower, but deeper, support. Because volunteers worked for local sponsors—such as social service agencies and churches—these organizations developed a strong stake in VISTA: the program provided sponsors with resources and incentives to advocate for its continuation and growth. Further, sponsors typically belonged to national interest groups that aggregated and projected their support on the national stage. For example, when the Nixon administration proposed cutting OEO funding and eliminating VISTA, several dozen liberal national interest groups created an ad hoc "Save the OEO Committee."[59] Later, sponsoring organizations became the core of Friends of VISTA, which defended against Reagan administration attacks.[60] Finally, many more groups in VISTA's day actively supported federal social programs generally, largely because so many more of them existed. So even if, for example, the National Council of Jewish Women had no direct stake, it still supported VISTA.[61] Time and again, when VISTA came under attack in Washington, these supporters rallied, but they were never sufficiently powerful to prevent the attacks outright.

VISTA Volunteers. VISTA's work was often hidden, but its volunteers were not. Until the program began recruiting mostly "indigenous" volunteers, VISTAs were outsiders, conspicuous in the small towns and urban neighborhoods where they worked. As early officials noted, "VISTA operated in a goldfish bowl. Because of the high visibility of its volunteers, it was under constant scrutiny."[62] They drew attention on matters from the nationally consequential to the highly personal. During the 1967 riots, administrators had "to tell the volunteers there that one false step on their part could very well . . . destroy not only VISTA's image but [everything] . . . being spent on the VISTA program."[63] On the other hand, male volunteers' beards created enough local controversy to become a national policy issue.[64] Again, the CCC comparison is striking. Enrollees were conspicuous in local towns, but they were largely anonymous: they did not stay, and there were so many of them that the actions of one typically did not reflect on the whole. The program also had a highly structured, authoritative relationship with its enrollees. In the CCC, beards were not up for debate; they simply were not allowed.

Several factors undermined the formation of any strong relationship between VISTA and its volunteers. During its early years, the times worked against an authoritative bond, as young adults contested authority of all kinds. But more important was the program's structure itself. As this chapter shows later, VISTA strove to recruit capable, independent volunteers who would not need much guidance or oversight, and occasionally got those who would not accept either.[65] VISTA's decentralized training made communicating clear expectations difficult, and after training, this only became harder. For its first two years, VISTA had no "personnel that could provide the needed day-to-day link between the volunteers and the organization's upper echelons."[66] For one volunteer, very likely speaking for many, "VISTA didn't exist after the training was over."[67]

Adding local and regional supervisors gave VISTA a greater presence but did little to clarify or strengthen volunteers' accountability. In fact, it is not clear to what extent they were accountable. Volunteers were "trained to be opportunists," to get support wherever they could, which could easily translate into shunning constraints whenever necessary.[68] "From a community organizing perspective, it matters little who pays your salary or to what organization you must officially report."[69] Even if it did, an accountability conundrum remained: "The volunteer must walk a tight wire between three or more organizations"—VISTA, the sponsor, the poor, and their organizations—"all of which are often claiming the right to direct his steps."[70]

Asked "who had the right to direct volunteers' steps," career-long VISTA administrator Diana London said, "The sponsors" unequivocally.[71] Volunteers' relationships with their sponsors were always key, yet varied by time, place, agency, and volunteer. As a result, VISTA scholar Marvin Schwartz's descriptions of early volunteer-sponsor dynamics in Arkansas best illustrate not a norm but the potential and occasionally very real challenges—with volunteers accusing sponsors of being "too establishment" and one acknowledging that they "treated the local sponsors as obstacles."[72] Another recalled this conversation with a displeased small-town police chief:

Chief: Who is your boss?
Lynch: The federal government . . .
Chief: Don't you have a local boss?
Lynch: We're sponsored by the [local] CAP [Community Action Partnership] agency, but they're not our boss. They are simply our sponsor.[73]

This is not to say that volunteers embraced federal oversight. This too varied. Volunteers often viewed VISTA apart from the federal government and certainly did not see themselves as federal employees (although community members often did).[74] In most respects, by law, they were not. Still, VISTA hired them and signed their small paychecks, giving volunteers certain "employee-like" responsibilities. How this relationship played out both created problems for the program and helped ensure its survival.

In the first major survey of VISTA volunteers (who served from 1965 to 1969), researchers David Gottlieb and Carol Hancock Gold asked about their attitudes toward government. More than three-fourths did "not feel that the leaders of the U.S. really desire[d] to wage an all-out effort against poverty," and nearly half of the male volunteers were suspicious of government-sponsored programs for social change, although they typically supported VISTA.[75] The survey revealed that "the major internal stress for VISTA was that [volunteers] often were in an ambiguous role of working for VISTA as a movement and against VISTA as a government agency."[76] VISTA attracted not only "critics of the current social scene" but critics of the very government enabling their service.[77]

Volunteer resistance started early. In 1966 a small group created "VISTAs for Peace" to protest the Vietnam War. According to a VISTA memo, "Volunteers say that if VISTA is so shaky it cannot withstand this crisis, too bad. . . . They feel that . . . by identifying themselves as VISTA volunteers they will have a greater impact"—an illegitimate impact in administrators' view.[78] The volunteers resigned or were fired.

President Nixon faced by far the greatest organized volunteer opposition, directed not at policies outside the program but at VISTA itself. The National VISTA Alliance was founded in 1970 and quickly grew to represent 2,000 active and 10,000 former volunteers.[79] Organizers consciously turned the strategies they used in their work against Washington, arguing that "now is the time for VISTA volunteers to take in hand the self-determination we daily preach to poor communities and hurl it at the VISTA administration, the OEO, and the federal government."[80] VISTA had provided these volunteers with the resources, incentives, information, and meanings to develop a greater willingness and ability to defend their program. Their goal was to become a recognized union, but instead of bargaining over wages, they wanted a voice in policymaking, to better protect the poor.[81] The administration took a hard line, believing, as VISTA's director put it, that "we would make more friends than we would lose if we were real hard-ass."[82] It tried, unsuccessfully, to bypass the group by creating an in-house national advisory council and assumed, incorrectly, that the NVA was a passing fad.[83] Although the NVA never achieved union status and eventually disbanded, it lived to plague the Nixon administration for the duration.

Even after the NVA's demise, volunteers continued to be a force. Writing in 1985 on "the agency that will not die," the *New York Times* credited VISTA's survival "in good part to a lobby consisting of some of the 80,000 former VISTA volunteers," a lobby that former CCC enrollees never created to protect their program decades earlier.[84] Again, VISTA had policy feedback effects, providing former volunteers with incentives and meanings—including an identity as former VISTAs—that strengthened their capacity and disposition to protect the program. That much credit was also due to Friends of VISTA shows the critical role VISTA's staff played in its survival.

Managing Inside Relationships: VISTA Leadership and Staff

Unlike the story of the CCC's leadership, which featured two main characters (FDR and Director Robert Fechner) and a supporting cast that stuck to the script, VISTA's story is one of continuously rotating leads who often had to fight lesser, veteran players for the right to direct the show. As a result, administrations found their plans moderated, if not thwarted altogether.

VISTA's DIRECTORS. Because of VISTA's inception under Kennedy and its long life after Johnson, no president ever had a strong, personal commitment to it. And given its tiny size, it rarely made it onto any president's agenda. Administrations' priorities instead came from heads of VISTA's parent agency—the

Office of Economic Opportunity through 1974 and ACTION thereafter—
and VISTA's directors. This chapter covers the OEO and ACTION below;
here, suffice it to say that VISTA's directorship was a problem in its own right.
It never had the innovative, constituency-building director that political scientists Jameson W. Doig and Erwin C. Hargrove, or Daniel Carpenter find key
to successful programs' growth and institutionalization.[85]

The problems began even before VISTA's founding, with Kennedy's
National Service Corps. The *New York Times* reported that "the most critical
need . . . is for a man-in-charge of stature enough to move [it] through Congress."[86] The administration never found one, and the stature gap remained
for VISTA. Many of VISTA's directors were young: Nixon offered the job
to a 24-year-old, Carter appointed someone 29, others were in their 30s. But
more important, none was well known, most did not stay long, and a critical
few were only acting directors. In 1972 one reporter observed: "Constance
E. Newman is [VISTA's] director. . . . Before her there were Glen W. Ferguson, William H. Crook, C. Robert Lane, and Carol M. Khosrovi. Not one
a household word."[87] She forgot Padraic Kennedy, but the point remains.
VISTA never had the equivalent of a Sargent Shriver, the Peace Corps's well-
known, charismatic inaugural director. Certainly, the CCC's Fechner was
unknown, but the CCC was so large and its presidential support so visible that
it did not need a director to raise its profile. VISTA did.

For more than two years, spanning the critical Johnson-Nixon transition,
VISTA had no permanent director, only acting leaders.[88] Lane described the
problem thus: "Your opponents will infer that . . . management doesn't have
confidence in your judgment, therefore they pay no attention to you. . . . Or
fundamental policy decisions are met with the rejoinder: 'Shouldn't this wait
[for] the permanent chief . . . ?' "[89] Timing exacerbated these problems. The
first acting director, Padraic Kennedy, was appointed under Johnson and continued, with little support, under Nixon, possibly on the assumption of the
program's demise. Lane held office, "hobbled by the 'acting' tag," during the
tumultuous founding days of the NVA.[90]

Finally, the directors' roster highlights the problem of high turnover. VISTA
had six directors in its first seven years; under Reagan it had another five in five
years.[91] Political appointees' tenures are typically short, but not this short. One
director explained that she was just "trying to get this little piece through, that
little piece through [Congress]."[92] VISTA's lack of stable, consistent leadership,
well known and respected by members of Congress, probably made getting its
"little pieces" through more difficult. Even more critical than that, it hindered
the directors' attempts to lead the program's civil service staff.

VISTA's CIVIL SERVANTS. In his 1988 book on the politics of VISTA and the Peace Corps, management professor T. Zane Reeves argues that "for almost twenty years at VISTA, two warring groups have vied for ideological supremacy: on the one side, presidentially appointed administrators . . . ; on the other, career employees and former volunteers."[93] VISTA's civil servants generally saw eye to eye with Carter's appointees, but like the volunteers, they took issue with Nixon's and Reagan's. Their resistance is not surprising: 90 percent of VISTA's career staff were thought to be Democrats, and many had been with the program from its start and were thus deeply committed to its survival.[94]

Lane described the limits of the Nixon administration's power: "When I'm asked if we're turning down the screws in VISTA, I confess . . . but in government at least, the screw handles are kind of hard to find and the threads are kind of rusty."[95] In attempting to implement reforms, Lane's "major problem . . . was their unpopularity among his own staff."[96] At least once, bureaucrats' opposition veered outside the law: in 1970 "sympathetic individuals in the OEO/VISTA administration" gave to NVA organizers "a computer printout of old volunteer addresses and over 3,000 government-franked envelopes" to recruit members. Adding insult to injury, Lane—as acting director and ultimate authority—was fined $300 per envelope (the fines were later dropped).[97] On the other hand, the administration ran into legal trouble of its own for, among other things, allegedly "recruiting [Republican] Party loyalists [and] . . . discriminating against classified employees who were active Democrats," both of which violated civil service laws.[98]

With more to fear from a possible Reagan administration, Carter appointees started Friends of VISTA (officially to commemorate its fifteenth anniversary) while he was still in office—an example of policy providing resources to help organize support on its own behalf. It continued to draw support and assistance (though no charges of lawbreaking) from VISTA's civil servants after they left.[99] Neither VISTA's bureaucrats nor the outside groups they supported were able to prevent all of Nixon's and Reagan's unwanted changes. However, through internal bureaucratic intransigence and external network-building, VISTA's civil servants were able to blunt the worst of them, acting as an effective "opposition within government."

Managing Inside Relationships: VISTA's Status

Like VISTA's leadership and staff, its status within the national government posed challenges. VISTA's institutional structure and location, its funding, and threats to its existence all interacted to influence the program's ability to fulfill its purposes, and allowed its specific purposes to change.

VISTA AND THE OEO—UNDER JOHNSON. Kennedy planned his National Service Corps to be independent; VISTA, however, was always part of a larger structure. Its first home was in the Office of Economic Opportunity, which affected its development for better and for worse. Philosophically, under the Kennedy plan, providing opportunities for volunteers to help the poor was the emphasis; under Johnson and the OEO, helping to eliminate poverty through volunteer action was the goal. The difference was subtle but went to the heart of the conflict that surrounded VISTA for decades.

Organizationally, OEO placement both allowed VISTA to exist—after the NSC's defeat, passing as an independent agency was unlikely—and complicated its existence. VISTA's original authorization was buried in the Economic Opportunity Act's "administration" section, making it look like an afterthought or, as many characterized it, a neglected stepchild.[100] Furthermore, the act authorized volunteers to work, Cinderella-like, for other OEO programs, which then viewed the "VISTA volunteers as cheap labor to fill their own personnel gaps."[101] Moreover, OEO Director Shriver—the Peace Corps's founding director—was thought by some to "not really want VISTA to blur the appeal of the Peace Corps."[102] VISTA's leadership resented its subordination and jockeyed for better position. For example, regarding a proposed VISTA expansion, Padraic Kennedy explained, "It would definitely make VISTA the most exciting focal point. . . . We would eat into the Peace Corps pool significantly." As for loyalty to the OEO, he said, "As the OEO begin[s] to sag, VISTA's rise will be even more remarkable."[103]

Certainly VISTA's funding was always an issue: VISTA "had a budget in the first year of about two and a half million dollars," far less than 1 percent of OEO's total, "and a reputation that was really zero."[104] This had consequences. First, it was difficult to recruit staff. "Capable and knowledgeable administrators in Washington, wise to the ways of the bureaucracy, took one look at VISTA's niggardly budget and sought employment elsewhere."[105] Second, it created "a rush to get [volunteers] into the field and in the public eye," as *the* way to establish its reputation.[106] With CCC-like speed (although not numbers), VISTA had its first volunteers in the field within five months. However, with speed came inefficiency. For example, VISTA haphazardly contracted with dozens of training centers, with "the training center in Oregon . . . sending trainees all over the country, including to Florida, and the training operation in Florida . . . sending volunteers . . . to Oregon."[107]

Third, VISTA's position pushed the program to place volunteers "in every single state," giving each U.S. senator a stake and making VISTA a "national"—if still very small—program.[108] VISTA succeeded, quickly assigning volunteers everywhere except Mississippi (which for years refused them). But this too had its trade-offs, with Kennedy asking, "Does it strengthen us appreciably . . . or would it make more sense to . . . [have our volunteers] in a lesser number of states but with a greater degree of concentration, effectiveness, and impact[?]"[109]

Finally, all of these factors complicated volunteer supervision. Speeding volunteer placement increased the need for quality monitoring, but spreading volunteers over great distances made this more difficult and expensive. Given its budget (and the NSC plan), VISTA left project-level supervision entirely to the local sponsors.[110] The limits became evident as early evaluations showed that "supervision of the volunteer was the weakest link in the project chain."[111]

VISTA's funding improved, increasing to $30 million in 1968, or 1.7 percent of the OEO budget.[112] But it still suffered, first within the OEO itself. Losing "the internal OEO struggle over the allocation of new funds" left VISTA, in Kennedy's view, a "popular midget suffering from an artificially stunted growth."[113] However, VISTA may not have fared better on its own. VISTA's requests would still have been vetted by Johnson's Bureau of the Budget (BOB), which took the OEO's penurious requests and cut them further. Faced with funding the war in Vietnam, the BOB dramatically limited funding for the War on Poverty, including VISTA. For example, in 1967 the OEO requested $33 million for VISTA; the BOB approved $26 million, a cut of 21 percent, with prior and future years' requests cut similarly.[114]

In comparison, Congress treated VISTA mildly. VISTA had a fair amount of support in the Senate, which frequently voted more money for VISTA than the BOB-approved administration request.[115] Although the House was never so generous, the final compromises typically resulted in VISTA's getting what the BOB asked. That these requests were low was not lost on legislators; and if VISTA's leadership, at least, was hoping to earn points for frugality, they did not always succeed. In 1968 one representative used the small size of VISTA's requested increase as a reason not to give it any increase: "Now VISTA. Your request is $32 million, compared with $30 million this year. Since you are so modest, what is wrong with getting $30 million in 1969? . . . You only ask for an increase of $2 million. *Apparently you do not know the ropes around here* [emphasis added]. That makes us say to you, 'If you are doing so fine with $30 million, go ahead, do it again with $30 million.' "[116] As other members noted, the major stumbling block to funding was in the executive branch, and this was under the Johnson administration.[117] VISTA soon would have to survive under Nixon.

VISTA AND THE OEO—UNDER NIXON. Having campaigned against VISTA, Richard Nixon's short-term strategy was to rein it in. Given VISTA's position, its leaders had always pressed for autonomy—earning Shriver's respect and new OEO Director Rumsfeld's enmity.[118] Rumsfeld once complained that "at conferences, VISTA personnel had the unfortunate habit of identifying themselves as VISTA employees without any mention of . . . OEO. This had to stop."[119] To end this and other VISTA practices he considered nefarious, Rumsfeld created an Office of Operations empowered to overrule VISTA's director and demoted VISTA's associate directors and division heads.[120] These steps increased the administration's formal control over VISTA, but they also reinforced the "us versus them" mentality they were intended to quell. President Nixon's Office of Management and Budget (formerly the Bureau of the Budget) went even further. In 1970, to balance the budget, the OMB recommended cutting OEO funding by 40 percent and eliminating VISTA's funds entirely—recommendations the president approved.[121]

To save the program, VISTA's supporters successfully brought media, interest group, and congressional pressure to bear, strategies that would help them again in the future. However, as Pass expertly describes, the circumstances of VISTA's 1970 rescue were unique—life-and-death program decisions rarely turning on stolen memos or confirmation hearings. The memo in question detailed the proposed budget cuts. It was written by John Wilson, the OEO's associate director of plans, research, and evaluation, recently nominated to become the OEO's overall associate director. Wilson left the memo in a photocopier; it was found by a former VISTA employee and given to NVA leaders. Senate confirmation hearings became the forum: just two weeks after the NVA received the memo, the team newly nominated to run the OEO and VISTA came before a Senate committee for approval. In the intervening days the NVA mobilized its members and got the word out, the League of Women Voters organized fifty organizations into a "Save the OEO Committee," and high-profile media covered the proposed cuts. Facing a Senate committee stacked with liberals (both Democrats and Republicans), Wilson denied writing the memo; and the OEO director-designate, Carol Khosrovi, denied reading it—and promised to push for "adequate" OEO funding and to protect VISTA from disproportionate cuts. She kept her word. VISTA's budget was reduced by a proportional 8.8 percent, to $33 million.[122]

VISTA AND ACTION—UNDER NIXON. While not guaranteed, the lobbying effort for VISTA was not unanticipated. In the stolen memo itself,

Wilson conceded that "I do not think the agency can politically eliminate this program. [It] would have to be terminated in the context of a much broader governmental reorganization."[123] So reorganize they did. Just weeks after the memo incident, in a speech at the University of Nebraska, President Nixon announced his plan to create a single "all-volunteer" agency—ultimately called ACTION—that would "give young Americans an expanded opportunity" to serve by increasing domestic volunteer funding; link domestic and international service; help "forge an alliance between the generations" by connecting youth and senior-oriented volunteer programs; and broaden volunteers' service to include "cleaning up the environment, [and] combating illiteracy, malnutrition, suffering, and blight."[124] More important, the plan gave the administration a positive vision for service and a constructive rationale for reorienting and restructuring programs. This was one reason for the additional funds: officials realized that "the press and Congress will quickly see through brave words combined with budget cuts."[125] Further, the administration chose reorganization, on which Congress routinely deferred to the executive, as the path of least resistance.[126]

The proposal's main problem was that key players within the administration opposed it. The Peace Corps director, Joe Blatchford, did not want his agency to lose its independence, and neither he nor VISTA Director Carol Khosrovi wanted his or her program overshadowed.[127] Nixon secured Blatchford's support the night before his speech by offering him ACTION's directorship, but officials had no agreed-upon merger plan. Nixon used his public announcement as an interdepartmental action-forcing mechanism. At issue was who would control ACTION's domestic programs and additional funds. As director of the government's largest domestic service program, Khosrovi assumed VISTA would set ACTION's domestic agenda.[128] Blatchford countered that "it was from Peace Corps that VISTA germinated, and it should be from Peace Corps that the expanded concept of American voluntarism draw guidance."[129] Regardless, VISTA was in for radical restructuring.

Khosrovi's plan was to turn VISTA into two hundred local volunteer resource centers, which would direct part-time volunteers to placements.[130] This idea reflected the president's priorities but amounted to a near-total repudiation of VISTA as it was. Consequently, it offended VISTA's staff and undermined VISTA's relevance as a model and source of expertise. Blatchford's plan was less radical—continuing with full-time volunteers—but was thus even more threatening. Under his plan, VISTA would "evolve into a series of 'corps'"—focused on safety, health, ecology, and economic development.[131] The administration backed away from this plan after VISTA officials leaked it to the press: with

"Nixon Envisages Abolition of VISTA in Merger Plan" plastered on the *New York Times'* front page, a repeat of the memo fiasco loomed.[132]

The administration finally submitted its reorganization proposal without any detail on VISTA's fate. Believing that any reorganization outcome would be bad, the NVA again led the opposition, identifying fourteen weaknesses in the plan—and, for balance, three strengths, possible through other means. One was that moving VISTA would signal a turn "away from actively working in poverty communities" and toward "getting thousands of people to volunteer" without regard to "the functions that volunteers will perform." Another was that ACTION's power to move funds between its programs meant "that the few dollars that VISTA has now could be transferred in whole or part to Foster Grandparents, the Peace Corps, or any other of the programs." Finally, the plan did nothing to assure that "VISTA will remain intact or that all the functions that VISTAs perform will be continued."[133] In the NVA's view, reorganization threatened VISTA's purpose, funding, and very survival, and it was not alone in its opposition to it.

To assuage concerns, the administration pledged to designate an "associate director for domestic and anti-poverty operations"; "retain [VISTA's] name, identity, image, sponsors, programs, and commitments"; and "preserve [its] community organization" focus.[134] However, the administration backpedaled on allocating VISTA extra funds (promising instead to spend the money on "VISTA-type" programs) and gave ACTION's director authority to "rearrange [the agency's] internal structure."[135] Given the reorganization bill's utter lack of detail, the administration was asking Congress, and VISTA's supporters, to trust it. Congress gave it the benefit of the doubt, with some of VISTA's supporters voting in favor of it out of fear that VISTA would face reprisals if it remained in the OEO over the administration's objections, more so than it would if it shifted into ACTION with the administration's blessing.[136]

Ultimately, the ACTION move did not affect VISTA as significantly as the administration hoped or supporters feared. VISTA's authorization—at first remaining in the Economic Opportunity Act and later included in the Domestic Volunteer Service Act of 1973—retained its core elements. Further, its volunteer strength remained relatively stable, at a little over 4,000. In no way had VISTA been "reorganized out of existence"; it had not even been appreciably altered. Its survival powerfully demonstrated the ability of its supporters to protect their program from a hostile administration. However, nothing they did convinced Nixon to be less hostile. Having failed to eliminate VISTA outright and through reorganization, the administration tried yet a third strategy: replacement.

As Moynihan had explained years earlier, "There is more than one way to kill a program in Washington. To withdraw funds and favor is only the most obvious. Establishing a competing program is certainly more elegant, and usually more effective."[137] VISTA's alternative was the University Year for ACTION (UYA), which engaged enrolled college students in full-time VISTA-type work in exchange for college credit and a stipend. From the administration's view, UYA had several advantages: it was a new program, and the administration could easily keep organizing and other objectionable emphases out of it right from the start; its volunteers were committed students and so thought to be more mature (unlike their VISTA peers, who were taking time off to "find themselves"); and they were supervised by both agency and university personnel, which the administration thought would be a restraining influence (professors apparently not yet having their radical reputation).[138] From VISTA supporters' perspective, UYA was a weak substitute funded at VISTA's expense.[139] By 1974 UYA had grown to nearly 1,700 volunteers.[140]

VISTA AND ACTION—UNDER FORD AND CARTER. Although UYA never supplanted VISTA, Gerald Ford proposed defunding VISTA—but not UYA—in his final budget. Had Ford won the 1976 election, VISTA again would have had to fight for its life, without being able to argue that it uniquely filled the full-time, anti-poverty volunteer niche. The Carter administration instead phased out UYA and strongly supported VISTA. President Ford had allowed VISTA's volunteer force to drop significantly; Carter built it back up to more than 4,000.[141] VISTA's budget increased, from $22.3 million in 1976 to $32 million in 1980, an increase that exceeded the high inflation rate.[142] At the same time, Congress allowed VISTA to spend up to 20 percent of its appropriation on a new community-advocacy-oriented National Grants program, which funded multistate grassroots coalitions targeting specific poverty-related problems and building the capacity of less "established" institutions to become VISTA sponsors.[143] This new program gave Carter's officials their best chance to reflect their values, and thus it drew the greatest ire from conservative opponents. One characterized it as "$4 million . . . channeled . . . to an assortment of leftist activist organizations," spent on "blatantly political activities."[144] ACTION's director defended the program, arguing that "any time you're out organizing the poor to speak for themselves, you'll have charges of politicization."[145] Conservatives' solution was not only to end VISTA's organizing but to end the program altogether. Carter's strong support turned out to be no more than a four-year reprieve, and one that helped set the stage for VISTA's next trial.

VISTA AND ACTION—UNDER REAGAN. In his first inaugural address, Ronald Reagan proclaimed that "government is not the solution to our problem," but *is* the problem. Of the many programs his appointees slated for demise, they considered VISTA especially egregious. That it was an ineffective waste of taxpayers' money ("cruelly unrelated . . . to the day-to-day needs of the truly poor") was the least of its offenses.[146] It was also inappropriately ideological ("a home for . . . social revolutionaries"), arrogant (who were volunteers to "tell people what's wrong with their lives and prod them into changes they don't really want"?), and fraudulent (perverting the true "neighbor helping neighbor" meaning of voluntarism).[147] Reagan's ACTION appointees made no secret of their intent to do away with it.

One of Burnley's first public statements as VISTA director was "I'm working as hard as I can to be the last VISTA director" and "after the phaseout, I'll . . . not give it a second thought."[148] This criticism contrasts with the Nixon appointees' conciliatory early comments (in 1969 Rumsfeld said that he "had a very favorable impression of VISTA"), but then Reagan's officials intended to succeed where Nixon's had failed.[149] With Reagan having won a resounding presidential election victory, with a new Republican-controlled Senate and more Republicans in the House, they had reason for optimism.

The plan was to rescind part of VISTA's appropriation, drastically cut its funding over the next two years, and end the program in 1984. In 1985 a reporter summarized the administration's accomplishments: "[VISTA's] recruitment program has been curtailed, its budget has been slashed . . . , [and] its volunteers have been cut . . . to 2,000"—significant changes. But on its main objective—VISTA's demise—the administration had failed.[150] Why?

Much of the fault was its own. In his zeal to purge VISTA of radicalism, ACTION's director created a "hit list" of thirty-nine projects whose sole common denominator was not that they were all radical hotbeds (some were traditional United Way affiliates) but that they used suspect language, such as "community organizing," in their project descriptions (in keeping with Carter officials' preferences, if not their own).[151] The fact that just "using the wrong words can land you in trouble with the Reagan administration" was widely and negatively reported.[152] Further, the courts slapped down a rule prohibiting VISTA from participating in any demonstration as a First Amendment violation.[153] Officials removed VISTA's name from agency newsletters and stationery well before its expected demise: the combination of executive branch overreach and over-confidence did not sit well with Congress.[154] Beyond all of this, the administration chose to seal VISTA's fate in 1983, the year President Reagan declared the National Year of Voluntarism.[155] Although officials believed that VISTAs were not "genuine" volunteers, opponents made much of the apparent hypocrisy. Even much smaller missteps, such as ACTION's failure to heed *Federal Register* rules when eliminating "community organization" as a required VISTA activity, were used by opponents to show that the administration's efforts to destroy VISTA knew no bounds.[156] According to Friends of VISTA Director Mimi Mager, "The truth is, had the Reagan administration gone about it in a legal and ethical way, the program would have been gone. . . . Because they did it illegally, unethically, and politically, . . . that gave us the hook to get the Hill involved, to get the media involved, to expose it."[157]

VISTA officials did not simply shoot themselves in the foot; they handed ammunition to others well positioned to shoot back. Chief among the defenders was Friends of VISTA. As a group dedicated to protecting and promoting VISTA, FOV had advantages over both the Nixon-era NVA and the "Save the OEO" coalition. FOV had a broader constituency than the volunteer-based NVA, including officeholders, academics, project sponsors, and social organizations, and it always had bipartisan cochairs.[158] Its mission was also less ideological: NVA was committed to VISTA's community-advocacy approach; FOV was committed to VISTA, period. This sole and permanent commitment also differentiated it from the "Save the OEO" coalition.[159] Finally, Director Mager had been a Carter-era VISTA appointee, so she knew the program inside and out, and had connections inside and out.

Relationships with VISTA's civil servants were especially critical. As Mager explains, "We were smoke-and-mirrors . . . the vision was always that Friends of VISTA was this huge organization . . . and hell, [all] we had was a telephone and an old typewriter. . . . But what we really had was a network of career people across the country."[160] This was typical of interest groups of the time: power came much less from numbers than from professional connections.[161] Civil servants were loyal to VISTA, not the administration—just like their counterparts in the Nixon years—and so "sabotage[d] . . . Reagan's plans from within" through leaks, "strict adherence to orders when this would prove disadvantageous to the Reagan cause," and "covert disobedience" otherwise.[162] In Mager's view, "You can't do what you want to do without really bringing in the career people, and particularly [those] who know how to make . . . your vision happen and do it within the law."[163] In policy feedback terms, VISTA as a program gave its civil servants the resources, incentives, and meanings—in this case an identity as a VISTA employee—that furthered their ability and willingness to protect the program. Coming largely from outside the Washington bureaucracy, Reagan's appointees were especially at the mercy of the civil servants, and given their goal, they were especially unlikely to be offered help. Even more skillfully diplomatic appointees would have been stuck, which helps explain why programs are so hard to kill: how do you convince people to show you how to destroy their life's work?

Ultimately, however, VISTA's fate rested not with its civil servants but with Congress. For two years it agreed to cut VISTA's funding—by 1983 it was a mere $8 million. But then, not only did it not agree to end VISTA, it increased its funding.[164] In so doing, the Republican Senate majority broke ranks with the administration. House Republicans showed greater loyalty but had less power; VISTA's Democratic supporters controlled the House and voted accordingly.[165] The Senate story is the more interesting. For VISTA's hearing before the Labor and Human Resources Subcommittee on Family and Human Services, chair Jeremiah Denton (R-Ala.) invited six witnesses: five spoke in VISTA's favor, one—ACTION's director—spoke against.[166] In full committee, chair Orrin Hatch (R-Utah) did Denton one better, recommending millions more in funding than Denton's already noteworthy proposed increase.[167] Hatch's committee approved VISTA's reauthorization and funding proposal by a vote of 16 to 2, and the Senate passed it on a voice vote.[168] In the committee hearings, there was "no evidence" of "any concerted effort . . . to eliminate VISTA."[169] And as for a Senate debate, what is most notable is that there was no debate: conservative Republicans stood idly by while the chamber's most renowned liberals—Edward Kennedy (D-Mass.) and Alan Cranston (D-Calif.)—praised the bill as a step toward "the promise of one day restoring [VISTA] to the strength it once enjoyed."[170] And thus, the administration's plan for VISTA's demise met its own demise.

Never again would VISTA's existence be so threatened: the settled consensus, at least within Congress, was that the federal government had a role to play in supporting full-time volunteer efforts against poverty. But what those efforts would look like remained an open question. As the conservative Heritage Foundation had warned before Reagan's VISTA fight, "VISTA is an established program with much support . . . it [will] be far easier to change the character of VISTA than eliminate it."[171] So, thwarted just as the Nixon administration had been so many times earlier, the Reagan administration responded in kind. "If VISTA had to remain, let it be as a conservatives' VISTA," starting with the work it would support and the remainder of its policy elements.[172]

8

VISTA's Tools, Rules, and Targets

Like VISTA's purpose and role for government, its tools, rules, and targets—the service work it supported, its educational goals and content,
the type of participants it recruited, and its obligations and inducements—
influenced its political support and viability and communicated lessons to
participants and the public, in large part through policy feedback dynamics.
In short, these lower-level policy elements further shaped the politics and civics of the program, which in turn influenced future policy development. Consistent with the findings discussed in the previous chapter, VISTA's design
details—including its association with critical citizenship—generated high
levels of controversy that worked against deep institutionalization; administrations typically altered these elements to bring the program in line with their
priorities, often either before or after trying to eliminate it. VISTA suffered
politically and civically from the ensuing conflicts, as well as from its neglect
of citizenship as an explicit goal for the program and its work.

VISTA's Work

Compared with the CCC's work, VISTA's was a mixed blessing, civically and
politically. Civically, it allowed volunteers to contribute their time and talents
to solving important national problems. Expectations, however, often exceeded
accomplishments, undermining the work's ability to strengthen volunteers'
sense of citizenship and convince the public that government and citizens
could address serious challenges together. Politically, VISTA's work helped

build deep, but narrow, support. Much more than the CCC's, VISTA's work was controversial, hard to see, difficult to quantify, and challenging to evaluate. Many supporters saw these obstacles as necessary consequences of VISTA's very purpose, while others—supporters and opponents alike—saw them as problems to be solved. At the same time, VISTA's work was more flexible than the CCC's: fighting poverty encompassed a broader range of activities than did conservation, which helped VISTA adapt and survive changing times.

As mentioned earlier, a significant amount of VISTA's work—particularly in community organizing and advocacy—stirred controversy. Certainly, just as foresters embraced the CCC, so most social service providers embraced VISTA for the same reason: it did not displace social workers or other "helping professionals" ("nondisplacement" is a sine qua non of civilian national service) and often assisted their practice, giving them an incentive to support the program. However, their support for VISTA, unlike the foresters' response to the CCC, revealed conflicts in the VISTA model. Former VISTA administrators William H. Crook and Ross Thomas explain professionals' support thus: "Most of [the VISTA volunteers] work with a minimum of supervision and are eagerly welcomed by the professionals who, until the VISTAs began to appear, frequently had to depend upon local, part-time volunteer[s]."[1] In fact, VISTA volunteers needed greater supervision ("the weakest link in the project chain") and were supposed to be replaced in short order by local, part-time volunteers. That Crook, a former VISTA *director*, failed to see the conflict between the goals of the program and these core supporters is startling.

VISTA's challenges extended to the public, where the need to build support typically pulled the program toward direct service. First, as always, was the controversy. Although some projects avoided controversy at the expense of effectiveness and others embraced it at the expense of political viability, still others negotiated a balance. One sponsor explained: "A point of view I adopted was to tie social change with delivery of service that people needed. While consciousness-raising was important . . . it was [more] difficult to attack delivery of services to little retarded kids."[2] This strategy also prevailed at the national level, especially during the Nixon years. From OEO Director Donald Rumsfeld's perspective, it was "going to be a lot easier . . . to market VISTA in the country if we [could] point to the fact that there [were] X number of VISTAs doing something specific that [could] be understood."[3] Direct service projects were easier for most people to understand, and accept. So while the shift away from community organizing was certainly an ideological choice, officials also believed it would help build support. If they had to keep the program, better to make it a credit to the administration.

Second, VISTA struggled to build a record, with severe consequences: leaders blamed its limited growth on its inability "to provide data on our program accomplishments."[4] At the start, all that VISTA could report were volunteer numbers, followed by anecdotal stories. The numbers were not insignificant—1,477 volunteers were placed in the program's first eleven months, twice the Peace Corps's rate—but not unquestionably impressive.[5] VISTA's anecdotal reports were also mixed. For every positive story touted by officials, critics could point to a negative one, and media coverage was similar. For example, the *New York Times* ran a story headlined "Tribe Wants Back 2 Girls It Ousted." Tribal leaders forced the volunteers out after the volunteers had "enraged some of the older, established authorities" (including a local priest who called them "volunteers in service to the devil") but asked them to return after reservation residents signed a petition in their favor.[6] This was a small incident, but it spoke volumes about the conflict in and ambivalence about the program.

However, within two years, VISTA officials had data, not just stories. And these data showed, for example, that two hundred migrant children were enrolled in VISTA preschool programs in Arizona, five thousand Pittsburgh residents had formed a credit union with VISTA assistance, and six hundred mental hospital patients in West Virginia had been released early because of VISTA services (saving the state $81,000 a year).[7] These lists were an improvement over anecdotes, but they had drawbacks. One, the inventory was not overwhelmingly impressive. Unlike the CCC, which measured its accomplishments in millions of trees planted and thousands of dams built, VISTA, with its meager volunteer contingent, yielded far fewer accomplishments. Two, VISTA could not claim exclusive credit for its achievements, because they "were often a mixture of contributions made by interlocking organizations, such as the CAAs [Community Action Agencies], the school districts, health departments, etc."[8] On the one hand, this was VISTA's intent and strength; on the other, it made credit-claiming difficult and even risky, opening the program to charges of overstating its work. Finally, the lists were incomplete: they did not capture all of the work that volunteers did and arguably missed their most important work, much of which was not quantifiable.

This last point brings us to the next challenge, that most of VISTA's work was neither visible nor concrete. In the words of an early volunteer: "My job is . . . to change attitudes. . . . I ask [people], 'Why can't you change this?' or 'Have you ever seen anything changed before?' It's sort of indirect therapy."[9] Another explained the situation thus: "A typical day, nothing great accomplished, nothing tangible done that you can point to and say, 'That person was given a new start, or next week he'll have a better job.' It's not that kind of program."[10] The problem was that "people . . . want to see something for their money, and you can't see relief, [or] hope."[11]

Furthermore, as Marvin Schwartz explains, even when "volunteer influence brought measurable improvement . . . the community organizing efforts that helped initiate those gains [were often] intangible. . . . How does one credit the volunteer . . . time spent writing, editing, and printing copies of CHANGE, the newsletter of the Committee for Representative Government [or] . . . the volunteers who consulted N. H. Hilliard in his near-successful campaign for a Texarkana School Board position?"[12] For average citizens this work was invisible and its value ambiguous; in fact, they might see it as objectionable. In sharp contrast, citizens could see the CCC's work, whose value was self-evident. Yet at the same time VISTA volunteers themselves were visible, working with the public in public, which denied VISTA the CCC's autonomy. In policy feedback terms, VISTA's work failed to create strong incentives for public support and in some cases actively created disincentives.

Finally, VISTA's work was especially challenging to assess at a time when evaluation standards were increasing. The CCC's main goals were to provide temporary work and to conserve natural resources. By definition it succeeded at the first—no need for evaluation there—and its conservation work, from planting trees to saving acres from erosion, was assessed simply by counting, another criterion that did not require evaluation. VISTA's goal was to provide full-time volunteers to help local organizations eliminate poverty. Simply tallying the number of volunteers and the people they served might have sufficed during the New Deal, but it was wholly insufficient for meeting the Great Society's technocratic evaluation standards. So if it appears that I am holding VISTA to a higher standard of accomplishment than I did the CCC (see chapter 5), it is because VISTA was in fact held to a much higher standard. VISTA needed to "devise totally objective standards for the evaluation and quantitative measurement of the relative effectiveness of volunteers and projects," standards the CCC could not have met—and never had to—and that were exceptionally difficult for VISTA to reach.[13]

Two years in, VISTA official Padraic Kennedy explained that "VISTA research and evaluation will be primarily directed toward determining the effectiveness of the volunteer in helping the poor change their motivation and condition."[14] VISTA would not be evaluated on its effect on volunteers, although its effect on them was an "important by-product."[15] Still, how to evaluate volunteer-initiated changes in the lives of the poor was complicated, as shown in this quasi-scientific cost-benefit formula the program devised in 1967:

$$\frac{\textit{Efficiency of Volunteer}}{\text{\$ Spent}} \quad \times \quad \frac{\textit{Vol/Project}}{\text{Supervision Ratio}}$$

$$\overline{\text{Coefficient of Social Gain}} \quad \overline{\text{Aspiration of Client Population}^{16}}$$

How evaluators chose to "totally objectively" quantify the "aspirations of the client population," among other things, is unclear.

Partly in response, the Nixon administration shifted VISTA's emphasis "toward more service- and problem-oriented projects—with successes and failures more easily assessed."[17] This approach continued under Ford. For example, VISTA's 1976 Project Survey assessed delivery of services, resource generation, and increased community self-reliance.[18] Excerpts of its findings are worth presenting in detail. The study found that

> A vast majority of VISTA volunteer tasks (95 percent) were seen as related to project objectives. Assuming that the objectives reflected community needs, it can be said that VISTA volunteers are providing effective human services. . . .
>
> The amount of resources generated . . . was quite high. Dollar values were given wherever possible [for] . . . construction materials, space, grants, welfare benefits, legal settlements [and other resources]. . . . A conservative estimate of the average amount generated per volunteer would be $46,822. . . .
>
> Although it was a difficult concept to measure, the findings of this study tend to show that community self-reliance has increased. The VISTA supervisors, VISTA volunteers, and interviewers all agreed that there was growth occurring in almost all (95 percent) of the projects. . . . Nonetheless, the concept of a limited period of involvement of VISTA volunteers . . . is either not understood, not taken seriously, or not acceptable to sponsoring organizations.[19]

The study concluded that "VISTA [was] accomplishing its legislated purpose with a high degree of success," but these excerpts show how difficult this was to document. The conclusion that VISTAs delivered worthwhile services was based on the assumption that project tasks met community needs. The finding that community self-reliance had increased was admittedly sketchy and was weakened by the fact that many organizations were unprepared to phase out their VISTA volunteers. Finally, many of VISTA's leveraged resources came from other government sources. Whereas the CCC could credibly argue that its work generated national wealth, VISTA was in the less enviable position of arguing that its work "generated" welfare payments for the needy and project grants that the government was awarding anyway.

Absent agreed-upon evaluation criteria and solid data, people could easily come to radically different conclusions about VISTA's effectiveness. Some argued that VISTA had been "very successful and, therefore, government officials quickly moved to reduce its effectiveness."[20] Others held that "anyone taking the time to examine VISTA's activities would come to understand how cruelly unrelated they [were] to the day-to-day needs of the truly poor."[21] Like most other disagreements about VISTA, these centered on different understandings of its purpose. Those committed to community-advocacy viewed ministering to the poor's "day-to-day needs" as merely applying a Band-Aid; those committed to compensatory-service viewed "rocking the boat" as more likely to toss the poor overboard than to rescue them.

That VISTA's work was often controversial, invisible, difficult to quantify, and hard to evaluate affected the volunteers; after all, they were the ones doing the work. Controversy—and efforts to quell it—led them to question the government's commitment to ending poverty in a way that the CCC's enrollees never questioned the government's commitment to its goals. Furthermore, the intangibility of volunteers' work led them to doubt the value of their work, even as they fought to do it. Volunteer Frances Wood remarked, "I always had doubts about what we had done . . . about raising hopes and not following through."[22] She served in VISTA in 1969, a time when "only a slight majority of the vol[unteers] (55 percent) felt that their own VISTA service had [had] an impact on the social conditions of the specific areas in which they worked."[23] Wood also did more community-advocacy work than compensatory-service, as did many other volunteers at the time. That also is likely to have influenced her perception. As she explains, with "community empowerment or advocacy," the "long-range impact on volunteers is often one of frustration and doubt."[24] On the other hand, direct service projects "most often result in positive VISTA memories, because the volunteer is able to assess his contribution."[25] The change brought by the Nixon administration is dramatic: in 1976, instead of being asked whether their work had an "impact on social conditions," volunteers were asked whether they were "providing important services"; 91.8 percent thought they were.[26]

That the Carter and Reagan administrations would argue in turn that their predecessors were asking the wrong questions again demonstrates the ongoing battle over VISTA's purpose. However, VISTA was flexible enough to be reframed; both administrations were able to alter VISTA's work to more or less accommodate their ideological commitments and the day's pressing issues. Carter's involved volunteers in energy conservation; Reagan's created the VISTA Literacy Corps. As a separate VISTA program dedicated to means and ends that conservatives supported, the Literacy Corps allowed VISTA to grow despite the administration's overall negative view of VISTA.[27] Opportunities like these helped the program survive, allowing domestic civilian national service to remain an option for thousands who wished to serve.

VISTA's Volunteers

Although VISTA did not exist for its volunteers, as the CCC did for its enrollees, it was made up of volunteers whose demographics mattered. VISTA's policies, set by administrations and implemented by the national office and local sponsors, determined VISTA's makeup with respect to age, sex, race, class, and education. Blessed with many more applicants than positions (nearly five times more at its 1969 peak), VISTA had to be selective.[28] Civically, the selection criteria and results influenced volunteers' experience and their view of government. At the same time, administrations determined VISTA's policies according to their perceived political consequences.

The CCC decided that its participants were "enrollees"; later, VISTA's planners had to decide what its participants were. In VISTA's case, "volunteer" came easily. Even before it incorporated *volunteers* into its name, it drew on Peace Corps precedent: in both cases participants were volunteers because they chose to participate and were not paid a market wage. The title emphasized their self-sacrificing, other-regarding nature and communicated a civic lesson. Politically, the title gave participants a moral standing missing from *employees* or *workers*, which groups such as the National VISTA Alliance used to their advantage. It is remarkable that no one questioned the appellation until the Reagan administration, when officials narrowed the definition of a "genuine volunteer" (in the civilian context) to exclude anyone receiving any remuneration. Since then, what to call national service participants—and whether to call them volunteers—has been a battle fought over the relationship between voluntarism and national service in the broad sense.

Nationally and Locally Recruited Volunteers

Following the Peace Corps model, the typical early VISTA volunteer was a young, well-educated, upper-middle-class white, sent far from home. Within several years, however, the program began recruiting older, less well-off, and, often, minority volunteers to serve in their local communities. This shift was striking in that the left, the right, and the technocratic center all supported it. As a result, locally recruited volunteers' [LRVs] numbers increased steadily regardless of which administration was in the White House. LRVs, who were introduced under Johnson, grew to 20 percent of VISTA's force in 1970, overtook nationally recruited volunteers (NRVs) by the end of Nixon's administration, expanded to nearly 75 percent of the force under Carter, and became the only volunteers under Reagan.[29] Tracing the administrations' different reasons for preferring LRVs sheds further light on their varying goals.

VISTA based its original recruitment strategy on the premise that the poor needed "outside catalysts [to] intervene"—that if they were able to change their communities and themselves on their own, they would not *be* poor.[30] VISTA administrators never wholly abandoned that premise, but they quickly realized that "outsiders" had weaknesses and "insiders" strengths. First, local volunteers could increase VISTA's efficiency and effectiveness: new national volunteers had to "establish themselves, gain credibility, and understand local needs," things that local volunteers could help them do.[31] For years this was the LRVs' main task, and it led to "different roles for different types of people."[32] Schwartz found local volunteers to be generally patient and humble; national volunteers, idealistic and impatient. "Working together, . . . the national would gain in humility and local awareness; the local would gain a sense of personal pride and . . . [learn] how to assert himself."[33] Furthermore, officials hoped that local volunteers would help projects continue after VISTA support ended.[34] They also were responding to political pressure. On the one hand, "urban poverty communities no longer welcomed assistance from outsiders," and on the other, "establishment leaders" saw national volunteers as "outside agitators."[35] The Nixon administration built upon these reasons, formalizing new VISTA "teams" of professionally skilled, generalist, and local volunteers.[36] Local volunteers would bring "the knowledge, experience, and identity which makes communication possible," and just as important, their communication styles would be less confrontational than those of "radical national volunteers" with no local connections and nothing to lose.[37] At the same time, however, the most radical national volunteers—those involved with the National VISTA Alliance—were pushing in the same direction. In the name of "community control," rather than pacification, the NVA imagined an eventual "phasing out of the original white, middle-class reformers."[38]

The NVA's vision inspired Carter's officials to increase local recruitment to almost 75 percent. In Sam Brown's words, "the volunteers are different, how they do what they do is different, and the renewed emphasis on self-help—on poor people helping themselves—is starting to take hold."[39] Later, Reagan officials were still concerned with the remaining 25 percent, those "who were more easily used for political activities because of their temporary status in the communities."[40] Although no data compare national and local volunteers' "political activities," data did show NRVs to be more critical of VISTA than LRVs were.[41] To further "defund the left" and as a step toward terminating VISTA, the Reagan administration decided that it made strategic sense to eliminate volunteers who complained and who it believed were the most "political." In addition, ending national recruitment reduced the federal government's administrative role and made the program less symbolically "national."

The shift to local recruitment solved all of these problems, but it complicated VISTA's mission as national service. The CCC could easily give its enrollees a "sense of the nation" simply by moving them to a different part of the country and intermingling them with enrollees from yet other areas. As NRVs became the minority, for VISTA to give its volunteers a "sense of the nation," it would have had to explicitly and forcefully connect volunteers' local work to the *nation's* commitment to end poverty. It did not.

Age and Sex

President Kennedy's speech on the National Service Corps shows both how much national service was associated with youth and how much Kennedy hoped to change that connection. On the one hand, Kennedy announced the NSC in his "Special Message on Our Nation's Youth," reinforcing the expectation that young people would be an "important [NSC] age group."[42] On the other hand, he intentionally tempered this focus by saying that the NSC would "not be limited to young people" and would include "all ages" (mentioned twice).[43] He further stated—twice—that "many of our senior citizens [have] indicated their willingness to participate."[44] In fact, he closed his remarks on the NSC with those words.

The reasons for this "senior" focus were programmatic and political: planners intended to recruit those "best qualified," which easily included seniors, and they knew that appealing to elders might bring another constituency to the New Frontier. Most aspects of the NSC's design, however, worked against significant senior involvement, especially living at the poverty line and being sent to any corner of the country. As a result, "VISTA [became] a young person's organization by both design and accident."[45] The numbers bore this out, despite how frequently VISTA advertised that volunteers ranged "from 18 to 85," and later "92."[46] In its first two years, more than 75 percent of VISTAs were under 25, and 15 percent under 20.[47] In David Gottlieb and Carol Hancock Gold's study, only 11 percent were over 30.[48] However, just as the program shifted toward recruiting local volunteers, so it moved toward recruiting older ones; in fact, the former was largely responsible for the latter. In 1976 most (62 percent) NRVs were under 25, but only 22 percent of LRVs were that young.[49] With rising proportions of local volunteers, VISTA "grew up": volunteers' median age in 1969 was almost 24 (an increase from earlier), in 1978 it was 27, and by 1987 it was 35.[50] Although VISTA never attracted a large senior contingent, over time it became more "adult."

Aiding its aging process was a decision to limit VISTA's youngest volunteers—those 18 and 19—who, according to Padraic Kennedy, typically "lacked the maturity, judgment, and humility to handle an exceedingly tough job."[51] Between 1966 and 1970, the proportion of teenage volunteers dropped from 15 to 3 percent.[52] VISTA's 1969 recruitment pamphlet explained: "Most VISTAs are young. *All* must be mature. . . . VISTA is no place for people trying to work out hang-ups [emphasis added]."[53] The pamphlet was titled "If you're not part of the solution, you're part of the problem"; for many youth the issue was that they were *thought* to have too many problems to be part of the solution. The contrast with the CCC is obvious: its administrators expected the CCC experience to instill maturity. Maturity was not a prerequisite for "being part of the New Deal solution."

Another contrast between the CCC and VISTA was in gender. The CCC was exclusively male; VISTA, predominantly female. Between 1966 and 1969—when VISTA routinely recommended draft deferments—54 percent of volunteers were women, a number that increased to 66 percent in 1977 and 77 percent in 1992.[54] Again, this shift was driven by the increase in LRVs: in poorer areas, more women had the deep community connections, the education, and the clean records that VISTA wanted. In 1972 women accounted for 62 percent of LRVs compared with 53 percent of NRVs; in 1980 the numbers were 73 and 63 percent, respectively.[55] Yet even among national volunteers, women were always the majority. The striking gender difference between VISTA and the CCC raises important questions about the constituency for different types of civilian national service and changing gender expectations.

Race and Class

Locally recruited volunteers diversified VISTA not only by gender but by race and class. In its first two years, "minority members . . . were conspicuous only by their absence."[56] In Gottlieb and Gold's study, 95 percent of respondents were white, and almost half reported yearly family incomes above $12,000 (almost $67,000 in 2010 dollars).[57] As T. Zane Reeves explains, one virtue of this upper-middle-class orientation was that volunteers could better "serve as resources in planning social change; after all, they understand how the economic and political system functions."[58] David Pass looks on the flip side, observing that "few [volunteers] had ever seen poverty close-up and far fewer had experienced living in poverty 24 hours a day."[59] This combination created a unique cross-class learning experience, first between VISTA volunteers and community members, later between national and local volunteers, for whom poverty was not a novelty. For local volunteers, VISTA offered a different type of learning experience.

The LRV shift also altered VISTA's racial and ethnic composition. By 1976 minorities made up almost 25 percent of the volunteer force, increasing to 42 percent in 1992.[60] At the same time, the national volunteer contingent remained more significantly white: in 1980 the vast majority (88 percent) of NRVs were white, compared with 51 percent of LRVs.[61] While VISTA had somewhat increased the racial and ethnic diversity of its original volunteer constituency—the young, college-educated, middle-class—most of its diversity came from recruiting local volunteers and from mixing local and national volunteers.

Education and Skills

In announcing his NSC proposal, Kennedy explained that the program was for those "whose present skills, jobs, or aptitudes enable them to serve their community in meeting its most critical needs."[62] In VISTA's early years, aptitude and idealism prevailed over skills and jobs, which had become suspect. As one 1967 brochure explained, volunteers "arrive in the nation's slums equipped not with a briefcase full of plans for urban renewal, but with the conviction that they can help."[63] Few had full-time work experience, and fewer still had professional credentials.[64] What they typically had was a college education, taken as a rough proxy for aptitude. Between 1965 and 1969, most volunteers (93 percent of the women and 80 percent of the men) had attended college, although in 1968 only 25 percent had graduated.[65] While these standards were obviously different from the CCC's—many CCC enrollees had not graduated from high school—they shared a notable similarity: the key criteria were aptitude and desire, not experience or demonstrated skill.

The CCC never wavered from this approach, but by the late 1960s VISTA had. Beginning under Johnson and continuing under Nixon, VISTA altered its selection criteria. By 1970 aspiring volunteers were told that idealism was necessary but no longer sufficient: "All [volunteers] must qualify as skilled." Certainly, "natural ability and a well-rounded education" might suffice, but "many [will be] skilled in a more specific way."[66] This shift resulted in a volunteer contingent with fewer college students, more local community members, and more professionals.

First, the program recruited fewer national volunteers who had yet to finish college, preferring those with degrees. By 1970 the percentage of college graduate volunteers had more than doubled, to over half.[67] While this change went hand in hand with reducing the teenage contingent, graduates were also thought to be better qualified and less apt to cause trouble. Still, both administrations were concerned that "B.A. generalists" were prone "to drift into community organization without sufficient experience and without fully understanding the political implications."[68] Although for years the B.A. generalists continued to dominate, the program strongly recruited others in the hope that they would be more productive and less problematic.

Among them were local volunteers, specifically those "known and accepted in the neighborhood."[69] These volunteers were less likely to have attended or graduated from college, but they had the experience the program needed and they knew the community. At the other end of the spectrum was VISTA's third category, professionally trained volunteers. Between 1969 and 1970, the number of volunteers with legal, business, health, education, or architecture training increased from 310 to 1,392, or 24 percent of volunteers.[70] Professionals had the virtue of having "the simple expectation of doing the job for which their education had prepared them," unlike many generalists, and of doing work that "had a clear objective," typically quantifiable and unobjectionable.[71] As one VISTA physician explained, "I expected to heal sick patients in . . . one of the ten poorest counties in the U.S. We accomplished this."[72] This fit perfectly with the Nixon administration's shift toward more "service- and problem-oriented projects—with successes and failures more easily assessed and local political toes less easily bruised."[73]

Although the Nixon administration's "team" concept included all three types of volunteers, the ideal emphasized partnership between specially skilled and local volunteers, such as the project that paired VISTA volunteers from the Stanford School of Business and local recruits to assist "ghetto businessmen."[74] However, this was not conceived as an *equal* partnership: local volunteers were needed "on the premise that the effectiveness of the *skilled* volunteer depends on his acceptance by the poor [emphasis added]."[75] The assumptions of the early Peace Corps and VISTA model still held, even if their form had been questioned. Under the Carter and Reagan administrations, the original model itself was rejected.

From the perspective of Carter's ACTION director, "VISTA's [original] goal was to help give people a voice about their own destinies through community organization. This became diluted . . . with a major influx of professionally and technically skilled VISTA volunteers delivering services."[76] So VISTA scaled back its recruitment of professionals and increased the number of local volunteers, who were given greater responsibility in the name of community self-help. As the Carter administration gave way to Reagan's, the rationale for recruiting local volunteers changed but the outcome did not. Unlike Carter officials, members of the Reagan administration firmly believed in volunteers delivering services, but like Carter officials, they moved toward a volunteer contingent composed entirely of local volunteers. For Reagan's appointees, a program of locally recruited, nonprofessional VISTA volunteers was just one step away from their ultimate goal—a *nonprogram* of locally recruited, nonprofessional volunteers.

Education for and through VISTA

A central point of this work is that all elements of policy design act as pedagogy, teaching participants and the public about their relationship to government and the meaning of citizenship. VISTA's policy design emphasized personal sacrifice, government as catalyst, and critical and service approaches to citizenship. In addition, VISTA had explicit educational components: it trained volunteers for their service and volunteers learned *from* their service. But unlike the CCC, which highly valued training and education, VISTA treated educational components as peripheral. Training was instrumental, necessary only to help already well-qualified individuals become better VISTA volunteers (and to weed out those not up to par). What volunteers might learn from their service was typically disparaged as "making VISTA about the volunteers." This view limited VISTA as civic education and weakened the civic lessons the volunteers did learn.

VISTA Training

Before volunteers officially became VISTAs, they were trained. The focus of training, like that of other program elements, shifted over time to reflect the accumulation of experience, changing volunteer demographics, and new administration priorities. The majority of VISTA's six-week pre-service training, and all of its on-the-job and in-service training, was practical, designed to impart specific service-related skills, and was conducted by volunteers' sponsors or similar organizations. Another portion, ranging from two weeks early in VISTA's history to several days later on, was conceptual, devoted to orienting volunteers to VISTA's program and philosophy.

In keeping with the Peace Corps model, Johnson's officials intended VISTA training "to help [volunteers] become barely acceptable subprofessionals whose energy and enthusiasm [would] compensate for their lack of academic training and experience."[77] As explained by Crook and Thomas, training had several specific goals. First, it "expose[d] the trainee to actual conditions of poverty," which was part test (trainees could be "de-selected") and part preparation.[78] Second, it provided "an intensive course in the history of VISTA, poverty in America, [and] the programs . . . designed to cure it."[79] Third, it "increase[d] the trainee's awareness of people and the techniques and dynamics of working with them"—critical given that VISTA's biggest challenge was teaching volunteers to not do things *for* people but to understand that "any permanent change . . . must come from the people themselves."[80] Finally, it should "assist the trainee in gaining a better understanding of himself, . . . his own commitment, his strengths, and his needs."[81] The overall intent was instrumental, designed to increase volunteers' effectiveness and lay the foundation for lifelong service. However, because Nixon officials believed that it was not instrumental enough, especially the last point, they concluded that "changing volunteers [in ideologically suspect ways] was the real goal of VISTA."[82]

In keeping with plans for the National Service Corps and its own frenetic start, VISTA did not develop its own training but rather hired universities and private organizations. By mid-1967 VISTA had contracts with forty-two training providers and granted each much autonomy.[83] As a result, the understaffed Washington leadership knew little of what its volunteers were taught or how well, and training could not provide volunteers a common experience. Further, the administrative inconsistencies associated with training volunteers all around the country and then moving them all around again for placement looked very much like incompetence. Subsequently, training was consolidated to one training center in each of the Office of Economic Opportunity's seven regions, with volunteers trained and placed within the same region.

This was the training regime Michael Balzano, Nixon's future ACTION director, studied for his 516-page Georgetown University doctoral dissertation.[84] Regionalization did not reduce trainers' autonomy, so Balzano studied two programs with divergent approaches, one at the University of Maryland and the other at the University of Colorado.[85] His question was whether they conformed to VISTA's intent as embodied in Kennedy's National Service Corps plan.

Balzano found the Maryland program entirely contrary to NSC goals. Specifically, it trained volunteers to "confront the status quo"; "bring about racial justice"; think "that federal, state, and local governments are inflexible and unresponsive"; and believe that they were "not part of the establishment."[86] In short, the Maryland program trained volunteers to be highly critical citizens. In practice this translated into a higher percentage of VISTA projects in Maryland's training region experiencing conflict or controversy: 29 percent compared with 23 percent nationwide.[87] While Balzano and Nixon's VISTA appointees equated discord with a lack of effectiveness, the conflict and controversy study itself found no such relationship.[88] Even so, controversy was civically and politically consequential for the program, projects, and volunteers.

In contrast, Balzano found the University of Colorado program "uncontestably" in harmony with NSC goals. Specifically, it trained volunteers to believe "that confrontation . . . hurt[s] the poor"; "that economic and social mobility . . . can be enjoyed by [all] if we work at it"; "that our political system . . . is basically sound, flexible, and responsive . . . [when] needs are perceived"; and that volunteers "are agents of the establishment and are working to improve it."[89] In short, the Colorado program stressed service and constitutional citizenship themes. In practice, this translated into only 17 percent of the Colorado region's projects experiencing conflict and controversy at the same time that these projects were working in the area (rural) and with the populations (migrants and Native Americans) that were statistically most prone to conflict.[90] Again, Balzano equated harmony with effectiveness without evidence; nonetheless, concord had its own implications.[91]

Balzano had reason to believe that most VISTA training programs, if not exactly like Maryland's, were not at all like Colorado's.[92] The Gottlieb and Gold study confirmed this view, finding that "most volunteers initially were politicized by the agency itself" through training that "[taught] political values that were *even more radical* than those generally held by poor people or college students."[93] The VISTA conflict and controversy study authors also focused on training, arguing for a national curriculum to ensure that trainers communicated a clear, consistent mission. They also recommended that "all training centers have . . . an attitude-producing approach that approximates that of the University of Colorado."[94] Balzano supported a national curriculum based on Colorado's approach, but he took issue with the conflict and controversy study's understanding of VISTA's mission, which varied from "any mission is better than none" to politically empowering the poor.[95] For Balzano the latter was a perversion of VISTA's NSC-based true purpose.

Balzano's study is open to challenge, particularly his premise that the only way for VISTA to honor its legislative mandate was to adhere to the National Service Corps's principles. Congress did pass VISTA on that basis, and the resulting program was different. However, the changing nature of the times all but ensured this, as did Congress itself by placing VISTA within the Office of Economic Opportunity. But it is important to note that members of Congress had the opportunity to force VISTA to conform to NSC principles through appropriations and oversight. That Congress gave VISTA its overall stamp of approval (if only by giving it money) while imposing restrictions on specific activities (as explained below) indicates that Congress actively expressed its intent over time.

The VISTA National Curriculum was completed in mid-1970, well before Balzano's ACTION tenure or even ACTION's creation, but fit well within the ACTION framework. The curriculum gave trainers an extensive outline and case studies its authors deemed necessary, though insufficient, for preparing effective volunteers. The materials heavily stressed service and constitutional citizenship themes. Volunteers were told that they "must be willing to put aside for a year [their] personal concerns and ambitions, to set aside [their] own 'agenda' " and become servants of the poor.[96] This orientation was differentiated from a work understanding thus: "You can't establish a job and set a salary which would require that the person live in the poverty community, share the life of the people there. . . . It's not something anyone will do for money. But some will volunteer."[97]

The curriculum also stressed volunteers' connection to VISTA as an OEO government program. It states that "a clear presentation of the OEO . . . will be the foundation on which the VISTA volunteer builds his identity," develops "commitment and loyalty to OEO," and has his "decision to work within . . . 'the system' " reinforced.[98] Further, volunteers were not to see "the system" or "the power structure" as the enemy; "the enemy [was] poverty and the lack of opportunity."[99]

Even before the end of Johnson's presidency, VISTA reduced its two weeks of "theoretical, classroom-oriented training" to five days, allowing for more pre-service "on-the-job training."[100] The national curriculum fit within this shorter classroom structure; the Nixon administration also added specialized training, in keeping with its emphasis on providing communities with highly skilled volunteers.[101] When Carter took office, his officials found VISTA's training regime lacking, believing that "those being helped often wound up giving all the training to our volunteers. . . . We do not feel that those being helped should have to help the helper."[102] As a result they requested a significant increase in training funds and developed a new curriculum for center-based training, presumably more consistent with the Carter program's emphasis on organizing and advocacy.[103]

In addition to pre-service training, volunteers had ongoing on-the-job and in-service training, focused on skill development for their assignments. However, with passage of the Domestic Volunteer Act in 1973, Congress mandated that low-income locally recruited volunteers also receive career development counseling, to aid their transition to regular employment.[104] This provision moved VISTA training in the direction of the CCC, although without the CCC's explicitly civic language connecting job-holding to citizenship. It also moved VISTA slightly toward a basis in reciprocity—to the idea that both the server and the served should benefit—and somewhat away from the principle of sacrifice, but only slightly: since these were low-income volunteers from VISTA's target communities, they were "being served" and "serving" at the same time. A bigger step came in 1979, when career counseling was made available to all volunteers.[105]

VISTA's career development program was one of its first official acknowledgments of the potential educative value of the VISTA experience for volunteers themselves. However, from its conception the program was intended to influence its participants; it did so, but in some ways not at all intended by its founders.

Education through VISTA Service

Unlike the CCC, with its enrollee-focused civic education emphasis, VISTA had a civic agenda focused mainly on the public and those served. One NSC goal was that full-time volunteers "would motivate many more Americans to participate" part time, prompting the "haves" to fuller citizenship.[106] Later, focus shifted to the "have-nots." For example, under Carter VISTA was "succeeding in giving poor people back their citizenship; their belief that they can help themselves."[107] Still, VISTA also influenced volunteers, acting as "experiential education," with strong civic implications.[108]

Under Johnson, officials saw VISTA's effect on volunteers' "continuing commitment to serve the poor in [their] community and through [their] subsequent profession [as an] . . . important by-product."[109] They stressed VISTA's service and work effects; it had critical and constitutional citizenship effects as well. Further, like the CCC enrollees, VISTAs were to learn principally through their work; however, VISTA only rarely professed in positive fashion that "those who join VISTA gain as much as they give."[110] Because VISTA was premised on sacrifice, and because some volunteers admitted to gaining more than they gave, officials soon downplayed its impact on volunteers.[111] Nonetheless, its impact was real, with civic and political consequences.

"Service" was key to Kennedy's National Service Corps and to VISTA, and NSC planners especially hoped that the program would "stimulat[e] a longtime respect for volunteer service" in volunteers.[112] In its recruiting material, VISTA promised that "the communities to which [volunteers] return after VISTA [will be] the beneficiaries of [their] newly found knowledge and confidence."[113] In the Gottlieb and Gold study, three-quarters of respondents stated that "VISTA ha[d] strengthened their commitment to end this country's social problems" and "had a positive effect on their desire to be involved," demonstrating that volunteers at least believed the program to have positive policy feedback effects on their future intended civic engagement.[114] Schwartz saw evidence of this in 1988, finding that "former volunteers . . . possess[ed] a distinct sense of community involvement."[115] Twenty years later, in a survey of VISTA's pre-1992 volunteers, almost half "reported that their VISTA experience influenced their volunteering activities"—and a staggering 95 percent had volunteered in the past year.[116] However, given that 94 percent of a comparison group—people accepted into VISTA but who left during training—had also volunteered in the previous year, their generosity was less likely the result of VISTA service than something typical of the volunteers VISTA recruited. At the same time, given the numbers, there was little more for VISTA to add.

"Attracting more Americans into helping professions" was another explicit goal for NSC planners.[117] In Schwartz's estimation, "many volunteers were already headed in that direction, [but] . . . with VISTA providing the last bit of thrust, many volunteers . . . moved into service careers. Almost unanimously, these former volunteers have identified their VISTA service as the single most influential event in determining their career directions."[118] In VISTA's 1980 evaluation, more than one-third of volunteers said that their service had altered their career plans, and in 1993 more than a third identified "career development" as their primary personal benefit from VISTA.[119] Further, in 1980 more than half planned to continue doing the same or similar work after they finished VISTA. Given that more than half of VISTA-sponsoring agencies had former VISTAs on staff, for a number of volunteers VISTA led directly to a job.[120]

Unlike volunteering, neither the NSC planners nor VISTA administrators framed volunteers' choice of a "helping" career as a necessary part of good citizenship. However, by highlighting and furthering this goal, VISTA communicated that citizens' paid work could contribute to the public good, a key principle of the public work citizenship approach. Further, VISTA emphasized bringing together people from diverse backgrounds to address public problems, also a central public work idea. On this score, VISTA also appears to have had influence: in a 1993 survey, 22 percent of former volunteers identified "community awareness" as their primary benefit from VISTA, understood as "enhanc[ing] their awareness of the issues, problems, and needs of local communities and develop[ing] better understanding of diverse community groups."[121]

VISTA volunteers also developed a better understanding of America's political system.[122] In Crook and Thomas's assessment, "the VISTA experience offers . . . a postgraduate course in practical politics. The volunteers, of necessity, learn all about the power structure and how to use it."[123] Part of this structure was inherent in VISTA itself—its place within the federal government and its relationship to the administration, Congress, state and local governments, and local agencies. And although early volunteers' experience may have led some to question our constitutional system, neither they nor those who followed turned away from it: an overwhelming 95 percent report voting in the first presidential election following their service, and 96 percent in the 2004 election.[124] Like the generosity of lifelong volunteers, the loyalty of faithful voters says less about VISTA service and more about the program's ability to attract a certain kind of person. VISTA service did affect the voting propensity of African Americans and Latinos: compared with blacks and Latinos who were accepted into VISTA but did not serve, volunteers' voting rates were 8 and 11 percentage points higher, respectively.[125]

This brings us to VISTA's most controversial lessons, those in critical citizenship. Just as VISTA recruited those with a developed commitment to service, so it recruited "critics of the current social scene."[126] And just as VISTA experience reinforced and strengthened commitment to service, it reinforced and strengthened ideology, particularly in its first decade. As one recruiter explained, "I'd tell people that if they went into VISTA as a conservative, they'd come out a liberal. If they went in as a liberal, they'd come out as a radical. And if they went in as a radical, they'd come out and go live on a mountaintop."[127] Mountaintops aside, the Gottlieb and Gold report supported this view. Specifically, they found that "the VISTA experience [had] a radicalization impact" that "generally embitter[ed] [volunteers'] attitudes toward social agencies and local and federal government."[128]

The report went on: "Over three-fourths of those who [held] a 'radical left' position state[d] that VISTA was an important reason," citing the following experiences:

—observed economic and political oppression of the poor;
—observed corruption at the local and federal levels;

—[were] shocked at how the system operated to enhance poverty and racism;

—became more politically aware of social and political injustice and the need for political action;

—learned that the national power structure is an obstacle to the solution of poverty;

—[were] shocked by the depth and extent of poverty in this country; and

—became frustrated with the uselessness and inadequacy of VISTA.[129]

One Republican summed up conservative reaction to the report: "VISTA is just a federally financed, $36 million-a-year 'hate Nixon' postgraduate school. What would you do with it if you were us?"[130]

By instilling a commitment to the program in conflict with commitment to the larger structures of which it was a part, VISTA created a strong constituency not just for itself but for a highly ideological version of itself. This all but ensured a strong conservative counterreaction, which undermined expansion and institutionalization and nearly cost VISTA its existence on multiple occasions. The contrast with the CCC is striking: through their experience, CCC enrollees learned that the power structure—and not just the CCC—could be a positive force against poverty and had a conservatizing influence on those who came in with radical beliefs.[131] Partly as a result, the CCC had much broader conservative support than VISTA. On the other hand, the CCC lacked the depth of commitment among enrollees that VISTA volunteers brought to their program's defense.

What political influence VISTA had on future volunteers is unknown because later evaluations did not ask; however, changes in VISTA practices and the broader culture make it unlikely that VISTA had this strong "left-pulling" influence consistently over time. Still, Crook and Thomas's early assessment may have held true, that volunteers' "critical sense will have been heightened and honed. . . . They will be quick to spot inequities and flaws, and they will be just as quick to do something about them."[132]

Probably the most important and positive civic lesson VISTA taught was that volunteers "can be total citizens in an increasingly complex society. They learn that the status quo is not sacrosanct and that if it needs changing, they have a responsibility as citizens to change it."[133] Its principal civic failing was its inability to effectively inculcate a nonideologically loaded conception of critical citizenship, or as scholar and future Corporation for National and Community Service CEO Leslie Lenkowsky put it, to communicate the idea that "calling America to live up to its ideals does not mean that you must hate America for its failures. In fact, it means you must love her enough to want to correct them, even to take risks to correct them."[134] Many VISTA volunteers took those risks, enduring threats and violence to help improve the lives of the poor. But often they suffered from the same affliction as CCC leaders decades earlier, the belief that criticism and patriotism are fundamentally incompatible. Certainly, VISTA volunteers were not alone in holding this view, particularly in VISTA's early years, and the VISTA leadership was not solely responsible for teaching the alternative view. But given that volunteers typically came to VISTA with a strong belief in service and high levels of civic knowledge and skill, its greatest potential civically may have been to remind volunteers that they were *citizens*—in this case citizens working for the government to improve the lives of others—and not only service providers, organizers, and advocates. This might also have helped the program politically, by making it seem less like government financing its own opposition.

Obligations and Inducements

Obligations and rewards were part of VISTA, just as they were part of the CCC. They were consistent with national service—VISTA provided subsistence pay in exchange for short-term service—but they fell in between the more familiar categories of unpaid volunteer and government employee. As a result, they were challenged by those who thought they made VISTA too much like a regular job and those who saw no reason it should not be more so. These challenges made it harder for VISTA to be recognized and institutionalized as national service.

VISTA's Obligations

True to VISTA's intent, participants were under no obligation to serve: the program recruited a small contingent, quite the opposite of universal conscription. But for national service advocates, universality remained the ideal, especially when the draft was imposing unequal service burdens. So VISTA fell far short in their eyes, limiting its influence on their plans.

However, optional participation did not preclude other requirements; VISTA imposed several. The first was that volunteers had to take the federal oath of service, pledging to "support and defend the Constitution and laws of the United States."[135] Given that many volunteers did not even appreciably recognize VISTA as part of government, let alone connect themselves with government, the oath could have clarified these relationships and placed VISTA service within America's tradition of public service.[136] Although

VISTA training did come to emphasize the program's institutional place, little attention was paid to linking volunteers' service to the principles and structure of America's political system. As a result, the oath's potential to serve larger civic purposes went unrealized.

Volunteers' next obligation was to serve for at least one year (two maximum). As VISTA's recruitment brochure explained, those "serving in VISTA are volunteers. You may resign, but . . . you have made a commitment."[137] Crook and Thomas cite an attrition rate of under 15 percent; most of those who left did so because of illness or family emergencies and others because they could not "stomach" bitter poverty, found themselves on the "losing side in a fight against city hall," or "simply decide[d] that they [had] joined the wrong outfit."[138] Their percentage is probably low: in the late 1960s the problem was sufficiently bad that administrators strengthened selection and training to "weed out those who can't make it . . . [rather] than have them quit [later]. That gives VISTA a black eye."[139] While Crook and Thomas, as supportive former VISTA administrators, may have downplayed attrition, Reagan's appointees may have played it up: in 1981 officials reported that "35 percent . . . failed to complete even a year of service," using this "black eye" to help justify VISTA's demise.[140] On the other side of the ledger, about one-third of volunteers reenlisted and extended their service.[141]

While a one- to two-year term is typical for civilian national service, the one-year standard was a source of controversy, in a number of ways. As one volunteer explained, "There was an urgency . . . we had only one year. . . . Our diplomacy was not very high, but we didn't care . . . we weren't afraid of getting fired."[142] They also would not have to live with the fallout. Another volunteer framed the problem differently: "One year? Forget it. This is the delusion of VISTA. Change the face of poverty with people in a year's time? You're nuts."[143] For these reasons, both the conflict and controversy study authors and the National VISTA Alliance, in rare agreement, recommended lengthening VISTA's standard enlistment to two years.[144] This would have been in line with the Peace Corps, but other proposed changes would not. For example, some objected to the two-year *limit* on service. In a 1976 survey, more than half of VISTA sponsors recommended extending the limit beyond three years, with most thinking that no limit was necessary.[145] While no comparable figures are available for volunteers, this shows that at least one VISTA stakeholder group did not fully accept VISTA's national service framing, preferring an employment frame.

VISTA's third obligation was that volunteers "live among and at the economic level of the people served."[146] Volunteers were to make ends meet (or not) by living on their stipends and were barred from drawing on another job, their savings, or help from family.[147] The rationale was that "volunteers [would] gain a fuller appreciation and awareness of the day-to-day problems encountered by community members."[148] The goal was to influence volunteers' attitudes and make them more effective. As one volunteer explained, "When you live with roaches, the john gets plugged up. . . . I say, 'Oh, you middle-class softie—think what it is like to be a mother with five kids.' "[149]

In this requirement, VISTA contrasts sharply with the CCC, whose goal was precisely the opposite: to take enrollees out of their impoverished surroundings and introduce them to middle-class standards. But volunteer poverty had its limits: until the program began recruiting local volunteers, VISTAs were precluded from being "mothers with five kids" or having any dependents at all. After the recruitment change, children were allowed, but they could not be supported (even if it were possible) by the VISTA stipend; they needed alternative support.[150] Again, the CCC had the opposite requirement: that enrollees have dependents (typically parents and siblings) who needed their financial contributions.

Just like length of service, VISTA's residency and living standard requirements caused controversy, again in multiple ways. As one early volunteer explained, "You can't pacify and hide the truth from a formerly brainwashed suburbanite if you put him in a poverty area. He'll learn what all poor people know: that this government is a farce, and that this government has to go!"[151] Nonetheless, even as VISTA officials tried to recruit fewer militant and more professional volunteers, these expectations remained.[152] Still, not everyone agreed; and, it is important to say, not everyone complied. In 1969 one journalist found "some [volunteers] admit[ting] privately that they receive[d] extra money from home and 'commute[d]' to their slum job."[153] Further, in a 1977 survey, "18 percent of volunteers indicated that they did not live in the target community," with "some supervisors and volunteers question[ing] the [policy's] relevance."[154]

This noncompliance raises an important question about policy enforcement. With volunteers accountable foremost to their sponsors and sponsors accountable only to small regional offices, VISTA had difficulty ensuring that anyone followed its rules. In fact, in 1967 an exasperated William Crook "observed a general indifference on the part of sponsors and volunteers toward stated VISTA policies." But in a memo to his regional administrators, all he could say was: "At the approaching meeting . . . an entire morning will be set aside to discuss policies. . . . In the meantime, you will please bring your immediate staff, *all* sponsors, and *all* volunteers into compliance with *every* stated VISTA policy [emphasis added]."[155] While this directive was backed by the threat of sending VISTA evaluation teams, without notice, to check for compliance, VISTA had hundreds of projects, few evaluators, and little money to send them anywhere. To a much greater extent than the CCC, VISTA had to enforce its rules by memorandum.

VISTA's fourth obligation, even harder to enforce, was that volunteers "remain available for service without regard to regular work hours," or at least full time.[156] However, the lack of work-time boundaries—and the nature of VISTA's work—appear to have made it as likely that volunteers would work less than full-time as more. For example, in 1968 Padraic Kennedy admonished: "Too many volunteers are not really committed. Some surveys have shown . . . volunteers are only working fifteen to twenty or twenty-five hours a week. . . . [They] may start out a "house [on] fire," but there is a definite downswing. . . . Commitment diminishes with the [enormousness] of problems and the frustration of trying to bring change."[157] Whether the problem was lack of commitment or was inherent in VISTA's structure and tasks (or some combination), it proved intractable: while 38 percent of volunteers worked forty-three hours a week or more in 1980, another 32 percent worked thirty-seven hours or less.[158]

Aside from the matter of volunteers' actual work hours, the ambiguous "without regard" requirement complicated their final obligation, which was to abide by the political prohibitions of the Hatch Act. While not generally considered federal employees, volunteers were covered by the Hatch Act, which barred them from "engaging in partisan political activities of any sort, at any time during [their] service."[159] Volunteers, like federal employees, could be politically active on their personal time, but VISTA's statute was unclear on whether volunteers had any strictly personal time. Many early volunteers opposed the VISTA Hatch Act application for this reason, believing that it could prohibit their involvement in anti-war efforts. However, they were equally opposed to the ban on their VISTA-related political activity, which was the prohibition's intent.

Although Kennedy administration planners expected the Hatch Act to cover National Service Corps volunteers, it was not originally applied to VISTA; governors' veto power and VISTA policies were considered sufficient and more flexible safeguards.[160] However, within two years Congress brought volunteers under the act, with VISTA's supporters accepting the change as the lesser of many evils that congressional conservatives otherwise had in mind.[161] Many volunteers were not so accepting. Gottlieb and Gold found that "many vol[unteer]s complained . . . [that] it was impossible to accomplish the goal of helping the poor to help themselves without engaging in political action of some sort."[162] Specifically, the Hatch Act provisions and related VISTA policies barred volunteers not only from engaging in "unlawful demonstrations" or election activity but also from "publicly taking sides on political issues . . . prominently identified with a party platform or policy."[163] The problem was that many poverty issues were prominently identified with a political party. Further, many critics interpreted the prohibition even more broadly, to encompass any type of policy advocacy, even nonpartisan. And of course, one outcome of nonpartisan political action (whether intended or not) is to raise an issue's profile sufficiently to turn it into a partisan issue. As VISTA officials acknowledged, "there are no easy answers," and therefore "it is the responsibility of all volunteers to exercise their own judgment."[164] The judgment of some volunteers led them to press the prohibitions beyond their limits.[165] Although exact figures are not available, simply the perception that volunteers' work—especially in community organizing and advocacy—violated federal law contributed to and provided justification for the Nixon and Reagan administrations' attempts to end the program.

VISTA's Inducements

Because VISTA was based on sacrifice rather than reciprocity, it offered fewer inducements and rewards than the CCC. Still, it provided volunteers a living allowance and health insurance, an end-of-service cash award, and a draft deferment recommendation for male volunteers. These benefits were framed to minimize VISTA as regular employment and to emphasize service and sacrifice. Even the psychic benefit of social approval was downplayed: given the controversy VISTA engendered, it often was not available.

One early benefit of VISTA service was its routinely approved draft deferment recommendations, which were based on VISTA service being "in the national interest." This policy was controversial, however, some thinking it went too far and others not far enough. The National VISTA Alliance, for one, wanted VISTA service to be considered a full-fledged alternative to military service.[166] The NVA believed that fighting in the war on poverty, compared with fighting in Vietnam, was superior national service. Others agreed with Rumsfeld, that "it's just plain wrong for VISTA to be a haven for draft-age people of middle-class backgrounds. If they don't go into the military service, poor people have to go in their places."[167] Despite this view, the draft deferment remained and clearly encouraged young men's participation; the percentage of men in VISTA, compared with the number of women, dropped after the draft's end.[168]

Other inducements were offered to everyone. To cover living expenses, VISTA gave volunteers a stipend of $208 per month in 1969 ($1,223 in 2010 dollars). Although the stipend was subject to taxation, VISTA training materials differentiated it from pay, explaining that "monies provided . . . are not salaries; they are not recompense for services rendered."[169] For VISTA's middle-class volunteers—unaccustomed to living on crackers at month's end—the allowance was less inducement than part of their obligation to experience poverty.[170] For some locally recruited volunteers, given the dearth of job prospects in low-income communities, the stipend (and health insurance) may have been an inducement. However, most LRVs were less satisfied than were the national volunteers with this benefit: 75 percent of them believed the allowance was inadequate, compared with 59 percent of NRVs.[171] Still, majorities in both groups believed it was too low. As one volunteer explained, "I have had a wonderful experience as a VISTA . . . I only wish that the pay was higher."[172]

Another part of VISTAs' pay was the end-of-service award, a lump-sum cash payment of $50 per month served, later raised to $75 and finally $100 per month. While the amount was not insignificant, given inflation it was always far less than the CCC's $30 per month, in keeping with the programs' different purposes.[173] Instead of money to support dependents, it was described as equivalent to the Peace Corps's "readjustment allowance" or a gift of thanks for service; given that it was subject to taxation, the IRS considered it deferred income. VISTA training, contrary to the rationale it provided to volunteers about the living stipend, did not communicate any particular understanding about the service award. Certainly, by the time Reagan took office, most conservatives saw the award as wholly inconsistent with the service ethic.

Because many conservatives, and others, had long disapproved of VISTA, volunteers were cautioned not to expect what one would think a common reward—widespread social approval and appreciation. Even VISTA's recruitment brochure warned that "the poor will not all love you. The affluent will not all admire you. Militants will charge you do too little, reactionaries that you do too much."[174] VISTA's national training curriculum went even further, reminding trainers to prepare volunteers accustomed to "approval, reinforcement, and reward" for the "considerable doubt, disapproval, denigration, and undermining [that] can come from every direction: a hostile press, a doubtful Congress, even angry and frustrated people in the community."[175]

Box 8-1. *VISTA at a Glance*

Dates	1964–93 (when it became part of AmeriCorps)
	First proposed by JFK as the National Service Corps
Enrollment	6,000/year at peak
	More than 170,000 total
Purposes	Help eliminate poverty through full-time volunteer service
	Stressed compensatory-service and community-advocacy approaches
Government role: Administration	Operated through a national government-local organization partnership
	Housed in Office of Economic Opportunity and later ACTION
Government role: Outside relationships	Publicly not well known, locally sometimes known and supported
	Well supported by interest groups, including staff and volunteers
Government role: Status within government	Limited support in the Johnson administration
	Nixon, Ford, and Reagan tried to eliminate, then altered work to compensatory-service
	Carter supported and directed work to community-advocacy
Work	Wide range of anti-poverty efforts: direct service, local organization capacity building, community organizing; gave the program flexibility
	Work could be controversial, and hard to see, quantify, and evaluate

VISTA's leadership appeared to treat this lack of appreciation as inevitable, something neither volunteers nor the program could significantly ameliorate—although volunteers were warned that their missteps could certainly make it worse. And given VISTA's policy design, perhaps it was inevitable. Even when administrations tried to make changes to appeal to a broader constituency, they necessarily offended those invested in VISTA as it was. This trade-off seriously complicated efforts to build a base of support broad

Participants	Nationally recruited volunteers; typically white, middle-class, college-age
	Locally recruited volunteers more often of color, lower income, older
	Largely female
Education	Training for service
	Learning through service
Obligations and inducements	Voluntary one-year, full-time plus term of service; maximum two years
	Live at economic level of the poor
	Refrain from political activity on the job
	Received living stipend, health insurance, and end-of-service award
Main civic points	Based on sacrifice and government as catalyst
	Stressed service and critical citizenship perspectives, but did not have an explicit civic development agenda for volunteers
Main political points	Not deeply institutionalized, because of increased program demands, presidential party change, insufficient leadership, and centrism
	Survived because of flexibility, local penetration, and organized support.
	Failed to influence future programs, because of small size, stagnation, Great Society tie, and limited reputation

and strong enough to successfully press for expansion and much deeper institutionalization.

Conclusion: The Politics and Civics of VISTA

VISTA was America's smallest and most controversial civilian national service program; it is also its longest-living program, continuing to the present day.

These facts make teasing out its civic and political lessons especially important. The key questions are first, how did VISTA act as national service and public policy for democracy? Second, why was VISTA's institutionalization so limited? Third, why was VISTA's influence on future national service policymaking so limited?

National Service and Citizenship in VISTA

VISTA has always had strong national service elements: it was a federal program that engaged mainly young volunteers in full-time, short-term, subsistence-wage work that filled a public need. However, because it was non-military and far from universal, it was typically not recognized as national service. The result was that it had little influence on future policymaking: national service advocates at best saw VISTA as a small part of the much larger and broader program they envisioned. VISTA's lack of an explicit volunteer-centered civic agenda also constrained its influence: even advocates who justified national service on the basis of its work, such as military sociologist Charles Moskos, valued civic benefits to participants more than VISTA did. Other advocates, such as William Buckley Jr. and political theorist Benjamin Barber, wholly justified civilian national service on this basis. Their view made VISTA seem even less suited as a national service model.

VISTA's lack of civic attention also made what civic lessons it did impart highly contested, which in turn hindered its institutionalization. VISTA primarily supported the service and critical citizenship perspectives, with its service aspects highlighted under Republican presidents and its critical aspects emphasized under Democrats. As part of the Great Society, created by a Democrat amid great social upheaval, VISTA was destined to exhibit a strong bent toward critical citizenship in its early years. This early inclination became significantly formative, influencing the program. While little in VISTA required this critical perspective, there was equally little in its structure—especially its decentralized training and supervision—that would allow administrators to limit it. At the same time, it is unclear how much they wanted to. As a result, decisions and actions made by volunteers and officials, more than VISTA's structure, led to its reputation for conflict. The perception that through VISTA the federal government was training its own opposition was repugnant to many officials, especially conservatives, who responded accordingly. Consequently, for most of VISTA's pre-AmeriCorps history, cycles of policy conflict prevailed over settled acceptance and downsizing over growth.

Still, VISTA did act as public policy for democracy—influencing how volunteers, community members, and the public understood poverty and what citizens and government could do to address it, stressing the volunteers' sacrifice and government's catalytic role. At its best VISTA helped create "images of the future" and "an optimism about our country's future."[176] As a small program operating in a more complex political and social context, VISTA was not able to influence the larger culture on the CCC's scale, but like the CCC, VISTA both reflected and contributed to the civic ideals of its time. The fact that over VISTA's lifetime these ideals changed—and not smoothly—contributed to the battles over its ends and means; but equally important is that its ends and means were malleable enough to survive and reflect these changing ideals.

The Politics of National Service in VISTA

How VISTA fit changing definitions of national service and citizenship is not the only reason it was not institutionalized or used as a model for future national service policymaking. There were also political reasons, those unique to the times and the changing nature of the times, and those that affect national service policy consistently across time.

INSTITUTIONALIZATION. VISTA was not deeply institutionalized for several reasons of both types. One time-dependent reason was that program demands had become increasingly sophisticated. Instead of addressing the problems of millions by employing 400,000 or more, as the CCC had, VISTA employed 4,000, who were expected to catalyze additional community efforts that would help eliminate the causes (not just the consequences) of poverty—working simultaneously for the national government, local sponsors, and the poor themselves—and to do so in a way that allowed the results to be quantified in a seven-part equation. In contrast with the CCC's simple "hammer and nail" model, VISTA was a Rube Goldberg machine. As such, its successes were harder to come by, ascertain, and publicize, which complicated the goal of becoming publicly and politically well recognized, accepted, and supported. In VISTA's case, policymaking based on complex interrelationships undermined institutionalization—especially in its early years, when administrators had little experience to draw upon.

Other undermining reasons followed. One was the ping-ponging of the presidency between the parties; with their sharply divergent views of VISTA's purpose, VISTA was unable to develop a settled approach. Another was the changing definitions of *liberal* and *conservative*. When Kennedy proposed the National Service Corps, solidly grounded in compensatory-service principles, it was considered solidly liberal. During the Johnson administration, this approach became solidly conservative and the community-advocacy approach liberal, a framing that held through the Nixon and Carter eras. However, by Reagan's election, the compensatory-service approach, at least when practiced by full-time, paid national service volunteers, was not conservative enough. In a sense, VISTA had been planted in ground that continued to shift ideologically, making it difficult for the program to grow and flourish.

Institutionalization was also thwarted for reasons that civilian national service programs have faced time and again. One is its centrism. This may sound odd given VISTA's reputation, but the problem was well summarized in VISTA's warning to volunteers that the poor (its intended constituency), the affluent (those with most political influence), and reactionaries and militants (those who make the most noise) might all turn against them. They often did. That VISTA simultaneously managed to offend a good number of the vast middle left it with a very small core constituency. Insufficient leadership is another problem recurring across programs. In VISTA's case its directors were transient, not well known, and not especially effective. While inspired, effective leadership is rare, VISTA's many challenges suggest that it was in particular need of exactly that.

On a good number of measures VISTA was never deeply institutionalized, especially compared with the CCC. VISTA was not nearly as well known, accepted, or supported. However, on the most basic measure of institutionalization—survival—VISTA succeeded where the CCC had failed. This basic fact of comparative national service history demands explanation. The answer is partly found in the program's nature, with VISTA's purpose being more malleable, a *benefit* of its complex charge and design that helped insulate it from the charge of irrelevance. However, most of the explanation is developmental, based on changes in American politics between the New Deal and the Great Society. First, the structure of federalism changed. While the CCC was a huge federal program that blanketed the nation, like a blanket it was laid on top of society; it could easily be lifted off and folded up when national conditions changed. VISTA, conversely, was not laid atop society; it penetrated it. Switching analogies, VISTA may have been planted in shifting sands, its roots may have been thin, but they were deep, reaching far down into local communities. These roots were also strong, anchored by interest groups intent on saving the program. This is another significant change: the CCC had broad support, but no organized support. Even the CCC's administrators were not well positioned or resourced to take up its cause. By the time VISTA came under attack, the interest group universe had exploded: the program was defended by organized groups of volunteers and sponsors, professional associations, and its civil service staff. The result is striking: a popular Franklin Roosevelt could not save the CCC, his well-known, widely approved, successful program; a popular Ronald Reagan could not eliminate VISTA, a relatively unknown, not very well regarded, questionably successful program. The basic premises of programmatic survival had fundamentally changed.

Future Influence

Changes in American government allowed VISTA to survive but did not guarantee its influence over future national service program development. A variety of factors limited the CCC's influence, and the same thing happened to VISTA. At any point, any effort to significantly expand VISTA would have had to surmount its founders' own arguments: they envisioned it growing to only 5,000 volunteers at most. From the 1970s on, VISTA's expansion and influence were further constrained by its association with the Great Society, just as the CCC's influence was limited by its association with seemingly outdated New Deal policymaking approaches. VISTA's approach to national service—how it framed its purpose, the role it gave to government, its work, education program, participants, benefits and obligations—and that it was not widely seen as national service were products of its time. Later its approach changed, but only so much; VISTA was flexible, but only to a point. VISTA's influence was also constrained by its reputation for generating conflict. Given that many conservatives had moved to opposing civilian national service on principle, even a strictly compensatory-service-oriented program would face harsh opposition; anything more controversial was untenable. As the program aged further, it was limited by a new reputation—for being old, tired, and all the more set in its ways for having survived multiple near-death experiences. Civilian national service has always been a "big idea"—embraced by presidents who seek to inspire, as did Franklin Roosevelt and John Kennedy. VISTA was billed as a "domestic Peace Corps," but it never captured the public imagination as its international sibling had. As a result, any future president who sought to follow in the footsteps of Roosevelt and Kennedy would want something new and different. When civilian national service next found a presidential champion in Bill Clinton, instead of being used as a model, instead of being venerated, VISTA was ignored.

Part

III

AmeriCorps

Since 1994 more than 775,000 Americans have served in AmeriCorps, working to meet the nation's pressing educational, public safety, health, environmental, and other needs. AmeriCorps both drew on and is distinct from its predecessors: it incorporated VISTA as one of its programs, included another—the National Community Conservation Corps (AmeriCorps*NCCC)—that had been modeled on the CCC, and created a major new program (AmeriCorps*State and National). Because AmeriCorps is the nation's main domestic civilian national service program, understanding its creation, its development over time (including through President Obama's first years), its place in national service history, and its lessons as public policy for democracy is vital for assessing its current state and future possibilities.

Like its predecessors, AmeriCorps influences how its participants and the public understand their relationship to government and the meaning of citizenship. Central to AmeriCorps are the principle of reciprocity, a commitment shared by the CCC, and the idea of government as catalyst, shared by VISTA. The belief that both the nation and the program's participants should benefit was especially strong under AmeriCorps's founding administration, and it has continued while administrations' commitment to government's investing in and building the capacity of local institutions has grown.

With respect to citizenship, AmeriCorps draws on multiple traditions: it strongly emphasizes the service perspective, as VISTA did, but also incorporates aspects of the constitutional, patriotic, and work perspectives, as the CCC did. Further, in its attention to citizenship, AmeriCorps shares similarities with both programs. Like the CCC, AmeriCorps has an explicit, formative civic goal: to strengthen participants' sense of citizenship and civic responsibility. However, AmeriCorps, following VISTA's example, recruits many participants who join precisely because they already have strong civic commitments and skills. These multiple strands present AmeriCorps with a unique civic challenge.

Politically, AmeriCorps's policy design shows both the difficulties and possibilities of institutionalizing civilian national service, to build a deep and durable policy into the future. The CCC's influence and VISTA's presence are clear but programmatically small. Further, AmeriCorps itself has been difficult to institutionalize. For much of its first decade, its very survival was in question, complicating efforts to make it a well-recognized, strongly supported policy option for addressing the nation's needs and a practical life option for large numbers of young adults. On the other hand, by 2009 its enrollment had grown to 75,000 members a year and was authorized to grow to 250,000 a year by 2017, which would move it slowly toward the CCC's scope. Like the CCC, AmeriCorps both benefited and suffered from its close association with its founding president and party, yet survived a hostile Congress and lived to be supported and expanded by future presidents, including one of the opposing party. These facts testify to the ideological malleability of civilian national service and the deepening of post–New Deal political structures. These same factors saved VISTA, but did not allow it to flourish. AmeriCorps has done far better, but its future, and the future of national service more broadly, remains equal parts accomplishment and possibility.

9

AmeriCorps's Roots and Relationships

I n his first inaugural address, Bill Clinton challenged "a new generation of young people to a season of service."[1] Seven months later, he signed the legislation creating AmeriCorps to help them do just that.[2] Housed in the Corporation for National and Community Service (CNS or CNCS), it has three components: AmeriCorps*VISTA, AmeriCorps*NCCC, and AmeriCorps*State and National. As part of AmeriCorps, VISTA retains its focus on serving low-income communities and its administrative structure, while growing to approximately 7,300 members in 2011. AmeriCorps*NCCC, much like the CCC, combines civilian service with certain military-type elements. Its approximately 1,200 uniformed members live together and work on team-based, short-term service and disaster relief projects. The bulk of AmeriCorps members—about 74,000 in 2011—work through the State and National component, which awards grants to programs chosen by the CNCS or by individual states. AmeriCorps differs from earlier programs by letting state commissions largely determine their projects, and the federal government does not choose or directly pay individual State and National members. Members can serve for up to two years and receive a stipend for living expenses, health insurance, and child care if they need it. They also earn a $5,350 voucher for higher education for each full-time year served, which provides the basis for AmeriCorps's principle of reciprocity—help with educational expenses in exchange for service.[3]

AmeriCorps's Roots

In advocating for a new national service program, Clinton highlighted one very old one—the CCC, which was not even recognized as national service during its lifetime. He explained, "Twice before in this century, Americans have been called to great adventures in civilian service."[4] His would represent the third; the CCC was the first. The Peace Corps had been the second.

AmeriCorps and the CCC

At the signing of AmeriCorps's legislation, Clinton acknowledged "the roots of our history," explaining that "the CCC . . . gave Americans the chance not only to do meaningful work so that they could feed themselves and their families but so that they could build America for the future."[5] He then signed the National and Community Service Trust Act of 1993 with Franklin Roosevelt's bill-signing pen.

The CCC influenced AmeriCorps through inspiration—through stories told by its elderly alumni, plaques honoring its work, and volumes of history. Rhetorically, Clinton sought to place AmeriCorps within an American tradition, drawing legitimation from what had come before. He also sought to legitimize AmeriCorps's principles of reciprocity and citizenship. Thus, as the CCC had been based on "the idea that people should be asked to serve and be rewarded for doing it," so would AmeriCorps.[6] And just as the CCC had instilled in its enrollees citizenship in its various forms, so would Ameri-Corps, giving young people the opportunity to fulfill their civic responsibilities and "bonding each to the other with the glue of common purpose and real patriotism."[7]

The CCC also influenced AmeriCorps programmatically, through Ameri-Corps's National Civilian Community Corps (NCCC). The similarities are striking. Like the CCC, the NCCC is residential. It gives participants a "24-hours-a-day, seven-days-a-week" experience with approximately two hundred other young adults from around the country. Like their CCC predecessors, the NCCC's participants wear uniforms and work in teams, the better to build esprit de corps, and engage in environmental and disaster relief work (although the NCCC also does other work). Finally, the CCC was and the NCCC is strongly national; based on federal property (public lands for the CCC, downsized military bases for the NCCC); and funded, organized, and run by the federal government. As Senator John McCain (R-Ariz.), an NCCC supporter, explained, "AmeriCorps's NCCC members know they are part of a national effort to serve their country. The communities they serve know that, too."[8] However, the differences are equally striking, and none more so than their size: at its peak, the CCC enrolled more than 500,000 participants; the NCCC, 1,200. As a result, while NCCC participants and the communities they serve may know they are part of a larger national effort, the nation as a whole does not know of it at all.

So what accounts for the CCC's relatively limited influence? The answers are found in the programs themselves. For the CCC, the main reason is simple: it ended. It could influence AmeriCorps inspirationally but not institutionally. There was no ongoing program that could be incorporated, no administrators who could be transferred, or even consulted. The CCC had not disappeared from the country—from the forests or from the public's memory—but it had disappeared from government. For AmeriCorps, the main reason is its founding date. By the early 1990s, massive federally run programs had fallen into disrepute. Clinton, while lauding the CCC's outcomes, distanced himself from its methods. In his words, "What will set [AmeriCorps] apart from other similar efforts in the past . . . is that it will totally eliminate the federal government bureaucracy. And believe me, no one will miss that."[9] Maybe not, but there are trade-offs in terms of communicating to participants and the public that AmeriCorps is national service, or that it even exists, and that the national government itself can do good things.

Given these factors, perhaps it is better to ask why the CCC had the influence it did. The answer is that its public impression survived. Again, it had disappeared from government but not from society. National service advocates understood this, which explains in part their attraction: they themselves learned of it through its history and lasting tangible accomplishments, and they wanted their programs to leave a similar legacy (without the CCC's demise). But again, this goal highlights a challenge for AmeriCorps. After it had been in existence for as long as the CCC ever was, only a third of Americans knew about it.[10] Not only did the CCC have near-universal recognition during its lifetime, but that familiarity stuck: over a third of Americans knew of it *more than fifty years later.*[11] Of course, this recognition was insufficient for keeping the CCC alive and is, in fact, no longer necessary for keeping programs afloat. On the other hand, recognition is probably necessary if AmeriCorps is to reach the goal that Clinton set for it, to change the country both for the better and forever.[12]

AmeriCorps and VISTA

Following Roosevelt's, America's second call to service was John F. Kennedy's. Just as VISTA was inspired by President Kennedy's Peace Corps, so was

AmeriCorps. And just as VISTA had been billed the "domestic Peace Corps," so has AmeriCorps. But what happened to America's first domestic Peace Corps? VISTA supporters once again saved their program, this time not from national service opponents but from its supporters. As Arkansas's governor and as president, Clinton acknowledged VISTA's contributions but never as effusively as the CCC's or the Peace Corps's. Because he placed his call to service in the generational context of the 1930s, 1960s, and 1990s, VISTA was, rhetorically, the odd program out. Programmatically, though, it was the odd program in.

In the preface to Marvin Schwartz's book on VISTA's first twenty years in Arkansas, then-Governor Bill Clinton wrote: "The VISTA concept was ingenious. . . . [It] taught us about the importance and power of people building within."[13] He ended with the hope that Schwartz's work might "rekindle an awareness and provide new vigor to public service programs."[14] When designing his own national service program, however, Clinton drew only sparingly on VISTA. It mainly influenced AmeriCorps just by continuing to exist. For simplicity's sake, VISTA could have been dissolved into AmeriCorps and not remained a distinct program; for politics' sake that was untenable.[15] Given the strength of VISTA's supporters, it almost certainly would have failed, and in the attempt, Clinton would have alienated key constituencies whose support he would need to pass and implement his larger program. As it was, ACTION employees (including VISTA's) mobilized against proposed Corporation work rules. As one observer noted, "Here they were trying to shepherd through a new service bill against inevitable Republican opposition, and they were getting slammed by, of all people, the employees at the existing service programs!"—and this was just about changing work rules, not eliminating programs.[16] So the administration's policymakers could not afford to move against VISTA, but neither were they willing to build AmeriCorps upon it. Unlike the CCC or the Peace Corps, VISTA was not well known and not always strongly supported. As a result, VISTA was "a piece of the puzzle that had to be fit in."[17] As part of AmeriCorps, VISTA grew, but like the NCCC remained a relatively small part of a much larger program.

Primary Influences

So what inspired the heart of AmeriCorps, the State and National component, often referred to simply as AmeriCorps? VISTA survived because of supporters who were committed specifically to it, but others were committed not to a particular program of national service but to the idea—people such as Charles Moskos, William Buckley, and Donald Eberly, who had been spearheading the national service movement since before VISTA's founding. These proponents and others reclaimed the CCC as national service and acknowledged VISTA's contribution, but their vision—which inspired AmeriCorps—was different. Their goal was to create a comprehensive program that incorporated both military and civilian service, and extended GI Bill benefits to civilian servers. They envisioned a civilian component at least as large as the CCC but engaged in a wider range of tasks, and that would broaden enrollment beyond the previous constituencies, namely the disadvantaged and the well-to-do, to create an all-American national service institution.[18]

Within a few short years after civilian national service reached its nadir with Reagan's cuts in VISTA and the Peace Corps, it reached critical mass as "an idea whose time had come."[19] Reagan's successor, George H. W. Bush, even established the first-ever White House Office of National Service. However, while Bush and some other Republicans were warming to the idea of national service, it had an even bigger impact on the party out of the White House. Moderate Democrats in particular were attracted to its principle of reciprocity, believing that their party had lost public support by focusing too much on rights and too little on responsibilities. National service became part of a larger agenda designed not only to help meet the country's social and environmental needs but to do so in a way that would meet the Democratic Party's political needs and, arguably, the nation's welfare state reform needs. To this end, in the 1980s the head of the centrist Democratic Leadership Council, Will Marshall, made national service a cornerstone of the DLC's platform, and in 1992 Clinton, as the DLC's presidential candidate, made it a cornerstone of his campaign.[20]

Yet questions remained about whether and how a new national service program might work. The answers came partly from two young Harvard Law graduates who developed City Year as a model national service demonstration project, one that they and others could use to leverage new federal policymaking.[21] Founded in Boston in 1988, City Year recruits a multiethnic, cross-class corps of young adults who engage in group service projects throughout the city for a year in exchange for a living stipend and an education award.[22] City Year's members quickly became well known, for their distinctive uniforms and early-morning calisthenics in front of Boston's Federal Reserve building as well as for their solid record of service.[23] And despite being a small, local nonprofit backed by private sector funds, the program quickly had a policy impact, highlighted by national service champion Senator Edward Kennedy (D-Mass.), influencing Bush administration officials and later becoming a model for Clinton.[24]

In 1990 Senator Kennedy introduced, Congress passed, and President Bush signed the National and Community Service Act of 1990. This act established the Commission on National and Community Service, which funded service programs, provided training and technical assistance grants, and developed a national service strategic plan.[25] Despite its small size—overall funding for commission programs reached only a modest $75 million—it "laid the groundwork" for future policymaking under President Clinton.[26]

Clinton's connection with AmeriCorps was like Franklin Roosevelt's with the CCC. He was essential to its creation, and multiple influences led him to it. From the perspective of AmeriCorps chronicler Steven Waldman, "Each stage of Clinton's development seemed to reinforce the importance of service": living through the Kennedy presidency as a teen; attending Georgetown, a university that stressed service as a religious obligation; contemplating civilian alternatives to military service in Vietnam; and later governing Arkansas, a state with far greater need for public services than money to fund them.[27] Clinton's personal experience not only lent itself to support for service, but more than any other policy goal, national service embodied his political philosophy. Translated into his campaign theme language, national service would "offer opportunity, reward responsibility, and build community." It is not surprising that Clinton said, "No proposal . . . means more to me than national service."[28] As president-elect, he publicized his support by wearing a City Year sweatshirt on his frequently televised jogs.

This combination of theory, practice, politics, and personality, both fueled and tempered by political realities, resulted in AmeriCorps's creation in 1993. Less comprehensive than its advocates had hoped, AmeriCorps was nevertheless the country's largest civilian national service program since the CCC. However, unlike the CCC's or even VISTA's creation, AmeriCorps's founding did not go unchallenged. While support for national service had grown in some quarters, the conservative criticism—marshaled by people such as Doug Bandow of the Cato Institute, Bruce Chapman of the Discovery Institute, and Martin Anderson of the Hoover Institution—was deepening. From their perspective, on principle "fulfillment of an obligation to government . . . is not true service."[29] In fact, "government-run volunteerism is a contradiction in terms."[30] Further, they recognized that a large, comprehensive national service program could have serious political implications, both increasing the size of the state and decreasing citizens' distance from it. These deep-seated beliefs contributed to the early Reagan-era assault on VISTA and set the stage for a battle over AmeriCorps, waged from its inception. In President Clinton, domestic civilian national service found its strongest advocate and defender since Franklin Roosevelt. But just as FDR's strong support proved a double-edged sword for the CCC, so did Clinton's support for AmeriCorps: it immensely benefited—and imperiled—his signature program.

AmeriCorps as National Service, or Not

AmeriCorps, like the CCC and VISTA before it, comprises clearly defined national service elements: it is a federal program that engages many of its participants, mostly young adults, in full-time, short-term, subsistence-wage work that fills pressing public needs. Further, AmeriCorps's national service framing—like its predecessors'—nonetheless fits uneasily with military and Jamesian national service definitions. However, unlike before, these definitions no longer characterize the national service universe: comprehensive national service, combining both military and civilian options, has become a more widely accepted category and goal, if not yet a programmatic reality—even with AmeriCorps's creation. Moreover, unlike its predecessors' national service identity, AmeriCorps's identity has been strongly asserted and contested—by both AmeriCorps's supporters and its critics—and not ignored. To an unprecedented extent, the debate over AmeriCorps has been a debate over the meaning and value of national service.

AmeriCorps and the Military

Of America's three main civilian national service programs, the CCC had the closest military association. In keeping with this history, of AmeriCorps's three programs, the NCCC also has the closest military association. Created in 1992, under President Bush, through the fiscal year 1993 Defense Authorization Act, the NCCC was to be a strong "substitute for traditional military service in periods of military downsizing" by "combin[ing] the best features of military and civilian service."[31] The program has been led in part by former military personnel and operates out of downsized and closed military bases, which tangibly connects it to the armed services. Further, its members experience some of military life's demands. As one official explained, "True to its roots, NCCC adheres in part to a military model—members wear uniforms, work in teams, participate in a physical fitness regimen, and serve in a highly structured and tightly disciplined environment."[32]

Small as the NCCC is, those who want AmeriCorps to become a civilian variant of military service have argued for its expansion and increases in AmeriCorps*State and National awards to "corps"-based programs, such as City Year, that share some of its principles. More broadly, advocates such as

Moskos believe that "the more closely a civilian program can approach the form of the military model, the more successful it will be."[33]

Short of creating a civilian variant, and garnering more support, is the goal of making AmeriCorps a civilian equivalent of military service, complete with GI Bill–type benefits. As one national service leader explained, "If we are willing to ask young people to die for their country, we should be willing to ask them to live for their country."[34] A review of AmeriCorps's conception and birth, however, shows how difficult achieving this equivalence is.

Under the original Moskos-inspired DLC plan, young adults would have been able to serve in a civilian capacity for one or two years or in the military for two years. The civilian option would have carried a $10,000 award for each year served; the military option, $2,000 more for each year because of "the longer commitment of time required . . . and the higher risks involved."[35] Even as the Clinton campaign, and later his administration, changed the details—for example, keeping the military program as it was and lowering the civilian service benefits—veterans groups insisted that the disparity be even greater and, as Waldman explains, were in fact "poised to launch a full-scale assault against national service" if it were not.[36] As a result, the education award was lowered to $4,725 per year, or 80 percent of the lowest GI Bill benefit, with the living allowance set at approximately one-third of the lowest military pay.[37] Still, many opponents in Congress believed that the rewards for civilian national service, compared with those for military service, were too high and dismissed outright the possibility of a civilian variant of military service. Representative Bill Goodling (R-Pa.) put it this way: "Now, to those who like, somehow or other, to mix this up with GI benefits—can you imagine volunteering for this national service program and then, somehow or other, saying it has something to do with serving in the military? All of a sudden to be called up and go to the Middle East[?]"[38]

Opponents were also concerned that instead of complementing the military, a civilian program might actively undermine it by offering "the best and brightest" of potential military recruits "a better deal."[39] For this reason military leaders have often been skeptical of civilian national service, despite their deep service commitment. As a result of these factors, military service retained its pride of place, continuing to influence the political support and civic lessons of national service more broadly.

AmeriCorps and William James

Advocates' goal of creating a civilian equivalent to military service reflects William James's ideal, as does their goal of making national service "a common expectation and common experience of all young people."[40] In addition, more so than either the CCC or VISTA, AmeriCorps had founders who were historically mindful, routinely acknowledging James's contribution to the cause. On the other hand, their acknowledgments typically stressed their differences with James's plan more than the similarities. The DLC's *Citizenship and National Service* blueprint provides an example: "In proposing [a] Citizen Corps, the DLC seeks, in James's phrase, 'to enflame the civic temper' in America. Rather than impose public service on all, however, we believe that voluntary enlistment in either military or civilian service, strongly encouraged by GI Bill–style benefits, best suits the American tradition of individual choice and freedom."[41] Given that James was a pacifist whose national service ideal was universal and compulsory, the DLC's caveats left little of James at all.

For many, however, this is all to the good, as they find James's legacy problematic at best. In Moskos's view, "It is by no means clear whether James's effort was an important breakthrough or an unfortunate detour . . . to making national service a reality."[42] James's views and place in history make it easy for opponents to paint all advocates with a Jamesian brush, as being dangerously anti-military and simultaneously dangerously pro-conscription, even when they are not. The problem, however, lies not solely with James. Some civilian service advocates do have problems with the military, and Moskos himself, among others, is in favor of mandates. The substance of advocates' diverse beliefs and "the long shadow of William James" combine to complicate the politics and civics of national service.

AmeriCorps and National Service Writ Large

The fact that AmeriCorps grew out of advocates' vision for comprehensive national service but differs significantly from their ideal raises questions about AmeriCorps *as* national service. To what extent has it been seen as national service? And to what extent has national service been considered a good thing?

More so than either previous program, AmeriCorps was not only billed as national service in its planning stages (as VISTA was) but has largely been able to keep that framing over time. The language of national service was especially prominent during the Clinton administration. In Clinton's many speeches on the topic, he never failed to connect AmeriCorps the program to national service as an idea. Officials within the Corporation for National and Community Service shortened its name to simply the Corporation for National Service. And this rhetorical emphasis seeped down to AmeriCorps members, whose T-shirts were emblazoned with the program's seal: a circle with the words *AmeriCorps National Service*.

On the other hand, in its design AmeriCorps was the least national of America's three programs. As AmeriCorps policymaker Bill Galston explained, "This program was designed as a federal, and not a national, program. It was a program designed to be run substantially at the state level" as well as the local level, with "communities . . . hav[ing] the flexibility to make their own programs work."[43] For this reason, some have found AmeriCorps's national service aspects lacking. "Indeed," national service scholar Michael Sherraden argues, "AmeriCorps . . . is not a national service program at all." Instead it is a "loose affiliation of a tremendous range of service programs. . . . All AmeriCorps [members] wear an insignia, but their primary identification is with particular programs," not with the national program.[44] Within the Republican Party, "national greatness" conservatives—most prominently McCain—have shared this view and strongly advocate "putting the 'national' in national service."[45]

On the other hand, "civil society" conservatives such as Leslie Lenkowsky, President Bush's first Corporation head, found the Clinton administration's "national" emphasis excessive, preferring greater stress on community. As a result, Lenkowsky reintroduced *Community* into the Corporation's title and *National Service* was taken off AmeriCorps's seal. But given many Republicans' antipathy to both the idea and fact of civilian national service, it is more surprising that the changes were so few. The Bush administration continued to positively identify AmeriCorps as national service, to a greater extent than the CCC or VISTA ever was.

Still, the debate continues, over whether national service is truly a good and whether AmeriCorps is truly national service. While Clinton's officials saw decentralization as a strength that certainly did not preclude AmeriCorps from being national service, from Sherraden's perspective AmeriCorps needs fundamental restructuring to become national service. For others, the issue is not AmeriCorps's structure but its size. Although the number of participants fell short of Clinton's goals and he pressed for more, he still proclaimed it "national service." However, the bar keeps rising—just as it kept rising in VISTA's day. In 2002 UPI ran an article titled "AmeriCorps Can *Become* National Service [emphasis added]." Its opening states: "The United States needs a viable national service program, and can establish it by expanding the Clinton-era AmeriCorps program by at least 50 percent."[46] In 2009, well after AmeriCorps had achieved this goal, some still spoke of national service as an aspiration, not a reality, as when conservative media personality Glenn Beck cited the 2009 Edward M. Kennedy Serve America Act as "part of [President] Obama's goal of establishing a national service program."[47] The benchmark for what counts as national service continues to shift, still making it less an existing program than, for supporters, an elusive aspiration or, for opponents, a looming threat.

How administrators and participants, elites, and the broader public have framed AmeriCorps has influenced its effectiveness as public policy for democracy and its place in policy history. The same was true about the CCC and VISTA. AmeriCorps's framework has proven controversial but strategically effective, enabling the program not only to survive but to grow, even with changes in administrations and governing ideologies—although challenges to its institutionalization remain. AmeriCorps's framework, however, has not been solely responsible for these successes and challenges; its programmatic elements have contributed as well.

10

AmeriCorps's Purpose and Government's Role

A ll programs, AmeriCorps included, are composed of multiple, overlapping elements that influence their political support and viability and communicate lessons to participants and the public, in large part through policy feedback dynamics. In short, these elements shape the politics and civics of the program, which in turn influence future policy development. Drawing again on Anne Larason Schneider and Helen Ingram's framework, these elements (as in the CCC and VISTA) include the program's purpose and the role it gives to government, as well as how government's role is organized and supported. This chapter focuses on these elements, and the next chapter on the program's "tools, rules, and targets"—the service work it supports, its educational goals and content, the type of participants it recruits, and its obligations and inducements.

Politically, AmeriCorps's policy design has allowed for slow but steady growth in both its size and political support, albeit in the face of significant opposition. Civically, AmeriCorps embodies the principle of reciprocity and the idea of government as catalyst, and most of the program's controversy has centered on whether either of these tenets is ideologically acceptable. For although AmeriCorps intentionally seeks to inculcate a widely accepted service understanding of citizenship (as well as constitutional, patriotic, and work approaches in smaller measure), opponents believe that it undermines this very goal, starting with its purpose.

The Purpose of AmeriCorps

As a program, AmeriCorps has been likened to a Swiss Army Knife: a multi-faceted policy tool that can serve multiple ends, including providing needed services, solving community problems, instilling an ethic of service, teaching civic and work skills, bridging racial and class divides, and expanding educational opportunity, to name just the most frequently cited.[1] This makes AmeriCorps the broadest of our national service programs, different from both the CCC and VISTA. Notably, AmeriCorps has neither of the previous programs' poverty focus: it is neither limited to those in poverty, like the CCC, nor dedicated to addressing poverty, like VISTA. To the extent that it has members who are poor and does service with and for the poor, its understanding of poverty's sources and solutions is also different. Fitting the times, AmeriCorps's emphasis is on education and skills for the global economy, as seen through its rewards for higher education and support for education reform programs. In this way and others, comparing AmeriCorps with the CCC and VISTA is instructive in attempting to untangle the various strands of AmeriCorps's purpose and determine their civic and political implications. Understanding their similarities and differences, and the relative strengths and weaknesses of their main goals at varying points, can help put AmeriCorps's survival and growth, after its difficult start, in context.

Clinton's Proposal: Service and Education

In his first major policy address as president, Bill Clinton explained that we "face profound challenges . . . from city streets plagued by crime and drugs . . . to hospital wards where patients need more care. . . . For those who answer the call and meet these challenges, I propose that our country honor your service with new opportunities for education."[2] From its inception, AmeriCorps embodied this dual purpose: accomplishing service and providing education aid. In this, AmeriCorps paralleled the CCC, with its twin goals of work relief and conservation. However, AmeriCorps's initial framing was less effective—politically, civically, and as policy—than the CCC's and led to early challenges.

The CCC's work and conservation focus effectively guided the program's development as a whole, specifically regarding its policy design details. For example, its work focus suggested that enrollees be paid and be recruited from those most in need of a job, while its conservation focus narrowed the scope of possible projects and indicated the government departments to be involved. For several reasons, AmeriCorps's original framing did not provide such clear guidance. The focus on service left open the question of what kind of service and thus how the program should be organized and supported. The focus on educational opportunity did suggest certain design details, like recruiting those most in need of student aid, but even these details were contested.

So why was Franklin Roosevelt better able to articulate more effective policymaking purposes than Bill Clinton? The critical difference is that FDR had a virtual free hand and Clinton did not. In 1932 there were no existing youth employment programs, focused on conservation or anything else. Further, federal government experience with social policy of any kind was limited. Finally, the idea for the CCC had not grown out of any larger movement, so there were few individuals or groups, inside or outside government, with interests to be accommodated or who had learned lessons to be heeded.

Sixty years later, the political landscape had been transformed. Large numbers of youth service, and youth-serving, programs flourished, encompassing a wide range of emphases. Within government, social policies had proliferated, some with outcomes that called into question the efficacy of means-targeting, among other lessons. And for twenty-five years a diverse array of advocates had worked to create a new national service program, giving them a vested interest in Clinton's proposal. As a result, AmeriCorps's purposes had to be broad enough to, at the very least, not alienate these interests. The trade-off was that most policy design questions were left unanswered. As this chapter explains in detail, postponing these decisions did not make them easier to resolve.

Beyond policymaking, programs' purposes have political effects. As just noted, AmeriCorps's goals served the political purpose of not offending potential supporters within the service and education communities. However, political tasks extend beyond placating interest groups to building public and party support. For the public, national service's dual-purpose framing worked well. As Steven Waldman describes, in campaign focus groups "neither service nor loans [for education] *alone* stirred much excitement," but together they did: "When tied to service, the loans did not seem like profligate liberalism, because Clinton was asking for something in return. . . . Conversely, the service program no longer seemed elitist, because it was helping middle-class working families send their kids to college."[3] On the downside, the proposed program was easier to describe in paragraphs than sound bites. In his first two addresses on national service, Clinton never captured its essence in a single, media-friendly phrase, along the lines of FDR's description of the CCC as "conserving not only our natural resources, but our human resources."[4] Further, when administration officials tried, they fell one purpose short. At the proposal's unveiling, they hung a banner proclaiming "National Service Means Educational Opportunity."[5]

The single-message banner highlights another reality: even multipurpose programs need an overriding goal. As chapter 2 describes, prioritizing goals facilitates policymaking, accountability, and public relations. Without question, the CCC's most important justification was work relief. Given the Great Depression, it could be no other. Happily for the country, in 1993 neither America's need for service nor rising college costs were crises on par with the Great Depression. This left AmeriCorps, however, unlike the CCC, without a patently obvious, and thus universally agreed upon, principal purpose. In fact, there was disagreement on its main purpose both within the administration and between the administration and congressional Democrats—which created a wide opening for Republican opposition.

The administration, and specifically the White House staff, was split between those who believed that "service was really at the heart of the president's proposal"—mainly policymakers in the White House Office of National Service—and those who felt that "the proposal's popularity stemmed from its ability to tap into middle-class anxiety about college costs"—mainly White House political strategists.[6] As the banner at the unveiling indicates, the political strategists prevailed, at least at the proposal stage. However, giving pride of place to the proposal's student aid aspects created as many political problems as it solved. Because the administration was unsure how many students would be helped or by how much, marketing national service principally as a student aid program could create expectations it might never meet. It also roughened the road through Congress. Representative Dave McCurdy (D-Okla.), a long-time national service advocate, for one, took issue with this framing, saying: "The administration's national service plan is too often described as a student loan program. It is not. The educational benefit . . . is important, but the basic purpose of national service is to allow young Americans to exercise their responsibilities as freely as they exercise their rights."[7]

This situation gave opponents two openings for attack. To the extent that supporters billed the program foremost as student aid, a critic such as Representative Dick Armey (R-Texas) could charge that it was "not a noble attack upon greed. It [was] more akin to a welfare program for . . . aspiring yuppies." To the extent that the proposal's supporters challenged this framing, Armey could charge that the proposal had "an identity crisis. [Was] it a service program or a [student] loan program?"[8]

The proposed program's twofold purpose thus cut both ways politically. However, civically, its dual focus was more uniformly positive. Like the CCC, it embodied the principle of reciprocity—that citizens should contribute to and benefit from the commonwealth—and communicated a sense of citizenship from multiple perspectives. The National and Community Service Trust Act spoke of citizenship when it called for its programs to "renew the ethic of civic responsibility and the spirit of community throughout the United States."[9] Talking about citizens "taking time out to serve," "work[ing] together to solve our common problems," and thus demonstrating "real patriotism," President Clinton regularly invoked citizenship in its many forms.[10] What distinguished Clinton's remarks from those of FDR—and led to the act's emphasis on civic renewal—was their cultural resonance. FDR's language reinforced civic understandings common to the culture; Clinton was trying to change the culture so that it better reflected these principles. In an era of low voter turnout, falling organization memberships, declining neighborhood involvement, and other signs of civic distress, Clinton, and AmeriCorps, faced a much greater civic challenge.[11]

Clinton's Program: Getting Things Done

In the year between the National and Community Service Trust Act's passage and the swearing in of AmeriCorps's first members, Corporation for National Service staff members had to flesh out AmeriCorps's policy design, including refining its stated purpose. In doing so they both expanded upon and prioritized what they had inherited.

In unveiling AmeriCorps, Corporation CEO Eli Segal identified and explained four purposes for the program "dedicated," as he put it, "to core American values."

> First, *getting things done* to make our streets safer, our schools better, our families healthier, our environment cleaner. Second, *strengthening communities*, showing how Americans from diverse backgrounds can work together for the common good. Third, *encouraging responsibility*, teaching young people to take care of themselves, take care of their families and take care of their communities. And fourth, *expanding opportunity*, giving the young people who do their part with America's future the new skills and a hand for college [emphasis added].[12]

Of these four, "getting things done"—doing valuable service work that directly addressed real problems—was primary and became the program's motto.[13] The other three were additional priorities, framed in the language of the president's campaign—and subsequently governing—themes. This language served to show how central even AmeriCorps's secondary goals were to the Clinton presidency, while simultaneously placing service center stage.

Why did the service emphasis prevail? One reason was the importance of earning public support, a critical element of the administration's hoped-for policy feedback loop. AmeriCorps's founders had a grand vision of what the program could become, in terms of size, impact, and legacy, all dependent upon its continuation and growth. The program's continuation and growth in turn depended upon increasing its congressional support, which depended in good part upon increasing its public support. Further, a public impressed by his signature program would help secure Clinton's reelection, a good in itself from his appointees' view, but which would also give AmeriCorps four more years of guaranteed presidential support. The problem was, how to impress a public convinced that government can do almost nothing right? To succeed, "national service would have to produce a product in which 'the public would delight,' " which in its creators' view depended upon participants doing "real, useful work."[14]

Further, at least some policymakers shared the CCC founders' belief that only by accomplishing real, valuable work could the program accomplish its other goals. As Shirley Sagawa, the Corporation's first executive director, explained, "Getting things done is absolutely the most important thing this program can do, and it is the piece that makes the other parts possible."[15] Make-work does not build community or instill civic responsibility or justify a reward. In the words of Harris Wofford, Segal's successor as CNS head, an "emphasis . . . on very concrete goals that can be measured and reported"—evidence of getting things done—was critical "so that the public will understand, but also so that the participants in the program will have a sense of achievement and know what they have done."[16] Finally, President Clinton made the connection between working to get things done and being a citizen, when he explained that "we need to take some time out to serve, to be citizens, to work together to solve our common problems."[17] From this view, a focus on service outcomes and impacts is entirely compatible with an emphasis on citizenship, especially from the service- and work-oriented citizenship perspectives.

Although these goals were decided upon early, they remained unclear and contested for years, even among those intimately familiar with the program. For example, in his 1996 testimony before the Senate Committee on Labor and Human Resources, Wofford (himself a former committee member and Democratic senator from Pennsylvania) used his time to tell his former colleagues the "untold story of national service." The first untold chapter concerned the "products" of AmeriCorps—its very purpose. It is worth quoting Wofford at length.

> The primary product of AmeriCorps is *not* giving young people an opportunity to further their education—although AmeriCorps has provided 45,000 opportunities for Americans to do just that. . . .
>
> The primary product of AmeriCorps is not teaching reciprocity—although the idea that a young American should give something to his or her country in return for aid is powerful and enduring. . . .
>
> The primary product of AmeriCorps is not giving a rewarding experience to those doing service—although many AmeriCorps members have reported their year or two of intense service to be a life-changing experience. . . .
>
> The primary product of AmeriCorps is not instilling an ethic of service—although there are already signs that those who give full-time service this year will give continuous service throughout their lifetimes. . . .
>
> The primary product of AmeriCorps is not even bringing people of different backgrounds together in a common mission—although I am moved whenever I see service programs build bridges between races. . . .
>
> Taken together, these by-products make national service a vital and worthwhile investment, but none of them is its primary product.
>
> The primary product—and the primary purpose—of AmeriCorps . . . is helping communities solve some of the critical problems of our country.[18]

The lack of clarity about AmeriCorps's core purpose can be chalked up in part to the fact that it had been refined in practice: "helping communities solve critical problems" puts "getting things done" into a much stronger community context than Segal's original framing. It also deepens the concept of "strengthening community" beyond "showing how diverse Americans can work together" to actively helping them do so. Still, Wofford's refined statement of priorities was far from a novel, wholesale redesign, and was unequivocal at that.

Nonetheless, a year later—so three years into AmeriCorps's history—national service experts were still questioning its central purpose. One commented that "it comes down to . . . the basic problem of goals: Is the primary goal to help the poor, at-risk children, and people in crisis, or is it to promote citizenship?"[19] More bluntly put, "What is the aim here? Is it problem solving or is it duty?"[20] Whether these questions were prompted by a lack of understanding of AmeriCorps's primary purpose or disagreement with it is unclear. Either way, the proffered alternatives are significant: citizenship and duty, not student aid, were the competing values. That citizenship could be seen as AmeriCorps's primary purpose suggests the strength of the program's civic mission, even as the connection between "getting things done" and citizenship was challenged.

There are parallels between this situation and that which the CCC faced at a similar age. By 1937 a critical mass of elite opinion believed that the CCC's conservation focus was undermining its ability to train future citizen-workers, as opposed to epitomizing it. The major difference is that the CCC had had several years to establish itself, programmatically, publicly, and politically, before its means and ends were seriously contested. AmeriCorps never had such a honeymoon.

The second "untold story of national service" that Wofford highlighted in 1996 was its "success in recruiting, organizing, and otherwise leveraging unpaid volunteers."[21] While not explicitly included as a goal, this had become central to AmeriCorps's mission—and survival. One of the Republicans' key criticisms was that national service would undermine traditional voluntarism. After all, they asked, why volunteer for free when you can get paid to serve?

The Corporation's initial response was to differentiate between voluntarism and service, between part-time, occasional volunteer efforts and full-time, year-round service commitments, and to support both. After Republicans won control of the House in 1994, however, AmeriCorps's leaders had to do more than argue that service and voluntarism were different but complementary. Arguing that Republicans should support a program they despised simply because it did not, in fact, kill that which they held dear was hardly persuasive. However, early in AmeriCorps's operation it became clear that it did more than complement traditional volunteer efforts; it expanded them. In Wofford's words, "Initially, the proposition that [AmeriCorps] could help nonprofit volunteer programs work better was greeted with skepticism. One such skeptic was Millard Fuller, founder and president of Habitat for Humanity International. . . . Today, he is a strong supporter because he has seen how AmeriCorps increased the number and efficiency of Habitat's traditional volunteers."[22] Although "a substantial portion of AmeriCorps assignments [already were] directly geared to enlisting and organizing the volunteer service of others," Wofford vowed to make this "an even higher priority."[23] It certainly did not hurt that Habitat for Humanity was the favorite charity of House Speaker Newt Gingrich (R-Ga.).

Under Bush: Corporals in the Armies of Compassion and Homeland Defense

When the 2000 presidential election was finally resolved, the key question facing AmeriCorps was whether it would continue to serve any purpose at all. With both the presidency and Congress in Republican hands, AmeriCorps's opponents saw an opportunity to finally do away with it. History suggested that George W. Bush, as a Republican president, would not have balked. Both Nixon and Reagan would have dispensed with VISTA had Congress assented. Only Bush's father had supported VISTA, but unlike his predecessors, or his son with regard to AmeriCorps, he had inherited the program from a fellow Republican. VISTA was saved in part by its ideological malleability, that conservatives could redirect it to fit their priorities. AmeriCorps also exhibited that flexibility: in the new millennium, it would contribute to Bush's program of "compassionate conservatism" and provide an outlet for civic engagement following the September 11 terrorist attacks.

Although Bush barely mentioned AmeriCorps during his campaign, he spoke frequently of increasing federal government support for community and faith-based organizations—a centerpiece of his "compassionate conservative" governing philosophy. In Leslie Lenkowsky's view, "National service fit well with this vision. One in seven AmeriCorps members, it turned out, was already serving with faith-based groups, and even more were serving with community-oriented secular ones."[24] This is not to say that Bush was prepared to accept Clinton's signature program without revision; there would be a "shift in thinking": "In contrast to the Clinton administration, which placed a priority on counting the number of children tutored . . . and the like—what it called 'getting things done'—the Bush administration will give more emphasis to building the capacity of nonprofit organizations to involve their communities in addressing local needs."[25]

As the president's top service officials explained, "The organizations mobilizing the armies of compassion need corporals and sergeants"—people like those in AmeriCorps, who can "take on long-range tasks and responsibilities that ordinary volunteers cannot."[26] So while Clinton's AmeriCorps's leaders celebrated its success at leveraging traditional volunteers, Bush's leaders made leveraging a funding requirement. They also pushed the program to go beyond leveraging, to include a broader range of organizational capacity-building activities, including administrative, financial, and technological assistance.[27] And they made this—the extent to which AmeriCorps members supported the work of community and faith-based organizations—as opposed to the extent to which they "got things done" directly—the primary purpose and justification for the program.

Surprisingly, this led Bush's national service policymakers to single out VISTA for praise, stating, "Since [VISTA] was created in 1965, members . . . have focused their efforts on mobilizing and managing teams of volunteer[s] . . . , developing or expanding programs, and implementing administrative and accounting systems. Those efforts equip nonprofits . . . to do more of the work they already do."[28] Clinton's policymakers had specifically prohibited (non-VISTA) AmeriCorps members from doing much of this work, partly in hopes of avoiding some of the political problems that had plagued VISTA for so many years. Ironically, Bush's officials criticized Clinton's AmeriCorps for attempting to anticipate and avoid traditional Republican criticism of national service by adopting Republicans' historically preferred strategy of direct service, and advocated changing the laws governing AmeriCorps to more closely resemble VISTA's.

However, in contrast with VISTA pre-AmeriCorps, AmeriCorps in the Bush administration stressed developing members' sense of citizenship, even more strongly than it had under Clinton. Although the Clinton administration made ample use of civic language, Bush's policymakers integrated civic engagement requirements into the program as a whole. Further, they placed a special emphasis on constitutional citizenship, in addition to the service and patriotism themes stressed earlier.[29]

That AmeriCorps could support the president's "compassionate conservative" ideology saved it from retrenchment or demise. However, it would take the events of September 11, 2001, and their aftermath to pave the way for expansion. After struggling to define a productive role for a public eager to respond, in his 2002 State of the Union address Bush called on citizens to give 4,000 hours of service to their communities or country over their lifetimes, either through part-time volunteering or full-time national service. From the president's perspective, "acts of goodness and compassion in one's community . . . would be an appropriate way of responding to the 'evils' of September 11."[30] Service could also contribute to homeland defense. To this end, Bush announced plans to increase AmeriCorps's work in public safety, public health, disaster relief, and other homeland security tasks, and to make the program part of his newly created USA Freedom Corps.[31]

By framing and broadening AmeriCorps's purpose to respond to the post-9/11 environment, the Bush administration both tapped into and reinforced the connections between patriotism, service, and citizenship. At the same time, this civic message served a political need—for the president to speak to

Americans' heightened sense of patriotism and desire to contribute. However, the greater political task was not convincing the public that AmeriCorps had value but convincing skeptical conservatives in government. By increasing AmeriCorps's support for traditional voluntarism and adding a homeland security focus, AmeriCorps's Republican supporters hoped to accomplish two critical, and related, political tasks. First, by connecting AmeriCorps to President Bush's top priorities, they hoped to raise AmeriCorps's profile and priority within the administration. Second, this allowed them to argue to Republicans, especially those in Congress, that Bush's vision for AmeriCorps was both different from and better than Clinton's, and therefore worthy of conservatives' support. It was a tough sell.

Under Obama: Meeting Demand and National Challenges

As uncertain as AmeriCorps's future was in 2000, it was ensured over the course of the 2008 presidential campaign: both parties' standard-bearers—Republican John McCain and Democrat Barack Obama—were strong advocates, supporting legislation that would triple AmeriCorps's size. To a large extent, well before Obama's Election Day victory, national service had already won.

Unlike Bill Clinton, who had to establish AmeriCorps's purposes, and George W. Bush, who had to shift its purposes, Obama did not have to create or alter their substance—just argue that more should be done to achieve them. He made that clear during the presidential campaign, charging that "we're not keeping pace with the demand for those who want to serve, and we're not leveraging that commitment to meet national challenges."[32] He proposed remedying the first shortcoming by increasing AmeriCorps from 75,000 to 250,000 members a year, which would represent the largest increase in civilian national service since FDR's 1935 CCC expansion. He proposed addressing the second by "establishing five new Corps" within AmeriCorps—a "Classroom Corps," "Health Corps," "Clean Energy Corps," "Veterans Corps," and "Homeland Security Corps."[33] However, of these, four were already AmeriCorps priorities, reflected above in Segal's statement that AmeriCorps would "make our streets safer, our schools better, our families healthier, our environment cleaner" and Bush's post-9/11 homeland security emphasis. Only the veterans focus was new, reflecting their rising numbers and needs after eight years of war.

Within his first hundred days as president—and with unprecedented bipartisan congressional support—Obama made good on his campaign promise, signing legislation that authorized increases in AmeriCorps enrollment to 250,000 per year over eight years, increased the AmeriCorps education award, and established five "service corps" within AmeriCorps*State and National (although substituting an economic development-focused "Opportunity Corps" for the one focused on homeland security).[34] Regarding AmeriCorps, the Edward M. Kennedy Serve America Act was a historic achievement both for how much it changed—foremost, AmeriCorps's projected size—and for how little it changed—namely, AmeriCorps's stated goals. AmeriCorps's purposes—and more broadly the belief that it served a good purpose—had gone from hotly contested to settled question.

Government's Role

By definition, supporters of national service see some role for government in providing citizens opportunities to serve. That said, AmeriCorps's creators envisioned a much smaller role for the federal government than had either the CCC's or VISTA's. Nonetheless, AmeriCorps's national leadership still had to manage its relationships with other levels of government, communities, and service organizations, as well as organize and support the program within the federal government itself. How this all worked influenced AmeriCorps's effectiveness, its political standing, and the civic lessons it imparted.

A "Federal" Program

In deciding how to manage AmeriCorps, policymakers had several options. They could follow the CCC's model and vest authority almost exclusively in the national government. This was the choice (unchanged from the George H. W. Bush administration) for AmeriCorps*NCCC. Or they could create a "local" national program whereby the federal government and community organizations shared responsibility. This was the structure for AmeriCorps*VISTA (which was still governed by VISTA's earlier mandate). Or they could come up with something new, which they did in creating AmeriCorps*State and National. As part of its larger effort to "reinvent government," the administration created a *federal* program in the term's original sense, with roles for both the national and state governments. Further, the national government role would be small, as would government's role overall, with most of the work done through community organizations.

In creating the CCC and VISTA, policymakers expanded federal government authority into new territory. In creating the new AmeriCorps program, policymakers did the opposite: not only did they not want to expand the federal government's role, for both programmatic and political reasons, they wanted to roll it back. President Clinton himself "distrusted the abilities of the federal government—even his federal government—and did not want to leave himself open to attack for being a typical big-bureaucracy Washington liberal."[35] The question then was, how do you run the largest civilian national service program since the CCC with the smallest role ever for the national government? The main answer was to give more responsibility than ever to state governments and community organizations.

The most authority that states had over the CCC or VISTA was the power to say no—a veto over projects—and not always even this. With AmeriCorps, policymakers gave states the power to say yes—to choose many, even most, of their state's projects. In doing so, they hoped to give governors—who, if so motivated, "could find thousands of creative ways to quietly sabotage the local projects"—an incentive to support and work for the program's success. So in part this was a policy design decision geared toward furthering a positive policy feedback dynamic. However, this power-sharing approach was not without its perils, captured well by Waldman: "As a former governor, [Clinton] liked the idea of the states playing a large role." However, Clinton no longer was a governor, he was the president, and he had decided to allow "the program [he] hoped would be his abiding legacy [to] be largely shaped by the governors, some of whom were his political enemies, some of whom didn't give a whit about service, and some of whom couldn't design a quality service corps if you paid them." At the same time, because he had created it and his federal government was funding it, "if the governors allowed volunteers to pick up gum wrappers, Clinton would get blamed."[36] It was a risk Clinton was willing to take.

Beyond this, the administration created new, limited administrative structures: the Corporation for National and Community Service at the national level (CNS under Clinton, CNCS under Bush and Obama, described in greater detail below) and governor-appointed commissions at the state levels. The Corporation and state commissions can be quite small, because they leave program delivery to others, mainly nonprofit organizations. A key principle of the 1990s "reinventing government" movement is that government should "steer, not row"—so set policy but not implement policy itself.[37] As a result, AmeriCorps was designed essentially as a grant program, providing funds on a competitive basis and largely according to how much and how well programs contributed to AmeriCorps's goals. In "reinventing government" language, this meant that programs needed to be "results-oriented." In CNS language, it meant they must "get things done."

Clinton hoped that "reinventing government" would make government more efficient, effective, and responsive, and through national service in particular would "empower young people and their communities, not . . . empower yet another government bureaucracy."[38] Politically, the administration hoped this strategy, combined with giving states, localities, and community organizations significant authority, would help build public support for national service and for the administration. The risk, however, was that the national government role would be so small—with the integration into local organizations so full and responsibility so diffuse—that AmeriCorps would be invisible, unaccountable, or both.

The administration's civic goals were related and the risks similar. It hoped to counter Republicans' claim that AmeriCorps, "from first line to last," was "calculated to increase the American people's dependence upon, and gratitude to, big government."[39] Instead of big government, it wanted smaller. Instead of dependence, it wanted collaboration. In Clinton's words, "National service recognizes a simple but powerful truth, that we make progress not by governmental action alone, but . . . when the people and their government work . . . in genuine partnership."[40] It did not even want gratitude, at least toward government in general (as opposed to the Clinton administration in particular). When someone suggested that "one of the measures of AmeriCorps's success is whether it increases public trust in government," Corporation head Wofford dissented, saying "I [have] never heard anyone point to that as one of the aims of AmeriCorps—nor do I think it should be. In fact, I believe the purpose, in a sense, is just the opposite, to build public trust in the idea that people have the ability to take action, and that action, if done well, can help really solve problems."[41] Both are examples of possible policy feedback affecting citizens' political and civic engagement, but they are premised on the program's sending different messages—or "meanings" in Paul Pierson's usage—to the public.

Wofford's perspective highlights the paradox of public distrust with respect to national service, especially in context of the times. When designing AmeriCorps—or any new program—policymakers faced an incredulous, weary, and wary—if not downright hostile—citizenry. In early administration research on national service, a focus group of politically diverse suburban voters was "profoundly unimpressed . . . they figured the government would devise some creative way of screwing up even something so promising."[42] In fact, when asked to name "*any* government program that worked well," they responded with the Peace Corps, the space program—and otherwise, total silence.[43]

On the political front, policymakers recognized that it would be difficult to create, sustain, and grow AmeriCorps in the face of such deep distrust—not impossible, but difficult.[44] On the civic side, citizens' distrust would make it harder to build the citizen-government partnerships—partnerships requiring trust—on which AmeriCorps was premised, again, not impossible, but more difficult. "Reinventing" government to work better could help restore public confidence, but citizens' lack of faith was a stumbling block in itself to elements of reinvention, generally and through AmeriCorps specifically. At the same time, any explicit effort to rehabilitate citizens' views of government would open the administration to conservatives' criticism and could undermine the central, civic action message of national service, all while probably failing.

This tension is partly inherent in national service and partly a product of the times. In 1933 the head of the CCC could publicly state that one of the CCC's aims was to "instill in [citizens] a greater faith in our government": in the context of the Great Depression, the people's faith in government and faith in themselves were not seen as mutually exclusive but, rather, interdependent.[45] Sixty years later, this was no longer the case, even for a Democrat as sympathetic to active government as Wofford.

In sum, AmeriCorps's "reinventing government"–inspired federal structure and small role for government held both high promise and high risk, politically and civically. Even more so than with the CCC or VISTA, how well AmeriCorps worked would depend on how well relationships outside and inside the program were managed.

Managing Outside Relationships

Given its structure and guiding principles, it is not surprising that Ameri-Corps's external relations—with the general public and local communities, its state partners and grantee organizations, and its member participants—were complex and critical. While some relationships, especially with the broad public and with members, remain tenuous, those with governors and grantees gave the program a solid foundation on which to build.

THE GENERAL PUBLIC. Like VISTA, and in contrast with the CCC, Ameri-Corps is disadvantaged in building strong public support. Although Ameri-Corps puts thousands more participants into the field than VISTA did, they are still spread thin over the country and are well integrated into the organizations and communities they serve. This makes them hard to see and recognize as AmeriCorps members, even at the local level where they work. Further, the proliferation of government programs and, more generally, increased social complexity mean that in the fight for public attention AmeriCorps has many more competitors than the CCC or even VISTA had earlier. As a result, AmeriCorps would have had to invest more resources to achieve the same level of public recognition. However, "in response to budget cuts and congressional critics who charged that AmeriCorps was trying to displace local volunteer groups," officials temporarily suspended AmeriCorps's public relations program early in its history.[46] Even when the public relations and recruitment budget was reinstated, it was less than a quarter of the corresponding budget in the Peace Corps, an already well-known program recruiting far fewer volunteers.[47]

The results were significant: a 1995 survey found that "only 24 percent of respondents said they had heard or read anything about AmeriCorps, compared with 91 percent who recognized the Peace Corps and 40 percent who recognized the Civilian Conservation Corps (CCC) and Volunteers in Service to America (VISTA)."[48] Six years and 200,000 AmeriCorps participants later, the numbers had not significantly improved, with two of three Americans still never having heard of it.[49] These statistics backed up the program's anecdotes of anonymity, such as this 1998 story: "In Washington last month, with the Lincoln Memorial as a backdrop, nearly 100 AmeriCorps members formally marked the end of their year of service. When curious tourists inquired about the ceremony, their inevitable next remark was 'What is AmeriCorps?' "[50]

That said, there was also evidence of public approval. In the 1995 survey, among those who knew of AmeriCorps "only 5 percent said they had a bad impression of it," and when it was described for the uninitiated, 83 percent were in favor of it.[51]

How much any of this matters is open to debate. Supporters typically see AmeriCorps's invisibility as a liability, as, in Wofford's words, "a challenge to all of us . . . to do better in telling the story of national service."[52] The reasons are both civic and political. Civically, AmeriCorps's lack of recognition limits its lessons to its direct participants and beneficiaries; and although they number several hundred thousand, advocates hope that AmeriCorps will help spread the gospel of national service and citizenship nationwide. As McCain lamented, "a program few have heard of will obviously not be able to inspire a new ethic of national service."[53] Politically, the danger is analogous: a program that few have heard of will be equally unable to inspire significant constituent support and thus put pressure on its opponents in Congress. Especially early on, "the sort of wide and deep public support that could help AmeriCorps weather future storms remain[ed] elusive."[54]

On the other hand, some believe that invisibility can have political benefits "because you can't target a program you can't find."[55] The problem is, the program is not invisible—at least as a budget item—to its critics, especially those in Congress. They can find it just fine. But a larger question is, as put by one advocate, whether it is appropriate to "equate national recognition of a program with programmatic success."[56] On this score AmeriCorps certainly suffers from its frequent comparisons with the CCC and the Peace Corps, but both its model of service and its times are markedly different. As I mentioned above, a decentralized program promulgated amid the morass of decades of accumulated programs, in a society more complex by many degrees of magnitude, is going to have a much harder time penetrating the public consciousness than those that are not facing the same circumstances. But this says nothing about the program's effectiveness or efficiency in fulfilling its purpose—in AmeriCorps's case, getting things done. While not dismissing the importance of increasing its public profile, AmeriCorps is bound to fail if it aspires to, or is held to, a standard achievable only by a different kind of program in a different time.

GOVERNORS. Although aspects of AmeriCorps's design work against building political support, other elements have given it a strong and vitally necessary political base. Policymakers took a risk in vesting so much authority in states' hands, but this chance paid off handsomely. Just two years into AmeriCorps's tenure—while congressional Republicans were trying mightily to kill it—Republican governors were singing its praises. New Hampshire Governor Steve Merrill called AmeriCorps "a great success." Michigan Governor John Engler said AmeriCorps "captures the promise found in all citizens." Arizona Governor Fife Symington said he was "enthusiastic and impressed with the work of AmeriCorps." And Massachusetts Governor William Weld called it "one of the most intelligent uses of taxpayer money ever."[57]

The reason for governors' support is clear: they received services for their states on the federal dime, and with AmeriCorps, unlike the CCC and VISTA, they controlled much of the spending themselves through their state commissions. What's not to like? And their backing was crucial. It allowed the administration to claim early, bipartisan support for the program around the country at a time when it was conspicuously absent in Congress. In addition, governors' approval came organized: unlike most of the small, local groups receiving AmeriCorps funding, governors have a lobbying presence on Capitol Hill. As a result, "the states . . . emerged as the principal political supporters of the CNS in Washington," second only to President Clinton himself.[58] And given that Clinton would not be president forever, their support had the potential to be even more important. While the fact that forty-nine governors, the majority Republican, went on record in 2000 supporting AmeriCorps did not guarantee its future, it made it easier to defend, especially because one of these governors was George W. Bush.[59]

GRANTEES. Even more important than its relationship with the states—and much more complex—is AmeriCorps's relationship with the hundreds of organizations it funds. Unlike the states, these groups implement virtually the entire program, making it difficult even to separate AmeriCorps from them. In fact, Wofford went so far as to say: "Except for the 1,000-member National Civilian Community Corps . . . which we're accountable for, City Year and 400 other programs, *are* AmeriCorps. We don't have the strategy; they have the strategy."[60] This perspective raises several questions. First, to what extent is it true? Second, to what extent is it beneficial?

It is true that neither the Corporation nor state commissions run their own AmeriCorps programs, the NCCC excepted, and that neither has a "strategy," understood as a specific approach or model of national service. However, AmeriCorps's policymakers do have a broad understanding of what they want AmeriCorps to be and, more important, have the power not only to influence but in many cases to determine which organizations become and remain part of AmeriCorps. As a result, the relationship between AmeriCorps and its grantees is simultaneously top-down and bottom-up.

This relationship has generated many of the civic and political benefits policymakers intended but also has had some drawbacks. On the positive side, AmeriCorps has largely lived up to President Clinton's promise that it would "be your programs at your levels with your people," that it would support grassroots organizations and programs already known to work instead of reinventing them.[61] However, AmeriCorps's structure has made it difficult for some grassroots organizations to become part of AmeriCorps at all. The decision to run AmeriCorps as a grant program and to keep the administrative offices small means that organizations seeking AmeriCorps funds must be able to navigate the application process, abide by federal regulations, and manage federal funds with minimal assistance. Further, the long lead times, delays in receiving promised funding, and uncertainty of receiving any funding at all—because of the nature of competitive grants and, early on, Congress's frequent attempts to eliminate AmeriCorps's funding altogether—mean that organizations often cannot depend on these funds and so need backup resources.[62] As a result, organizations lacking professional management and other funds are disadvantaged, even though they may be "especially close to the grassroots and adept at reaching underserved populations"—and therefore precisely the kind of organizations (among others) that the program intends to support.[63] In response, and in keeping with its emphasis on supporting local faith-based and community initiatives, the Bush administration took steps to make AmeriCorps more administratively "grassroots-friendly," but the nature of federal funding makes it difficult to even the playing field.[64]

At the same time, AmeriCorps's grant structure and small administrative offices also created problems for AmeriCorps itself. Keeping the program simple, by giving organizations lump sums and then letting them hire Ameri-Corps members with the funds led to serious accounting challenges. Some-times organizations cannot find anyone to hire, which leaves slots unfilled and money left over, or they do not find someone until late in the program year. Organizations could decide after receiving their grants whether to hire members full time or part time, paid or "education award only," even though these choices affect the likelihood of members' earning or using their educa-tion award and thus the funding needed for the education award trust.[65] Cor-poration accountants have formulas to anticipate enrollments and outlays, but when they are off the mark—as they were in 2002—the consequences can be dire.

And if the Corporation has had trouble knowing how many people it sup-ports, some of those being supported do not know it, or focus on it, them-selves. Senator McCain captured the problem well in 2001: "The ability to provide skilled and motivated manpower to other organizations is what makes AmeriCorps so effective. But it also creates a problem. . . . Staffers at non-profit groups sometimes call AmeriCorps headquarters looking for support for their organizations, only to find out that *their own salaries* are being paid by AmeriCorps."[66] On the one hand, this problem could in fact be a benefit. One of conservatives' key concerns about nonprofits receiving federal support is that they "become less responsive to their clients and more responsive to the bureaucrats."[67] However, if the funding mechanism is such that an organiza-tion's workers are unaware that they even are receiving funds, they will not alter their behavior—and potentially neglect their core mission—to ensure its continuation. At the same time, they cannot give credit where it is due, even if the funding is helping them to further their mission.

This is a fear with AmeriCorps, and one that goes well beyond funding ignorance. Even those who know that their organizations are receiving and benefiting from AmeriCorps funding can forget to highlight it. One exam-ple, recounted by Wofford, will illustrate. In the mid-1990s, Representative John Kasich (R-Ohio) visited the AmeriCorps-supported Rheedlen Cen-ters for Children and Families in Harlem, acclaimed for its success working with inner-city kids.[68] Impressed, he said, "I'm going to be writing a book on volunteer service, and I think I'll start with this as the prime example of what really works." As he was leaving he turned to Geoff Canada [the center's director] and said, "Damn it. This is the sort of thing AmeriCorps ought to do." And Geoff Canada said, "This is AmeriCorps. We wouldn't have this program but for these 55 AmeriCorps people you've been with all morning."[69]

Wofford told this story to emphasize the supportive, yet critical, role AmeriCorps plays in helping local organizations. However, the story simultaneously raises troubling questions. How could an organization's director let a major congressional leader all but walk out the door without knowing that it was benefiting from a much-needed federal program, especially when that program was under threat from Congress and opposed by this very member? Further, how could someone—anyone—spend an entire morning visiting a program with fifty-five AmeriCorps members, and meeting these members, and never know it?

AMERICORPS MEMBERS. One possible answer to the last question is that the AmeriCorps members may not have seen themselves—and so did not present themselves—as AmeriCorps members. This was another of McCain's concerns, that "members often take on the identity of the organizations they're assigned to. In the process, they often lose any sense of being part of a larger national service enterprise," namely, AmeriCorps itself.[70] Certainly, compared with either the CCC or VISTA, AmeriCorps has a less direct relationship with its members: it neither hires, places, nor directly pays any of the thousands of members serving through its State and National program.

This is not to say that policymakers have been content to let members think of AmeriCorps as nothing more than the agency that would soon give them money for college. The AmeriCorps pledge, logo-printed T-shirts, group-training activities, and other program elements are designed to give members a common bond across the diversity of their service assignments. Some, such as McCain, believe that these efforts have fallen short; others, however, have thought they go too far. For example, Representative Pete Hoekstra (R-Mich.) lamented that AmeriCorps was engaged in "'national identification activities'—that is, promoting the name of AmeriCorps," with members "wearing nationally identifiable uniforms, using common language and definitions, and handing out palm cards to promote the national organization." From his perspective, this made AmeriCorps "a national army of sorts . . . much bigger than the individual programs that [were] involved" when he had "envisioned a simple program with local kids working in their own communities on local problems."[71]

McCain's and Hoekstra's concerns are civic—McCain's stemming from his "national greatness" conservative philosophy, Hoekstra's from the "civil society" conservative perspective. However, Hoekstra's concern was also political: a national army could be mobilized for the political benefit of AmeriCorps, its grantee organizations, and the commander-in-chief—official prohibitions notwithstanding.

And there are official prohibitions. To avoid the conservative backlash against VISTA that followed its eras of political advocacy, AmeriCorps's founders banned members from lobbying or otherwise participating in political events and activities in connection with their service. These restrictions certainly affect their service work, which this chapter discusses below, but they also affect members' relationship to AmeriCorps itself: as one member "noted banefully . . . AmeriCorps membership even restrained her own ability to support her program"—an example of how a program's rules can undermine a participant's ability to become politically engaged.[72] Specifically, members are not allowed to organize in defense of AmeriCorps's appropriation, which was regularly on the Republican Congress's chopping block. Indeed, "some members of AmeriCorps [felt] helpless because the budget [was] up for debate year after year, and they [couldn't] say anything about it."[73]

Some critics believed they were engaged anyway, and with official blessing. For example, in 1995 Hoekstra cited "a rally at the White House" with "similar activities . . . taking place simultaneously throughout the nation . . . with AmeriCorps members clapping in rhythm for President Clinton as he decried our efforts to carry out our required [oversight] duties." As Hoekstra put it, "We appear to disagree on what our definitions of 'political' are."[74] However, in subsequent years advocates appeared quite mindful of Republicans' views—and AmeriCorps members were conspicuously absent from rallies. For instance, in response to the 2003 funding crisis, advocates sponsored Voices for AmeriCorps: 100 Hours of National Service Testimony (see more about this event below). This Capitol Hill event featured more than seven hundred speakers testifying on AmeriCorps's importance—and it appears that not one was a current AmeriCorps member.[75] The official AmeriCorps alumni association has taken the political activity ban even further, issuing the following disclaimer: "The Corporation for National and Community Service does not endorse and is in no way affiliated with the AmeriCorps Alums Advocacy Center. Furthermore, current AmeriCorps members are expressly forbidden to engage in any advocacy efforts, including *visiting the AmeriCorps Alums Advocacy Center* [website], while in service [emphasis added]."[76]

Had policymakers not included an advocacy ban, it is virtually certain that Congress would not have passed AmeriCorps and none of the civic lessons and benefits that it imparts would have been realized. However, the ban also has had costs, further widening the distance between members and Ameri-Corps itself.

INTEREST GROUPS. AmeriCorps's policy design affected not only members' and individual grantee organizations' relationships with the program, it also affected efforts to create supportive interest groups. Given policy feedback dynamics, one might have expected such groups to grow in the wake of Ameri-Corps's creation, especially after it came under threat. This happened with VISTA, and it was a much smaller program. By funding the work of hundreds of nonprofits and by graduating tens of thousands of alumni each year, AmeriCorps had even greater potential to "rally broad-based political support . . . by bringing together the supporters of many individual programs."[77] Early on, AmeriCorps created an alumni association in part to do just that, encouraging former members to advocate for the program and for national service more broadly. Alums also started their own advocacy organizations, such as ServeNext, which organizes grassroots support for national service. But the same constraints that prompt many members to see themselves as part of their organizations, more so than part of AmeriCorps, affect former members—and probably even more than members, because alums are no longer directly *part* of the program. For these reasons, organizing grantee organizations for advocacy has had greater political potential.

However, AmeriCorps's policy design, especially its multitiered, competitive grant structure, has made it harder for organizations to cooperate with one another and thus harder to realize this political potential. For example, when National grantees worked to increase the percentage of AmeriCorps's budget awarded directly by the Corporation, those organizations funded through state commissions were not amused. At the same time, National and State grantees compete among themselves for limited funds. Such rivalry is a key reason there was no "organized 'industrywide' group to advocate for national service" for most of AmeriCorps's first decade—even in the face of congressional opposition that might have hurt them all."[78] That President Clinton was willing and able to successfully fight for AmeriCorps perversely made it less necessary for groups to set aside their differences and fight for the program themselves.

This changed in 2003 when a funding crisis threatened an 80 percent cut in the program. Although the reduction would be temporary (the details are below), the consequences for grantees would be severe, including, for some, closure. To pressure Congress for emergency funds, City Year's Alan Khazei and AnnMaura Connelly started the Save AmeriCorps Coalition, bringing together heads of AmeriCorps's grantee organizations, former Corporation leaders and other government officials, several governors and state service commission members, academics, and corporate CEOs, backed by private foundation funding.[79] (On the positive side, that grantees must raise nongovernment funds to supplement or match their AmeriCorps funding meant that these nonprofit leaders had strong private sector connections and that business and philanthropic leaders had a vested interest in the fate of AmeriCorps-funded programs.) The coalition's efforts over a short seven weeks included getting 44 governors and 147 mayors to sign letters to President Bush and congressional leaders to restore AmeriCorps's funds; placing full-page ads in the *New York Times* and *Financial Times*, signed by 250 business and philanthropic leaders; and getting more than 50,000 citizens to sign an online petition.[80] This work contributed to passage of the Strengthen AmeriCorps Program Act, which resulted in lesser cuts to the program—55 percent instead of 80 percent—but the coalition fell short of its goal of making the program whole.

With one battle over, the coalition—now mobilized—turned its attention to the next: AmeriCorps's funding for the upcoming year. Khazei and the coalition, again within two months, organized Voices for AmeriCorps: 100 Hours of National Service Testimony, "and it worked. Not only did Congress restore all of the [AmeriCorps's] funding . . . in the next year's budget, they added, per President Bush's urging, a $100 million increase in order to fulfill his promise to grow AmeriCorps from 50,000 to 75,000 members."[81] Although "'lobbying by the Save AmeriCorps Coalition'" was not the only factor contributing to the increase, it had introduced "a new 'dimension' to the politics of the Corporation's budget appropriation."[82]

Turning to longer-term goals, coalition members then created Voices for National Service as a permanent organization to influence funding and policy. Several years later, Khazei's new outfit, Be the Change Inc., launched a campaign called Service Nation, which eventually gathered the support of more than one hundred national organizations. Coinciding with the 2008 presidential campaign, Service Nation included a national summit, complete with a presidential candidate forum and presentation of major new national service legislation, and a National Day of Action. The summit, held over the anniversary of 9/11, drew a bipartisan cast of political heavyweights and Hollywood notables. Senator Orrin Hatch (R-Utah) unveiled the Serve America Act he had just authored with Senator Edward Kennedy (D-Mass.) with Service

Nation encouragement. Both presidential nominees, McCain and Obama, spoke about their commitment to national service, and both agreed to co-sponsor the Serve America Act. Cable outlets covered the candidate forum live; *Time* magazine ran a cover story on national service. Two weeks later, the Service Nation Day of Action engaged more than 250,000 citizens in events across the country.[83]

After Barack Obama's election, Service Nation, Voices for National Service, America Forward (a coalition promoting social innovation and entrepreneurship), and others organized for inclusion of funds for AmeriCorps in the economic stimulus package and passage of the Serve America Act.[84] With Congress's Democratic majorities and AmeriCorps's growing bipartisan support, passage was on their side, but outside groups' advocacy efforts very likely helped the legislation achieve its overwhelming victory. Fighting for the funds to accomplish the act's goals, especially after the Republican gains in the 2010 elections, has proved to be a tougher battle. However, the fact that such extensive and well-organized coalitions exist clearly differentiates the politics of AmeriCorps's first decade from its second, with no sign of abatement.

Managing Inside Relationships: AmeriCorps's Leadership

Like Franklin Roosevelt and the CCC, Clinton made his national service program a high priority. Unlike FDR, but largely courtesy of the changes he initiated, Clinton was not nearly as involved in determining his program's details: with a vastly expanded portfolio of responsibilities, Clinton had less time to devote to even a "pet" program. As a result, it is surprising to see how involved he was in deciding AmeriCorps's policy matters.[85] However, even FDR relied primarily on his CCC director, and similarly Clinton relied on those he chose to lead the Corporation for National Service, first Segal and later Wofford.

Segal came to the position from a political and business background. He had worked on several (failed) Democratic presidential campaigns and was a prodigious party fundraiser before Clinton, a friend for more than twenty years, tapped him to head his presidential campaign. At the same time, Segal had earned millions, owning and running successful publishing, toy, and game companies. This background contributed to Segal's successes and struggles as the Corporation's CEO.

By choosing Segal first to head the White House Office on National Service and then the Corporation, Clinton was signaling his personal commitment to national service.[86] Segal's political experience prepared him to deal with the Democratic Congress, while his corporate background enabled him to "converse with Republicans in the universal language of business-speak" and helped ensure that AmeriCorps would reflect business-inspired "reinventing government" principles.[87] Even his lack of service experience was seen as a benefit: not coming in committed to any particular service model, he was willing and able to challenge the assumptions of those steeped in the service culture.[88] As Segal later explained, "I try to go in with as blank a slate as I can on a subject and just ask a billion questions."[89]

But there were drawbacks to Segal's background. He could ask the tough questions but had to rely on others for the answers. Waldman asked, "Could someone so ignorant of how service programs worked—including the scams— know how to guarantee real work?"[90] The answer turned out to be yes. Segal's lack of service expertise resulted in neither poor program design nor poor implementation; it did not present a policy problem.[91] It did, however, compound a political problem. National service advocates, including Clinton, billed national service as a bipartisan, even nonpartisan, way to address the nation's ills—a claim many congressional Republicans seriously doubted. Had Clinton appointed a recognized service expert to lead the effort, Republicans' concern that AmeriCorps was more about serving the president's reelection needs than the nation's needs might have been assuaged, or at least not exacerbated. Instead, he chose his top campaign manager—and, as far as many Republicans could tell, for precisely that reason.[92] Even Segal's business acumen was called into question when the merger of programs and agencies into the new CNS structure created so much confusion that its books were determined unauditable.

Segal deserves high praise for what was accomplished during his two-and-a-half-year tenure: AmeriCorps alone—just one of many Corporation programs—went from campaign promise to 20,000 members ready to begin a second year of service. But he bequeathed his successor, Wofford, a mighty challenge: to take a program intimately associated with the Democratic president and help it to survive and thrive in the face of the hostile, Republican-controlled Congress that came to power with the 1994 elections.

Wofford was available for the head Corporation job only because of the Republicans' success in the 1994 elections: he lost his U.S. Senate seat to Republican Rick Santorum, who skewered AmeriCorps in his campaign for paying kids for "picking up trash in a park and singing 'Kumbaya' around the campfire."[93] Nonetheless, availability was the least of Wofford's qualifications. He had been a national service leader for more than thirty years. As a Kennedy White House staffer, he helped Sargent Shriver plan and organize the Peace Corps, later becoming director of operations in Ethiopia and Peace Corps associate director. Wofford then turned to domestic service, creating the Committee to Study the Idea of National Service. Later, as Pennsylvania's secretary of labor and industry, Wofford established the PennServe service-learning initiative, managed the Pennsylvania Conservation Corps, and assisted U.S. senators in passing the National and Community Service Act of 1990, under the first President Bush. After becoming a U.S. senator, Wofford was instrumental in creating the NCCC, also under Bush, and in securing passage of the National and Community Service Trust Act when Clinton took office.[94]

Wofford recognized the challenge he faced as Corporation CEO: his top priority, stated in his confirmation hearing, was to "get national service established in the public mind as a nonpartisan institution." To this end he promised "[his] Republican colleagues . . . that [his] party partisanship ha[d] ended for the duration."[95] Segal could have said these words and meant them, but Wofford could say them and not be dismissed out of hand. Further, his subsequent priorities—paying increased attention to the Corporation's other, non-AmeriCorps programs and to the relationship between the Corporation's programs and their nonprofit counterparts—while justified on policy grounds were also politically strategic.[96]

None of the Corporation's other programs was so closely identified with President Clinton or the Democratic Party; by stating his intent to focus on them, he made it clear that he was not going to tend Clinton's baby to the neglect of the Corporation's other children. As for AmeriCorps, his third priority suggested he intended to raise it with values Republicans could respect, by targeting its work even more on expanding part-time, unpaid volunteer service and reducing the federal government costs.[97]

From this base, Wofford went about converting Republicans to the cause of national service, and if he did not convince the leadership, he did manage to win over other key members. These included McCain, Kasich, and even Santorum. Expanded political support translated into an expanded program: when Wofford left office in 2001, AmeriCorps had grown to 50,000 members a year. This was a remarkable success and worthy legacy for someone who had invested decades in the cause of national service. Whether it could be sustained, this time under a unified Republican government, would be its next big hurdle.

This challenge fell to Leslie Lenkowsky, who came from the academic and foundation worlds and longtime service on the Corporation board. One of the Corporation's key "corporate" features is its board of directors, whose members are appointed by the president but whose makeup by law is bipartisan.[98] By requiring no fewer than "50 percent minus one" of board members be

Republican, the Corporation ensured a degree of Republican representation and support—and thus bipartisan legitimacy—from its otherwise overwhelmingly Democratic inception, and included Republicans willing and able to argue its merits when first Congress and then the presidency shifted to Republican hands. It is not surprising that Bush's first Corporation head came from the board.

Lenkowsky had two major tasks. First, he had to convince a lukewarm President Bush that his administration would have a distinct, and distinctly better, vision for AmeriCorps—that by supporting the program over the objections of many Republicans he would be doing more than wasting political capital to preserve his *predecessor's* legacy.[99] That Lenkowsky is a well-respected conservative intellectual, with clearly thought-out ideas on the philosophy that Corporation programs should reflect, worked to AmeriCorps's advantage. Lenkowsky succeeded by arguing that AmeriCorps could be reformed to more fully reflect the president's "compassionate conservative" approach to social betterment.[100] Further, his approach emphasized government's role as "serving a broader consensus based in the private sector; based in communities; based in corporate, foundation, nonprofit, civic organization desires for federal government involvement"—so not eschewing government's role altogether but framing it in a way more acceptable to conservatives.[101] As a result, Lenkowsky saved AmeriCorps from VISTA's earlier trials at the election of Republican presidents: first they tried to kill it, and only when that failed did they seek to reform it. With Lenkowsky's influence Bush spared AmeriCorps the first step and went directly to the second, which is all the more significant because unlike VISTA, AmeriCorps would not have survived to see the second step had it been subjected to the first.

Lenkowsky's second major task was to implement that more conservative vision, and although none of the changes were as fundamental as earlier Republican changes to VISTA, they were significant. They ranged from bringing the "community" back into use in the Corporation's name to further increasing AmeriCorps's role in leveraging volunteers, from stressing evaluation and accountability for results to encouraging history and civics as part of the program's citizenship training. Further, in response to 9/11 he supported expanding AmeriCorps from 50,000 to 75,000 members a year—a historic increase both in size and precedent, making Bush the first president to press for expansion of a national service program not of his own making.

However, it was an inadvertent increase in AmeriCorps's size that tarnished Lenkowsky's tenure. As this chapter explains below, Lenkowsky presided over a bureaucratic perfect storm: a grant structure that made it impossible to predict and even difficult to know AmeriCorps's exact enrollment; decisions that left the trust for members' education awards underfunded; and a surge in enrollments attributable to the post-9/11 patriotic upswing and economic downturn.[102] As a result, instead of a dramatic increase, the program had to dramatically contract for a year to cover its prior obligations. None of this resulted from affirmative decisions made on Lenkowsky's watch, but that it happened on his watch and had been neither anticipated nor prevented led to calls for his resignation.

In the short term, the funding shortfall revealed a serious weakness in AmeriCorps's decentralized management system and insufficient commitment on the part of the president and Congress to provide extra funds, but also significant vocal, organized support from the organizations and communities faced with losing AmeriCorps members. A longer-term perspective shows even more, namely just how much AmeriCorps's leadership—especially the Corporation's three CEOs—had accomplished: the funding shortfall did not presage AmeriCorps's demise or even significantly derail its future growth as it might have just several years earlier. That Lenkowsky's successor, AOL Time Warner Foundation head David Eisner, came in with a mandate to strengthen AmeriCorps's administration—and not to fundamentally alter its approach or preside over its dismantling—is another indication of the extent to which AmeriCorps had surpassed VISTA's earlier trials and its own troubled history with Congress to achieve a strong degree of political support.[103]

Managing Inside Relationships: AmeriCorps's Standing with Congress

Despite the fact that Democrats controlled Congress in 1993 and, after twelve years of Republican presidential rule, had a vested interest in President Clinton's success, passage of Clinton's national service legislation was in no way guaranteed. In addition to holding the votes of congressional Democrats, the administration needed Republican votes—both to demonstrate national service's bipartisan bona fides and to foreclose a possible filibuster by Senate Republicans. That AmeriCorps's road to creation was this rocky foreshadowed even more serious problems to come.

Granted, the national service bill had some Republican support.[104] In fact, Representatives Chris Shays (R-Conn.) and Steve Gunderson (R-Wis.) worked hard to bring their co-partisans along, arguing that national service was a "basic Republican idea," "that the president's proposal [was] structured as a Republican would have structured it," and that thus "it deserve[d] broad Republican support."[105] However, the vast majority of Republicans were opposed, for a mix of reasons. Some were opposed on principle and would not have supported any type of paid, government-run service program. Others were opposed to the specifics of Clinton's plan, believing that it was "too costly, too bureaucratic, too prescriptive and [that] it misdirect[ed] education resources."[106] Finally, many were loath to give President Clinton a legislative win: Senator Alfonse D'Amato of New York, for one, "warned that a victory on national service, coming soon after a possible budget win, would give Clinton too much political momentum."[107] However, Republicans did have to worry about opposing such an "apple-pie issue"—and so attacked national service not from the right but from the left.[108]

That the administration had stressed national service's student aid aspects gave Republicans an opening. One strategy was to push for means-testing, so that the poor would qualify for more national service slots just as they qualified for more student aid; another was to press for a funding "trigger," which would deny funds to national service until Pell Grants were fully funded.[109] The goal was to give Republicans political cover; gain liberal Democrats' support for the changes; and if they were successful, turn moderate and conservative Democrats against the bill by making it little more than an old-fashioned Democratic anti-poverty program—which Republicans would then also vote against in the end. As Waldman wryly notes, "The spinmeisters' insistence on selling national service as a student aid program was now jeopardizing the entire effort."[110] It took unequivocal statements of support for Clinton's centrist plan from venerated, unreconstructed liberals—Marian Wright Edelman of the Children's Defense Fund and Senator Claiborne Pell (D-R.I.), for whom Pell Grants are named—to keep congressional liberals from temptation.[111]

Beyond these statements of support, House passage required guaranteeing Corporation employees traditional civil service protections (to assuage labor Democrats) and placating the veterans lobby by reducing the education grant to well below what those in the military earned.[112] These matters addressed, the House passed the national service bill 275 to 152, with twenty-six Republicans joining all but five Democrats. However, greater concessions were needed in the Senate, where the Republican minority was both more strongly opposed and had more power—namely the ability to filibuster and thus prevent the measure from even coming to a vote.

With fifty-six Democrats in the Senate, four Senate Republicans cosponsoring the bill, and two additional Republicans voting for the bill in committee, the administration thought it had more than the sixty votes needed to prevent a filibuster. They were wrong: the Republican leadership was able to peel off four of the six Republicans, including two of the cosponsors. This gave opponents the power to demand concessions, but also drew media attention: "While the media had barely covered the national service proposal before, they finally had something they could recognize: a partisan brawl."[113] News stories and editorials blasting the Republicans as obstructionists took their toll, but not before the GOP leadership was able to negotiate a shorter authorization period (from five to three years, giving the program less time to prove itself) and a cut in funding (from $3 billion to $1.5 billion over three years).[114] In the end the administration got its vote and its program but, despite courting and concessions, gained only seven Republicans' support.

These numbers did not bode well when the Republicans won control of both chambers of Congress the next year. The problems began immediately: just six months after AmeriCorps's first members were sworn in, the House voted to rescind three-fourths of the program's existing appropriation, which would have prevented most of the then-20,000 members from completing their service.[115] Later that year both the House and Senate voted to eliminate funding for the upcoming year, which the House did again in 1996, 1999, and 2000.[116] In 1997 the House relented and voted merely to halve the requested funds.[117] (Because the House, compared with the Senate, gives more power to its majority, it was more supportive of AmeriCorps when it was controlled by the Democrats and more strongly opposed when it was controlled by the Republicans.)

The new Congress also took issue with how specific monies were being spent. That AmeriCorps members would meet the president's plane when Clinton flew in to visit their communities, opponents took as "federal funds [being] used to run the permanent campaign."[118] A grant to the ACORN Housing Corporation and other liberal groups led critics to charge that AmeriCorps was "just a tool or a vehicle to funnel money to the left wing, or the president's political friends," echoing Republican complaints about VISTA during the Carter years.[119] That federal agencies could apply for AmeriCorps grants (to encourage "reinventing government" through the integration of community service into their programs), opponents saw as nothing more than "backdoor funding . . . to help [these agencies] do more 'rowing' than their appropriated funds allowed."[120] In response, the Corporation ended these practices and canceled certain grants.

In other cases, critics put the Corporation in a no-win situation. A major complaint early on was the cost of each AmeriCorps member to the federal government—by some counts $28,000.[121] In response, the amount was lowered to $15,000, with grantees having to make up the difference by raising other funds. Later, however, critics held the grantees' successful fundraising against the program. Citing the "tremendous nonfederal support for national service initiatives," congressional opponents said that "AmeriCorps [grantees] could be increasingly sustained by the corporate and community sector."[122]

These stands raise two key questions. Republicans had not controlled Congress as a whole for forty years, and to make up for lost time, they had an ambitious, even revolutionary, agenda. How and why did AmeriCorps—a relatively minor and, budgetwise, positively minuscule program—come to top the list not just for a thoroughgoing critique but for elimination? And given that it did, how did it survive?

AmeriCorps became a target because national service is never just a program: for supporters, it is a symbol of how government should work with citizens and communities anew, and for opponents a dangerous perversion of exactly that. As a *New York Times* article explained, AmeriCorps "takes up about a 30th of a percent" of the nation's budget, but "small as it is, it makes a perfect bull's-eye. From the moment that President Clinton called the corps a 'proud achievement' that is 'changing the way government works,' Republican congressional leaders started taking aim."[123] Further, Clinton hoped that AmeriCorps would become for him what the Peace Corps became for President Kennedy, a mainstay of his legacy. However, Republicans—with an eye on upcoming presidential elections—had a greater stake in undermining Clinton's legacy than helping to secure it. In the view of Republican critic Senator Charles Grassley of Iowa, "The president hasn't done the cause of AmeriCorps any good by calling it the so-called monument of his administration. He raised the political stakes. So it's easier to take potshots."[124]

Finally, because AmeriCorps was such a high, personal priority for the president, Republicans could use it strategically, by basically taking it hostage. For example, Republicans "could eliminate national service in May and offer to restore it in October in exchange for some major Clinton concession."[125] At the same time, by fighting harder and giving more to save AmeriCorps than other key social programs under fire, Clinton offended congressional liberals—some to the point that they voted with Republicans to eliminate the program in hopes of saving others.[126]

In each instance AmeriCorps survived the attacks in large part by the threat or reality of a presidential veto—which simultaneously saved the program and kept it in the crosshairs by tying it further to Clinton. Without Clinton's devotion, AmeriCorps would not have been created nor would it have survived, but neither would it have come under such withering assault. Presidential backing can be a double-edged sword, which raises the intriguing possibility that a president can support a program too much.

At the same time, the president's veto pen was not the only weapon defending AmeriCorps. Over time, the program won a measure of Republican backing, especially in the Senate. As noted earlier, credit is due to budget and policy changes implemented by Wofford but also to the work of the program itself. For much of AmeriCorps's history, even opponents rarely objected to what its members do. (It differs from VISTA in that way.) For example, while leading the charge against the program in 1995, Senator Grassley acknowledged that he "hadn't seen a single nonworthy project."[127] The next chapter discusses in more detail how AmeriCorps achieved this feat, but for now suffice it to say that the result was typically positive reviews of AmeriCorps's work on the ground. While the program's work accomplishments were not enough to overcome Grassley's philosophical and political objections, they were for others. In policy feedback terms, sometimes politics influenced policy views more than views about the policy influenced politics, and sometimes not. McCain was the most prominent and outspoken convert, who explained in 2001,

> When Clinton initiated AmeriCorps in 1994, most Republicans, myself included, opposed it. We feared it would be another "big government program" that would undermine true volunteerism, waste money in "make-work" projects, or be diverted into political activism.
>
> We were wrong. Though AmeriCorps's record is not untarnished, the overall evidence for its effectiveness is hard to deny. . . . Having seen results . . . and having often seen AmeriCorps members work on the ground—more and more of my GOP colleagues have changed their minds about the program.[128]

All told, President Clinton and national service supporters had reason to both hope and fear for AmeriCorps's future under a new president. With membership more than 50,000 strong, growing Republican support, and Clinton out of the equation, the Republican leaders might relent and let AmeriCorps continue unharassed. Or they might press their advantage against the program, knowing that neither Republican candidate George W. Bush nor Democratic candidate Al Gore had anywhere near Clinton's stake in rescuing it. The likeliest scenario fell in between, with the program facing real cuts.[129]

UNDER PRESIDENT BUSH. As it turned out, the rosier scenario came to pass. Shortly after taking office, Bush proposed continuing support for AmeriCorps at its existing level.[130] His stance did not magically bring congressional Republicans on board; majority leader Dick Armey (R-Texas) still found the program "obnoxious."[131] But it did have an effect: in a noted "change from previous years," and in fact a major change from just six months earlier (when the Senate voted to cut and the House to eliminate AmeriCorps), both chambers passed budget resolutions funding AmeriCorps at Bush's requested level.[132] The result was much stronger support for the status quo. This may not sound like much, but the fact that AmeriCorps had survived the transition intact was a historic achievement—and one that would be topped less than a year later.

In his 2002 State of the Union address, President Bush asked Congress to expand AmeriCorps by an unprecedented 50 percent, to 75,000 members, and to reform and reauthorize the program by passing the Citizen Service Act of 2002. Here Congress balked. Even Bush's post-9/11 rationale for expanding AmeriCorps (and his post-9/11 popularity) could not persuade Congress to acquiesce. As for the reauthorization legislation, it acted as a magnet, attracting the interest—and amendments—of friends and foes alike. Conservatives wanted to ban members from working in family-planning programs, liberals objected to proposed changes in VISTA, grantee organizations opposed the administration's new funding formula, and so on.[133] As a result, the act never came up for a vote.

Despite congressional inaction, Bush was still largely able to get what he wanted through executive order, bypassing Congress altogether.[134] And without doing anything at all, he saw AmeriCorps's enrollment surge to a record 70,000. At first blush, this was all to the good: Americans were heeding the president's call to service. With online applications rising 50 percent in the month after the State of the Union address, grantees were better able to fill their authorized slots and benefit from AmeriCorps members' work.[135] And because all authorized slots were funded, the Corporation could afford the program costs. What it could not afford was the projected cost of members' education awards.

Ultimately, how the education award shortfall came to pass and precipitate the crisis it did can be traced backed to AmeriCorps's always difficult relationship with Congress. At AmeriCorps's founding, the Corporation placed in a trust the full value of a member's education award for every position it authorized. Because not all authorized positions were filled, not all members fulfilled the requirements to earn an award, and not all who earned an award redeemed it, a huge overfunding of the trust resulted. By estimating yearly trust outlays, Corporation officials could free up additional funds to increase enrollments without having to ask an unreceptive Congress for more money. So far, so good, but a series of future decisions—all justified in and of themselves—soon led things astray.

Even after reducing trust deposits, congressional appropriators saw the still-large trust fund balance as a waste; and so for fiscal years 2000 and 2001 they rescinded a total of $110 million and put it into other programs. However, beyond the laudable goal of increasing funding efficiency, AmeriCorps supporters—including Corporation leaders—saw other, more nefarious motives: "Indeed, the rescissions were seen by some not as a technical, accounting decision but as a subtle but powerful way for congressional opponents of AmeriCorps to limit its growth" or even "another way to kill it." At the same time, the Corporation decided not to ask for any new trust funds for fiscal 2001. It did so believing that "the end of the Clinton administration likely portended budget cuts for AmeriCorps—and that the best way to maintain (or even increase) its level of enrollment was to put the entire budget into programming, none into the trust, which, indeed, appeared to have adequate reserves." The financial implications of this decision were compounded when Congress, failing to pass the fiscal year 2002 budget, had to fund the government through a continuing resolution—an action that simply extends the previous year's funding. Because the prior year's funding for the trust had been nothing, no new funds were placed in the trust for an additional six months. "And so it was that two years of budget rescissions were followed by eighteen months of zero funding"—at the same time that enrollments, and thus trust fund obligations, were skyrocketing.[136]

In response, the Corporation suspended enrollments in the fall of 2002 and evaluated its options. First, simply to cover the award obligations that had already been incurred, Congress appropriated $64 million in emergency funds.[137] Next, the Corporation had to figure out what to do with its planned 2003 enrollment of 50,000 new members, given that it already had 20,000 deferred members waiting to serve. The Government Accountability Office, an arm of Congress, believed that the Corporation was legally bound to go back to making full deposits for every authorized position, unless Congress approved otherwise. Reverting to this old standard would require so much money as to virtually halt new enrollments, dropping total enrollment for 2003 to 25,000—the 20,000 deferred members plus 5,000 new enrollees. The Office of Management and Budget, in the executive branch, supported a conservative estimation formula that would allow more members to serve—the 20,000 deferred members plus up to 30,000 new ones. Congress gave its stamp of approval to this approach by passing the Strengthen AmeriCorps Program Act in July 2003.[138]

Although in the aggregate this would result in 50,000 members serving in 2003, as Congress intended, it would wreak havoc on the allocation of enrollees to grantee organizations. To accommodate the 20,000 carry-over members already placed, other organizations would see their authorized positions drop; some would lose their positions altogether. Preventing this would require $100 million in supplemental funding to support an additional 20,000 new members. With pressure from the Save AmeriCorps Coalition's campaign, congressional support for the supplemental was strikingly high. The proposal passed the Senate 71 to 21, and 233 (of 435) House members signed a petition in support.[139] However, the Bush administration never endorsed the supplemental appropriation, and the House leadership refused to bring it up for a vote.[140]

Just months later Congress had to vote again, this time to decide Ameri-Corps's funding for 2004. As he had for the previous two years, Bush requested funds to support 75,000 members, and for the first time, Congress agreed. Explanations for this major funding increase, coming so close on the heels of the White House's and Congress's refusal to support an infusion of lesser funds, vary. Manhattan Institute scholar Howard Husock, in his case study on the funding crisis and its aftermath, notes that "some believe that the Corporation's willingness, as one official puts it, to 'pay a price' for its apparent 'mismanagement,' as well as its willingness to wait for a new budget cycle, bought it support from the White House and Capitol Hill. Others, however, believe the high-profile [Save AmeriCorps] Coalition vastly increased pressure on both."[141] Through the end of his presidency, both Bush and Congress continued to support AmeriCorps at 75,000 members.

While Bush and the congressional majority were content with AmeriCorps as it was, others had loftier goals. For example, shortly after 9/11, Senators Evan Bayh (D-Ind.) and McCain introduced the Call to Service Act, which proposed expanding AmeriCorps to 250,000 members, and in 2007 Representative Carolyn McCarthy (D-N.Y.) and thirty-two cosponsors introduced the Generations Invigorating Volunteerism and Education (GIVE) Act, which called for 100,000 members. While neither these nor similar proposals were passed, they laid the groundwork for what would pass.

UNDER PRESIDENT OBAMA. In fall 2008 Senators Kennedy and Hatch introduced the Serve America Act, which (among other purposes) reauthorized AmeriCorps, created new "service corps" within it, increased its education award, and set enrollment goals (contingent on yearly appropriations) that would bring AmeriCorps to 250,000 members a year in eight years.[142] This bill, reintroduced at the start of the Obama administration and renamed in Kennedy's honor, passed in record time and with record bipartisan support:

79 to 19 in the Senate, with more Republicans voting in favor—21—than against—19, and 321 to 105 in the House, with 70 Republicans voting in favor. President Obama signed it before the end of his first one hundred days. After years of controversy, AmeriCorps had finally achieved solid bipartisan support and was poised to approach the Civilian Conservation Corps in scale.

Neither accomplishment would last, at least over the short term. Ameri-Corps did grow for a time, temporarily adding 13,000 members with funding through the 2009 American Recovery and Reinvestment Act (the economic stimulus package), but the Republican House victory in the 2010 elections and concern over the deficit kept AmeriCorps's appropriation far lower than its authorized increases.[143] In a replay of votes taken by the new Republican majority in the 1990s, in 2011 the House voted to eliminate AmeriCorps's funding altogether.[144] To a degree, AmeriCorps had been dragged back more than a decade, with the program imperiled by the House and saved by the Senate and president. But there are differences, shown clearly in the votes of the sixty Republicans who supported AmeriCorps's expansion in 2009 and then supported its elimination just two years later.[145] Given that AmeriCorps had not appreciably changed, the issue now, in contrast to the 1990s, was much less the program than the Republican Party's budget priorities: the vote did not signal a total loss of the political support AmeriCorps had built over the years. Still, it amply demonstrates just how precarious that support can be. When it weakens, AmeriCorps loses potential participants and accomplishes less work.

11

AmeriCorps's Tools, Rules, and Targets

A long with its purpose and role for government, AmeriCorps's tools, rules, and targets—the service work it supports, its educational goals and content, the type of participants it recruits, and its obligations and inducements—influence its political support and viability and communicate lessons to participants and the public, in large part through policy feedback dynamics. In short, these lower-level policy elements further shape the politics and civics of the program, which in turn influence future policy development. Consistent with the findings in the previous chapter, AmeriCorps's design details have allowed slow but steady growth in the program's size and political support, albeit in the face of significant opposition. Civically, these details have both contributed to and constrained AmeriCorps's teachings, for participants and for the larger public.

AmeriCorps's Work

AmeriCorps's work—its whole range of diverse service activities—has provided many of the same civic and political benefits as the CCC and VISTA work programs did, while avoiding some of their drawbacks. AmeriCorps has accomplished this in part because it encompasses both earlier programs' work agendas (and more) and in part because program leaders had learned from experience. Civically, AmeriCorps allows members to contribute their time and talents to issues of national concern while they also strengthen community capacity. Politically, the nature of AmeriCorps's work has helped build significant and growing support, providing incentives through policy feedback. Although the program has suffered from its work's relative invisibility, it has largely avoided VISTA's other early challenges: like the CCC, its work is less controversial and easier to quantify and evaluate. At the same time, it shares VISTA's flexibility. Unlike the CCC, it has a broad range of tasks that has allowed it to adapt and survive changing times. So although the nature of AmeriCorps's work is in tension with building wide public recognition, in other ways it has worked to the program's civic and political advantage.

When the CCC and VISTA were founded, their work's focus was clear; at AmeriCorps's founding, the focus of its work was an open question. President Clinton came to office committed to national service and what it could accomplish, but without a concrete agenda for what exactly it should accomplish. He was unlike FDR and LBJ, whose conservation and anti-poverty commitments, respectively, motivated their national service aspirations. In short, after deciding AmeriCorps's motto would be "Getting Things Done," its founders still had to determine what those things would be. One question was whether the program should focus on a single area, as the two earlier programs had, or have multiple emphases. Focusing all AmeriCorps members' work in one area—improving education, for example—would allow for greater impact and give members a shared mission, which could create significant political and civic benefits. On the other hand, although the education community would cheer, the environmental groups, housing organizations, and health services would be left out in the cold. As Shirley Sagawa explained, if, as she feared, "support for national service was 'a mile wide and an inch deep,' . . . to focus the issue would 'cut off three-quarters of the mile.'"[1] Even if Clinton had had a strong, singular vision for AmeriCorps's work, the realities of interest group politics—realities FDR and even LBJ had not faced—might have pushed the program to its ultimate destination, with emphases on education, the environment, health, and public safety.

One interest FDR did have to placate was labor, and it remained a force. AmeriCorps's founders assuaged unions' concerns by giving labor representatives guaranteed seats on state commissions and the Corporation board, allowing them to veto grants to union-staffed organizations, and banning AmeriCorps members from "displac[ing] workers or duplicat[ing] their functions." Steven Waldman, for one, holds that such concessions "risked undermining [the] goal of producing real work," yet experience shows that such accommodations are both necessary for program creation and insufficient to undermine work accomplishments. The CCC—whose work Waldman rightly lauds—went so far as to appoint a union leader as its director to receive labor's much-needed blessing.[2]

Beyond securing service groups' and unions' support, AmeriCorps's founders were highly attuned to the need for public support, to "produce a product in which 'the public would delight,'" as noted earlier. This concern contributed to the decision to focus AmeriCorps's work in multiple areas so "the president [could] go to a community hard-hit by a defense base closing and say, 'We're going to put National Conservation Corps people here,' or go to a crime-ridden area and say, 'We're going to put volunteers here to help make your streets safer.'"[3] It also contributed to the emphasis on "direct" service.

As the program's regulations explain, direct service "provide[s] a direct benefit to the community where [it is] performed or . . . involve[s] the supervision of [those] whose service [does so]." To meet this standard, the service must bring "participants face-to-face with residents of the community served or in contact with the physical [service] environment." The only indirect service allowed had to be "incidental" to a participant's direct service. So "physical projects such as renovating low-income housing or creating a playground in a vacant lot, as well as less tangible projects such as tutoring, mentoring, and conflict resolution" counted as direct service, and acceptable indirect service included surveying community residents to determine who was in need of Meals on Wheels, which members would then deliver.[4]

Direct service has the benefit of being visible: the public can watch a playground being built, teachers and students see their tutors. Given that other policy design decisions, such as working through existing service organizations, tend to hide AmeriCorps's role, making the work visible would at least not exacerbate the problem. Further, direct service's value is easily understood. Given public distrust that government could do anything worthwhile and Republicans' distrust of the entire enterprise, this was not inconsequential. Finally, a direct service mission could help AmeriCorps earn "a reputation for doing tough, hard, rewarding work," worthy of respect on this basis alone.[5]

These considerations motivated Clinton's AmeriCorps policymakers, but the Bush administration took a different view. With its even greater emphasis on national service's "community" and local organization aspects, policymakers expanded the sphere of allowable indirect activities: instead of a member's indirect service having to be incidental to his or her own direct service, it could now be incidental to the service program's direct service.[6] Thus AmeriCorps members could be hired for the purpose of providing indirect service, to "build the administrative and technological capacities of grassroots groups."[7]

Indirect service has the benefit of being catalytic. As Bush's policymakers explained, by "mobilizing and managing teams of volunteer[s] . . . , developing or expanding programs, and implementing administrative and accounting systems," AmeriCorps members better "equip nonprofits . . . to do more of the work they already do."[8] As a result, AmeriCorps members leave more behind when they finish—not only the work they accomplished but their organization's ability to do more without them than it did before they arrived.

In VISTA's early years, critics charged that its indirect, capacity-building service too often merely increased organizations' capacity to make trouble, with volunteers engaged in questionable or outright illegal political and policy advocacy. The Clinton administration emphasized direct service in part to help avoid such charges, and the Bush administration certainly was equally opposed to capacity building of this kind. From its founding, regulations barred members from engaging in "any effort to influence legislation" or "the outcome of an election to any public office," as well as "organizing protests, petitions, boycotts, or strikes" on AmeriCorps's time (or while wearing Ameri-Corps insignia).[9]

These prohibitions were less contested than they had been in VISTA's early years, but they still created "difficulties and dilemmas" for grantees and members.[10] At heart were differing understandings of community, democracy, and citizenship. For example, one program manager asked, "How do you differentiate between community service and what the leaders of the community do? It seems to me you all need to work together in the community, but it's a nationally funded program and you can't take sides. But, try to split community service from democratic participation—it doesn't work."[11] An Ameri-Corps member addressed the "community service-democratic participation split" from another angle, explaining, "It almost feels like censorship. . . . I understand them not wanting us to lobby, but I feel as though we should be allowed to say, 'Hey, this is what's going on here, and this is what needs to happen.' We're putting in those hours; we're right on top of the situation. . . . We could give great insight, but in this program it can't happen."[12]

Others took a sharply different view, seeing the "split" as wholly beneficial. One program manager put it this way:

> Maybe it was a really intelligent person, who thought, Let's do something about this innately American behavior to have someone else solve the problem: "Okay, I have a hole in the front of my house. Let's get a politician to [fix] it." Making a separation makes it possible for us to do

community building in the truest sense. Let's do something about this hole—not demonstrate about it, not write a letter about it, but just figure out what resources we can use in the community to solve this problem.[13]

The civic benefits of AmeriCorps's advocacy ban clearly are open to debate. Not so its political benefits: without question it helped AmeriCorps avoid much of the controversy that hurt VISTA's early attempts to build broad public and political support. That politicians opposed to AmeriCorps very rarely oppose its work laid the foundation for key Republican conversions. As for the public, when people have known of AmeriCorps's work, they have liked it.

It is hard to overemphasize the extent to which AmeriCorps's leaders have prioritized the accomplishment of valuable service work and the need to accurately measure and evaluate it. "Getting Things Done" was the start. Ensuring that what "got done" made a real difference was next: both Clinton and Bush officials emphasized that AmeriCorps's work should "help communities solve critical problems" and "address real community needs."[14] President Obama went one step further, insisting that AmeriCorps's work add up to something even larger, that it serve as "a vehicle to meet national goals."[15] More so than either the CCC or VISTA, by far, AmeriCorps devoted resources to assessment, funding research to determine what the program's work was accomplishing. This task was doable because so much of AmeriCorps's work is concrete and readily quantifiable.

From the first year, Eli Segal and Harris Wofford were able to cite specific examples of AmeriCorps's work around the country: the twenty-eight AmeriCorps members who helped close forty-four Kansas City, Missouri, crack houses; the nineteen members in Simpson County, Kentucky, who helped raise struggling second graders' reading scores by three grade levels; the group in Vermont that helped 1,300 women and children victimized by domestic and sexual violence.[16] Within several years, evaluators were able to aggregate AmeriCorps's work to provide a broader picture. For example, in its study of 381 AmeriCorps projects (employing 11,099 members), Aguirre International determined that more than 9 million people had directly benefited: 1.9 million students received educational services; 75,000 young children received care, instruction, or immunizations; 70,000 families were helped; 25,000 parents were trained; 3.3 million others received education, human need, public safety, or environmental services; another 3.7 million benefited from community improvements.[17] Beyond these accomplishments, the study described work impossible to associate with specific, individual beneficiaries. For example, it cited "282 community policing programs [that] were initiated, expanded, [or] maintained" and "80,727 acres or miles of trees planted in parks and public lands."[18] VISTA was able to present similar data in its early years as well; but with many fewer participants, its numbers were less impressive. AmeriCorps's numbers were closer to those posted by the CCC and were used in like fashion by supporters, as evidence of the program's success. However, Will Marshall and Marc Porter Magee note in their meta-analysis of AmeriCorps's effectiveness that such "figures do not speak to the quality or value of the work performed."[19] AmeriCorps had more to prove.

The Corporation's funding of Aguirre International's "Making a Difference" evaluation is one early example of how hard it worked to make Ameri-Corps's case. To assess community views of AmeriCorps's effectiveness, these outside evaluators interviewed community representatives who knew about AmeriCorps projects: between 82 and 85 percent rated the overall project impact, quality, community impact, and achievement of project goals and objectives as outstanding, excellent, or very good.[20] Asked specifically about *civic* impact, majorities also rated AmeriCorps's ability to strengthen commu-nities (68 percent), encourage civic responsibility among groups (69 percent), and help organizations work better together (57 percent) as outstanding to very good.[21] Finally, evaluators conducted a cost-benefit analysis of forty-four programs. They found that the programs' benefits (direct service benefits plus future economic benefits to members) outweighed the costs (members' sti-pends, education awards, and program operating expenses) by a ratio of 1.66-to-1, meaning that every dollar spent on the program generated $1.66 in ben-efits.[22] Even alone, the direct service benefits outweighed the costs.[23] Six other cost-benefit analyses, each focused on two or three AmeriCorps programs, also found that benefits exceeded costs: the resulting average ratio was 1.95-to-1.[24]

With the increasing emphasis on producing specific outcomes that address critical needs, evaluations have focused on this goal as well. To give just one example, Abt Associates' AmeriCorps Tutoring Outcomes Study assessed the effect of AmeriCorps's literacy tutoring programs on struggling first-, second-, and third-grade students' reading ability.[25] Evaluating 869 students in sixty-eight AmeriCorps programs, the study found that the programs were suc-cessful in bringing their students up to grade level. In 2002 the Corporation went further, funding a study of its outcomes, indicators, and data sources to improve its ability to show results not just in periodic evaluations but on an annual basis for all of its programs: the goal was "to make the Corporation a results-oriented agency."[26]

AmeriCorps's growing inventory of work and results did not persuade all of its critics, many of whom focused on the absolute costs—almost $27,500 a member in 1995—to the exclusion of the generated benefits and outcomes.[27] Nonetheless, supporters were able to employ this evidence and the scholarly consensus in AmeriCorps's favor as ammunition during the program's ongoing political battles. They did not guarantee victory, but AmeriCorps's continuation and growth would have been infinitely harder without them.

The nature, amount, and impact of AmeriCorps's work have also had a positive effect on AmeriCorps members because they are the ones *doing* the work. One member's story will illustrate. Adam Herzog graduated from an Ivy League school with a "much-coveted degree in finance" and chose to defer his investment banking job offer for a year to participate in AmeriCorps*NCCC. As he recounts:

> AmeriCorps*NCCC sent me all over . . . completing projects like Habitat for Humanity, forest firefighting, wilderness reclamation, and FEMA [Federal Emergency Management Agency] crisis relief. . . . At some point over those ten months, I realized . . . I was loving every minute of it. . . . And believe me it wasn't the actual physical work . . . [I learned] that having a job that matters [is] the only thing that matters.[28]

AmeriCorps's work is more varied than either the CCC's or VISTA's, and its outcomes are more likely to be variable, at least more variable than the CCC's. Still, AmeriCorps's work program reflects the strengths of both previous programs. Like the CCC's work, its work is readily quantifiable, easily understood, and broadly valued. Like VISTA's work, its work encompasses a broad array of social concerns and thus has the flexibility to respond to new administrations' priorities. The combination of these characteristics largely accounts for AmeriCorps's success.

AmeriCorps's Members

Like the CCC and VISTA, AmeriCorps selects its members. Who they are, why they apply, and how they are chosen significantly influences the program. AmeriCorps's policies and grantee organizations' hiring decisions determine AmeriCorps's membership with respect to age, sex, race, class, and education. Given that the number of applicants has exceeded the number of available positions overall, the program—or at least a good many grantee organizations—can be selective. Civically, the choice of applicants and the resulting composition of the membership have influenced the participants' experience, especially as this experience relates to AmeriCorps's goals for racial and class diversity. At the same time, AmeriCorps's selection policies were determined in large part because of their perceived political consequences.

Like CCC and VISTA policymakers, AmeriCorps's policymakers had to figure out not only who the program's participants would be but what they would be. Specifically, should they be called *volunteers*, or something else? "AmeriCorps volunteer" remains in common usage by the media and others, but from the start, the program's leadership recognized that a "deep problem with national service is that by labeling it volunteerism, you've really chosen the one word that is absolutely unsatisfactory to either liberals or conservatives."[29] Conservatives in particular had latched onto the idea of "paid volunteerism" as a contradiction in terms, finding it a useful handle for declaring VISTA's illegitimacy. AmeriCorps's creators knew to avoid inviting such an attack and sought to parry it by labeling AmeriCorps's participants *members*.

The *members* appellation has civic as well as political virtues. It suggests that participants belong to a larger enterprise, one that links them with other participants working in different organizations, on different issues, in different parts of the country. Given AmeriCorps's highly decentralized design, this word is a small but still important reminder. It also fit with the intention to highlight the participants' working in teams and thus being *team members*. Given that the program has placed more of its participants individually than it had planned to makes *team member* a less accurate reflection of reality, but the phrase still demonstrates the need to make everything—language included—emphasize that AmeriCorps members are part of a larger shared effort.[30] Finally and most significant, *member* fits well with AmeriCorps's principle of reciprocity, much more so than the CCC's word *enrollee* did. Members—not just of service programs but of anything—are expected both to contribute to and to benefit from the groups they join. From this perspective, the language of membership is very much an accurate reflection of AmeriCorps's reality.

Sex and Age

Like President Kennedy before him, Clinton called on Americans of all ages to serve. But while Kennedy placed a special emphasis on the role he expected older Americans to play in what became, in its early years, a very youth-dominated VISTA, Clinton embraced young people's role in AmeriCorps, despite its solid recruitment of older adults. To a great extent these choices reflect the programs' different goals: AmeriCorps, much more than VISTA, has an explicit pedagogical intent, to inculcate values of citizenship through service and to further members' schooling through the education award. And education, even more than service, is considered the province of the young.

AmeriCorps's emphasis on youth is most evident in the NCCC, which limits participation to those who are 18 to 24 years old. Following the example set by the CCC, the NCCC's founders saw young adults as best able to benefit from and contribute to a residential, 24/7 program with travel requirements and other militarylike components. VISTA and State and National do not have these elements or an upper age limit. However, they have had notable differences in age: in keeping with changes and trends initiated more than twenty-five years earlier, in 1997 only 6 percent of VISTA volunteers were 21 or younger, while 55 percent were at least 30. In State and National, 23 percent were 21 or younger and 70 percent were under 30.[31] In Clinton's program, young people were indeed leading the way.

To the extent that national service is an activity of the young, it is equally the activity of women. AmeriCorps's NCCC parallels the CCC in many respects but not in size and not in sex. The CCC was 100 percent male; the NCCC was 68 percent female in 1999. AmeriCorps's two other programs have been even more predominantly female, with women making up 71 percent of the State and National membership in 1999 and 80 percent of VISTA in 1997.[32] Given that men make up approximately 85 percent of U.S. active-duty armed forces, to a notable degree America has a two-track national service system by gender: men in the military, women in civilian service. And while women's numbers and roles in the military have been topics of serious debate, the implications of their overrepresentation—and men's underrepresentation—within AmeriCorps have gone largely undiscussed.

Race and Class

More so than other factors, race and class have dominated debate and discussion of AmeriCorps's demographics. Indeed, one of the program's four key goals—strengthening communities—was originally defined as "showing how Americans from diverse backgrounds can work together for the common good."[33] Some early policymakers in fact saw diversity as a sine qua non of national service. Catherine Milton, executive director of the pre-Corporation Commission on National and Community Service, was questioned about YouthBuild, a highly regarded program engaging low-income youth in corps that are frequently racially homogenous: "Are you willing to say YouthBuild is not national service?" Her answer: "Yes . . . one of the characteristics that distinguishe[s] national service from antipoverty programs [is] race and class mixing."[34]

This view was contested by some national service advocates and policymakers, but given President Clinton's commitment to integration through service, the question was how far AmeriCorps would go in Milton's direction. Would programs have to be mixed? Mixing could threaten the whole enterprise: the nondiverse programs were politically well organized; without their support, national service might never be passed.[35] At the same time, there was the question of how to do it. "If the plan specified that a certain percentage of federal money go to diverse corps, that would be, well, a quota. And how does one define *diverse*? Is fifty-fifty black-Hispanic 'diverse,' or does the term require whites? Is a corps that mixes rich and poor whites considered diverse? What if it is class-homogeneous but race-heterogeneous?"[36] In the end the issue was addressed through AmeriCorps's regulations, which require programs to "seek actively"—but not "ensure"—that they "engage participants from diverse backgrounds."[37] Exceptions for programs such as YouthBuild are narrowly tailored.

On the whole, AmeriCorps has recruited a membership that is significantly more diverse than the nation's population. In 1997 State and National members were 45 percent Caucasian, 29 percent African American, 20 percent Hispanic, 2 percent Asian American/Pacific Islander, 2 percent Native American/Alaskan Native, and 3 percent other. VISTA had a higher percentage of whites (57 percent), somewhat fewer blacks (26 percent), and many fewer Hispanics (11 percent). The NCCC was the least diverse, with its membership 80 percent Caucasian, 7 percent African American, and 6 percent Hispanic.[38]

Given that AmeriCorps's goal is race mixing, diversity at the service site level is even more important than national statistics; two studies shed light on site-level diversity. In its 1997 *Study of Race, Class, and Ethnicity in Ameri-Corps Programs*, Macro International found that of 535 sites (each with at least ten members), 24 percent were highly diverse, with members of the largest racial or ethnic group making up less than 55 percent of total site membership. Another 46 percent of sites were moderately diverse, with the largest groups making up between 55 and 84 percent of the site's membership. The remaining 30 percent were relatively homogeneous, with 85 percent or more of their members sharing race or ethnicity.[39] These numbers suggest that more than two-thirds of sites with at least ten members gave participants a significant potential to work across lines of race and ethnicity. But another study places these results into a larger context. In a 1999 survey, Abt Associates found that 49 percent of members served as the only member at a service site and in only 40 percent of programs did members work in teams.[40] As a result, large numbers of AmeriCorps participants had no opportunity to work with other members regardless of their backgrounds, and even some who served alongside other members were not working with them. How these factors have influenced what members learn about diversity is addressed later in this chapter.

In terms of class, data are less readily available, but those that exist show greater economic diversity than found in the CCC or VISTA. In its survey of 422 members serving in program sites specifically chosen for their diversity, Macro International found that half of respondents self-identified as middle class, 35 percent as working class, and approximately equal numbers as upper class (7.4 percent) and lower class (7.7 percent).[41] These numbers obviously have their limits: the sample was not representative, and it is impossible to know how respondents defined these terms.[42] Abt Associates' larger, representative sample survey instead asked respondents for their previous year's personal and household incomes. The results for the NCCC show another stark difference between its members and the CCC's uniformly disadvantaged enrollees: NCCC members' average 1998 household income was $61,475, well above the national average of $51,855. State and National members' family incomes were lower, $32,683 on average, or only about 63 percent of the national average.[43] Still, with two-thirds of NCCC and State and National members overall coming from households with incomes over $20,000, AmeriCorps has avoided being a typical anti-poverty program. At the same time, with one-third coming from families with incomes below this level, it also has avoided narrowly recruiting the affluent, as the Peace Corps and VISTA had in their early years.[44] To a fair extent, AmeriCorps has achieved its goal of providing service opportunities for the broad middle class and creating opportunities for mixing across class lines.

Education

When unveiling his national service plan, Clinton presented it as a program for recent college graduates: "Opportunity for all means giving every young American the chance to borrow the money necessary to go to college and pay it back . . . with years of national service."[45] As the program moved from campaign promise to administration proposal, its target participant group broadened to include those who only aspired to go to college or who had no plans to attend college. As a result, educational diversity was added to the AmeriCorps mix. Abt Associates' survey of State and National and NCCC members found that "slightly more than a third (37 percent) have at least some postsecondary education . . . but have not obtained a bachelor's degree; slightly smaller percentages (31 and 32 percent, respectively) have either received a [four-year] degree . . . or have only a high school diploma or less."[46]

This mix gave AmeriCorps's grantee organizations the opportunity to choose members whose education and skills fit their needs, "making sure they get the right people to solve the problem at hand," and allowed AmeriCorps as a whole to focus on a broader range of work than did earlier programs.[47] Still, there was debate. For those who advocated national service from the flip side of Clinton's original view, those who wanted "to see national service offer more opportunities to people who have been shut out of the system," the high percentage of members who already had college experience was "worrisome."[48] However, that more than two-thirds were not college graduates did create opportunities not envisioned originally and added responsibilities as well, increasing the importance of training for AmeriCorps service and the role AmeriCorps could play in members' learning and development.

Education for and through AmeriCorps

A central point of this chapter, and those preceding it, is that all elements of policy design act as pedagogy, teaching participants and the public about their relationship to government and the meaning of citizenship. AmeriCorps's policy design emphasizes reciprocity, government as catalyst, and principally a service approach to citizenship (and constitutional, patriotic, and work perspectives to lesser degrees). In addition, AmeriCorps has explicit educational activities and goals, tied to its legislative mandate to renew an ethic of civic responsibility and expand opportunities for higher education. Although "member development" does not have as high a priority as it did under the CCC, it has received greater emphasis than it did under VISTA: the possibilities for training have been quite extensive, the value of learning through service has been emphasized, and higher education supported. All three of these components have civic elements and implications, which reinforces AmeriCorps's overall civic priorities.

Training

AmeriCorps's training is twofold: it provides training in skills specific to members' service placements (for example, in pedagogical strategies for tutors, or in construction basics for housing rehabbers) and training useful to members regardless of their service assignments. In both cases, local AmeriCorps directors and service supervisors set the training agenda, determining the what, when, where, how, and how much of their members' training, with support from state commissions, the Corporation, and various training providers and organizations. Up to 20 percent of a member's service hours can be fulfilled through training.

Much of what is known about AmeriCorps's training—a highly decentralized element in an already highly decentralized program—comes from the 2004 Abt study. Its findings show that local programs' attention to member development has been variable. For example, in their survey of State and National programs, Abt researchers found member orientation ranging from one to twenty-five days, with an average of around eight, and that almost equal numbers of programs offered "formal member development" weekly (26 percent), biweekly (24 percent), monthly (29 percent), and less than once a month (21 percent).[49]

The Clinton and Bush administrations emphasized service-specific skill development, which is reflected in the fact that 80 percent of programs offered such training for an average of 40 hours.[50] Given the Clinton administration's belief in the primacy of "getting things done," "the goal of [their] training [was] to improve the ability of national service programs and participants to get things done."[51] In the process, however, members' gains went beyond the instrumental. Member Ben Fritz says, "In just a month, I've gained the confidence and the skills to supervise the construction of a roof. I've gone from clueless to capable."[52] Others gained new career goals—Adam Herzog's switch from investment banking to public interest law, for example—while others gained career goals, period. Alicia Cayce explains, "In the beginning I just wanted some kind of training, but as time went by, I began to learn about water conservation, about recycling, and to be motivated to . . . do my degree in geology and hydrology."[53]

For non-service-specific training, a survey form to help gauge members' training needs gives an indication of the options. Members were asked to indicate in which of nineteen knowledge and skill areas they thought they needed or could provide training. The areas, grouped into categories, were learning about AmeriCorps (its history, procedures, and so on); working with communities; working in professional settings; goal setting and planning; team building; leadership; diversity; health (HIV/AIDS awareness, CPR); and citizenship—specifically "the responsibilities of citizenship."[54] Of these, Abt researchers found that programs most frequently offered team-building training and devoted more time to it, on average, than to any other non-service-specific training (96 percent offered it for an average of twenty-four hours).[55] Mediation, diversity, leadership, and communication training were all offered by at least three-fourths of programs, and first-aid, community resource knowledge, career awareness, job search, and interpersonal skills training were offered by more than half, and all for at least nine hours on average.[56]

While most of these training categories relate to citizenship in some way, the Abt researchers did not find "citizenship training" per se widely offered, despite the Clinton and Bush administrations' emphasis on citizenship. The reason may be partly due to the fact that both administrations strongly associated citizenship with the act of service itself, meaning that members could acquire citizenship training through their service. At the same time, neither administration was content to leave all civic learning implicit, especially Bush's.

At AmeriCorps's founding, enough academic debate about the relationship between service and citizenship was swirling close enough to the Corporation to prompt it and at least one state commission to sponsor the development of citizenship curricula specifically geared toward AmeriCorps members and their trainers. Minnesota's commission contracted with the Center for Democracy and Citizenship to create *By the People,* a guidebook for members focused on imparting public work–oriented civic concepts and skills.[57] CHP International, under contract with the Corporation, built on this work to create *A Facilitator's Guide for By the People,* which emphasizes both public work and service citizenship perspectives.[58] The Corporation also commissioned *A Facilitator's Guide to Effective Citizenship through AmeriCorps,* by the Constitutional Rights Foundation, which includes constitutional, service, and public work–oriented learning activities.[59]

The way Bush's Corporation appointees formulated citizenship training was similar to how they worked out other aspects of national service. They did not reject their predecessors' philosophy or approach so much as alter their emphases. With respect to citizenship training, this meant significantly raising its profile and stressing its constitutional and historical aspects. As the Constitutional Rights Foundation *Citizenship Toolkit* explained to grantee organizations, "Civic education deepens the experience of doing service, by connecting it to such fundamental American values as liberty, responsibility, and freedom. It has, therefore, become a priority for all AmeriCorps programs."[60] The Corporation used its 2003 program application guidelines to clarify its civic education goals, which were

—fostering within members positive attitudes regarding the value of life-long citizenship and service for the common good;

—enhancing the ability of members to discuss and explore their community and the people, processes, and institutions that are most effective in improving community conditions;

—enhancing the ability of members to plan effective service projects that respond to real community needs; and

—developing the social, cultural and analytical skills necessary to effectively participate in American democracy.[61]

The guidance then "recommended that applicants incorporate citizenship training into their member development plan." All plans were to "include opportunities for members to enhance and develop their knowledge about citizenship, their citizenship skills, and ultimately their civic attitudes" and "should consider including a service project"—beyond their regular service work—"and a discussion of the relevant principles of American democracy that it might illuminate."[62]

The Corporation also recommended *A Guide to Effective Citizenship through AmeriCorps* and *A Facilitator's Guide for By the People* (going so far as to send copies to every AmeriCorps program) and provided each member with "a selection of basic documents, including the Declaration of Independence, the Constitution, and the Gettysburg Address, which set out the nation's democratic principles."[63] The curricula and readings were linked through five new "thematic areas"—the rule of law; consent of the governed; rights and responsibilities; equality and liberty; and social capital and democracy—and predominantly emphasized constitutional and patriotic aspects of citizenship. The "consent of the governed" theme, for example, was framed in the following words.

> An important principle of American political thought is that citizens cede some of their rights to the state, which then governs in the people's name—that is, by the consent of the governed. How the nation shall be governed is settled by vote. This makes us aware of the primacy and meaning of majority rule. What does it mean to say that our government is of the people, by the people, and for the people (Gettysburg Address)? . . . What guarantees that the majority who rules and decides will guard and protect the rights of the minority? (Think especially about Federalist Papers #10 and #51, as well as the Constitution, in regard to this.)

At the same time, the themes allowed for discussion consistent with critical citizenship, for example, by asking about the meaning of equality or whether Americans have a right to health care.[64]

Just what impact citizenship training has had is an open question; two studies, both conducted shortly before the Bush administration initiative, suggest possibilities and challenges. In a 2001 study of civic engagement issues and training (*civic engagement* defined as synonymous with *citizenship*), former AmeriCorps program director and CNS national service fellow Elisa C.

Diller found AmeriCorps members very interested in public affairs, more so than other citizens. "The issue may be framed as not *whether* civic engagement training might be of interest to members but rather *how* to provide quality civic engagement training to [already interested] members." At the same time, she found that state commissions and program directors on the whole were not capitalizing on this opportunity: only 30 percent of state commissions and 60 percent of program directors surveyed provided civic engagement training to their members at least once a year.[65]

Why the relatively low numbers? First, some respondents were not sure what civic engagement entailed (it seems unlikely that "citizenship" would have been any clearer). As a result, they may have provided relevant training but not called it *civic engagement*. Second, some were concerned that "even discussing citizenship roles might lead to politicization of members" and thus run afoul of the ban on AmeriCorps-sponsored political action. As one state commission staffer explained, "We have not provided information [on civic engagement]. Our focus has been on emphasizing "prohibited activities.""[66] This view filtered down to the program level; in an earlier study, a project director explained, "I am scared to death of political anything. . . . They say we're supposed to encourage our members to register to vote, and I don't even want to get into that, because, really, that's close to a line of endorsing a candidate. It's such a big issue, that they're always sending us memos from Washington."[67] In this case, people had a definition of *citizenship* or *civic engagement*, but it conflicted with other program mandates: their fear was not that members would be insufficiently civic but rather that they would be too political. Third, some were missing the necessary training resources— fewer than half had received *By the People* or *Effective Citizenship*—or found these materials inappropriate for their program (they took too much time) or membership (the materials were too basic). Fewer than half of those who had received the curricula had used them.[68]

The Bush administration's citizenship efforts addressed some of these issues: programs were strongly urged to plan for citizenship training, all state commissions and programs were sent the curricula, and so on. However, given the Corporation's focus on the curricula, program directors' concerns about these materials remained relevant. In their evaluation of *A Facilitator's Guide for By the People* and *A Guide to Effective Citizenship*, researchers William Strang and Adrienne von Glatz assessed program directors' views of the materials and member outcomes from training. For citizenship training advocates, their results were disappointing: fewer than half of program directors found the curricula appropriate and engaging for most of their members, and members themselves showed no discernible civic gains from training.[69] So why did the materials not matter?[70] One reason is that the curricula were seen as too basic for a membership that included many people with a college education and long histories of civic activity. "The members, in other words, may already have been at the level that the curriculum was aiming for." Another possibility is that the curricula focused on the wrong things, "on 'nonpolitical' civic activities, [when] the members—as evidenced by their participation in AmeriCorps—are already there."[71] The authors recommend greater emphasis on discussion of policy options related to members' service areas, an idea in keeping with Diller's point that members might be more receptive to training "directly connected to the change that they want to create within the community."[72]

This perspective was possible under the Bush administration's new framework, as it was earlier, but was not the focus of its changes. In some ways, citizenship training under AmeriCorps has faced the same pitfalls that it had in the CCC. Implemented by (often rightly) controversy-averse program directors, abstracted from members' service work, and insufficiently challenging for many, what members learn of citizenship is probably more powerfully taught through their overall AmeriCorps experience.

Education through the AmeriCorps Experience

Well beyond training, AmeriCorps was designed to be broadly educative; evidence shows that it largely has met this goal. Qualitative and quantitative studies, including Aguirre International's early, short-term evaluation and Abt's longitudinal study, as well as members' personal testimonies show that AmeriCorps service has had significant effects.[73] So what have members learned and what difference has it made, civically and politically?

Like the CCC throughout and VISTA in its later years, AmeriCorps aspires to develop members' "life skills"—"general skills which enable a person to make effective use of their school, life, family, employment, and service experience in pursuit of careers, working with others . . . overcoming personal challenges, and participating in society as informed citizens."[74] Aguirre International's researchers paid particular attention to life skills and concluded that AmeriCorps participation led to substantial life skill gains for more than three-quarters of its members, with often-dramatic gains among those who started with the least developed skills.[75] It was not the case of "those who had got more" to the exclusion of those who had little. Further, they determined that these gains came through the AmeriCorps experience; comparable non-members did not make similar gains.

Life skills are applicable outside the civic sphere, but they are absolutely necessary for working within it. Aguirre International's communication indicators alone show this well: having the ability to "listen and respond to other people's suggestions or concerns"; "talk with people to get the information you need"; "express your ideas, feelings, and insights"; and "work closely with people different from you" are all fundamental citizenship skills, from multiple perspectives—needed for engaging in service, public work, and constitutional citizenship activities.[76] A Chicago program director gave an example: "We also partner with the city during cleanups. . . . Our members serve as coordinators . . . ; they need to know who to contact. They poll the community. . . . They go to the city. Ask councilmen for assistance. . . . It is becoming aware of being a citizen."[77] Member Michael Mandel provides a different example:

> One day in the not-so-distant future, we're going to be the ones who are leading. . . . And if we can have these ten-month, twelve-month experiences out in the field, out in our communities, we'll better able to see the issues that need to be dealt with and to learn how to deal with them. . . . We've learned the tools that will be with us for the rest of our lives.[78]

However, whether members as a whole use these skills for civic purposes, or even believe that doing so is important, is another question.

The Abt researchers evaluated members' civic engagement most thoroughly, assessing a wide range of civic attitudes, knowledge, and behaviors, from multiple citizenship perspectives. Overall, their results show that AmeriCorps developed its members as citizens. They found statistically significant, positive effects for nine out of twelve civic engagement indicators in their 2004 State and National study (six for the NCCC) and further found that for several indicators effects either persisted or developed over time.[79] Moreover, these gains applied "on average, to all AmeriCorps members, regardless of demographic characteristics, program characteristics, or program experience, which shows that the AmeriCorps model is effective for a broad population," a conclusion consistent with Aguirre International's more limited civic involvement results.[80]

The Abt study revealed two unexpected findings of note, one regarding the NCCC and the other regarding diversity. Of AmeriCorps's three sub-programs, the NCCC was expected to have the greatest civic power. Specifically, Leslie Lenkowsky believed that "the residential structure of AmeriCorps*NCCC . . . contributes to a far more intense citizenship development experience."[81] More generally, Suzanne Goldsmith Hirsch, who wrote a book on City Year, believes that the corps [model] can be a laboratory for practicing the arts of citizenship and democracy and community building. Teams have to learn to get along. . . . Opportunities abound for group decisionmaking. . . . And acceptance of authority as well as . . . respectful dissent are part of the experience. These are all critical to survival in the corps environment, and not surprisingly, they're also key elements of effective citizenship and civic engagement.[82]

However, this logic was not strongly reflected in the study results. Abt found that State and National participants made more gains on more civic indicators than did NCCC members in the 2004 study, and after the passage of additional time, NCCC members came out only slightly ahead.[83]

With regard to diversity, one of AmeriCorps's key goals is to show how Americans from different backgrounds can work together (both with other AmeriCorps members or with community residents). In fact, 15 percent of members cited "to learn about or work with different ethnic or cultural groups" as one of their top two reasons for joining.[84] Although fewer members worked in diverse teams and fewer worked outside their home communities than originally anticipated, "the overall result [has been] a program of some substantial diversity," with positive effects on individual participants.[85] One member explained: "For me race has been a huge issue in my placement. . . . It has been a huge eye-opener and learning experience, in dealing with racism for the first time, and learning from a culture I'm not used to."[86]

This said, the Abt studies failed to find that members overall increased their appreciation of cultural and ethnic diversity.[87] State and National members showed only a statistically insignificant gain, and NCCC members showed a statistically strong loss, compared with control groups.[88] Four years later, neither program's members showed any significant difference in appreciation of diversity compared with control groups.[89]

The studies found evidence of other expected civic engagement outcomes, however. Given AmeriCorps's emphasis on citizenship through service—on developing a lifelong commitment to volunteering—and the belief of some opponents that AmeriCorps might undermine such a commitment by rewarding participants monetarily, Abt's finding that NCCC members were more likely to volunteer after completing AmeriCorps than were similar nonmembers, and State and National members equally likely—with a substantial 64 percent volunteering in the preceding year—was an important validation of the program.[90] However, AmeriCorps's civic lessons went further, increasing

members' (self-assessed) connection to their communities and their understanding of their communities' problems; their belief in the importance of
being involved in their neighborhoods and "the feasibility of starting a grassroots effort to meet a range of community needs"; and their actual post-service
community activism.[91] These findings held over the two-year short term, and
several over the eight-year longer term, and showed AmeriCorps's support not
only for a service understanding of citizenship but for a work-based understanding as well.[92] People who had served in AmeriCorps were more likely
than those who had not to pursue a career in a public service job—and to
believe in the importance of their choice.[93]

Abt's surveys did not directly focus on patriotic or critical citizenship
themes, but they did assess AmeriCorps's effect on constitutional citizenship,
with disappointing but not surprising results overall. After completing their
service, members' belief in the importance of voting and jury service and the
"frequency with which [they] participate in activities intrinsic to the political
process, including learning about candidates and voting," was statistically no
different from the belief of nonmembers, short term or long term.[94] Another
study also found "no evidence that AmeriCorps mobilizes people politically"
(and "equally little evidence that [it] channels engagement away from politics").[95] The one constitutional citizenship-related outcome that AmeriCorps
service did affect was members' belief in "the feasibility of working with local
or state government to meet a range of community needs."[96]

These findings, both positive and negative, reflect AmeriCorps members'
experience in the program: they often work in partnership with government,
but, as Segal and Wofford explained to Congress, "political advantage isn't on
the mind of an AmeriCorps member closing a crack house in a neighborhood
she calls home. The next election isn't the priority of an AmeriCorps tutor
bending over a torn book and a tired second grader. . . . They aren't politiciz-
ing AmeriCorps"—and neither are they learning to engage in politics or the
political process.[97]

Clearly, something of the AmeriCorps experience "sticks," making members on the whole more civically engaged than similar people who did not
join. And, it is important to note, the things that stick are more likely to be
connected to their service work—developing a greater commitment to their
communities; believing in the efficacy of grassroots, local, and state government responses to community problems; continuing their volunteer work or
pursuing public service careers—compared with those things that are not connected to it, such as learning about political candidates or voting.

Higher Education

President Clinton's national service plan began as the centrist-Democrat-approved way for students to earn federal money for college. Along the journey from idea to law, "AmeriCorps [became] a *service* program with an educational *component* [emphasis added]"—with greater emphasis placed on service than on student aid.[98] As Segal explained, the administration "wanted to avoid a debate—which [it] would end up losing—that this was an expensive Pell Grant."[99] Indeed, in determining the education award amount, the major point of reference was the GI Bill benefit—not the Pell Grant—and because of veterans groups' demands, the award was significantly less than GI Bill benefits.[100] Not until the Kennedy Serve America Act was passed in 2009 was the award changed and pegged to the Pell Grant, strengthening AmeriCorps as an education access program, both substantively and symbolically.

Nonetheless, even before the 2009 change, AmeriCorps's education award component—renamed in Segal's honor following his death—was important in both practical and symbolic terms. Practically, the $4,725 that members could earn for each year of full-time service (from the program's start until 2009; with lesser amounts available for fewer service hours) helped many of them reach their educational goals: 42 percent cited "to get an education scholarship" as one of the two most important reasons they joined the program; among State and National members, 60 percent reported that the education award was "very important" to furthering their education, another 11 percent said it was "important," and similar percentages "indicated that as a result of their AmeriCorps experience they were in fact more likely to continue with their education."[101] Although two years after finishing their AmeriCorps service members were no more likely to have earned or to be working toward a college degree than were demographically similar nonmembers, 76 percent did redeem their award—with NCCC members' rates as high as 89 percent.[102] These figures are comparable to those for veterans' use of the original GI Bill benefit (80 percent) and significantly higher than later Army reservists' use of Montgomery GI Bill benefits (42 percent).[103]

Symbolically, the education award has been one of the few things that make AmeriCorps, AmeriCorps. Unlike the CCC's enrollees, members do different kinds of work for different kinds of sponsors. Unlike VISTA's earlier volunteers, they work full time or part time, some for pay, some not. Regardless, all AmeriCorps members can earn money for college, and both the Clinton and Bush administrations worked to expand the award's reach. With Republican encouragement, Clinton's Corporation created the "education award only" program, in which sponsoring organizations paid member stipends (or not) and other costs, leaving the federal government responsible only for the education award.[104] This strategy reduced the government's cost per participant, allowing it to enroll more members without added appropriations. The Bush administration, for its part, pressed for a change to increase the award's user rate. To make the award relevant to those without further educational aspirations or loans to repay, such as senior citizens, it proposed to allow them to transfer their awards to others—their grandchildren, for example, or even children they tutored.[105] The Serve America Act does not permit transfers to tutees, but it does allow transfers to children or grandchildren.[106]

Beyond expanding access and usage, maintaining the education award's value has been the biggest challenge for those focused on expanding educational opportunity. The maximum award of $4,725 a year was set in 1993; by 2007 its value had declined 30 percent, to $3,303 in constant 1993 dollars. At the same time, college costs had risen by almost 80 percent, even at the nation's public universities—from $6,365 to $11,441 per year.[107] Even two full-time awards—the maximum allowed—would not cover one year of tuition. (The 2009 increase, to $5,350, with future increases assured as Pell Grants increased, helped, but still did not reinstate the award's original purchasing power.) To compensate, the Corporation worked to supplement the award by persuading colleges and universities to match their students' AmeriCorps awards or give them academic credit for their service work. As of 2004, about half of the country's colleges and universities agreed.[108]

So, did AmeriCorps open doors to higher education? The evidence is mixed. High percentages of members said it did and used their awards, yet similar nonmembers managed to earn degrees in comparable numbers. Politically, Congress has been committed to keeping the award focused solely on education, which, given the role that higher education plays in fostering civic engagement of all kinds, has civic benefits.[109] But it has been equally committed to keeping its funding obligations in check, limiting the power of the education award—including its civic power—to no more than that of other college funding options.

Obligations and Inducements

AmeriCorps membership, like membership in the CCC and VISTA, carries both obligations and inducements. Some of these, like AmeriCorps's education awards, are unique, but on the whole the key differences are those of extent: AmeriCorps offers fewer inducements than did the CCC and imposes fewer obligations than either previous program. The principle of reciprocity still applies—public benefits in exchange for public service, as it did in the CCC—but AmeriCorps operates with a much lighter touch.

In each program's era, the idea of universal service—that all young Americans might have an obligation to serve—was discussed in theory and dismissed in practice. What distinguishes AmeriCorps, however, is that it has always been seen as national service. This increased the chance that national service advocates—those who believe in mandates and those who want opportunities expanded without mandates—would be able to build on AmeriCorps, instead of having to create a new program as others had to in the past. That as strong a national service advocate as Barack Obama went this route made this approach even more likely.

Still, that participation is optional has not precluded at least a few other requirements, including that members take an oath of service. The pledge was written specifically for AmeriCorps, largely by Robert Gordon, then a young Clinton administration national service staffer.[110] Every member promises

> I will get things done for America—to make our people safer, smarter, and healthier. I will bring Americans together to strengthen our communities.
> Faced with apathy, I will take action.
> Faced with conflict, I will seek common ground.
> Faced with adversity, I will persevere.
> I will carry this commitment with me this year and beyond.
> I am an AmeriCorps member, and I will get things done.

Along with the chance to earn an education award, taking this pledge has been one of the few experiences shared by all AmeriCorps members, and one that serves "as a reminder of why they signed up and as a guide for their lives after AmeriCorps."[111] It also strongly reinforces both service and public work understandings of citizenship.

The AmeriCorps pledge replaced VISTA's long-standing oath—the same one that federal employees take—which the Bush administration later tried to reinstate for AmeriCorps.[112] AmeriCorps's congressional opponents supported the move; they believed all along that AmeriCorps members were really nothing more than misnamed government employees.[113] Given the federal oath's (optional) "So help me God," critics of "messing with the pledge" contended that it "reflect[ed] the efforts of the Bush administration to invoke the name of God . . . in public life" and "would have the effect of dividing people rather than uniting them."[114]

However, the belief that national service should inculcate traditional constitutional and patriotic citizenship values, reflected in the federal oath's language that adherents "support and defend the Constitution" and "bear true faith and allegiance to the same," was most likely a stronger motivation than anything to do with religion. Under VISTA, the federal pledge's civic education potential went largely unnoticed and thus untapped; Bush's AmeriCorps leaders might have done better, but the idea's rollout suggests probably not. No one made the civic case for the federal pledge (beyond "but everybody else does it"), and when AmeriCorps's director, Rosie Mauk, was asked, she merely stated that it would be optional and could supplement the original pledge.[115] In any event, faced with vocal opposition from AmeriCorps alumni and failure of the reauthorization bill containing the change, they did not get the chance.

AmeriCorps members' second obligation is to complete their term of service, typically a year, with the option of a second. In the program's early years (1994 to 1998), overall attrition was high, averaging 28 percent—a fact that opponents cited as evidence of AmeriCorps's failure.[116] Attrition rates were higher among men, minorities, and those with less education, and while the overall rates were comparable to the Peace Corps's and military's, AmeriCorps's programs required commitments half as long.[117] Accounting for attrition, the Abt study found that 26.3 percent of its 1999 State and National sample left early: 67 percent for health, personal, or financial reasons (including to take a job); 19 percent because of dissatisfaction; and 4 percent because they were asked to leave.[118] By 2003 attrition rates had declined to 21.3 percent in State and National (and were 10 percent and 6.2 percent in NCCC and VISTA, respectively) and remained in that general ballpark, with an overall attrition rate of 20.1 percent in 2006.[119]

AmeriCorps members' final major obligation is to abide by the Hatch Act and other AmeriCorps-specific policies that prohibit advocacy and other political activities on members' service time. As I mentioned earlier, these restrictions had a political rationale and significant civic implications, affecting how members relate to the program, how they do their work, and what they learn. At the same time, they raised much less debate than similar restrictions on VISTA had a generation earlier. Beyond differences in the times' political cultures were differences in the programs' purposes: "Both members and employers are more likely to characterize AmeriCorps as a service program rather than an advocacy or change-oriented program," as many VISTA volunteers, especially in its early years, characterized their program.[120] As a result, scholar Jon Van Til found that "even though the restrictions on advocacy seem weird to many participants, they tend to learn to work within them such that their effect is minimal on the basic relationship that counts for them: their relationship to the individuals in the communities they serve."[121]

In exchange for their service and agreement to abide by these obligations, AmeriCorps members receive benefits: they earn money for education; many receive a living stipend and health insurance; those in need can receive help for child care. These inducements form the flip side of the program's principle of reciprocity, but they also show the strength of the principle of sacrifice. More so than AmeriCorps's obligations, these inducements have been controversial, both politically and civically: some on the right find them counter to the very definition of service; some on the left find them insufficient to permit the poor to serve or fully reflect the value of members' service. However, while controversy has flared at the ideological edges, most policymakers, program administrators, and members have found in them an appropriate balance.

AmeriCorps's largest and most contentious inducement is its living stipend, approximately equal to minimum wage and below poverty level even for a single person, but still something. The argument for stipends is straightforward: as Senator Edward Kennedy put it, "Volunteerism shouldn't just be limited to those who have the resources to be able to volunteer."[122] The counterargument is equally straightforward: "Acceptance of a government job," in Bruce Chapman's words, cannot be called "true service."[123] (Bush's Corporation officials had to devise a conservative response to this conservative criticism, and they did so by arguing that taking on "responsibilities that ordinary volunteers cannot . . . justifies paying some [members] a small stipend.")[124] Members support both ideas. For those of modest means, subsistence support is often necessary to allow a substantial service commitment. As one member stated, "If I wasn't getting the living stipend, I wouldn't be able to put the amount of time I put into AmeriCorps."[125] However, another explained, "I don't want to make $30,000 a year—that would be like a real job and would defeat the purpose of service."[126]

As a program that combines the demographics of the CCC and early VISTA programs—including both the disadvantaged and the well-off— AmeriCorps has ended up combining their foundational principles, targeting them to different constituencies. For the disadvantaged, the stress is on reciprocity. Malik, an AmeriCorps member, captured this emphasis well: "We talk to other people around the neighborhood . . . we let them know it's not all about the stipend. . . . AmeriCorps can give me a chance, so I want to give something back to them. I'm going to help build up the community."[127] For the well-off, the idea of sacrifice—even among those arguing for stipends and other inducements—is dominant. The late Nick Bollman, co-founder of the Funders' Network, said:

> The notion that compensation or no compensation is the test of whether this is volunteerism . . . is wrong. The idea is, compared to what—the college graduate who . . . gets the $60,000-a-year job . . . and doesn't do a whit of service for anyone? Compared to the college graduate who takes a $7,500-a-year job as an AmeriCorps participant? It seems to me, this is the right comparison. This is the person who is making an enormous sacrifice.[128]

That said, these divergent ideas hold more in principle than in practice. For the disadvantaged, reciprocity goes only so far: AmeriCorps's stipends still leave them poor. In one member's words, "It seems strange that a lot of us have to turn to public aid."[129] In the CCC, enrollees' work took the place of public aid. That was its purpose. At the same time, unlike VISTA for much of its history, AmeriCorps does not require that members live in poverty; well-off members do not have to make that sacrifice, and poor members do not have to continue to live in poverty. Members do not have to make ends meet solely with their stipends; they can receive public assistance, hold jobs, or get help from parents—and many do.[130] The stipend's low level was set not by pedagogical principles—the idea that servers need to share the circumstances of those they serve—but by philosophical, political, and pragmatic concerns: it maintains the distinction between service and "a job" and helps keep costs in check.

In Van Til's assessment, AmeriCorps strikes the right balance in what it asks of and provides to its members: "AmeriCorps clearly gives the citizenry something it highly values—a program that harnesses the energies of youth to social renewal. But it also gives its workers a set of incentives and a level of compensation that they find appropriate." Thus, "perhaps the most important reason that AmeriCorps works is that it has succeeded in constructing that rarest of human organizations: one that is based on the needs of its members"— and, I would add, one that is also based on their capacities.[131]

Conclusion: The Politics and Civics of AmeriCorps

As of 2012, AmeriCorps is the United States' main civilian national service program, the largest since the Civilian Conservation Corps, the longest-lived since VISTA, and the first to grow under presidents not responsible for its creation. These facts make teasing out its civic and political lessons critically important. The key questions are, first, how has AmeriCorps acted as national

Box 11-1. *AmeriCorps at a Glance*

Dates	1993–present
	Comprises State and National, VISTA, and NCCC programs
Enrollment	Peak: 88,000/year in 2009 (75,000 through regular appropriation; 13,000 one-time Recovery Act positions)
	More than 775,000 total by 2011
Purposes	Clinton: Service and higher education funding, "Getting Things Done"
	Bush: Leveraging part-time volunteers, homeland defense
	Obama: Better meeting demand and public needs
Government role: Administration	Funded by the national government; grantees chosen mainly by state commissions; program mainly run by nonprofit groups
	Housed in the Corporation for National and Community Service
Government role: Outside relationships	Not publicly well known
	Well supported by governors, grantee organizations, and interest groups
Government role: Status within government	Not well supported by congressional Republicans during 1990s, built support over time
	Supported by Bush, pushed to expand post-9/11
	Supported by Obama, pushed to expand to 250,000 members/year
Work	Health, education, public safety, environment (Bush added homeland security, Obama added veterans and economic opportunity)

service and public policy for democracy? Second, why has AmeriCorps's institutionalization been limited? Third, why has its institutionalization gone well beyond that of its predecessors?

National Service and Citizenship in AmeriCorps

From its inception AmeriCorps has always had clear national service elements. It is a federal program that engages many (although not all) members, mostly

Work (*continued*)	Leveraging part-time volunteers
	Direct and indirect, capacity-building service
	Flexibility, quantifiability aided support, low visibility detracted
Participants	Mainly young, majority female, diverse in race and class
	Equally split between high school grads, college grads, those with some college
Education	Training for service and life skills
	Learning through service
	Earn money for college
Obligations and inducements	Voluntary one-year term of service; two-year limit
	Minimum-wage pay, health insurance, and $5,350/full-time year of service for higher education
Main civic points	Based on reciprocity and government as catalyst
	Encouraging civic responsibility is a key goal
	Emphasizes service, as well as patriotic, constitutional, and public work perspectives
Main political points	Strong association with Clinton, Democrats undermined Republican support; giving governors a large role helped build it
	Flexibility, interest group support, experience with civic practice helped build support

young adults, in full-time, short-term, subsistence-wage work that fills public needs. And more so than any previous program, AmeriCorps has been recognized as national service. However, for AmeriCorps as for previous programs, this label has remained contested. For much of its first decade, the extent to which AmeriCorps qualified as national service, and the extent to which that was considered a good thing, were challenged. Debate over the relative merits of national and community service might have undermined AmeriCorps's continuation and growth, especially with the advent of the Bush administration. That it did not was testimony both to AmeriCorps's design and to its leadership. Debate over whether AmeriCorps even qualified as national service could have prompted advocates to turn away from AmeriCorps and promote a new alternative, as they had after VISTA's creation. That this did not happen was largely due to AmeriCorps's explicit national service framing, which led national service advocates to press for AmeriCorps's expansion and development to make it "real" national service. That this came to pass contributed to its growth.

Like the country's earlier national service programs, AmeriCorps has influenced how its participants and the public understand their relationship to government and the meaning of citizenship. Like the CCC, AmeriCorps has a strong formative civic mission for its members, one grounded mainly in the principle of reciprocity. AmeriCorps has emphasized multiple citizenship perspectives—including service, patriotic, constitutional, and public work perspectives—that it communicates through program participation and reinforces through training. By engaging members in work supported by the national government and the private sector, chosen (mainly) by states, and implemented through local government and civil society, AmeriCorps has provided real-life examples of federalism, public-private partnerships, and active citizenship. By engaging members in work in education, the environment, economic opportunity, health, public safety, and more, AmeriCorps has shown how government, nonprofits, and citizens can work together to address serious public problems. By recruiting members who differ in age, gender, race, ethnicity, class, and education, AmeriCorps has emphasized that everyone has something to contribute to the commonwealth. That it offers educational awards to all has emphasized that everyone can benefit from it as well. That citizenship is too often defined solely as voting—and that members are barred from registering voters or engaging in political or policy advocacy—have obscured some of these lessons. The prevailing alternative definition—citizenship as service, often abstracted from a broader public context—has obscured them as well, as has the frequent failure of programs and training to connect members' work to relevant public policy. Still, by making citizenship an explicit priority within a program structured as it is, AmeriCorps has been able to influence members' civic development in ways not seen since the days of the CCC.

As a relatively small program operating in a highly complex political and social context, AmeriCorps, like VISTA, has not been able to influence the larger culture on a scale as wide as the CCC's; but like the other two programs, it reflects and has contributed to the civic ideals of its time. That it is authorized to grow significantly will not turn back the clock to New Deal civic time, but it may give AmeriCorps a chance to have a greater civic impact in twenty-first-century America.

The Politics of National Service in AmeriCorps

Politically, AmeriCorps's policy design and history show how difficult it has been to institutionalize civilian national service. The CCC and VISTA influenced AmeriCorps, but it developed largely along a different path, and one fraught with as much danger as opportunity. Its survival was in question for much of its first decade as increases in ideological opposition to national service combined with the recurring complication of strong presidential identification to create a powerful anti-AmeriCorps Republican congressional contingent. It took significant time for AmeriCorps to gain the bipartisan support necessary for institutionalization, and a portion of this support has been soft, limited to good economic times. While some supporters see AmeriCorps as an important policy tool for surviving hard times by providing work and services to those in need, others see it as a luxury we cannot afford: nice, but not necessary.

That it survived a hostile Congress and lived to be accepted by a new, Republican president—and then his Democratic successor—is testimony to civilian national service's ideological malleability and the deepening of post–New Deal political structures, most notably cooperative federalism and public-private partnerships. For good political and programmatic reasons, both the CCC and VISTA largely bypassed state governments. On both counts AmeriCorps has benefited from the national and state governments' increased ability to work together. Similarly, it has benefited from its administrators' increasing effectiveness on the ground. In this AmeriCorps gained from VISTA's experience, as nonprofits have become better at working with government and within communities over time. Both of these factors helped AmeriCorps avoid the earlier programs' fate. Unlike the CCC, AmeriCorps lived past its founding president's term; unlike VISTA, it was neither downsized nor pulled toward policy extremes with the presidency ping-ponging between the parties. The result by 2012 has been steady, significant growth, with expansion planned—albeit delayed—that in better economic times may well achieve what has remained elusive for more than seventy-five years: the creation of an American domestic civilian national service institution.

Part

IV

Conclusion

12

Making Sense of the Past and Its Lessons for the Future

I n the United States, domestic civilian national service has been difficult to create and just as hard to maintain and expand. The CCC was America's first, largest, most highly esteemed, and most explicitly civic of national service programs, but it was also the shortest-lived. VISTA was, and remains, our longest-existing program, but also our smallest and most controversial. AmeriCorps has done much better, expanding in political support and size to become the first domestic civilian national service program to grow under presidents who were not responsible for its creation. But whether AmeriCorps will be widely recognized and strongly supported as a feasible policy option for addressing the nation's needs and a practical life option for significant numbers of young adults remains to be seen.

Further, the CCC, VISTA, and AmeriCorps's main State and National program are all strikingly different—in purpose, government role, work, number and background of their participants, educational goals, and obligations and inducements. As policymaking for national service progressed over the years, earlier or existing programs were not used as the starting point for future program development. Presidents Kennedy and Johnson explicitly distanced VISTA from the CCC, and Clinton implicitly distanced AmeriCorps from VISTA. He did pay homage to the CCC, but its practical influence was limited.

The lack of deep institutionalization of any individual program and of a clear policy pathway connecting the three programs is worth explaining in its own right, because it deviates from the experience of many New Deal and post-New Deal social programs and runs counter to political scientists' emphasis on the importance of path dependence in understanding policymaking over time.[1] The CCC and VISTA show evidence of path dependence; but instead of increasing returns, the CCC hit a dead end, while VISTA crawled along a road heading nowhere that national service advocates wanted to go. As a result, path dependence in these programs led to a lack of path dependence in national service policymaking overall: advocates had to start over, twice. It is only with AmeriCorps, and very recently at that, that path dependence as it is typically understood may be in evidence. The lack of institutionalization and interprogram continuity are also worth explaining because they influence national service's ability to act as public policy for democracy, especially how participants and the larger public understand their relationship to government and the meaning of citizenship. The politics of national service affect the civics of national service, and vice versa.

Understanding the dynamics of national service policymaking requires that we look at both developmental changes that occur over time and factors that have remained consistent despite passage of time. On the one hand, focusing on consistency over time helps us identify the durable—although not immutable—regime characteristics that have influenced national service policymaking and the durable—again, not immutable—characteristics of national service policymaking itself. These include national service's centrist appeal and its lack of concentrated, broad-based support, the powerful association between specific programs and their founding presidents and parties, and the changing definition of national service itself. On the other hand, a developmental perspective helps us gauge the influence that changes in the size and scope of government action, the nature of federalism, the civic experience of government and community organizations, the organization of interest groups, and the meaning and strength of liberal and conservative ideologies have had on national service policymaking.

Together these two perspectives help explain why policymakers designed programs as they did at varying points, and how these programs developed, up to the present. Given AmeriCorps's growth in size and support, it is especially important to gauge whether (helpful) developmental changes affecting national service policymaking have significantly altered its (unhelpful) consistent characteristics. Have the politics of national service fundamentally changed? Understanding these dynamics can give us insight into where national service may be headed and help us draw lessons for future policymaking. These lessons include improving program quality by paying more attention to the fit between members and their service placements (but not through narrowing AmeriCorps's focus), increasing AmeriCorps's visibility, and expanding the program so that every young adult is able and encouraged to enroll (but is not mandated to do so). These lessons also include tying AmeriCorps's civic education to members' service work, emphasizing the many ways that people can act as citizens, and more clearly identifying Ameri-Corps with government, while remaining mindful of the limits of fostering political participation through AmeriCorps itself. The goal is to understand what the experience of the past nearly eighty years can teach us about maximizing the possibilities (while acknowledging the limits) for civilian national service to become a civically powerful, well-known, and strongly supported program for ever-growing numbers of young adults to contribute to their communities and country.

Consistent Factors Affecting National Service

In the United States, presidents have created domestic civilian national service programs in generational cycles—in the 1930s, 1960s, and 1990s. While the programs were products of their times, certain factors have influenced their creation and history time and again. These consistent factors are characteristics of either the American regime or of national service policymaking itself, and typically they have worked against the deep institutionalization of any individual program and the development of a clear policy pathway connecting programs over time. These factors include the centrist appeal of national service and its lack of concentrated, broad-based support; the intense association between specific national service programs and their founding presidents and parties; and the changing definition of national service itself.

First, as a policy area civilian national service has been in some sense "surrounded" by hostile ideological stands and interest-based claims, from the right most notably but also from the left. Ideologically, support for national service most often (but not always) has come from centrists, those less leery of activist government than those on the right and equally less afraid to speak the language of civic duty and obligation than those on the left (or the libertarian right). This centrist appeal has helped national service advocates win public support, but it has hurt their attempts to build political support: typically neither party finds it in its interest to press for programs that simultaneously offend some of its most committed supporters and appeal to significant numbers of the opposition, because these partisans will share credit for legislative success. Centrist programs are often caught in this bind. With national service, this pattern played out on several levels. For example, Democratic presidential candidates Walter Mondale and Michael Dukakis were unwilling to campaign for national service, for fear of offending liberal interest groups.[2] At another level, Republican House Leader Dick Armey refused to bring President Bush's Citizen Service Act to a vote in 2002 because, as a senior associate explained, "It would [have been] a difficult vote for many of our members, and it would [have] alienate[d] our base less than 100 days before the [midterm] election."[3]

Second, national service has suffered from a lack of concentrated, broad-based support. It certainly has public appeal: surveys typically register high levels of support. But they rarely ask how important people believe it to be or where people rank it relative to other spending priorities. So national service could be a big applause-line when Bill Clinton campaigned in 1992 and yet remain a program no one asked for when Representative Curt Weldon (R-Pa.) met with citizens from around the country.[4] Public support has been wide but not deep, because national service has been seen as nice but not necessary.

Interest group support has been even more tenuous. National service advocates have few natural interest group allies, groups that see national service as essential to their success or a first-order priority for their members. As a result, in the constellation of groups affected by national service—business, labor, the military and veterans, nonprofit organizations, colleges and universities, and youth-serving and youth-service groups—none has supported national service out of hand. As the head of the National Social Welfare Assembly testified regarding the Kennedy NSC plan, "A National Service Corps, *under certain conditions*, can make significant contributions [emphasis added]."[5] This perspective has held over time. In many cases support or at least neutrality could be negotiated, but it could not be assumed. Support has been highly contingent. This is largely the story of AmeriCorps's journey from idea to law: administration officials negotiating with unions to protect service-sector jobs, with veterans groups over the size of the education award, with existing service corps regarding race- and class-mixing requirements, and so on.[6] Once a particular program is in place, interest groups, especially those that tangibly benefit, defend it fiercely; but building a coalition for a new program has been much more difficult.

Not only does this dynamic complicate national service policymaking, it means that support for national service has first been built and generated within government. Advocates such as Charles Moskos and Donald Eberly may come from the outside, but their energy focused on influencing politicians and bureaucrats as opposed to assembling a coalition of supportive interest groups or creating a mass-based national service pressure group. In fact, in an effort that was becoming more common, Kennedy's cabinet-level national service study group all but created the Citizens' Committee for a

National Service Corps, a privately funded group formed to generate public and congressional support. It was co-chaired by a much more than average citizen, Malcolm Forbes.[7]

Third, the constraints of centrism and the need for within-government support have combined to make presidents *the* key actors in creating national service programs, but this very support has compromised the programs' futures. Neither the CCC nor AmeriCorps would have been created without their respective presidents; AmeriCorps would not have survived without President Clinton's support.[8] However, the personal presidential investment that has allowed national service programs to exist at all has made them a convenient target for presidential opponents who wanted to make a point. In 1937 House Democrats denied the CCC permanence principally to chastise FDR. In 1995 House Republicans voted to rescind AmeriCorps funding primarily to humiliate Clinton.[9] "Because Clinton loved the program so much," House Speaker Newt Gingrich knew that "AmeriCorps could become a useful hostage."[10] Further, this dynamic has had consequences beyond a program's founding administration. Presidents who inherited a civilian national service program and who either did not try to kill it or did not succeed in killing it, typically went out of their way to differentiate it under their administrations and distance it from its founder. Bush's support for AmeriCorps hinged on his policymakers being able to do exactly this.

Strong presidential identification has also served to tie the programs to their founding presidents' party, so that national service programs have suffered from the drawbacks of both political centrism and partisanship without gaining many benefits. Opponents have been concerned that national service will act as a recruiting mechanism for the party that created it—to date, the Democrats. Some politicians, however, Democrats and Republicans alike, have been concerned that administrations may use it to support their party, which, about half of the time, will not be the politicians' own. Their fear lies not only, or even principally, in the possibility that participants will engage in partisan political activities through their service work. This problem did come up with VISTA, but generally it is amenable to bureaucratic solution, through project selection, job descriptions, training, and supervision. But what is the solution when the other party is getting all the gratitude? As a Young Americans for Freedom representative testified in 1963, "It is impossible to ignore the political implications of 5,000 roving welfare corpsmen who owe their jobs to the president," to say nothing of the tens of thousands served, who may thank the party for providing assistance by giving their support.[11] Regarding AmeriCorps, this dynamic was multiplied threefold just at its founding, and its advocates aspired for much more. Clearly the phenomenon is not limited to national service. However, because national service mainly recruits the young and intentionally aims to socialize them—certainly into a commitment to service but also quite possibly into an understanding of the proper role of government—partisan concerns have been particularly powerful.

Finally, it has been difficult for programs to be institutionalized or to act as models for national service, because the definition of national service has kept changing. Today the CCC is recognized as national service, but it was not during its lifetime. Advocates then argued that it could become national service if enrollees were trained as military reserves or, alternatively, if the program was changed to reflect William James's "moral equivalent of war." The War on Poverty was such a moral equivalent, but one fought with very few troops. Just two years after Kennedy's National Service Corps proposal was realized through the founding of VISTA, the *New York Times* published "The Case for a National Service Corps." The key question was how to enroll all young Americans.[12] This vision inspired AmeriCorps, but because of its structure and limited numbers, the idea that AmeriCorps had merely the potential to become national service had its adherents. However, unlike either previous programs' officials, AmeriCorps's officials—notably, in all three of its administrations—called it national service. Doing so helped AmeriCorps survive and grow by channeling national service advocates' energies to its defense. And because AmeriCorps did survive and grow, advocates did not have reason to abandon the program and work to create national service anew. Two words—and the many other factors that contributed to AmeriCorps's success—may have broken the cycle.

Overall, consistent elements affecting national service have posed serious challenges for national service policymaking. They have made it harder for advocates to create programs, made it harder for programs to gain broad bipartisan acceptance and support, and made it harder for programs to expand or build on one another over time. Combined with—and in fact ameliorated by—the developmental factors described below, this situation suggests a number of lessons that policymakers and advocates might heed to increase the likelihood that civilian national service will become deeply institutionalized and act as public policy for democracy.

Developmental Factors Affecting National Service

While certain characteristics of policymaking endure over time, domestic civilian national service programs are also products of their times—created in response to unique problems and opportunities and influenced by their political and cultural contexts. Developmental changes in the nature of American politics and government have combined with time-bound events—ranging from war on the largest scale to the scheduling of a vote in Congress on the smallest—to account for new national service policy designs. Along with the consistent factors discussed above, these developmental changes also account for programs' fates.

The Civilian Conservation Corps

The CCC was created to respond to massive youth unemployment caused by the Great Depression and did so directly, by giving hundreds of thousands of young men meaningful public work. Its design was in keeping with the New Deal approach to policymaking, giving the lead role to the federal government working directly with citizens, and its simplicity contributed to its success. By definition the program succeeded at its principal task, providing jobs, and the focus of its efforts led to its success in its other main task, accomplishing significant conservation work. That design, and a broadly amenable culture, further helped the program accomplish its *civic* task, influencing how its participants and the larger public understood their relationship to government and the meaning of citizenship. The program was based on the principles of reciprocity and citizenship understood as public work; both ideas communicated the belief that citizens—program participants and others—should contribute to and benefit from the commonwealth.

However, over the course of the CCC's lifetime, these principles came into question. As CCC scholar John Salmond approvingly noted, by the late 1930s the CCC was expected to accomplish "more-sophisticated functions—tasks concerned with the welfare and training of youth"—than simply work relief and conservation.[13] This development diminished the CCC as national service and, as it gained force over the following decades, obscured the CCC as a model for future national service policymaking. This is a case where political development, namely increasing expectations for program sophistication, worked against deep institutionalization, policy path development, and public policy for democracy.

In other cases, the lack of development worked against accomplishing these goals. When World War II made jobs plentiful and the national budget tight, Congress eliminated the program—in essence declaring its mission accomplished. Today the thought of terminating a popular, successful program is hard to conceive under any circumstances. In fact, we rarely eliminate unpopular or failed programs. One reason that post–New Deal programs survive is that powerful organized interests within society and government itself protect them. Such groups had yet to forcefully emerge during the CCC's lifetime. This lack of protection, combined with events of the times, such as Roosevelt's court-packing plan that circuitously derailed the CCC's chance for permanence in 1937 and, most significant, the country's entry into the war, led to the CCC's demise. In the language of path dependence, the CCC's chosen path—and its inability to branch off in more promising directions in the face of obstacles—led to a dead end.

VISTA

At VISTA's creation, policymakers were committed to an alternative model based on a different understanding of service, a different approach to addressing poverty, and a different understanding of federalism. Unlike the CCC, VISTA was based on the principle of sacrifice. VISTA volunteers were to gain from participation, but the balance of benefits was to accrue to the poor—those being served. This principle was reflected in VISTA's approach to poverty, which was based on providing the poor not with work but with a volunteer who was expected to catalyze local efforts to address poverty's underlying causes. VISTA's goal was significantly more ambitious than the CCC's—addressing the problems of millions by employing several thousand as opposed to several hundred thousand—and its causal mechanisms significantly more sophisticated. VISTA was to be small and smart. It was also local. VISTA operated in cooperative fashion with the national government and localities, in keeping with the program's goals and new understandings of federalism.

Developmental changes in American politics led policymakers to set high expectations for how much VISTA could accomplish with so little and within its structure. At the same time, these changes were new enough—had not matured fully enough—that those responsible for policymaking and implementation at both the national and local levels lacked the extensive experience necessary to meet these expectations. As a result, VISTA's successes were harder to come by, ascertain, and publicize—and were not always even seen as successes. These facts complicated VISTA's ability to be institutionalized and to effectively act as public policy for democracy, with respect to volunteers and the larger public.

Following VISTA's creation, other developmental factors worked against these goals. One was that the definitions of *liberal* and *conservative* changed. When the Kennedy administration proposed the National Service Corps, solidly grounded in compensatory-service principles, it was considered solidly liberal. By late in the Johnson administration, this approach had been redefined as solidly *conservative* and the community-advocacy approach *liberal*. By President Reagan's election, however, the very idea of civilian national service was considered liberal and there was no solidly accepted conservative approach. Time-bound events such as the social upheaval of the late 1960s contributed to these shifting definitions, and frequent party changes in the White House exacerbated the challenges to VISTA's institutionalization and civic teachings. Not only did presidents of different parties markedly alter VISTA to reflect their own ideology, Republican presidents from Nixon through Reagan tried to end it.

If developmental changes impeded VISTA's institutionalization and even threatened its existence, they were also responsible for its survival. VISTA's approach to federalism embedded the program into local community organizations. The exponentially increased number and strength of local and national interest groups—in VISTA's case, organized groups of volunteers, sponsors, professional associations, and its civil service staff—ably defended it when it came under attack. Finally, VISTA's complex, multijointed design gave the program flexibility. Even opposing administrations could turn it to their own purposes, which made it less likely that they would fight to the death. Nonetheless, VISTA's survival did not ensure its deep institutionalization, its influence on future policymaking, or its success as public policy for democracy. From a path dependence perspective, VISTA avoided being stopped in its tracks, in part because its supporters were powerful enough to push it forward and in part because it could maneuver to the right and left as circumstances dictated. But the path its founders set it on and the road it ultimately traveled could not reach national service advocates' desired destination. They needed a new path, and a new vehicle.

AmeriCorps

In creating AmeriCorps, policymakers faced an even more challenging political environment than had VISTA's. The growth of welfare state entitlements had shrunk the proportion of public resources available for discretionary programs (among them civilian national service), and the rise of interest groups dedicated to protecting existing discretionary programs (among them VISTA) had shrunk the resources available for new ones. The same development that had saved VISTA threatened AmeriCorps: programs had become harder to kill, but also harder to create, especially on an ambitious scale.[14] The New Deal gave us not only the CCC but also the Works Progress Administration; the Agricultural Adjustment Administration; the Securities and Exchange Commission; the Federal Housing Administration; the National Labor

Relations Board; the Civil Aeronautics Authority; the Federal Communications Commission; and of course Social Security, with its programs for retirees, the unemployed, dependent children, and the blind and disabled. The Great Society gave us not only VISTA but also Head Start, Job Corps, the Food Stamp program, Medicare and Medicaid, the Equal Pay Act, the Clean Air Act, the Wilderness Act, the Civil Rights Act, and the Voting Rights Act, among others. But by the 1990s, the list of landmark legislation had shrunk significantly: the Americans with Disabilities Act, the Family and Medical Leave Act, perhaps a few others. AmeriCorps had to jump hurdles that were much higher than previous ones; and with few other new programs closing in on the goal line, more eyes—especially disapproving ones—were focused on it. AmeriCorps's creators faced the full force of ideological opposition to civilian national service and, unlike VISTA's founders, had to do so from the program's inception, without benefit of the protection that comes from having been in operation for several years.

While developments in American politics made AmeriCorps especially hard to create, they also influenced how it was designed and how well it has worked. Civically, AmeriCorps is based on reciprocity, as was the CCC. However, in the CCC reciprocity was consistent with prevailing political and cultural norms, and in AmeriCorps it is going against the grain. Over the intervening decades, government programs' animating principle had become rights, and service's animating principle, sacrifice. That AmeriCorps attempts to balance rights and responsibilities, benefits and contributions, makes its work as public policy for democracy even more important but also more difficult.

On the other hand, certain organizational developments, including those in federalism and civic practice, have had the opposite effect. More than any other program, AmeriCorps is federal, providing the largest role ever for states to determine projects and control funding. It has given governors a stake in success that no other civilian national service program had given them. That many of these governors have been Republican has helped broaden AmeriCorps's partisan and ideological appeal, countering some of the drawbacks associated with its consistent centrism. Beyond the large role for states, the "reinventing government" ethos of the times led to an even larger role for nonprofit and community-based organizations, those that would actually implement the program. Importantly, by the time AmeriCorps was founded, the likelihood that a national service program would succeed in states and communities had improved. As sociologists Carmen Sirianni and Lewis Friedland document, professionals at all government levels and in nonprofits are significantly more skillful at designing, implementing, and supporting effective civic practice, including that done through national service, compared with their 1960s counterparts.[15] Their more sophisticated skills further expanded Ameri-Corps's partisan and ideological support, as some opponents were won over by evidence that the program really did work for their constituents. Combined with the flexibility that AmeriCorps shares with VISTA—that its work could be steered toward the priorities of a new, conservative administration (without jeopardizing its future after the Democrats' subsequent return)— these factors have helped the program overcome its early political challenges and set the stage for its growth.

That the 9/11 attacks, the war on terror, and the Afghanistan and Iraq wars prompted AmeriCorps's expansion highlights another potential developmental change in the effect of war on civilian national service. World War II largely sealed the fate of the CCC; the Vietnam War, by siphoning resources from the War on Poverty, contributed to VISTA's stagnation; but America's most recent wars have led to AmeriCorps's expansion. Bush not only tapped Americans' post-9/11 civic spirit through its expansion but put AmeriCorps members to work on homeland security tasks, while Obama created a Veterans Corps to help address the needs of military personnel returning from fighting abroad. In both cases, civilian servers contribute to war-related efforts. While it is too early to tell what influence this new, positive relationship between civilian and military service will have on policymaking over the long term, it is currently providing a new rationale and broadening the constituency for expanding domestic civilian national service programs.

So where does this leave AmeriCorps and national service more broadly? These developmental factors, reflected in AmeriCorps, have largely blunted the negative impact of national service's consistent factors. AmeriCorps's structure and work accomplishments have broadened its ideological and partisan support, allowing it to suffer less from the drawbacks of centrism while still gaining its benefits—and what is also important, helping it to survive and grow. That it survived and grew under the Bush administration loosened its tight ties to Bill Clinton and the Democratic Party, creating a virtuous circle of increasing Republican congressional support. That it grew also expanded its support among organized interests, creating another virtuous circle and rendering national service's lack of natural interest group allies—as opposed to AmeriCorps's—moot. That it grew and is slated to grow substantially over the next several years, budget politics allowing, has the potential to increase its public recognition and significantly increase the number of young people, and others, who will reap its benefits, civic benefits among them. Finally, that it grew and is slated to grow further has kept national service advocates in the fold: not only do they recognize AmeriCorps as national service, they believe it is on a path that can lead them to their desired policy goal. Although advocates do not all agree on the exact final destination, they share the idea that AmeriCorps should be institutionalized—that it should be considered a viable policy option for addressing the nation's needs and a practical life-option for large numbers of young adults.

Lessons for Future Policymaking

Just because AmeriCorps is on a path to deep institutionalization does not guarantee its arrival. That it has had to fight to keep its funding and enrollment stable just a few short years after the Kennedy Serve America Act authorized it to grow significantly is particularly worrisome. Neither does its path guarantee that it is fulfilling its promise as public policy for democracy. What lessons can advocates and policymakers learn from this history to make AmeriCorps's growth and civic accomplishments more likely?

AmeriCorps's success on the ground is its greatest strength, both politically and civically. Its effectiveness in local community organizations has provided the foundation for broadening political support, most notably among state governors but also among members of Congress. By continuing to pay attention to the quality and quantity of AmeriCorps's work, administrators can ensure that it continues to play this vitally important role. To improve the quality of AmeriCorps's work (among other benefits), researchers Peter Frumkin and JoAnn Jastrzab advocate more careful matching of member applicants to available AmeriCorps positions.[16] This is an important point: their research and others' findings have shown that mismatches are too prevalent.[17] Incompatibility can occur when service site staffers themselves do not select members. This can happen when a larger organization, such as a United Way affiliate or a university, receives an AmeriCorps grant to hire and place members at smaller, local nonprofits that do not have the infrastructure to apply for federal funding on their own. As scholars Ann Marie Thomson and James L. Perry suggest, requiring grantees to involve service site staff, who know their organizations' needs best, in member selection and placement could ameliorate this problem.[18] A thorough review of potentially more detailed member applications, with referrals to grantees beyond those identified by the applicant, could reduce mismatches that occur despite direct member hiring.

To further improve the quality of AmeriCorps's work, Frumkin and Jastrzab also recommend narrowing its focus, for example to education, rather than trying to manage programs focused on education plus the environment, economic development, health, and veterans.[19] This streamlining would help by allowing AmeriCorps to develop better substantive expertise; the program would know better how to match applicants and positions, identify organizations to fund, train members, and evaluate results. A narrower focus would also give AmeriCorps a clearer substantive identity. To be sure, there would be trade-offs. For one, not everyone interested in national service is interested in, say, education. Focusing on only one area would limit AmeriCorps's appeal to a narrower range of Americans and potentially detract from its goal of recruiting a diverse membership. That said, if programmatic concerns were the only considerations, the case for a narrow focus might prevail. But programmatic concerns are not the only considerations. Politically, narrowing AmeriCorps's focus would be disastrous.

As I mentioned earlier, AmeriCorps's policymakers decided to work in a range of areas in good part because of their concern that, in Shirley Sagawa's words, "support for national service was 'a mile wide and an inch deep,' [and] to focus the issue would 'cut off three-quarters of the mile.'"[20] Over AmeriCorps's history support has deepened considerably, but the larger dynamic remains: significantly narrowing its focus would just as significantly narrow its base of support. Advocates might argue that support would simply shift, from say, conservation groups that currently receive funding to a greater number of funded education organizations. What this view neglects to consider is organized interest group support. Education interest groups already support AmeriCorps, and their numbers will not increase; environmental advocacy groups and others do as well, but if education were to become AmeriCorps's sole focus, they would have no reason to. Given that AmeriCorps's advocates have had to fight not just to increase AmeriCorps's funding but often simply to maintain it, this is support that the program cannot afford to lose.

Further, such a move would be likely to undermine AmeriCorps's development well into the future. First, it would decrease the program's flexibility and thus its ability to respond to new priorities, most important, those supported by new presidents. Presidents as far back as Richard Nixon have altered national service programs' priorities to respond to their values and interests; narrowing AmeriCorps's scope would not eliminate this strategy but certainly would limit the strategy's range. This limitation could significantly reduce not only AmeriCorps's ability to secure future presidents' support but, even worse, its ability to moderate a hostile president's opposition. Second, although narrowing AmeriCorps's focus would increase its substantive identity, it would undermine its national service identity. Again using an education-focus example, the rationale for moving the program to the Department of Education and eliminating the Corporation for National and Community Service would be persuasive. Even without this move, national service advocates would be likely to shift their energies away from growing the "AmeriCorps Education Program" to pushing for a more encompassing program, just as they did in the decades following the CCC's demise and the years following VISTA's creation. This shift could well reignite the "start, stop, start, then start over again" dynamic that has characterized the history of U.S. national service policymaking to its detriment.

Finally, just a concerted attempt to narrow AmeriCorps's focus to a single priority would divide the program's supporters when they need to be united to defend and expand the program. The infighting over which priority should win, where to draw the lines around the chosen priority ("Yes, we are a conservation program, but we educate about conservation, so we should still qualify!"), and other details could be even more damaging than the aftereffects of the policy change itself.[21] Improving the quality of AmeriCorps's work is important, but given that its quality is already a strength, policymakers should focus on areas such as member-placement matching, training, and evaluation, and avoid large-scale changes whose benefits come at huge political cost.

Beyond quality, AmeriCorps's officials need to recognize that AmeriCorps's work, unlike the CCC's, does not speak for itself, especially to the public. Therefore they also need to pay attention to the visibility of AmeriCorps members and their work. Increasing the number of people who see what the program does, and does well, can help the program politically, as elected officials respond to constituent support. It can also help civically, as the public sees how government and citizens can work together to address public problems.

Given that many AmeriCorps members work out of the public eye, integrated into their placement sites, increasing their visibility has its limits. Policymakers need to be mindful of any trade-offs between visibility and the effectiveness of service rendered. However, there are ways to increase public awareness of the program. Advertising is one. Placing "AmeriCorps Members at Work" signs outside schools where they tutor—and anywhere else—could increase its visibility. So could increasing AmeriCorps's size. The CCC was not well known simply because its work was visible. Not many people ever saw the physical results of the CCC's work, and far fewer ever saw CCC enrollees at work. But most people knew, or knew of, someone who had been in the program. This fact gave the public, located in towns and cities far from the forests where the CCC operated, an appreciation of the program that a smaller program would not have given them. As the number of AmeriCorps members grows, so will the number of people who know about them, the work that they do, and the program itself.

Of course increasing AmeriCorps's size would have other effects, both on the public (through the work accomplished) and on members themselves. AmeriCorps acts as a direct lesson for its participants on public policy for democracy, influencing their understanding of the relationship between citizens and their government and the meaning of citizenship; increasing the size of the program would spread these lessons more broadly. With national service, as long as its administrative capacity increases accordingly, bigger is in fact better.

The benefits of increased size raise the question of whether national service, with AmeriCorps as a major component, should grow large enough to accommodate all young Americans. It is safe to say that national service advocates in general believe that all who want to serve should have the opportunity, and all should be encouraged. But whether national service should be required is still contested. As chapter 2 explains, both sides marshal civic and political arguments in favor of and against a national service mandate; putting these arguments into historical context lends support to the opponents. The CCC came closest to universality yet insisted that it wanted only enrollees who were eager to participate. The success of both its work program and camp living environment depended in large measure on enrollees' voluntary cooperation. Even without a residential component, a mandatory program today would be hard-pressed to inspire good work from the disgruntled, even if they made up just a small percentage of those serving. A small percentage of a large group is still a large number, certainly dwarfing the number of convicts sentenced to do community service, and unlike those who are sentenced, those forced to undertake such service would lack the threat of a jail term to encourage compliance. A sanction would have to be monetary, but this would allow opponents with means to buy their way out of the requirement while others could not. In sum, the challenges would be enormous—as would the costs. This book focuses solely on civic practice through national service, but many other types of civic efforts could also benefit from public dollars; investing so much in national service would leave little to nothing for these and other deserving programs.[22] Finally, politics is involved. It has taken AmeriCorps its entire history to develop significant, albeit often tenuous, support among conservatives and Republicans, support it needs to continue growing. If the possibility of creating a mandate enters the picture, the backing from conservatives and Republicans—and from many liberals and libertarians—is likely to disappear. Outside the context of a military draft (in which some are required to serve, and thus fairness might dictate that all should serve in some capacity), a concerted effort to mandate service is more likely to undermine the growth and institutionalization of AmeriCorps, and national service in general, than to encourage them.

The question remains as to how best to encourage national service participation and accommodate all comers. Beyond advocating that Congress fund AmeriCorps at levels sufficient to meet the Kennedy Serve America Act's enrollment goals—reaching 250,000 members a year—and then pressing for expansion beyond this, is there another way to institutionalize AmeriCorps's growth? A group of national service leaders has developed such a plan, one that would encourage participation and provide a new incentive for Congress to appropriate the necessary funds. They call it the National Service American Dream Account (NSADA).

The NSADA idea was developed by leaders from City Year (Michael Brown, AnnMaura Connelly, and City Year co-founder Alan Khazei); Teach for America (Wendy Kopp); the Points of Light Foundation (Michelle Nunn); the White House Office of National Service (former Director Gregg Petersmeyer); and the Corporation for National and Community Service (former executives Shirley Sagawa and Harris Wofford), who elaborated on it in their 2008 *American Interest* magazine article, "A Call to National Service." Their basic idea is that the federal government would place $5,000 into a tax-free investment account, similar to a Roth IRA or 529 education account, for each American child at birth. By the time the child turns 18, the account would have grown to $18,000, assuming a 7 percent rate of return; by age 28, to $33,000. The money could be used to pay for college, buy a home, start a business or nonprofit, or invest for retirement—component parts of the American Dream—but it could not be used at all until the beneficiary had spent a year in service. If, by age 28, an individual had not completed the service requirement, the account would be forfeited, with the proceeds used to fund accounts for new babies.

The benefits of this proposal are significant. First, it provides a much greater incentive for service than AmeriCorps does currently, at approximately the same cost per participant—about $5,000 for the AmeriCorps education award and for the NSADA account. Second, by funding the accounts from birth, it creates the expectation early on that children will serve and earn the investment, making their participation more likely. Third, by creating the account in children's names, it is likely to produce what social scientists refer to as "asset effects"—the finding that "holding assets promotes a sense of personal control and future orientation that elicits positive attitudes and behaviors."[23] Having money set aside for goals, such as college, reinforces the idea that the child can and should go to college and thus do what it takes to get into college. Fourth, by putting an investment account in their name, it leads children and their parents to expect that the service opportunities necessary to access the funds will exist; Congress will have an incentive to respond. The alternative, again given the individual account structure, would be to provide access unearned—a huge financial giveaway. Finally, although the first account earners would not be serving for at least 18 years, policymakers would have an incentive to ramp up national service during that time, providing an increasing number of Americans with service opportunities while building service infrastructure. As Michael Brown and his co-authors explain, "This 18-year period provides an opportunity: to test out methods, to build capacity intelligently and efficiently, and to adjust our methods as we learn. We can scale up deliberately."[24]

Although the benefits are substantial, so are the costs. Most are the same that come with any major expansion of national service, namely the expenses associated with member stipends and defraying the training and other administrative costs incurred by service placement sites. Even with the value of members' service outweighing these costs, the absolute sums of money required will be significant. If one million individuals—approximately one quarter of the number of Americans who turn 18 each year—served each year, these costs are estimated to be $14 billion annually.[25]

Other costs are more closely associated with the NSADA structure itself. As the authors note, although experience and research should give policymakers some idea of how many young adults would serve to earn their accounts each year, we would not know for certain, which to a fair degree would make funding of the program's operating expenses an open-ended commitment. Further, the account mechanism suffers from two criticisms typically levied against the idea of private Social Security accounts. One is that the account's value will be subject to the vagaries of the market. This could be problematic especially if Congress replaced other forms of college financial aid with the NSADA; after a market drop, families may not have the money they were counting on to pay for school. Second, the government would have to "double pay" for 18 years— funding newborns' accounts while at the same time paying the education awards of current servers. While the program would become more than self-sustaining after this point, with each forfeited account funding approximately six new accounts, the expenses up to that point again would be substantial.[26]

While the costs of the NSADA plan are high, the benefits would far outpace them. If AmeriCorps's average cost-benefit ratios were to hold in this much expanded program, the value of the work accomplished would continue to outweigh the program's cost. Beyond this, the proposal's account structure would create the benefits accrued from a citizenry better able to afford higher education, start a business, or fund retirement, while increasing the visibility of national service and the expectation that citizens will serve. Finally, by exponentially increasing the number of Americans engaged in service, the program would gain the political and civic benefits mentioned above. For national service advocates, it is an idea worthy of strong consideration and support.

Whether AmeriCorps expands or stays at its current size, policymakers must also focus on its effectiveness as public policy for democracy. Given widespread concerns over the state of civic engagement in the United States, especially among youth, the program's civic lessons deserve serious attention. By placing members' service work in its larger civic and political context, by more clearly connecting service to other aspects of citizenship, and by more clearly highlighting the role played by nonprofit organizations and especially government, AmeriCorps can better fulfill its potential as public policy for democracy.

Like the CCC, AmeriCorps has an explicit civic mission—to increase its members' ethic of civic responsibility—and accomplishes that mission through its overall policy design and specific citizenship curricula and programming. Also like the CCC, AmeriCorps has made concerted efforts on the curricula and programming side—albeit with limited results—and has paid insufficient attention to its overall policy design's civic potential, which may prove more effective. For civic learning to be central to AmeriCorps, its leaders should build on what is most central to AmeriCorps members' experience, namely their service. When members, for example those who serve as tutors, learn how their service complements other governmental and nongovernmental efforts to improve education; when they become familiar with the views of various education-policy stakeholders; and when they develop the skills to work with (or bypass) these stakeholders, they have learned important civic lessons. When AmeriCorps's trainers and other officials focus on teaching these lessons, they build members' civic knowledge, skills, and attitudes from multiple perspectives, from constitutional citizenship to critical citizenship to citizenship understood as public work.

Beyond placing members' service work in a broader civic and political context, AmeriCorps's leaders could even more clearly place service in the broader context of citizenship and its various perspectives. Serving is one aspect of citizenship, whether full time through national service or part-time volunteering. Voting and otherwise participating in electoral politics is another. Advocating for an issue or cause is another, as is building a career in public service, whether in the public, nonprofit, or business sector. Emphasizing the many ways that people can work to address public problems, and thus act as citizens, can help members think more clearly and expansively about how they act as citizens while they are serving in AmeriCorps, and how they might in the future.

One way AmeriCorps has communicated an explicit civic message through its policy design is by highlighting the large role played by nonprofit, community-based organizations. The lesson that citizenship is not only about government is important, especially given the extent to which much of the public holds government in low esteem. However, if AmeriCorps's policymakers and advocates want the program to help counter cynicism about government, they would also do well to more clearly identify the program with the government that created and funds it. To the extent that participants and the public see the program as valuable, it represents what government can do well and encourages the respect necessary to foster civic and political participation. Further, to the extent that participants want to see changes in the program—including its growth—they need to understand that because it is a government program their active engagement in the political process is the way to make changes happen.

At the same time, with respect to all of these recommendations, policymakers and advocates need to be mindful of the limits of fostering political participation, in particular through the program itself. While an argument can be made that if policymakers want to encourage AmeriCorps members to vote, for example, having them serve by registering others to vote makes a good deal of sense. The problem with this strategy is that although it has the potential to build national servers' support for politics, it also has the potential to undermine political support for national service. As I mentioned above, AmeriCorps has developed Republican support but could easily lose it. Many would be concerned about the potentially negative political impact of voter registration and advocacy projects on their interests and values. Given AmeriCorps's tumultuous congressional history, this is a risk the program cannot afford. Any effort to improve AmeriCorps as a civic program must, at the very least, not jeopardize the civic lessons it now accomplishes, by making the program's survival and growth less likely. Policymakers and supporters must be mindful of both the opportunities and limits of national service to act as public policy for democracy.

My goal in this work has been to explain the politics and civics of domestic civilian national service in the United States and to use this understanding to draw lessons for future policymaking. The Civilian Conservation Corps, VISTA, and AmeriCorps all provided young Americans with the opportunity to contribute to the country; how they did so had political and civic consequences in their times and across time. The history of domestic civilian national service suggests that the challenges of making it a civically powerful, well-known, strongly supported, and widely available opportunity for the nation's young people—and the nation as a whole—are significant. It also suggests that the potential is greater now than at any previous time to make the next eighty years of national service history even more compelling than the last.

Notes

Preface

1. David Adamany, "Introduction," in *The Semi-Sovereign People,* edited by by E. E. Schattschneider (New York: Holt, Rinehart and Winston, 1975), p. ix.

2. Ibid., p. x.

3. James W. Ceaser, *Liberal Democracy and Political Science* (Johns Hopkins University Press, 1990), p. 2; Harvey C. Mansfield, *America's Constitutional Soul* (Johns Hopkins University Press, 1990), p. 1; Raymond Seidelman quoted in Gabriel A. Almond, *A Discipline Divided: Schools and Sects in Political Science* (Newbury Park, Calif.: Sage Publications, 1990), p. 19.

4. Bernard Crick, *In Defence of Politics* (University of Chicago Press, 1972), p. 195.

Chapter 1

1. For ease of reading and in keeping with common usage in newspapers and policy circles, I will use *national service* as shorthand for *domestic civilian national service,* although it is important to note that this study focuses only on the latter, more limited, category.

2. For a full explanation of *public policy for democracy,* see Steven Rathgeb Smith and Helen Ingram, "Public Policy and Democracy," in *Public Policy for Democracy,* edited by Helen Ingram and Steven Rathgeb Smith (Brookings, 1993), pp. 1–18.

3. See, for example, Walter W. Powell and Paul J. DiMaggio, eds., *The New Institutionalism in Organizational Analysis* (University of Chicago Press, 1991).

4. For discussion of army enlistment and college attendance as institutions, see Ronald L. Jepperson, "Institutions, Institutional Effects, and Institutionalism," in *The New Institutionalism in Organizational Analysis,* edited by Powell and DiMaggio, pp. 143–63.

5. Paul Pierson, "Public Policies as Institutions," in *Rethinking Political Institutions: The Art of the State,* edited by Stephen Skowronek, Daniel Galvin, and Ian Shapiro (New York University Press, 2006), p. 116.

6. In this I differentiate *institutionalization* from *programmatic entrenchment*, whereby a program becomes highly resistant to change or elimination because of strong interest group support, high transition cost, or other factors but does not necessarily have a broad or deep impact on society, the public, or even large numbers of beneficiaries.

7. Smith and Ingram, "Public Policy and Democracy," p. 1.

8. See, for example, Robert D. Putnam, *Bowling Alone: The Collapse and Revival of American Community* (New York: Simon and Schuster, 2000), and National Commission on Civic Renewal, *A Nation of Spectators: How Civic Engagement Weakens America and What We Can Do about It* (University of Maryland, 1998).

9. See, for example, ServiceNation, "Strategies for Becoming a Nation of Service: Policy Blueprint" (www.bethechangeinc.org/servicenation/policy/policy_blueprint); Richard Stengel, Jeremy Caplan, and Kristina Dell, "A Time to Serve," *Time*, September 10, 2007, pp. 48–67; and William A. Galston, "The Case for Universal Service," in *The AmeriCorps Experiment and the Future of National Service*, edited by Will Marshall and Marc Porter Magee (Washington: Progressive Policy Institute, 2005), chap. 6.

10. Paul Pierson, "When Effect Becomes Cause: Policy Feedback and Political Change," *World Politics* 45, no. 4 (July 1993): 595–628.

11. Anne Larason Schneider and Helen Ingram, *Policy Design for Democracy* (University of Kansas Press, 1997).

12. Suzanne Mettler, "Bringing the State Back in to Civic Engagement: Policy Feedback Effects of the GI Bill for World War II Veterans," *American Political Science Review* 96, no. 2 (June 2002): 351–65.

13. Suzanne Mettler, *Soldiers to Citizens: The GI Bill and the Making of the Greatest Generation* (Oxford University Press, 2007).

14. Paul Pierson, "Increasing Returns, Path Dependence, and the Study of Politics," *American Political Science Review* 94, no. 2 (June 2000): 251–67.

15. Eric M. Patashnik, *Reforms at Risk: What Happens after Major Policy Changes Are Enacted* (Princeton University Press, 2008).

16. Schneider and Ingram, *Policy Design for Democracy*.

Chapter 2

1. For a description and analysis of civilian national service from a comparative perspective, see Amanda Moore McBride and Michael Sherraden, *Civic Service Worldwide: Impacts and Inquiry* (New York: M.E. Sharpe, 2006), and Donald J. Eberly and Michael Sherraden, *The Moral Equivalent of War? A Study of Non-Military Service in Nine Nations* (New York: Greenwood Press, 1990).

2. Anne Larason Schneider and Helen Ingram, *Policy Design for Democracy* (University of Kansas Press, 1997).

3. Paul Pierson, "When Effect Becomes Cause: Policy Feedback and Political Change," *World Politics* 45, no. 4 (July 1993): 595–628; Suzanne Mettler, "Bringing the State Back in to Civic Engagement: Policy Feedback Effects of the GI Bill for World War II Veterans," *American Political Science Review* 96, no. 2 (June 2002): 351–65.

4. Eric M. Patashnik, *Reforms at Risk: What Happens after Major Policy Changes Are Enacted* (Princeton University Press, 2008).

5. Joel Westheimer and Joseph Kahne, "What Kind of Citizen? The Politics of Educating for Democracy," *American Educational Research Journal* 41, no. 2 (Summer 2004): 6.

6. See William A. Galston, *Liberal Purposes: Goods, Virtues, and Diversity in the Liberal State* (Cambridge University Press, 1991), p. 221, and Thomas A. Spragens Jr., *Civic Liberalism* (Lanham, Md.: Rowman & Littlefield, 1999), chap. 8. Galston uses the term *liberal state*, and Spragens *liberal regime* instead of *constitutional democracy*; however, the terms are close enough in meaning to serve the present purpose.

7. In addition, many rights and duties associated with citizenship—obeying the law, paying taxes, even registering for the draft—are not actually tied to legal citizenship. See Morris Janowitz, *The Reconstruction of Patriotism: Education for Civic Consciousness* (University of Chicago Press, 1983), pp. 4–5.

8. See, for example, Kay Lehman Schlozman and others, "Why Can't They Be Like We Were? Understanding the Generation Gap in Participation" (unpublished paper presented at Boston College, 1998); Cliff Zukin and others, *A New Engagement? Political Participation, Civic Life, and the Changing American Citizen* (Oxford University Press, 2006); and Harwood Group, *College Students Talk Politics* (Dayton, Ohio: Kettering Foundation, 1993).

9. Stephen Nathanson, *Patriotism, Morality, and Peace* (Lanham, Md.: Rowman & Littlefield, 1993), p. 38.

10. See, for example, ibid., and Joshua Cohen, ed., *For Love of Country: Debating the Limits of Patriotism* (Boston: Beacon Press, 1996).

11. Hilary Putnam, "Must We Choose between Patriotism and Universal Reason?" in *For Love of Country*, edited by Cohen, pp. 91–97.

12. Martha C. Nussbaum, "Patriotism and Cosmopolitanism," in *For Love of Country*, edited by Cohen, pp. 2–20.

13. Cohen, *For Love of Country*.

14. Charles C. Moskos, *A Call to Civic Service* (New York: Free Press, 1988), p. 14. Military service in the United States has had a long history of connection to state governments, but in times of war, state-based soldiers fought for the nation.

15. This is the author's estimate based on number of active duty personnel, National Guard and Reserve forces, veterans under age 65, and U.S. adult population under age 65.

16. See Emily Hoban Kirby, Karlo Barrios Marcelo, and Kei Kawashima-Ginsberg, "Volunteering and College Experience," CIRCLE Fact Sheet, August 2009, p. 2, and Mark Hugo Lopez and others, *The 2006 Civic and Political Health of the Nation: A Detailed Look at How Youth Participate in Politics and Communities* (College Park, Md.: CIRCLE, 2006), p. 10.

17. See Robert N. Bellah and others, *Habits of the Heart: Individualism and Commitment in American Life* (New York: Perennial Library, 1986).

18. Benjamin R. Barber, *Strong Democracy: Participatory Politics for a New Age* (University of California Press, 1984).

19. Harry C. Boyte, "Community Service and Civic Education," *Phi Delta Kappan* 72 (1991): 765–67; Westheimer and Kahne, "What Kind of Citizen?" 6.

20. Paul Rogat Loeb, *Generation at the Crossroads: Apathy and Action on the American Campus* (Rutgers University Press, 1994), p. 231.

21. See Judith N. Shklar, *American Citizenship: The Quest for Inclusion* (Harvard University Press, 1991), and Spragens, *Civic Liberalism*.

22. Harry C. Boyte and James Farr, "The Work of Citizenship and the Problem of Service Learning," in *Experiencing Citizenship: Concepts and Models for Service-Learning in*

Political Science, edited by Richard M. Battistoni and William E. Hudson (Washington: American Association for Higher Education, 1997), pp. 42–43.

23. Harry C. Boyte, "Civic Education as a Craft, Not a Program," in *Education for Civic Engagement in Democracy*, edited by Sheilah Mann and John J. Patrick (ERIC Clearinghouse for Social Studies, 2000), p. 65.

24. Harry C. Boyte and Nancy N. Kari, *Building America: The Democratic Promise of Public Work* (Temple University Press, 1996), p. 122.

25. William F. Buckley Jr., *Gratitude: Reflections on What We Owe to Our Country* (New York: Random House, 1990), p.113.

26. Ibid., p. 20.

27. Benjamin R. Barber, *A Place for Us: How to Make Society Civil and Democracy Strong* (New York: Hill and Wang, 1998), p. 106.

28. Benjamin R. Barber, "Service, Citizenship, and Democracy: Civil Duty as an Entailment of Civil Right," in *National Service: Pro and Con*, edited by Williamson M. Evers (Stanford, Calif.: Hoover Institution Press, 1990), p. 36.

29. Boyte and Kari, *Building America*, p. 21.

30. Harry C. Boyte, Benjamin R. Barber, and Will Marshall, *Civic Declaration: A Call for a New Citizenship* (Dayton, Ohio: Kettering Foundation, 1994), p. 4.

31. Doug Bandow, "National Service Initiatives," in *National Service: Pro and Con*, edited by Evers, p. 10.

32. Michael Sherraden, "Civic Service: Issues, Outlook, Institution Building," CSD Perspective 01-18 (Washington University, Center for Social Development, October 2001), p. 7.

33. Theda Skocpol, "How Americans Became Civic," in *Civic Engagement in American Democracy*, edited by Skocpol and Morris P. Fiorina (Brookings, 1999), p. 33.

34. Buckley, *Gratitude*, p. 50.

35. Jameson W. Doig and Erwin C. Hargrove, *Leadership and Innovation: Entrepreneurs in Government* (Johns Hopkins University Press, 1990), p. 16.

36. Mickey Kaus, *The End of Equality* (New York: Basic Books, 1992), p. 81.

37. See Deborah Stone, *Policy Paradox and Political Reason* (New York: HarperCollins, 1988), p. 124.

38. Buckley, *Gratitude*, pp. 38–39.

39. Barber, *Place for Us*, p. 59.

40. Moskos, *Call to Civic Service*, p. 2.

41. Ibid., p. 146.

42. Barber, *Place for Us*, pp. 105–06.

43. Buckley, "National Debt, National Service," *New York Times*, October 18, 1990.

44. Richard Danzig and Peter Szanton, *National Service: What Would It Mean?* (Lexington, Mass.: Lexington Books, 1986), chap. 2.

45. Ibid., p. 17.

46. Bruce Chapman, "Politics and National Service: A Virus Attacks the Volunteer Sector," in *National Service: Pro and Con*, edited by Evers, p. 136.

47. Danzig and Szanton, *National Service: What Would It Mean?* p. 19.

48. John Beilenson, "Looking for Young People, Listening for Youth Voice," *Social Policy* 24, no. 1 (Fall 1993): 10–11.

49. M. Kent Jennings and Richard G. Niemi, *Generations and Politics* (Princeton University Press, 1981), p. 230, and Sidney Verba, Kay Lehman Schlozman, and Henry E. Brady, *Voice and Equality: Civic Voluntarism in American Politics* (Harvard University Press, 1995), p. 305.

50. See, for example, Zukin and others, *New Engagement?*

51. Verba, Schlozman, and Brady, *Voice and Equality*, p. 304.

52. Scott J. Peters, "A New Citizenship in the Making?" *Social Policy* 24, no. 1 (Fall 1993): 49.

53. Robert Gordon quoted in Steven Waldman, *The Bill: How Legislation Really Becomes Law: A Case Study of the National Service Bill* (New York: Penguin Books, 1995), p. 112.

54. Buckley, *Gratitude*, p. 33.

55. Peters, "A New New Citizenship in the Making?" p. 49.

56. Eric B. Gorham, *National Service, Citizenship, and Political Education* (State University of New York Press, 1992), p. 195.

57. Ibid., p. 182.

58. See, for example, Moskos, *Call to Civic Service*, p. 3, and Buckley, *Gratitude*, p. 113.

59. Robert D. Putnam, *Bowling Alone: The Collapse and Revival of American Community* (New York: Simon and Schuster, 2000), chap. 14.

60. Martin Anderson, "Comment: The Dirty Work Philosophy of National Service," in *National Service: Pro and Con*, edited by Evers, pp. 244 and 247; Gorham, *National Service, Citizenship, and Political Education*, p. 209.

61. William James, "The Moral Equivalent of War," in *Memories and Studies* (New York: Longmans, Green, and Co., 1912), p. 290.

62. Moskos, *Call to Civic Service*, p. 136.

63. Don Wycliff, "Comment," in *National Service: Pro and Con*, edited by Evers, p. 18.

64. Moskos, *Call to Civic Service*, p. 134.

65. Ibid., p. 162; Martin Anderson quoted in Bandow, "National Service Initiatives," p. 8.

66. Moskos, *Call to Civic Service*, p. 37.

67. Anderson, "Comment," p. 247.

68. Moskos, *Call to Civic Service*, p. 126.

69. For Buckley's view, see *Gratitude*, p. 69.

70. Benjamin R. Barber, "A Mandate for Liberty," in *Education for Democracy*, edited by Barber and Richard M. Battistoni (Dubuque, Iowa: Kendall/Hunt Publishing, 1993), p. 201.

71. Chapman, "Politics and National Service," p. 134.

72. Gorham, *National Service, Citizenship, and Political Education*, p. 37.

73. See Daniel Hajdo, "The Debate over America's Civilian National Service, AmeriCorps: Whither From Here?" in *Politics in Action: A Reader in American Government*, edited by Jose de la Cruz, Becky de la Cruz, and Andrew J. Dowdle (New York: McGraw-Hill, 2001), chap. 15.

74. Donald Eberly quoted in Gorham, *National Service, Citizenship, and Political Education*, p. 33.

75. Moskos, *Call to Civic Service*, p. 181.

Chapter 3

1. Franklin D. Roosevelt, Inaugural Address, March 4, 1933, in *The Public Papers and Addresses of Franklin D. Roosevelt*, vol. 2, edited by Samuel I. Rosenman (New York: Random House, 1938), pp. 12–13.

2. The president was inaugurated on March 4, 1933. He asked Congress to authorize creation of a "civilian conservation corps" on March 21, which Congress did on March 31 when it passed "An Act for the Relief of Unemployment through the Performance

of Useful Public Works and for Other Purposes," Public Law No. 5, 73 Cong. 1 sess. (Washington: Government Printing Office, 1933). So empowered, the president created the Emergency Conservation Work program by executive order on April 5. The first men were enrolled on April 7 and in camp on April 17. The full contingent was enrolled and encamped on July 1, 1933 (Emergency Conservation Work, *Two Years of Emergency Conservation Work: April 5, 1933–March 31, 1935* [Washington, 1935]).

3. Franklin D. Roosevelt, "Three Essentials for Unemployment Relief," March 21, 1933, in *Public Papers and Addresses*, vol. 2, p. 80.

4. The Department of Labor's role was limited to "junior enrollees" and was later taken over by the CCC office. Veterans were selected by the Veterans Administration, and Native Americans were selected and supervised by the Interior's Office of Indian Affairs.

5. Kenneth Holland and Frank Ernest Hill, *Youth in the CCC* (Washington: American Council on Education, 1942). With regard to specific policy elements, other nations' programs may have had influence as negative models. For example, unlike the British vocational training centers, the CCC required enrollees to work; unlike the German youth camps, the CCC did not demand enrollment and was not explicitly partisan. See Kenneth Holland, "Education in CCC and European Camps," Special Edition on Education in the Civilian Conservation Corps, *Phi Delta Kappan* XIX, no. 9 (May 1937): 317–22.

6. John A. Salmond, *Civilian Conservation Corps, 1933–1942: A New Deal Case Study* (Duke University Press, 1967), p. 7.

7. Holland and Hill, *Youth in the CCC*, p. 22.

8. Roosevelt, "Three Essentials," p. 81.

9. Holland and Hill, *Youth in the CCC*, p. 22.

10. Frank Ernest Hill, *The School in the Camps: The Educational Program of the Civilian Conservation Corps* (New York: American Association for Adult Education, 1935), p. 8. Regarding public support, see Michael Sherraden, "The Civilian Conservation Corps: Effectiveness of the Camps," Ph.D. dissertation, University of Michigan, 1979, p. 219.

11. William James, "The Moral Equivalent of War," in *Memories and Studies* (New York: Longmans, Green, and Co., 1912), p. 290.

12. Salmond, *Civilian Conservation Corps*, p. 6.

13. Ibid., p. 8.

14. On the CCC's various names, see Leslie A. Lacy, *The Soil Soldiers: The Civilian Conservation Corps in the Great Depression* (Radnor, Pa.: Chilton, 1976), and Perry H. Merrill, *Roosevelt's Forest Army: A History of the Civilian Conservation Corps* (Montepelier, Vt.: 1981).

15. John Jacob Saalberg, "Roosevelt, Fechner, and the CCC: A Study in Executive Leadership," Ph.D. dissertation, Cornell University, 1962, pp. 142–43.

16. Ibid., p. 144.

17. Quotation from Ray Hoyt, *We Can Take It: A Short History of the CCC* (New York: American Book Company, 1935), p. 115. Labor unions were soon placated and became solid backers (Salmond, *Civilian Conservation Corps*, pp. 201–02), while many liberals and pacifists never supported the CCC, because of Army involvement (Saalberg, "Roosevelt, Fechner, and the CCC," chap. 7). Their pressure was sufficient to keep officials sensitive to the issue but not strong enough to secure the Army's removal.

18. Robert Fechner, "Radio Address at the 13th Women's Patriotic Conference on National Defense," January 26, 1938. In Articles and Speeches, Box 6, CCC Division of Planning and Public Relations, National Archives Record Group 35.

19. A. C. Oliver Jr. and Harold M. Dudley, eds., *This New America: The Story of the C.C.C.* (New York: Longmans, Green and Co., 1937), p. ix; Frances Perkins quoted by Fechner in Hearings before the House Labor Committee, "To Make the Civilian Conservation Corps a Permanent Agency," April 14–15, 1937, on H.R. 6180, 75 Cong. 1 sess., Washington, p. 20.

20. James McEntee, *8th Anniversary Story Material*, April 1941. In Articles and Speeches, Box 18, CCC Division of Planning and Public Relations, National Archives Record Group 35.

21. Jack J. Preiss, *Camp William James* (Norwich, Vt.: Argo Books, 1978), p. 242.

22. American Federation of Labor President William Green, quoted in Salmond, *Civilian Conservation Corps*, p. 14.

23. Indeed, Holland and Hill—the leading American scholars of work camps of their time—labeled a number of European work camp programs "national service" but never once so labeled the CCC (Holland and Hill, *Youth in the CCC*, p. 19; Hill, *The School in the Camps*; Holland, "Education in CCC and European Camps").

24. Editor of *Today* Raymond Moley, quoted in Oliver and Dudley, *This New America*, p. 32.

25. For a complete first-person history of the experiment, see Preiss, *Camp William James*.

26. *New York Times*, February 9, 1941, and Representative Albert Engel (R-Mich.), quoted in Salmond, *Civilian Conservation Corps*, pp. 205 and 206.

Chapter 4

1. Anne Larason Schneider and Helen Ingram, *Policy Design for Democracy* (University of Kansas Press, 1997).

2. Franklin D. Roosevelt, "What We Have Been Doing and What We Plan to Do," May 7, 1933, in *The Public Papers and Addresses of Franklin D. Roosevelt*, vol. 2, edited by Samuel I. Rosenman (New York: Random House, 1938), p. 162; Emergency Conservation Work, *Two Years of Emergency Conservation Work: April 5, 1933–March 31, 1935* (Washington: 1935), p. 1.

3. Scott Leavitt, "The Social and Economic Implications of Conservation," Special Edition on Education in the Civilian Conservation Corps, *Phi Delta Kappan* (May 1937): 326.

4. Robert Fechner, "Radio Address on the CCC's 4th Anniversary," given over WMAL on the *Farm and Home Hour*, April 2, 1937. In Articles and Speeches, Box 7, CCC Division of Planning and Public Relations, National Archives Record Group 35.

5. Cook quoted in Ovid Butler, *Youth Rebuilds* (Washington: American Forestry Association, 1935), p. 33.

6. Franklin D. Roosevelt, "Greetings to the Civilian Conservation Corps," July 8, 1933, in *Public Papers and Addresses*, vol. 2, p. 271.

7. See, for example, Hearings before the House Labor Committee, "To Make the Civilian Conservation Corps a Permanent Agency," April 14–15, 1937, on H.R. 6180, 75 Cong. 1 sess., Washington, pp. 93–95, 98–99.

8. Paul E. Williams, "Community and Camp Work Together for Guidance and Adjustment," Special Edition on Education in the Civilian Conservation Corps, *Phi Delta Kappan* (May 1937): 334.

9. Fechner quoted in Civilian Conservation Corps, *The Annual Report of the Director of the Civilian Conservation Corps: Fiscal Year 1939* (Washington: Government Printing Office, 1939), p. 10.

10. Roosevelt, "Greetings to Civilian Conservation Corps," p. 271.

11. It also affected the debate on the type of enrollee to accept. Some believed that "selection should . . . be on the basis of fitness to do the work and ability to profit by it." See W. Frank Persons, "Letter to Robert Fechner, October 13, 1936." In Department of Agriculture, 1935–37 File, Box 5, Permanent CCC Legislation, Records Relating to Legislation, CCC Division of Selection, National Archives Record Group 35. Others believed it should "be for those boys who most need its benefits rather than for those who would contribute most to the accomplishment of the work projects, or be most easily supervised, or perhaps even for those who would gain most from the experience." See Fred Morrell, Talk to the Society of American Foresters, January 1936. Sent to Dean Snyder, March 27, 1936 (same archive as above).

12. Robert Fechner, "The Educational Contribution of the Civilian Conservation Corps," Special Edition on Education in the Civilian Conservation Corps, *Phi Delta Kappan* (May 1937): 307.

13. Perkins quoted in W. Frank Persons, "Human Resources and the Civilian Conservation Corps," Special Edition on Education in the Civilian Conservation Corps, *Phi Delta Kappan* (May 1937): 325.

14. See, for example, Hearings before the House Labor Committee, "To Make the Civilian Conservation Corps a Permanent Agency," 1937, pp. 93–95.

15. Quoted in Frank Ernest Hill, *The School in the Camps: The Educational Program of the Civilian Conservation Corps* (New York: American Association for Adult Education, 1935), p. 67.

16. Franklin D. Roosevelt, "A Recommendation for Legislation to Make the Civilian Conservation Corps a Permanent Agency," April 5, 1937, *Public Papers and Addresses,* vol. 6, edited by Samuel I. Rosenman (New York: Random House, 1941), p. 144.

17. Harry C. Boyte and Nancy N. Kari, *Building America: The Democratic Promise of Public Work* (Temple University Press, 1996), p. 106.

18. John A. Salmond, *Civilian Conservation Corps, 1933–1942: A New Deal Case Study* (Duke University Press, 1967), p. 216.

19. G. H. Gilbertson, "Rehearsal for Defense" Pamphlet (GPO, 1941), pp. 1 and 4. In Publications, Box 4, CCC Division of Planning and Public Relations, National Archives Record Group 35.

20. Salmond, *Civilian Conservation Corps,* p. 216.

21. Franklin D. Roosevelt, Inaugural Address, March 4, 1933, in *Public Papers and Addresses,* vol. 2), p. 13.

22. Franklin D. Roosevelt, "Three Essentials for Unemployment Relief," March 21, 1933, in *Public Papers and Addresses,* vol. 2, p. 81.

23. Salmond, *Civilian Conservation Corps,* p. 15.

24. Robert Fechner, "Radio Address on the Columbia Broadcasting System," May 6, 1933. In Articles and Speeches, Box 1, CCC Division of Planning and Public Relations, National Archives Record Group 35.

25. A. C. Oliver Jr. and Harold M. Dudley, eds., *This New America: The Story of the C.C.C.* (New York: Longmans, Green and Co., 1937), p. viii. It isn't clear how the authors

expected "the meeting of East and West" to "bring a new appreciation of democracy" or how they defined *democracy*. What the quotation shows, however, is that they believed that the CCC served a larger public purpose than simply conservation and relief.

26. Robert Fechner, "What the C.C.C. Means," in *This New America*, edited by Oliver and Dudley, p. 18.

27. American Institute of Public Opinion cited in Salmond, *Civilian Conservation Corps*, pp. 70 and 103.

28. Salmond, *Civilian Conservation Corps*, pp. 34–35.

29. Michael Sherraden, "The Civilian Conservation Corps: Effectiveness of the Camps." Ph.D. dissertation, University of Michigan, 1979, p. 219.

30. Ibid., pp. 218 and 221.

31. See, for example, Hearings before the House Labor Committee, "To Make the Civilian Conservation Corps a Permanent Agency," 1937, p. 37. A National Association of CCC Alumni was finally founded in 1977 (see www.naccca.org).

32. Civilian Conservation Corps, "Minutes of the Advisory Council to the Director," March 20, 1939. In Minutes of the Advisory Council to the Director, April 13, 1933–July 1, 1942, Box 1, General Records, National Archives Record Group 35, p. 5.

33. Theda Skocpol, *Diminished Democracy: From Membership to Management* (University of Oklahoma Press, 2004), p. 129.

34. Ibid., p. 131.

35. Salmond, *Civilian Conservation Corps*, pp. 42–43, 77.

36. Fechner was CCC director from its founding until his death in January 1940. He was succeeded by James McEntee, the CCC's assistant director, also from its founding. Like Fechner, McEntee came from the ranks of labor; he held the CCC directorship until the CCC's demise.

37. Ray Hoyt, *We Can Take It: A Short History of the CCC* (New York: American Book Company, 1935), p. 19.

38. John Jacob Saalberg, "Roosevelt, Fechner, and the CCC: A Study in Executive Leadership," Ph.D. dissertation, Cornell University, 1962, p. 28; Salmond, *Civilian Conservation Corps*, p. 28.

39. Salmond, *Civilian Conservation Corps*, p. 76.

40. Ibid., pp. 28–29.

41. Civilian Conservation Corps, "Minutes of the Advisory Council to the Director," January 13, 1939. In Minutes of the Advisory Council to the Director, April 13, 1933–July 1, 1942, Box 1, General Records, National Archives Record Group 35, p. 3.

42. Fechner quoted in Salmond, *Civilian Conservation Corps*, p. 28.

43. The contrast between the CCC and the Social Security Administration, in terms of the education and expertise of their staffs, the deference accorded to them by Congress, their development over time, and their ultimate fate, could not be more striking. See Martha Derthick, *Policymaking for Social Security* (Brookings, 1979).

44. Kenneth Holland and Frank Ernest Hill, *Youth in the CCC* (Washington: American Council on Education, 1942), p. 30.

45. Walsh quoted in Salmond, *Civilian Conservation Corps*, p. 20.

46. Daniel Carpenter, *The Forging of Bureaucratic Autonomy* (Princeton University Press, 2001).

47. Roosevelt, "Three Essentials," p. 81.

48. Franklin D. Roosevelt, "Annual Address to Congress," January 4, 1935, in *The Public Papers and Addresses of Franklin D. Roosevelt*, vol. 4, edited by Samuel I. Rosenman (New York: Random House, 1938), pp. 22–23.

49. Salmond, *Civilian Conservation Corps*, pp. 104–06.

50. Emergency Conservation Work, *Annual Report of the Director of Emergency Conservation Work: Fiscal Year Ending June 30, 1936* (GPO, 1936). The president set an enrollment goal of 600,000, but as discussed later, new regulations limited the applicant pool, and the quota went unfilled.

51. Salmond, *Civilian Conservation Corps*, pp. 58, 63, and 67.

52. Ibid., pp. 66–67.

53. Murphy quoted in Hearings before the House Labor Committee, "To Make the Civilian Conservation Corps a Permanent Agency," February 9, 23, and 24, 1939, on H.R. 2990, 76 Cong. 1 sess., Washington, p. 105.

54. On conservation, see McEntee quoted in ibid., p. 47. On youth unemployment, see Fechner quoted in ibid., p. 18.

55. Ibid., pp. 23, 25–26, and 48.

56. Ibid., p. 23.

57. Representative Richard Welch (R-Calif.), quoted in ibid., p. 27.

58. Eric M. Patashnik, *Reforms at Risk: What Happens after Major Policy Changes Are Enacted* (Princeton University Press, 2008).

59. Hugh H. Bennett, chief of the Soil Conservation Service, Department of Agriculture, quoted in Hearings before the House Labor Committee, "To Make the Civilian Conservation Corps a Permanent Agency," 1939, p. 82.

60. Representative Gerald Landis (R-Ind.), quoted in ibid., p. 20.

61. Salmond, *Civilian Conservation Corps*, pp. 151–57.

62. Hoyt, *We Can Take It*, p. 19.

63. See, for example, Emergency Conservation Work, *Annual Report of the Director of Emergency Conservation Work: Fiscal Year Ending June 30, 1936*, p. 1.

64. Charles P. Harper, *The Administration of the Civilian Conservation Corps* (Clarksburg, W.Va.: Clarksburg Publishing Co., 1939), p. 31. The CCC office was officially called the Office of Emergency Conservation Work from its founding until 1937, when Congress changed its name to the name of its program.

65. Fechner quoted in Hearings before the House Labor Committee, "To Make the Civilian Conservation Corps a Permanent Agency," 1939, p. 15.

66. Salmond, *Civilian Conservation Corps*, pp. 177–78.

67. Ibid., p. 178.

68. Charles C. Moskos, *A Call to Civic Service* (New York: Free Press, 1988), p. 2.

Chapter 5

1. Franklin D. Roosevelt, "Three Essentials for Unemployment Relief," March 21, 1933, in *The Public Papers and Addresses of Franklin D. Roosevelt*, vol. 2, edited by Samuel I. Rosenman (New York: Random House, 1938), pp. 80–81.

2. Ibid., p. 80.

3. Regarding environmental organizations, for example, the Wilderness Society was founded in 1935 and the National Wildlife Federation in 1936, while the Sierra Club and Audubon Society were growing in membership and influence.

4. Emergency Conservation Work, *Annual Report of the Director of Emergency Conservation Work: Fiscal Year Ending June 30, 1937* (Washington: Government Printing Office, 1937), pp. 8–9.

5. Emergency Conservation Work, *Two Years of Emergency Conservation Work: April 5, 1933–March 31, 1935* (Washington: 1935), p. 5.

6. Like the CCC, the WPA was not framed as a national service program at the time, but unlike the CCC, it never gained this label in retrospect. This is due to the fact that the WPA more closely mirrored normal employment: its work had been done previously in the normal economy; there was no set term of service; and pay was set at prevailing wages and varied according to workers' skill level.

7. The relative attention given to WPA projects that were novel, like the Post Office Art Project and the Federal Writers' Project, is the exception that proves the rule.

8. Michael Sherraden, "The Civilian Conservation Corps: Effectiveness of the Camps," Ph.D. dissertation, University of Michigan, 1979, p. 219.

9. Frank Ernest Hill, *The School in the Camps: The Educational Program of the Civilian Conservation Corps* (New York: American Association for Adult Education, 1935), p. 50.

10. C. H. Blanchard, "I Talk With My CCC Boys," Special Edition on Education in the Civilian Conservation Corps, *Phi Delta Kappan* (May 1937): 354.

11. Quoted in Donald Dale Jackson, "To the CCC: Thanks for the Memories and Monuments," *Smithsonian* 25, no. 9 (December 1994): 76.

12. Ray Hoyt, *We Can Take It: A Short History of the CCC* (New York: American Book Company, 1935), p. 118.

13. John Jacob Saalberg "Roosevelt, Fechner, and the CCC: A Study in Executive Leadership," Ph.D. dissertation, Cornell University, 1962, pp. 205–06.

14. Ibid., p. 206.

15. Robert Fechner, "The Educational Contribution of the Civilian Conservation Corps," Special Edition on Education in the Civilian Conservation Corps, *Phi Delta Kappan* (May 1937): 307.

16. Ibid., p. 307. Fechner does not explain what he means by "democratic."

17. Ibid., p. 305.

18. Robert Fechner, "Statement before the U.S. Senate Special Committee to Investigate Unemployment, March 15, 1938." In Publications, Box 5, CCC Division of Planning and Public Relations, National Archives Record Group 35.

19. Ibid.

20. Hill, *The School in the Camps*, p. 47; Kenneth Holland and Frank Ernest Hill, *Youth in the CCC* (Washington: American Council on Education, 1942), p. 150.

21. Scott Leavitt, "The Social and Economic Implications of Conservation," Special Edition on Education in the Civilian Conservation Corps, *Phi Delta Kappan* (May 1937): 326.

22. Holland and Hill, *Youth in the CCC*, p. 150; Leavitt, "The Social and Economic Implications of Conservation," p. 327.

23. Holland and Hill, *Youth in the CCC*, chap. 10.

24. Ibid., p. 151.

25. Ibid., p. 253.

26. Hill, *The School in the Camps*, p. 8.

27. Robert Fechner, "CCC Has Enough Work to Keep Busy for 50 Years," *Daily Sentinel* (Grand Junction, Colo.), August 13, 1939. Reprinted in *The Nation Appraises the CCC: April 1933–September 1939*. In Federal Security Agency, CCC, Office of the Director,

Publications 1933–42, Box 4, CCC Division of Planning and Public Relations, National Archives Record Group 35.

28. Ned Dearborn, "Educational Opportunity for Enrollee," Special Edition on Education in the Civilian Conservation Corps, *Phi Delta Kappan* (May 1937): 301.

29. Kidwell quoted in Ovid Butler, *Youth Rebuilds* (Washington: American Forestry Association, 1935), p. 73; James McEntee, Article on Education, December 14, 1936. In Articles and Speeches, Box 4, CCC Division of Planning and Public Relations, National Archives Record Group 35; Holland and Hill, *Youth in the CCC*, p. 211.

30. Jackson, "To the CCC: Thanks for the Memories and Monuments," 76.

31. Harry C. Boyte and Nancy N. Kari, *Building America: The Democratic Promise of Public Work* (Temple University Press, 1996), p. 29.

32. Holland and Hill, *Youth in the CCC*, p. 231.

33. Robert Fechner quoted in A. C. Oliver Jr. and Harold M. Dudley, eds., *This New America: The Story of the C.C.C.* (New York: Longmans, Green and Co., 1937), p. 28.

34. Howard W. Oxley, "Growth and Accomplishments of CCC Education," Special Edition on Education in the Civilian Conservation Corps, *Phi Delta Kappan* (May 1937): 316.

35. Holland and Hill's study of 419 enrollees showed that 47.5 percent had never belonged to an organized group and that 60.9 percent of rural enrollees had never belonged to one (*Youth in the CCC*, pp. 68 and 89; see also p. 205). On enrollees becoming "joiners," see Hoyt, *We Can Take It*, p. 86, and Robert D. Putnam, *Bowling Alone: The Collapse and Revival of American Community* (New York: Simon and Schuster, 2000).

36. Kay Lehman Schlozman and others, "Why Can't They Be Like We Were? Understanding the Generation Gap in Participation" (unpublished paper presented at Boston College, 1998); Putnam, *Bowling Alone*.

37. Joel E. Nystrom, "Informal Educational Activities," Special Edition on Education in the Civilian Conservation Corps, *Phi Delta Kappan* (May 1937): 349.

38. Hoyt, *We Can Take It*, p. 81.

39. Oxley, "Growth and Accomplishments," p. 316; Holland and Hill, *Youth in the CCC*, pp. 200–01; Hoyt, *We Can Take It*, p. 81.

40. Hill, *The School in the Camps*, p. 56; Holland and Hill, *Youth in the CCC*, p. 227.

41. Holland and Hill, *Youth in the CCC*, p. 223.

42. On conforming citizenship, see Holland and Hill, *Youth in the CCC*, chap. 14. Contemporary scholars Westheimer and Kahne would call this "personally responsible" citizenship; see "What Kind of Citizen? The Politics of Educating for Democracy," *American Eductional Research Journal* 41, no. 2 (Summer 2004). "If I Were an Enrollee," Captain John F. More quoted in Oliver and Dudley, eds., *This New America*, pp. 49–50.

43. Holland and Hill, *Youth in the CCC*, chap. 14.

44. James McEntee, "8th Anniversary Story Material," April 1941. In Articles and Speeches, Box 18, CCC Division of Planning and Public Relations, National Archives Record Group 35.

45. Holland and Hill, *Youth in the CCC*, p. 230.

46. Saalberg, "Roosevelt, Fechner, and the CCC," pp. 191–95.

47. Holland and Hill, *Youth in the CCC*, p. 154. From 1933 to 1937 the CCC spent only $12 million on the education program in total; see Fechner, "The Educational Contribution of the Civilian Conservation Corps," p. 306.

48. Hill, *The School in the Camps*, p. 30.

49. Quoted in Hill, *The School in the Camps*, p. 32.

50. Fechner, "The Educational Contribution of the Civilian Conservation Corps," p. 306.

51. Emergency Conservation Work, *Annual Report 1937*, pp. 10–11; Saalberg, "Roosevelt, Fechner, and the CCC," p. 203.

52. Calculation based on data in Hill, *The School in the Camps*. He reports that 172,962 enrollees out of an approximate enrollment of 290,000 (p. 6) received instruction in June 1935 (p. 34).

53. Oxley, "Growth and Accomplishments," p. 313.

54. Holland and Hill, *Youth in the CCC*, p. 41.

55. Howard W. Oxley, "Trends in CCC Education," *School Life: Official Journal of the U.S. Office of Education*. Series of reprints from vol. 25, 1941. In Records Relating to the CCC Education Program, Box 6, Division of Selection, National Archives Record Group 35, p. 2; Saalberg, "Roosevelt, Fechner, and the CCC," p. 200.

56. Holland and Hill, *Youth in the CCC*, chap. 10.

57. 1939 *Camp Life Reader* quoted in Eric B. Gorham, *National Service, Citizenship, and Political Education* (State University of New York Press, 1992), pp. 138–39.

58. Ned Dearborn, *Once in a Lifetime: A Guide to the CCC Camp* (New York: Charles E. Merrill Co., 1936), p. 40. The CCC used this book but did not publish it.

59. Ibid., p. 162.

60. Holland and Hill, *Youth in the CCC*, p. 224.

61. Hill, *The School in the Camps*, p. 56.

62. Holland and Hill, *Youth in the CCC*, p. 224.

63. L. W. Rogers, "Training in Vocational Fundamentals," Special Edition on Education in the Civilian Conservation Corps, *Phi Delta Kappan* (May 1937): 355.

64. Fechner, "CCC Has Enough Work to Keep Busy for 50 Years."

65. M. Kent Jennings and Richard G. Niemi, *Generations and Politics* (Princeton University Press, 1981); Sidney Verba, Kay Lehman Schlozman, and Henry E. Brady, *Voice and Equality: Civic Voluntarism in American Politics* (Harvard University Press, 1995).

66. See Suzanne Mettler, "Bringing the State Back in to Civic Engagement: Policy Feedback Effects of the GI Bill for World War II Veterans," *American Political Science Review* 96, no. 2 (June 2002): 351–65, and Suzanne Mettler, *Soldiers to Citizens: The GI Bill and the Making of the Greatest Generation* (Oxford University Press, 2007).

67. Hill, *The School in the Camps*, p. 4.

68. Idaho's governor quoted in Hoyt, *We Can Take It*, p. 62; on a CCC for women, see Henry Goddard Leach, "Education for Patriotism," *Forum and Century* 93, no. 5 (May 1935): 258.

69. Olen Cole Jr., *The African-American Experience in the Civilian Conservation Corps* (University of Florida Press, 1999), p. 9. The worst year for unemployment during the Great Depression was 1933.

70. Emergency Conservation Work, *Annual Report of the Director of Emergency Conservation Work: Fiscal Year Ending June 30, 1936* (GPO, 1936), p. 23; Civilian Conservation Corps, *Annual Report of the Director of the Civilian Conservation Corps: Fiscal Year 1938* (GPO, 1938), p. 68.

71. Emergency Conservation Work, *Annual Report 1936*, p. 23.

72. Emergency Conservation Work, *Two Years*, section on Department of Labor, p. 2.

73. John A. Salmond, *Civilian Conservation Corps, 1933–1942: A New Deal Case Study* (Duke University Press, 1967), pp. 30 and 27.

74. Emergency Conservation Work, *Annual Report 1936*, p. 22; Salmond, *Civilian Conservation Corps*, p. 60.

75. Salmond, *Civilian Conservation Corps*, p. 63.

76. Ibid., p. 61.

77. Ibid., p. 63.

78. Hearings before the House Labor Committee, "To Make the Civilian Conservation Corps a Permanent Agency," April 14–15, 1937, on H.R. 6180, 75 Cong. 1 sess., Washington, p. 2.

79. W. Frank Persons, "Human Resources and the Civilian Conservation Corps," Special Edition on Education in the Civilian Conservation Corps, *Phi Delta Kappan* (May 1937): 324.

80. Ibid. More than half (52.2 percent) of enrollees came from rural areas or small towns; 43.8 percent of the total U.S. population lived in these areas.

81. Dearborn, *Once in a Lifetime*, pp. 203–11.

82. Robert Fechner, "Letter to FDR, October 24, 1936." In Articles and Speeches, Box 4, CCC Division of Planning and Public Relations, National Archives Record Group 35.

83. Holland and Hill, *Youth in the CCC*, p. 71.

84. Mettler, "Bringing the State Back in to Civic Engagement," and Joe Soss, "Lessons of Welfare: Policy Design, Political Learning, and Political Action," *American Political Science Review* 93, no. 2 (June 1999): 363–80.

85. Emergency Conservation Work, *Summary Report of the Director of Emergency Conservation Work on the Operations of Emergency Conservation Work, April 1933–June 30, 1935* (GPO, 1935), p. 47.

86. Cole, *The African-American Experience in the Civilian Conservation Corps*.

87. Ibid., p. 17. Data were not kept for Asian Americans or Hispanic Americans.

88. Salmond, *Civilian Conservation Corps*, pp. 90–91.

89. Cole, *The African-American Experience in the Civilian Conservation Corps*, pp. 14–15.

90. Ibid., p. 14.

91. Ibid., p. 20.

92. Ibid., p. 26. Exceptions were made only in those states with too few blacks to form an entire company.

93. Salmond, *Civilian Conservation Corps*, p. 92.

94. Ibid., pp. 92 and 95.

95. Cole, *The African-American Experience in the Civilian Conservation Corps*, p. 61.

96. Ibid., and Salmond, *Civilian Conservation Corps*, p. 101.

97. Salmond, *Civilian Conservation Corps*, p. 101. African American enrollees on average stayed five months longer than their white counterparts: fifteen months compared with ten.

98. Robert Fechner, "Radio Address on the Columbia Broadcasting System," May 6, 1933. In Articles and Speeches, Box 1, CCC Division of Planning and Public Relations, National Archives Record Group 35.

99. Holland and Hill, *Youth in the CCC*, p. 48.

100. Ibid., p. 55.

101. Jackson, "To the CCC: Thanks for the Memories and Monuments," p. 69.

102. Fechner, "Radio Address on the Columbia Broadcasting System."

103. The maximum allowed length of stay in the CCC varied over time, ranging from one to two years (Emergency Conservation Work, *Annual Report 1936*, p. 23).

104. Holland and Hill, *Youth in the CCC*, p. 127.

105. See, for example, Emergency Conservation Work, *Annual Report 1936*, p. 5, and Fechner, "CCC Has Enough Work to Keep Busy for 50 Years."

106. As a result, "unattached, homeless, transient men were not selected, because it was believed that the enterprise would be of more benefit to whole families than to single individuals" (Emergency Conservation Work, *Two Years*, section on Department of Labor, p. 2).

107. Estes quoted in Oliver and Dudley, eds., *This New America*, p. 63.

108. Ranney quoted in Butler, *Youth Rebuilds*, p. 118.

109. Quoted in Dearborn, *Once in a Lifetime*, p. 228.

110. War Department, "Regulations for Civilian Conservation Corps, Relief of Unemployment (1934)." In Publications, Box 5, CCC Division of Planning and Public Relations, National Archives Record Group 35, pp. 18–19. Docking of pay was limited to $3 per month.

111. Hoyt, *We Can Take It*, p. 114.

112. Fechner quoted in Hearings before the House Labor Committee, "To Make the Civilian Conservation Corps a Permanent Agency," 1937, p. 34.

113. Kantor quoted in Butler, *Youth Rebuilds*, pp. 67–68.

114. Canty quoted in Butler, *Youth Rebuilds*, p. 86.

115. Holland and Hill, *Youth in the CCC*, p. 47.

116. McMillan quoted in Butler, *Youth Rebuilds*, p. 161.

117. Morris Janowitz, *The Reconstruction of Patriotism: Education for Civic Consciousness* (University of Chicago Press, 1983), pp. 173–74.

118. Quoted in Butler, *Youth Rebuilds*, p. 72.

119. Holland and Hill, *Youth in the CCC*, pp. 236–37.

120. This view was not uncontested: the leader of Camp William James called it "a complete renunciation of every value for which the United States has ever stood" (Rosenstock-Huessy quoted in Jack J. Preiss, *Camp William James* (Norwich, Vt.: Argo Books, 1978), p. 222.

121. Enrollees were also given Election Day off to vote and were encouraged to do so.

122. Mettler, *Soldiers to Citizens*; Putnam, *Bowling Alone*.

123. This question of capable leadership has also affected other domestic civilian national service programs; it is a consistent, shared concern that works against institutionalization.

124. The Corps Network, "History" (www.nascc.org/index.php?option=com_content&view=article&id=85&Itemid=65).

Chapter 6

1. Eric B. Gorham, *National Service, Citizenship, and Political Education* (State University of New York Press, 1992), p. 50. The Corporation for National and Community Service, in its 2008 retrospective evaluation of VISTA, concurs, noting that "civic engagement of VISTA members was not an explicit part of the purpose of VISTA until it joined AmeriCorps" (Corporation for National and Community Service, Office of Research and Policy Development, *Improving Lives and Communities: Perspectives on 40 Years of VISTA Service* [Washington, 2008], p. 31).

2. Gorham, *National Service, Citizenship, and Political Education*, p. 140.

3. Volunteers' stipends allowed them to live at the living standard of the poor. The end-of-service award was set at $50 per month of service and was later increased to $75 and finally $100 per month.

4. John F. Kennedy, "Special Message on Our Nation's Youth," February 14, 1963. In Legislative Files, Box 52, President's Office Files, Kennedy Presidential Library, Boston, Mass., p. 4.

5. Sargent Shriver, "Introduction," in *Warriors for the Poor: The Story of VISTA, Volunteers in Service to America*, by William H. Crook and Ross Thomas (New York: William Morrow and Co., 1969), p. 8.

6. President's Study Group on a National Service Program, "In Consideration of a National Service Corps (Some Initial Staff Observations)," November 15, 1962. In Robert F. Kennedy's Attorney General Files, 1960–1964, Box 41, Kennedy Presidential Library, Boston, Mass.

7. Daniel Patrick Moynihan, *Maximum Feasible Misunderstanding* (New York: Free Press, 1970), p. 72.

8. Padraic Kennedy quoted in Crook and Thomas, *Warriors for the Poor*, p. 48.

9. Moynihan, *Maximum Feasible Misunderstanding*, p. 73.

10. Crook and Thomas, *Warriors for the Poor*, pp. 76–77.

11. Senate Committee on Labor and Public Welfare, "Minority Report," excerpts from Committee Report 382. Reprinted in *Congressional Digest* 43, no. 1 (January 1964): 15; also see *Congressional Digest*, "Con" articles in this same volume.

12. President's Study Group on a National Service Program, "A Report to the President," January 14, 1963. In Robert F. Kennedy's Attorney General Files, 1960–1964, Box 41, Kennedy Presidential Library, Boston, Mass., p. 2.

13. Ibid., p. 2.

14. The size was limited because "a huge national program [was] neither practical nor consistent with American tradition." President's Study Group, "A Report to the President," pp. 2 and 3.

15. Peter Marris and Martin Rein, *Dilemmas of Social Reform* (Chicago: Aldine Publishing Co., 1973), chap. 1.

16. Moynihan, *Maximum Feasible Misunderstanding*, p. 79.

17. David Jacob Pass, "The Politics of VISTA in the War on Poverty: A Study of Ideological Conflict," Ph.D. dissertation, Columbia University, 1975, p. 30. Among others rejected were VISA (for its foreign connotation), Domestic Peace Corps (because of a prohibition in the Peace Corps Act), and Volunteers for America (because of a similarly named Salvation Army program). The challenge of simply naming the program demonstrates on a small scale the increasingly dense governmental and social environment in which VISTA had to operate, especially in comparison with the CCC.

18. Robert Taft Jr. (R-Ohio) quoted in Pass, "The Politics of VISTA in the War on Poverty," pp. 14–15.

19. Marvin Schwartz, *In Service to America: A History of VISTA in Arkansas 1965–1985* (University of Arkansas Press, 1988), p. 12.

20. On the draft-dodging charge, see, for example, Donald Rumsfeld quoted in Robert Sherrill, "De-escalator of the War on Poverty," *New York Times*, December 13, 1970.

21. For quotations, see William James, "The Moral Equivalent of War," in *Memories and Studies* (New York: Longmans, Green, and Co., 1912), p. 290.

22. See Robert McNamara, "Address to American Society of Newspaper Editors," *New York Times*, May 19, 1966, and Marion K. Sanders, "The Case for a National Service Corps," *New York Times*, August 7, 1966.

23. The National Service Secretariat was led by Donald Eberly, a key figure in the Peace Corps's creation and a tireless advocate for national service for over fifty years.

24. McNamara, "Address to American Society of Newspaper Editors."

25. Gallup Opinion Index, Report #44, February 1969. In History of VISTA Files, 1965–1972, Box 7, Records of ACTION, National Archives Record Group 362. This requirement for both men and women was favored by 44 percent.

26. This was twice what the nation annually allocated for the entire War on Poverty. Calculation based on figures in Sanders, "The Case for a National Service Corps."

27. Ibid., p. 73.

28. Donald J. Eberly, *National Service: A Report of a Conference* (New York: Russell Sage Foundation, 1968); Sanders, "The Case for a National Service Corps."

29. "The New Volunteer Agency," Peace Corps Plan, March 1971. In Records Relating to the Proposed Reorganization of ACTION, 1971, Box 1, Records of ACTION, National Archives Record Group 362, p. 13.

30. Brown quoted in "Senate Confirms Turner for C.I.A.," *New York Times*, February 24, 1977.

Chapter 7

1. David Jacob Pass, "The Politics of VISTA in the War on Poverty: A Study of Ideological Conflict," Ph.D. dissertation, Columbia University, 1975, p. xix.

2. President's Study Group on a National Service Program, "Facts on the Proposed National Service Program," April 5, 1963. In Robert F. Kennedy's Attorney General Files, 1960–1964, Box 41, Kennedy Presidential Library, Boston, Mass., p. 1.

3. Ibid.

4. President's Study Group on a National Service Program, "In Consideration of a National Service Corps (Some Initial Staff Observations)," November 15, 1962. In Robert F. Kennedy's Attorney General Files, 1960–1964, Box 41, Kennedy Presidential Library, Boston, Mass., p. 7.

5. President's Study Group, "Facts on the Proposed National Service Program," pp. 11–14.

6. Ibid., pp. 6–10.

7. See Michael Balzano Jr., "The Political and Social Ramifications of the VISTA Program: A Question of Means and Ends," Ph.D. dissertation, Georgetown University, 1971, p. 80.

8. William Anderson quoted in Balzano, "The Political and Social Ramifications of the VISTA Program," p. 86.

9. Frank J. Lausche (D-Ohio), excerpts from addresses and debate. Reprinted in *Congressional Digest* 43, no. 1 (January 1964): 23; Senate Committee on Labor and Public Welfare, "Minority Report," excerpts from Committee Report 382. Reprinted in *Congressional Digest* 43, no. 1 (January 1964): 15.

10. Balzano, "The Political and Social Ramifications of the VISTA Program," pp. 92–94.

11. Pass, "The Politics of VISTA in the War on Poverty," pp. 39–40.

12. Lyndon B. Johnson, "Remarks to Members of VISTA," December 12, 1964, *Public Papers of the Presidents of the United States*, edited by the Office of the Federal Register, National Archives and Records Administration Staff (Washington: Government Printing Office, 1965), vol. 2, p. 801.

13. Robert Kennedy quoted in Douglas Robinson, "Kennedy, at Rally Here, Urges All to Join in Fight on Poverty," *New York Times*, August 13, 1965, p. 13.

14. Joseph Califano quoted in Merle Miller, *Lyndon: An Oral Biography* (New York: G. P. Putnam's Sons, 1980), p. 364.

15. Daniel Patrick Moynihan, *Maximum Feasible Misunderstanding* (New York: Free Press, 1970), p. 143.

16. Califano quoted in Miller, *Lyndon: An Oral Biography*, p. 364.

17. Padraic Kennedy, "Memo to Bill Crook," February 6, 1968. In History of VISTA Files, 1965–1972, Box 1, Records of ACTION, National Archives Record Group 362.

18. Jerry Budin quoted in John Kifner, "Dismissed VISTA Volunteers Stay on in Newark," *New York Times*, February 23, 1966, p. 46.

19. Unnamed VISTA volunteer quoted in William H. Crook and Ross Thomas, *Warriors for the Poor: The Story of VISTA, Volunteers in Service to America* (New York: William Morrow and Co., 1969), p. 20.

20. Ibid.

21. Jack Goldberg quoted in Pass, "The Politics of VISTA in the War on Poverty," pp. 61–62.

22. John Herbers, "The Nine Lives of the Poverty Agency," *New York Times*, December 21, 1969.

23. Eve Edstrom, "VISTA Overtakes Peace Corps at Colleges," *Washington Post*, March 4, 1969. Also see Richard Nixon's first inaugural address.

24. See Balzano, "The Political and Social Ramifications of the VISTA Program."

25. Jack Schaffer, "Memo to C. R. Lane, Re: VISTA Volunteers' Conflict and Controversy," March 30, 1970. In Records Relating to the Proposed Reorganization of ACTION, 1971, Box 1, Records of ACTION, National Archives Record Group 362.

26. C. Robert Lane quoted in "Nixon Seeking a Softer Image for VISTA," *New York Times*, June 14, 1970, p. 73.

27. Donald Rumsfeld quoted in Robert Sherrill, "De-escalator of the War on Poverty," *New York Times*, December 13, 1970. Weathermen were members of the Weather Underground, a radical left group founded in 1969 that advocated the violent overthrow of the U.S. government and was responsible for a campaign of bombing government buildings and banks.

28. Rumsfeld quoted in Herbers, "The Nine Lives of the Poverty Agency."

29. John Iglehart, "OEO Directs VISTA Volunteers to Aim at Less 'Noise,' More Service," *National Journal* 2, no. 22 (May 30, 1970): 1143. The newly named "community planning" projects were to be reduced from 19 to 5 percent of VISTA's total.

30. Balzano quoted in ACTION, "A Prototype of Pre-service Orientation for Full-time ACTION Volunteers," 1975. In AmeriCorps*VISTA Library, Corporation for National and Community Service.

31. "U.S. Agency Sued by VISTA Workers," *New York Times*, January 16, 1974, p. 42.

32. Sam Brown quoted in ACTION, *VISTA's Fifteenth Anniversary Publication* (Washington: 1980), pp. 5–6.

33. ACTION, *ACTION Annual Report, 1977* (Washington: 1977), p. 46; ACTION, *VISTA: A Louder Voice for the Nation's Poor*, recruitment pamphlet, 1978. In AmeriCorps*VISTA Library, Corporation for National and Community Service.

34. ACTION, *VISTA: A Louder Voice for the Nation's Poor*, p. 2.

35. Padraic Kennedy, "Draft Memo to President Nixon," 1969. In History of VISTA Files, 1965–1972, Box 3, Records of ACTION, National Archives Record Group 362;

ACTION, *VISTA: A Louder Voice for the Nation's Poor*, p. 4; ACTION, *ACTION Annual Report, 1977*, p. 46.

36. ACTION, *VISTA: A Louder Voice for the Nation's Poor.*

37. Representative Robert H. Michel (R-Ill.) quoted in Karen DeWitt, "U.S. Action Agency Is Assailed; Its Chief Senses Political Attack," *New York Times*, December 30, 1978, p. 13.

38. ACTION Director Tom Pauken quoted in ACTION, *ACTION Annual Report, 1981* (Washington: 1981), p. 21.

39. Donald Lambro, *Fat City: How Washington Wastes Your Taxes* (South Bend, Ind.: Regenry/Gateway, 1980), p. 170.

40. ACTION, *ACTION Annual Report, 1981*, p. 21.

41. James H. Burnley quoted in Marjorie Hunter, "Washington Follow Up: Next-to-Last Director," *New York Times*, March 29, 1982.

42. ACTION, *ACTION Annual Report, 1982* (Washington: 1982), p. 3; ACTION, *ACTION Annual Report, 1986* (Washington: 1986), p. 2.

43. ACTION, *VISTA Twenty-Fifth Anniversary Issue* (Washington: 1990), pp. 2–3.

44. President's Study Group on a National Service Program, "A Report to the President," January 14, 1963. In Robert F. Kennedy's Attorney General Files, 1960–1964, Box 41, Kennedy Presidential Library, Boston, Mass., p. 2.

45. John F. Kennedy, "Special Message on Our Nation's Youth," February 14, 1963. In Legislative Files, Box 52, President's Office Files, Kennedy Presidential Library, Boston, Mass., p. 5.

46. Moynihan, *Maximum Feasible Misunderstanding*, p. 73.

47. Richard M. Nixon, "Message to the Congress Transmitting Reorganization Plan I of 1971 to Establish ACTION," March 24, 1971, *Public Papers of the Presidents of the United States*, edited by the Office of the Federal Register, National Archives and Records Administration Staff (GPO, 1972), p. 467.

48. "A Day with VISTA: Shock and Toll," *New York Times*, June 20, 1965, p. 51.

49. Mimi Mager quoted in Barbara Gamarekian, "Despite Plans for Its Demise, Agency Hangs On," *New York Times*, September 9, 1985, p. A20.

50. Crook and Thomas, *Warriors for the Poor*, p. 60, citing a Gallup poll.

51. Marvin Schwartz, *In Service to America: A History of VISTA in Arkansas 1965–1985* (University of Arkansas Press, 1988), p. 4.

52. Lane quoted in Iglehart, "OEO Directs VISTA Volunteers to Aim at Less 'Noise,' More Service."

53. Schaffer, "Memo to C. R. Lane, Re: VISTA Volunteers' Conflict and Controversy."

54. See Schwartz, *In Service to America*, pp. 113–56, and Crook and Thomas, *Warriors for the Poor*, pp. 113–14.

55. Judy Lewis quoted in Crook and Thomas, *Warriors for the Poor*, p. 50.

56. VISTA Supervisor Lou Vitale quoted in ACTION, *VISTA's Fifteenth Anniversary Issue*, p. 39.

57. Crook and Thomas, *Warriors for the Poor*, pp. 127–29; Peter Kihss, "Loans for VISTA Sought," *New York Times*, November 7, 1967, p. 1.

58. Crook and Thomas, *Warriors for the Poor*, p. 129.

59. Pass, "The Politics of VISTA in the War on Poverty," p. 232.

60. Mimi Mager, interview with author, Washington, October 2, 2003.

61. Noted in Iglehart, "OEO Directs VISTA Volunteers to Aim at Less 'Noise,' More Service."

62. Crook and Thomas, *Warriors for the Poor*, p. 134.

63. Padraic Kennedy, "Memo to William H. Crook," July 21, 1967. In History of VISTA Files, 1965–1972, Box 1, Records of ACTION, National Archives Record Group 362.

64. Iglehart, "OEO Directs VISTA Volunteers to Aim at Less 'Noise,' More Service."

65. See Schwartz, *In Service to America*, p. 315.

66. Crook and Thomas, *Warriors for the Poor*, p. 173.

67. R. Thomas Preston quoted in Crook and Thomas, *Warriors for the Poor*, p. 98.

68. VISTA trainer Howard Higman quoted in Balzano, "The Political and Social Ramifications of the VISTA Program," p. 197.

69. Schwartz, *In Service to America*, p. 53.

70. Two unnamed former VISTA volunteers quoted in Crook and Thomas, *Warriors for the Poor*, p. 20.

71. Diana London, telephone interview with author, 2003.

72. VISTA volunteer Christel Brellochs quoted in Schwartz, *In Service to America*, p. 204.

73. VISTA volunteer Kathy Lynch quoted in Schwartz, *In Service to America*, p. 376.

74. Pass, "The Politics of VISTA in the War on Poverty," p. 123; Schwartz, *In Service to America*, p. 204.

75. David Gottlieb and Carol Hancock Gold, *VISTA and Its Volunteers—1965–1969. Summary Report* (Pennsylvania State University, 1970), p. 2. These findings were certainly influenced by their temporal context; that these questions were asked only during this time period and not in later surveys further indicates their particularity and precludes tracking changes over time.

76. Richard Parsons, "Review of VISTA Special Projects," November 25, 1970. In Program Planning and Research File, History of VISTA Files, 1965–1972, Box 9, Records of ACTION, National Archives Record Group 362, p. 1.

77. Crook and Thomas, *Warriors for the Poor*, p. 181.

78. Memo of February 1, 1966. In "VISTAs for Peace" File, History of VISTA Files, 1965–1972, Box 7, Records of ACTION, National Archives Record Group 362.

79. C. Payne Lucas, "Memo to Joe Blatchford, Re: NVA," February 3, 1971. In Records Relating to the Proposed Reorganization of ACTION, 1971, Box 1, Records of ACTION, National Archives Record Group 362.

80. VISTA volunteer Vincent Valentino quoted in Pass, "The Politics of VISTA in the War on Poverty," p. 135.

81. Ibid., p. 145.

82. Lane quoted in ibid., p. 150.

83. Ibid., pp. 146–47.

84. Gamarekian, "Despite Plans for Its Demise, Agency Hangs On."

85. Jameson W. Doig and Erwin C. Hargrove, *Leadership and Innovation: Entrepreneurs in Government* (Johns Hopkins University Press, 1990); Daniel Carpenter, *The Forging of Bureaucratic Autonomy* (Princeton University Press, 2001).

86. Hedrick Smith, "New Peace Corps Faces Opposition," *New York Times*, December 26, 1962, p. 4.

87. Louise Hickman Lione, "VISTA Today: Less Noise, More Action?" *Philadelphia Inquirer*, August 9, 1972.

88. From June 1968 through October 1970.

89. Lane quoted in Pass, "The Politics of VISTA in the War on Poverty," p. 94.

90. Ibid.

91. Gamarekian, "Despite Plans for Its Demise, Agency Hangs On."

92. Constance E. Newman quoted in Lione, "VISTA Today: Less Noise, More Action?"

93. T. Zane Reeves, *The Politics of VISTA and the Peace Corps* (University of Alabama Press, 1988), p. 1.

94. On party affiliation, see Pass, "The Politics of VISTA in the War on Poverty," p. 95.

95. Ibid., p. 101.

96. Ibid., p. 100.

97. Ibid., pp. 135–36.

98. Reeves, *The Politics of VISTA and the Peace Corps*, p. 75.

99. Mager interview.

100. Crook and Thomas, *Warriors for the Poor*, p. 134; Pass, "The Politics of VISTA in the War on Poverty," p. 45. In 1966 VISTA's authorization was given its own title, Title VIII, in the Economic Opportunity Act.

101. Pass, "The Politics of VISTA in the War on Poverty," p. 45.

102. Steve Mittenthal quoted in Pass, ibid., p. 31. Shriver would go on to become one of VISTA's strongest supporters.

103. Padraic Kennedy, "Confidential Memo to Glenn Ferguson," April 7, 1966. In History of VISTA Files, 1965–1972, Box 1, Records of ACTION, National Archives Record Group 362.

104. Padraic Kennedy quoted in Pass, "The Politics of VISTA in the War on Poverty," p. 51.

105. Crook and Thomas, *Warriors for the Poor*, p. 47.

106. VISTA northeastern region director Ernest Russell quoted in Francis X. Cliner, "New Vista for VISTA: The Stress is on Results," *New York Times*, December 12, 1969, p. 57.

107. Director of VISTA's program division Dr. Willard Hoing quoted in Balzano, "The Political and Social Ramifications of the VISTA Program," p. 98. VISTA had contracts with forty-two different agencies by mid-1967 (Crook and Thomas, *Warriors for the Poor*, p. 68).

108. Padraic Kennedy quoted in Pass, "The Politics of VISTA in the War on Poverty," p. 51.

109. Padraic Kennedy, "Memo to Glenn W. Ferguson," July 22, 1966. In History of VISTA Files, 1965–1972, Box 1, Records of ACTION, National Archives Record Group 362.

110. Pass, "The Politics of VISTA in the War on Poverty," p. 50.

111. Padraic Kennedy, "Transition Papers," 1969. In History of VISTA Files, 1965–1972, Box 3, Records of ACTION, National Archives Record Group 362.

112. Appropriation Hearing, April 1968. In History of VISTA Files, 1965–1972, Box 4, Records of ACTION, National Archives Record Group 362; Pass, "The Politics of VISTA in the War on Poverty," p. 206.

113. Padraic Kennedy, "Memo to Bill Crook," June 19, 1967. In History of VISTA Files, 1965–1972, Box 1, Records of ACTION, National Archives Record Group 362.

114. Pass, "The Politics of VISTA in the War on Poverty," p. 205.

115. Crook and Thomas, *Warriors for the Poor*, p. 135.

116. Representative Daniel Flood (D-Pa.) quoted in Appropriation Hearing, April 1968; emphasis added.

117. See Pass, "The Politics of VISTA in the War on Poverty," pp. 203–05.

118. On Shriver, see ibid., p. 46.

119. Rumsfeld quoted in ibid., p. 88.

120. Pass, "The Politics of VISTA in the War on Poverty," pp. 88 and 91.

121. Ibid., p. 212–13.

122. All cites in this paragraph: ibid., pp. 230–39.

123. John Wilson quoted in ibid., p. 234.

124. Richard M. Nixon, "Remarks to a Student-Faculty Convocation at the University of Nebraska," January 14, 1971, *Public Papers of the Presidents of the United States*, p. 33.

125. "A Bold New Proposal," unsigned, undated. In Records Relating to the Proposed Reorganization of ACTION, 1971, Box 1, Records of ACTION, National Archives Record Group 362.

126. Pass, "The Politics of VISTA in the War on Poverty," p. 245.

127. Ibid., p. 244.

128. Ibid., p. 248.

129. Joseph Blatchford, "Draft Memo to the White House," undated. In Peace Corps File, History of VISTA Files, 1965–1972, Box 7, Records of ACTION, National Archives Record Group 362.

130. Jamie Heard, "Agency Report/Plan to Merge VISTA, Peace Corps, Other Volunteer Programs Nears Approval," *National Journal* 3 no. 20 (May 15, 1971): 1049; Pass, "The Politics of VISTA in the War on Poverty," p. 249.

131. "The New Volunteer Agency," Peace Corps Plan, March 1971. In Records Relating to the Proposed Reorganization of ACTION, 1971, Box 1, Records of ACTION, National Archives Record Group 362, pp. 2 and 3a–6.

132. Jack Rosenthal, "Nixon Envisages Abolition of VISTA in Merger Plan," *New York Times*, March 12, 1971, p. 1.

133. National VISTA Alliance, March 29, 1971, Newsletter. In Records Relating to the Proposed Reorganization of ACTION, 1971, Box 1, Records of ACTION, National Archives Record Group 362.

134. Pass, "The Politics of VISTA in the War on Poverty," pp. 281–82.

135. Ibid., pp. 273–74 and 282.

136. Ibid., p. 284.

137. Moynihan, *Maximum Feasible Misunderstanding*, p. xiii.

138. Reeves, *The Politics of VISTA and the Peace Corps*, p. 61.

139. As a pilot, UYA was funded from VISTA's budget; when permanent, it competed with VISTA for funds.

140. ACTION, *ACTION Annual Report, Fiscal Year 1975* (Washington: 1975), p. 18.

141. ACTION, *ACTION Annual Report, 1977*, p. 46; ACTION, *ACTION Annual Report, 1980* (Washington: 1980), p. 2.

142. ACTION, *ACTION Annual Report, 1980*, p. 1.

143. Ibid., p. 6; ACTION, *ACTION Annual Report, 1977*, p. 46.

144. Lambro, *Fat City: How Washington Wastes Your Taxes*, p. 170.

145. Brown quoted in DeWitt, "U.S. Action Agency Is Assailed."

146. Lambro, *Fat City: How Washington Wastes Your Taxes*, p. 170.

147. On ideology, Lambro, *Fat City: How Washington Wastes Your Taxes*, p. 170; on arrogance, quote from Reeves, *The Politics of VISTA and the Peace Corps*, p. 118.

148. Burnley quoted in Hunter, "Washington Follow Up: Next-to-Last Director."

149. Rumsfeld quoted in Pass, "The Politics of VISTA in the War on Poverty," p. 87.

150. Gamarekian, "Despite Plans for Its Demise, Agency Hangs On."

151. Mager interview; Reeves, *The Politics of VISTA and the Peace Corps*, pp. 125–27.

152. *Boston Globe* editorial quoted in Gaynor Richards Strickler, "VISTA: A Study in Organizational Survival," Ph.D. dissertation, Bryn Mawr College, 1994, p. 273.

153. Strickler, "VISTA: A Study in Organizational Survival," p. 275.

154. Ibid., p. 273.

155. Ibid., p. 307.

156. Ibid., pp. 272 and 287.

157. Mager interview.

158. Ibid.

159. Strickler, "VISTA: A Study in Organizational Survival," pp. 304–05.

160. Mager interview.

161. See Theda Skocpol, *Diminished Democracy: From Membership to Management* (University of Oklahoma Press, 2004).

162. Strickler, "VISTA: A Study in Organizational Survival," p. 308.

163. Mager interview.

164. Strickler, "VISTA: A Study in Organizational Survival," p. 279.

165. Ibid., p. 280.

166. Ibid., p. 280.

167. Ibid., pp. 282–83. Jeremiah Denton proposed $11.8 million, and Orrin Hatch levels of $15 million, $17 million, and $20 million for 1984–86.

168. Ibid., p. 285.

169. Ibid., p. 284.

170. Representative Alan Cranston (D-Calif.) quoted in Strickler, "VISTA: A Study in Organizational Survival," p. 285.

171. Charles Heatherley quoted in Reeves, *The Politics of VISTA and the Peace Corps*, p. 125.

172. Ibid., p. 124.

Chapter 8

1. William H. Crook and Ross Thomas, *Warriors for the Poor: The Story of VISTA, Volunteers in Service to America* (New York: William Morrow and Co., 1969), p. 17.

2. VISTA volunteer Rev. David Stephens quoted in Marvin Schwartz, *In Service to America: A History of VISTA in Arkansas 1965–1985* (University of Arkansas Press, 1988), p. 127.

3. Donald Rumsfeld quoted in John Iglehart, "OEO Directs VISTA Volunteers to Aim at Less 'Noise,' More Service," *National Journal*, vol. 2, no. 22 (May 30, 1970): 1144.

4. Padraic Kennedy, "Transition Papers," 1969. In History of VISTA Files, 1965–1972, Box 3, Records of ACTION, National Archives Record Group 362.

5. John Herbers, "Shriver Hails VISTA Project," *New York Times*, September 28, 1965.

6. Nan Robertson, "Tribe Wants Back 2 Girls It Ousted," *New York Times*, December 24, 1965, p. 40.

7. OEO analysis quoted in David Jacob Pass, "The Politics of VISTA in the War on Poverty: A Study of Ideological Conflict," Ph.D. dissertation, Columbia University, 1975, pp. 78–79.

8. Ibid., p. 79.

9. VISTA volunteer Judy Lewis quoted in Crook and Thomas, *Warriors for the Poor*, p. 50.

10. VISTA volunteer Robert Dresser quoted in ibid., p. 21.

11. Arkansas OEO Director Robert Whitfield quoted in Schwartz, *In Service to America*, p. 50.

12. Schwartz, *In Service to America*, p. 151.

13. Crook quoted in Pass, "The Politics of VISTA in the War on Poverty," p. 77.

14. Padraic Kennedy, "Memo to Bill Crook," January 31, 1967. In History of VISTA Files, 1965–1972, Box 1, Records of ACTION, National Archives Record Group 362.

15. Ibid.

16. Illustrated in Pass, "The Politics of VISTA in the War on Poverty," p. 78.

17. C. Payne Lucas, undated paper. In Records Relating to the Proposed Reorganization of ACTION, 1971, Box 1, Records of ACTION, National Archives Record Group 362.

18. Melvin E. Beetle, "VISTA Project Study: FY-1976, Step I Report," Office of Policy and Planning, Division of Evaluation, March 1977. In AmeriCorps*VISTA Library, Corporation for National and Community Service.

19. Ibid., pp. ii–iv.

20. Kenneth Oldfield, "The Early Years of VISTA: The Political Alteration of a Successful Public Policy," *Journal of Volunteer Administration* 7, no. 1 (Fall 1988): 14.

21. Donald Lambro, *Fat City: How Washington Wastes Your Taxes* (South Bend, Ind.: Regenry/Gateway, 1980), p. 170.

22. VISTA volunteer Frances Woods quoted in Schwartz, *In Service to America*, p. 231.

23. David Gottlieb and Carol Hancock Gold, *VISTA and Its Volunteers—1965–1969*. Summary Report (Pennsylvania State University, 1970), p. 3.

24. Schwartz, *In Service to America*, p. 54.

25. Ibid.

26. Louise Frazier, Keith Jamtgaard, and Jacalyn Kalin, "VISTA Volunteer-Sponsor Survey," Office of Policy and Planning, Division of Evaluation, October 1976. In AmeriCorps*VISTA Library, Corporation for National and Community Service, p. III-8.

27. Mimi Mager, interview with author, Washington, October 2, 2003.

28. VISTA, "Fiscal 1970: Budget Justification—VISTA," VISTA Briefing Manual, 1970. In History of VISTA Files, 1965–1972, Box 6, Records of ACTION, National Archives Record Group 362, p. 2.

29. Iglehart, "OEO Directs VISTA Volunteers to Aim at Less 'Noise,' More Service"; Office of Economic Opportunity, "VISTA," Pamphlet 5000-2, April 1971. In Pamphlets, Posters, Manual Sections, Instructions, and Fact Sheets of the OEO on the

VISTA Program, Box 1, Records of ACTION, National Archives Record Group 362, p. 43; ACTION, *ACTION Annual Report, Fiscal Year 1974* (Washington: 1974), p. 9; ACTION, *Volunteers in Service to America 1980 Activities and Outcome Survey Final Report*, ACTION Evaluation, 1980. AmeriCorps*VISTA Library, Corporation for National and Community Service, p. 6; ACTION, *ACTION Annual Report, 1982* (Washington: 1982), p. 16. In 1980 "nearly three-quarters" of volunteers "reported coming from the community or area served by their project," although only 61 percent were recruited by their local sponsoring agencies. Because of the increase in the percentage of volunteers serving locally but recruited by the national office, the report cited replaced the term "locally recruited volunteer" with "local volunteer," which included all volunteers serving in their home community (ACTION, *Volunteers in Service to America 1980 Activities and Outcome Survey*, p. 6). National recruitment was reintroduced under the George H. W. Bush administration (Corporation for National and Community Service, Office of Research and Policy Development, *Improving Lives and Communities: Perspectives on 40 Years of VISTA Service* [Washington, 2008], p. 8). In 1992, 81 percent of volunteers were "local" and 19 percent "national" (Development Associates Inc., *VISTA: An Evaluation Report on Volunteers in Service to America,* May 1993. In AmeriCorps*VISTA Library, Corporation for National and Community Service, p. 12).

30. T. Zane Reeves, *The Politics of VISTA and the Peace Corps* (University of Alabama Press, 1988), p. 16.

31. Schwartz, *In Service to America*, p. 282.

32. Ibid., p. 283.

33. Ibid., p. 286.

34. American Technical Assistance Corporation, "Community Volunteers: A New Direction for VISTA," December 1969. In History of VISTA Files, 1965–1972, Box 9, Records of ACTION, National Archives Record Group 362.

35. Ibid.

36. VISTA, "Summary: Major Trends," VISTA Briefing Binder, FY 1969. In History of VISTA Files, 1965–1972, Box 6, Records of ACTION, National Archives Record Group 362. The "team" approach also reduced the number of volunteers working alone. Although Kennedy's NSC proposal envisioned volunteers working in large groups—groups of thirty were mentioned—VISTA was "implemented mostly by solo Volunteers," according to Schwartz (*In Service to America*, p. 42). Nixon officials worked to increase the size of project groups to five to ten volunteers (and decrease those with more than twenty) to facilitate supervision and project effectiveness (Jack Schaffer, "Memo to C. R. Lane, Re: VISTA Volunteers' Conflict and Controversy," March 30, 1970. In Records Relating to the Proposed Reorganization of ACTION, 1971, Box 1, Records of ACTION, National Archives Record Group 362).

37. Office of Economic Opportunity, "VISTA," Pamphlet 5000-2; Schwartz, *In Service to America*, p. 283.

38. Pass, "The Politics of VISTA in the War on Poverty," p. 145.

39. Quoted in ACTION, *VISTA's Fifteenth Anniversary Publication* (Washington: 1980), p. 6.

40. ACTION, *ACTION Annual Report, 1982*, p. 16.

41. ACTION, *Volunteers in Service to America 1980 Activities and Outcome Survey*, pp. 11 and 19.

42. President's Study Group on a National Service Program, "In Consideration of a National Service Corps (Some Initial Staff Observations)," November 15, 1962. In Robert F. Kennedy's Attorney General Files, 1960–1964, Box 41, Kennedy Presidential Library, Boston, Mass., review section.

43. John F. Kennedy, "Special Message on Our Nation's Youth," February 14, 1963. In Legislative Files, Box 52, President's Office Files, Kennedy Presidential Library, Boston, Mass., pp. 4–5.

44. Ibid., p. 5.

45. Crook and Thomas, *Warriors for the Poor*, p. 16.

46. John Herbers, "The Nine Lives of the Poverty Agency," *New York Times*, December 21, 1969; Frazier, Jamtgaard, and Kalin, "VISTA Volunteer-Sponsor Survey," p. III-1.

47. Pass, "The Politics of VISTA in the War on Poverty," p. 53.

48. Based on calculations in ibid., p. 108, with data from the Gottlieb and Gold study.

49. Frazier, Jamtgaard, and Kalin, "VISTA Volunteer-Sponsor Survey," p. III-4.

50. Benjamin Welles, "VISTA Positions Draw the Skilled," *New York Times*, July 6, 1969, p. 32; ACTION, *Volunteers in Service to America 1980 Activities and Outcome Survey*, p. 7; ACTION, *ACTION Annual Report, 1987* (Washington: 1987), p. 18.

51. Quoted in Pass, "The Politics of VISTA in the War on Poverty," p. 72.

52. Ibid.; Iglehart, "OEO Directs VISTA Volunteers to Aim at Less 'Noise,' More Service."

53. Office of Economic Opportunity, "If You're Not Part of the Solution, You're Part of the Problem," Recruitment Pamphlet, August 1969. In Pamphlets, Posters, Manual Sections, Instructions, and Fact Sheets of the OEO on the VISTA Program, Box 1, Records of ACTION, National Archives Record Group 362.

54. Pass, "The Politics of VISTA in the War on Poverty," p. 108; ACTION, *ACTION Annual Report, 1977* (Washington: 1977), p. 47; Development Associates Inc., *VISTA: An Evaluation Report*, p. 12.

55. Frazier, Jamtgaard, and Kalin, "VISTA Volunteer-Sponsor Survey," p. III-1; ACTION, *Volunteers in Service to America 1980 Activities and Outcome Survey*, p. 10.

56. Pass, "The Politics of VISTA in the War on Poverty," p. 54.

57. Gottlieb and Gold, *VISTA and Its Volunteers*, p. 1.

58. Reeves, *The Politics of VISTA and the Peace Corps*, p. 16.

59. Pass, "The Politics of VISTA in the War on Poverty," p. 108.

60. Frazier, Jamtgaard, and Kalin, "VISTA Volunteer-Sponsor Survey," p. III-1; Development Associates Inc., *VISTA: An Evaluation Report*, p. 7. The racial and ethnic groups reported typically included white, black, American Indian, Asian, and Hispanic, with a multiracial category added in 1992.

61. Development Associates Inc., *VISTA: An Evaluation Report*, p. 10.

62. John F. Kennedy, "Special Message on Our Nation's Youth," p. 4.

63. Office of Economic Opportunity, "Make the Scene. Better," Pamphlet 210-2, December 1967. In Pamphlets, Posters, Manual Sections, Instructions, and Fact Sheets of the OEO on the VISTA Program, Box 1, Records of ACTION, National Archives Record Group 362.

64. Pass, "The Politics of VISTA in the War on Poverty," p. 54.

65. Ibid., p. 105; Iglehart, "OEO Directs VISTA Volunteers to Aim at Less 'Noise,' More Service."

66. Office of Economic Opportunity, "VISTA Serves," Pamphlet 4100-3, November 1970. In Pamphlets, Posters, Manual Sections, Instructions, and Fact Sheets of the OEO on the VISTA Program, Box 1, Records of ACTION, National Archives Record Group 362.

67. Iglehart, "OEO Directs VISTA Volunteers to Aim at Less 'Noise,' More Service."

68. Pass, "The Politics of VISTA in the War on Poverty," p. 73.

69. C. Payne Lucas, "Memo to Joe Blatchford, Re: NVA," February 3, 1971. In Records Relating to the Proposed Reorganization of ACTION, 1971, Box 1, Records of ACTION, National Archives Record Group 362.

70. Office of Economic Opportunity, *Annual Report FY 1969–1970* (Washington: 1970), p. 43.

71. Schwartz, *In Service to America*, p. 175.

72. Dr. Robbie Wolf quoted in ibid.

73. Lucas, "Memo to Joe Blatchford, Re: NVA."

74. VISTA, "Summary: Major Trends"; Eve Edstrom, "VISTA Overtakes Peace Corps at Colleges," *Washington Post*, March 4, 1969.

75. Lucas, "Memo to Joe Blatchford, Re: NVA."

76. ACTION, *ACTION Annual Report, 1977*, p. 45.

77. Crook and Thomas, *Warriors for the Poor*, p. 74.

78. Ibid., p. 64. Approximately 10 to 20 percent of trainees were screened out or voluntarily withdrew during training, with different training programs having higher or lower rates. See Welles, "VISTA Positions Draw the Skilled."

79. Crook and Thomas, *Warriors for the Poor*, p. 69.

80. Ibid., p. 68.

81. Ibid., pp. 69 and 64.

82. Richard Parsons, "Review of VISTA Special Projects," November 25, 1970. In Program Planning and Research File, History of VISTA Files, 1965–1972, Box 9, Records of ACTION, National Archives Record Group 362.

83. Crook and Thomas, *Warriors for the Poor*, p. 68.

84. Michael Balzano Jr., "The Political and Social Ramifications of the VISTA Program: A Question of Means and Ends," Ph.D. dissertation, Georgetown University, 1971.

85. This despite the fact that the University of Maryland lost its contract because of problems with the volunteers it trained even before Balzano began his study.

86. Balzano, "The Political and Social Ramifications of the VISTA Program," pp. 391–93.

87. Ibid., p. 402; Schaffer, "Memo to C. R. Lane, Re: VISTA Volunteers' Conflict and Controversy."

88. Schaffer, "Memo to C. R. Lane, Re: VISTA Volunteers' Conflict and Controversy."

89. Balzano, "The Political and Social Ramifications of the VISTA Program," p. 390.

90. Ibid., pp. 401–02; Schaffer, "Memo to C. R. Lane, Re: VISTA Volunteers' Conflict and Controversy."

91. Balzano, "The Political and Social Ramifications of the VISTA Program," p. 412.

92. Ibid., p. 417.

93. Reeves, *The Politics of VISTA and the Peace Corps*, p. 48, citing Gottlieb and Gold. The Gottlieb and Gold study (1970) apparently was not published in time for Balzano to include it in his thesis.

94. VISTA Volunteers' Conflict and Controversy Study quoted in Balzano, "The Political and Social Ramifications of the VISTA Program," p. 451. At the same time it was

being cited as a model, the University of Colorado lost its contract for training volunteers for administrative reasons that Balzano questions. In his opinion, the true reason for its termination was that its "goals and approaches to training [were] far too conservative for the majority of the staff members in the Washington office" (p. 414). It is possible that the national curriculum was spearheaded by supportive political appointees, while training contracts were determined by unsupportive civil servants.

95. Ibid., p. 450; Schaffer, "Memo to C. R. Lane, Re: VISTA Volunteers' Conflict and Controversy."

96. VISTA, *Core Curriculum for VISTA Training Centers*, Summer 1970. In AmeriCorps*VISTA Library, Corporation for National and Community Service, p. 15.

97. Ibid., p. 11.

98. Ibid., p. 2.

99. Ibid., p. 21.

100. VISTA, "Fiscal 1970: Budget Justification—VISTA."

101. Office of Economic Opportunity, *Annual Report FY 1969–1970*, p. 45.

102. Kevin Sullivan, "Memo to Sam Brown, et. al., Re: Congressional Testimony," February 6, 1980. In AmeriCorps*VISTA Library, Corporation for National and Community Service, p. 4.

103. ACTION, *ACTION Annual Report, 1980*, p. 2. I have been unable to find a copy of the 1979 curriculum. Further, I have found no data on whether or how the Reagan administration altered VISTA's training, although one expects that it revised it in keeping with its principles.

104. Domestic Volunteer Service Act of 1973, Public Law 93-113, October 1, 1973; Frazier, Jamtgaard, and Kalin, "VISTA Volunteer-Sponsor Survey," p. III-16.

105. ACTION, *Volunteers in Service to America 1980 Activities and Outcome Survey*, p. 17.

106. John F. Kennedy, "Special Message on Our Nation's Youth," p. 5.

107. Brown quoted in ACTION, *VISTA's Fifteenth Anniversary Publication*, p. 7.

108. VISTA volunteer Rev. David Stephens quoted in Schwartz, *In Service to America*, p. 154.

109. Padriac Kennedy, "Memo to Bill Crook," January 31, 1967. In History of VISTA Files, 1965–1972, Box 1, Records of ACTION, National Archives Record Group 362.

110. Office of Economic Opportunity, "Make the Scene. Better."

111. Gertrude Samuels, "VISTAs in Navajoland," *New York Times Magazine*, September 11, 1968, p. 25; see VISTA, *Core Curriculum for VISTA Training Centers*.

112. President's Study Group, "In Consideration of a National Service Corps (Some Initial Staff Observations)," review section, p. 2.

113. Office of Economic Opportunity, "Make the Scene. Better."

114. Gottlieb and Gold, *VISTA and Its Volunteers*, p. 4.

115. Schwartz, *In Service to America*, pp. 4–5.

116. Corporation for National and Community Service, Office of Research and Policy Development, *Improving Lives and Communities*, pp. 35–36.

117. President's Study Group on a National Service Program, "Facts on the Proposed National Service Program," April 5, 1963. Robert F. Kennedy's Attorney General Files, 1960–1964, Box 41, Kennedy Presidential Library, Boston, Mass., p. 1.

118. Schwartz, *In Service to America*, p. 447.

119. ACTION, *Volunteers in Service to America 1980 Activities and Outcome Survey*, p. 40; Development Associates Inc., *VISTA: An Evaluation Report*, p. 35.

120. Frazier, Jamtgaard, and Kalin, "VISTA Volunteer-Sponsor Survey," p. II-2.

121. Development Associates Inc., *VISTA: An Evaluation Report*, pp. 35–36.

122. Frazier, Jamtgaard, and Kalin, "VISTA Volunteer-Sponsor Survey," p. S2.

123. Crook and Thomas, *Warriors for the Poor*, p. 180.

124. Gottlieb and Gold, *VISTA and Its Volunteers*; Corporation for National and Community Service, Office of Research and Policy Development, *Improving Lives and Communities*, pp. 33–34.

125. Corporation for National and Community Service, ibid., p. 34.

126. Crook and Thomas, *Warriors for the Poor*, p. 181.

127. VISTA recruiter Joann Rose quoted in Schwartz, *In Service to America*, p. 447.

128. Gottlieb and Gold, *VISTA and Its Volunteers*, pp. 3 and 4.

129. Ibid., p. 3.

130. Unnamed Republican official quoted in Ben A. Franklin, "Life in VISTA Called Radicalizing," *New York Times*, May 24, 1971, p. 1.

131. See Ovid Butler, *Youth Rebuilds* (Washington: American Forestry Association, 1935), p. 72.

132. Crook and Thomas, *Warriors for the Poor*, p. 181.

133. Ibid., p. 182.

134. Leslie Lenkowsky, keynote address, 2002 Governor's Conference on Civic Engagement, Billings, Mont., October 27, 2002.

135. Noncitizens could, with approval, become VISTA volunteers and take an alternative oath of service (Domestic Volunteer Service Act of 1973).

136. On volunteers' views of VISTA's relationship to government, see Gottlieb and Gold, cited in Pass, "The Politics of VISTA in the War on Poverty," p. 123.

137. Office of Economic Opportunity, "VISTA: Questions and Answers," recruitment brochure, June 1971. In Pamphlets, Posters, Manual Sections, Instructions, and Fact Sheets of the OEO on the VISTA Program, Box 1, Records of ACTION, National Archives Record Group 362.

138. Crook and Thomas, *Warriors for the Poor*, p. 21.

139. Padraic Kennedy quoted in Welles, "VISTA Positions Draw the Skilled."

140. ACTION, *ACTION Annual Report, 1981*, p. 21.

141. Crook and Thomas, *Warriors for the Poor*, p. 18; Development Associates Inc., *VISTA: An Evaluation Report*, p. 37.

142. Rose quoted in Schwartz, *In Service to America*, p. 40.

143. Christel Brellochs quoted in Schwartz, *In Service to America*, p. 40.

144. Pass, "The Politics of VISTA in the War on Poverty," p. 132; Schaffer, "Memo to C. R. Lane, Re: VISTA Volunteers' Conflict and Controversy."

145. Frazier, Jamtgaard, and Kalin, "VISTA Volunteer-Sponsor Survey," pp. II-3–II-4.

146. Office of Economic Opportunity, "Volunteer Housing and Living Conditions," Instruction 4400-1, May 8, 1969. In Pamphlets, Posters, Manual Sections, Instructions, and Fact Sheets of the OEO on the VISTA Program, Box 1, Records of ACTION, National Archives Record Group 362.

147. Office of Economic Opportunity, "VISTA Handbook," April 1970. In Pamphlets, Posters, Manual Sections, Instructions, and Fact Sheets of the OEO on the VISTA

Program, Box 1, Records of ACTION, National Archives Record Group 362, p. 1. Food stamps were allowed.

148. Development Associates Inc., *VISTA: An Evaluation Report*, p. 4.

149. Quoted in Pass, "The Politics of VISTA in the War on Poverty," pp. 108–09.

150. VISTA stipends did not count as income in determining a family's eligibility for welfare, so children of low-income volunteers could be supported through AFDC.

151. Quoted in Pass, "The Politics of VISTA in the War on Poverty," p. 126.

152. Padraic Kennedy, "Memo to VISTA Staff," October 22, 1969. In History of VISTA Files, 1965–1972, Box 1, Records of ACTION, National Archives Record Group 362.

153. Francis X. Cliner, "New Vista for VISTA: The Stress is on Results," *New York Times*, December 12, 1969, p. 57.

154. Beetle, "VISTA Project Study: FY-1976, Step I Report," p. vi.

155. William Crook, "Memo to VISTA Regional Administrators," September 6, 1967. In History of VISTA Files, 1965–1972, Box 1, Records of ACTION, National Archives Record Group 362.

156. Office of Economic Opportunity, "Volunteer Housing and Living Conditions."

157. Padraic Kennedy, "Memo to Bill Crook," February 6, 1968. In History of VISTA Files, 1965–1972, Box 1, Records of ACTION, National Archives Record Group 362.

158. ACTION, *Volunteers in Service to America 1980 Activities and Outcome Survey*, p. 25. A 1977 survey found that 29 percent of volunteers worked less than forty hours per week. See Beetle, "VISTA Project Study: FY-1976, Step I Report," p. v.

159. Office of Economic Opportunity, "Political Guidelines," Instruction 4010-3, March 20, 1969. In Pamphlets, Posters, Manual Sections, Instructions, and Fact Sheets of the OEO on the VISTA Program, Box 1, Records of ACTION, National Archives Record Group 362.

160. Balzano, "The Political and Social Ramifications of the VISTA Program," p. 86.

161. Pass, "The Politics of VISTA in the War on Poverty," p. 176.

162. Gottlieb and Gold, *VISTA and Its Volunteers*, p. 4.

163. Office of Economic Opportunity, "Political Guidelines."

164. Ibid.

165. See Schwartz, *In Service to America*, p. 151.

166. Pass, "The Politics of VISTA in the War on Poverty," p. 132.

167. Rumsfeld quoted in Robert Sherrill, "De-escalator of the War on Poverty," *New York Times*, December 13, 1970.

168. In its 2008 survey, 18 percent of volunteers serving between 1965 and 1972 stated that a primary reason for enrolling in VISTA was that they "wanted to avoid the draft." See Corporation for National and Community Service, Office of Research and Policy Development, *Improving Lives and Communities*, p. 13.

169. VISTA, *Core Curriculum for VISTA Training Centers*, p. 16.

170. See Pass, "The Politics of VISTA in the War on Poverty," p. 108.

171. Frazier, Jamtgaard, and Kalin, "VISTA Volunteer-Sponsor Survey," p. III-10. "Inherent in this difference may [have been] the lower educational level and older mean age (37 years) of the LRVs leading to their possible view of the VISTA allowance as income. Conversely the younger (mean age 27), well-educated NRVs conceivably accept[ed] it as a temporary stipend with their sites on prospective higher income in the future" (ibid.).

172. Development Associates Inc., *VISTA: An Evaluation Report*, p. 36.

173. VISTA's end-of-service award was worth a maximum of $342 per month in 2010 dollars ($50 in 1965); the CCC's pay was worth a maximum of $500 per month in 2010 dollars ($30 in 1933). CCC enrollees' living expenses were provided, while VISTA volunteers' expenses were covered by their stipends.

174. Office of Economic Opportunity, "If You're Not Part of the Solution, You're Part of the Problem."

175. VISTA, *Core Curriculum for VISTA Training Centers*, p. 22.

176. ACTION Deputy Director Mary E. King and Senator Charles Percy (R-Ill.) quoted in ACTION, *VISTA's Fifteenth Anniversary Publication*, pp. 20 and 60.

Chapter 9

1. William J. Clinton, "Inaugural Address," January 20, 1993, *Public Papers of the Presidents of the United States*, edited by the Office of the Federal Register, National Archives and Records Administration Staff (Washington: Government Printing Office, 1994–2001), vol. 1, p. 2.

2. The National and Community Service Trust Act passed Congress on September 8, 1993, and was signed into law on September 21. The first AmeriCorps members were inaugurated on September 12, 1994.

3. From 1994 through 2009, the education award was $4,725 for every year of full-time service. With passage of the Edward M. Kennedy Serve America Act in 2009, the award was set at the maximum Pell Grant level and will increase as Pell Grants do.

4. Clinton, "Remarks on Signing the National and Community Service Trust Act of 1993," September 21, 1993, *Public Papers of the Presidents of the United States*, vol. 2, p. 1544.

5. Ibid.

6. Clinton, "Remarks on National Service at Rutgers University in New Brunswick," March 1, 1993, *Public Papers of the Presidents of the United States*, vol. 1, p. 226.

7. Clinton, "Remarks on the National Service Initiative at the University of New Orleans," April 30, 1993, *Public Papers of the Presidents of the United States*, vol. 1, p. 549.

8. John McCain, "Putting the 'National' in National Service," *Washington Monthly*, October 2001.

9. Clinton, "Remarks on the National Service Initiative at the University of New Orleans," p. 549.

10. McCain, "Putting the 'National' in National Service."

11. Nancy Ethiel, *National Service: Getting It Right*, Catigny Conference Series (Chicago: Robert R. McCormick Tribune Foundation, 1997), p. 15. In a 1995 survey conducted by George Gallup, 40 percent of those surveyed knew of the Civilian Conservation Corps; at that time, 24 percent had not heard or read anything about AmeriCorps (ibid.).

12. Clinton, "Remarks on National Service at Rutgers University in New Brunswick," p. 225.

13. Clinton in Marvin Schwartz, *In Service to America: A History of VISTA in Arkansas 1965–1985* (University of Arkansas Press, 1988), p. xiii.

14. Ibid., p. xiv.

15. Peter Frumkin and JoAnn Jastrzab propose such a merger in *Serving Country and Community: Who Benefits from National Service?* (Harvard University Press, 2010), pp. 230–31.

16. Steven Waldman, *The Bill: How Legislation Really Becomes Law: A Case Study of the National Service Bill* (New York: Penguin Books, 1995), p. 163.

17. William A. Galston, interview with author, College Park, Md., March 5, 2003.

18. William F. Buckley Jr., *Gratitude: Reflections on What We Owe to Our Country* (New York: Random House, 1990); Donald J. Eberly, *National Service: A Promise to Keep* (Rochester, N.Y.: John Alden Books, 1988); Eberly and Reuven Gal, *Service without Guns* (self-published at Lulu.com, 2006); Charles C. Moskos, *A Call to Civic Service* (New York: Free Press, 1988).

19. Nunn quoted in Williamson M. Evers, ed., *National Service: Pro and Con* (Stanford, Calif.: Hoover Institution Press, 1990), p. xvii; Robert D. Hershey Jr., "The Ideal of Service by Youth Is Revived," *New York Times*, September 14, 1989, p. A18.

20. See Will Marshall, *Citizenship and National Service: A Blueprint for Civic Enterprise* (Washington: Democratic Leadership Council, 1988), drawing specifically on Moskos, *A Call to Civic Service*.

21. Alan Khazei, *Big Citizenship: How Pragmatic Idealism Can Bring Out the Best in America* (Cambridge, Mass.: PublicAffairs, 2010), pp. 109–10.

22. By 2012 City Year had expanded to twenty-three sites across the United States and to sites in Johannesburg, South Africa, and London, England.

23. Suzanne Goldsmith, *A City Year* (New York: New Press, 1993); Khazei, *Big Citizenship*.

24. Khazei, *Big Citizenship*, pp. 117–20.

25. Ibid., p. 121; *Congressional Digest* 72, no. 10 (October 1993): 228.

26. *Congressional Digest* 72, no. 10: 228; Khazei, *Big Citizenship*, p. 122.

27. Waldman, *The Bill: How Legislation Really Becomes Law*, pp. 7 and 11.

28. Clinton quoted in Stephen Bates, *National Service: Getting Things Done?* Catigny Conference Series (Chicago: Robert R. McCormick Tribune Foundation, 1996) p. 26.

29. Bruce Chapman, "Politics and National Service: A Virus Attacks the Volunteer Sector," in *National Service: Pro and Con*, edited by Evers, p. 134.

30. Representative Robert H. Michel (R-Ill.), excerpts from House floor debate, July 13, 1993. Reprinted in *Congressional Digest* 72, no. 10 (October 1993): 237.

31. Eli J. Segal, "Testimony of Eli J. Segal, Chief Executive Officer of the Corporation for National and Community Service, before the House Appropriations Subcommittee on VA, HUD, and Independent Agencies," March 15, 1994. Federal Document Clearing House, 1994.

32. Harris Wofford, "Prepared Statement of Harris Wofford, Chief Executive Officer, before the Senate Committee on Appropriations, Subcommittee on VA, HUD, and Independent Agencies. Subject: FY2000 Appropriation for the Corporation for National Service," March 11, 1999. Federal News Service, 1999.

33. Moskos quoted in Ethiel, *National Service: Getting It Right*, p. 9.

34. Khazei quoted in Ethiel, *National Service: Getting It Right*, p. 155.

35. Marshall, *Citizenship and National Service: A Blueprint for Civic Enterprise*, chap. 3, p. 1.

36. Waldman, *The Bill: How Legislation Really Becomes Law*, p. 100.

37. Ethiel, *National Service: Getting It Right*, p. 28.

38. Representative Bill Goodling (R-Pa.), excerpts from House floor debate, July 13, 1993. Reprinted in *Congressional Digest* 72, no. 10 (October 1993): 241.

39. Representative Bob Stump (R-Ariz.), excerpts from House floor debate, July 13, 1993. Reprinted in *Congressional Digest* 72, no. 10 (October 1993): 249.

40. Wofford quoted in Ethiel, *National Service: Getting It Right*, p. 78.

41. Marshall, *Citizenship and National Service: A Blueprint for Civic Enterprise*, ch. 4, p. 1.

42. Moskos, *A Call to Civic Service*, p. 9.

43. Galston, testimony, *Voices for America: 100 Hours of National Service Testimony* (Washington, September 2, 2003) (www.saveamericorps.org/vfa.htm); Clinton, "Remarks on the National Service Initiative at the University of New Orleans," p. 548.

44. Michael Sherraden, "Civic Service: Issues, Outlook, Institution Building," CSD Perspective 01-18 (Washington University, Center for Social Development, October 2001), p. 5.

45. McCain, "Putting the 'National' in National Service."

46. Christian Bourge, "AmeriCorps Can Become National Service," UPI, July 3, 2002, citing a Progressive Policy Institute study.

47. Glenn Beck, *Glenn Beck Program*, Fox News, March 26, 2009 (www.youtube.com/watch?v=EAx4OnfdJaI).

Chapter 10

1. Steven Waldman, *The Bill: How Legislation Really Becomes Law: A Case Study of the National Service Bill* (New York: Penguin Books, 1995).

2. William J. Clinton, "Remarks on National Service at Rutgers University in New Brunswick," March 1, 1993, *Public Papers of the Presidents of the United States*, edited by the Office of the Federal Register, National Archives and Records Administration Staff (Washington: Government Printing Office, 1994–2001), vol. 1, p. 225.

3. Waldman, *The Bill: How Legislation Really Becomes Law*, p. 12.

4. Franklin D. Roosevelt, "What We Have Been Doing and What We Plan to Do," May 7, 1933, in *The Public Papers and Addresses of Franklin D. Roosevelt*, vol. 2, edited by Samuel I. Rosenman (New York: Random House, 1938), p. 162.

5. Waldman, *The Bill: How Legislation Really Becomes Law*, p. 130.

6. Ibid., p. 129.

7. Representative Dave McCurdy (D-Okla.), excerpts from House floor debate, July 13, 1993. Reprinted in *Congressional Digest*, 72, no. 10 (October 1993): 242.

8. Representative Richard K. Armey (R-Texas), excerpts from House floor debate, July 13, 1993. Reprinted in *Congressional Digest* 72, no. 10 (October 1993): 243.

9. National and Community Service Trust Act of 1993, Public Law 103-82 (H.R. 2010), September 21, 1993, p. 4.

10. William J. Clinton, "Remarks to AmeriCorps Volunteers in Dallas, Texas," April 7, 1995, *Public Papers of the Presidents of the United States*, vol. 2, p. 578; "Remarks on the National Service Initiative at the University of New Orleans," April 30, 1993, *Public Papers of the Presidents of the United States*, vol. 1, p. 548.

11. Robert D. Putnam, *Bowling Alone: The Collapse and Revival of American Community* (New York: Simon and Schuster, 2000).

12. Eli J. Segal, "Press Briefing by the President and CEO for the Corporation for National and Community Service," September 8, 1994. White House Office of the Press Secretary, p. 2.

13. Segal came up with the idea for "getting things done," unaware that Harold Ickes Sr., FDR's interior secretary and father of President Clinton's then chief of staff, had used the same language, complimenting CCC enrollees for "really getting things done" (Eli J. Segal, interview with author, Boston, Mass., June 27, 2003; Harold Ickes, "Radio Broadcast to the Men of the CCC," July 17, 1937. In Articles and Speeches, Box 1, CCC Division of Planning and Public Relations, National Archives Record Group 35).

14. Segal quoted in Waldman, *The Bill: How Legislation Really Becomes Law*, p. 103.

15. Sagawa quoted in Nancy Ethiel, *National Service: Getting It Right*, Catigny Conference Series (Chicago: Robert R. McCormick Tribune Foundation, 1997), p. 35.

16. Harris Wofford quoted in Senate Labor and Human Resources Committee, "Confirmation of Harris Wofford to Be CEO of the Corporation for National and Community Service," September 7, 1995. Federal News Service, 1995, p. 10.

17. Clinton, "Remarks to AmeriCorps Volunteers in Dallas, Texas," p. 579.

18. Harris Wofford, "Prepared Testimony of Harris Wofford, Chief Executive Officer, Regarding the Corporation for National Service before the Senate Committee on Labor and Human Resources," May 21, 1996. Federal News Service, 1996, pp. 2–3.

19. Michael Gerson quoted in Ethiel, *National Service: Getting It Right*, p. 137.

20. Joseph Morris quoted in Ethiel, *National Service: Getting It Right*, p. 93.

21. Wofford, "Prepared Testimony before the Senate Committee on Labor and Human Resources," p. 13.

22. Ibid.

23. Wofford quoted in Senate Labor and Human Resources Committee, "Confirmation of Harris Wofford to Be CEO of the Corporation for National and Community Service," p. 8.

24. Leslie Lenkowsky, "The Bush Administration's Civic Agenda and National Service," *Society* 40, no. 2 (January-February 2003), p. 9.

25. Ibid., p. 7.

26. John M. Bridgeland, Stephen Goldsmith, and Leslie Lenkowsky, "Service and the Bush Administration's Civic Agenda," in *United We Serve: National Service and the Future of Citizenship*, edited by E. J. Dionne Jr., Kayla Meltzer Drogosz, and Robert E. Litan (Brookings, 2003), p. 56.

27. Lenkowsky, "The Bush Administration's Civic Agenda and National Service," p. 11.

28. Bridgeland, Goldsmith, and Lenkowsky, "Service and the Bush Administration's Civic Agenda," pp. 56–57.

29. Corporation for National and Community Service, "National Service Agency Launches 3 New Initiatives to Enhance Citizenship," Press Release, September 17, 2002; Corporation for National and Community Service, "National Service Agency to Co-Sponsor White House Forum on American History, Civics, and Service," Press Release, April 30, 2003.

30. Bridgeland, Goldsmith, and Lenkowsky, "Service and the Bush Administration's Civic Agenda," p. 55.

31. Ibid.; Dana Milbank, "Bush Tour Will Promote National Service," *Washington Post*, March 4, 2002, p. A2.

32. Barack Obama, "A Call to Service," speech delivered in Mt. Vernon, Iowa, December 5, 2007.

33. Ibid.

34. Corporation for National and Community Service, Office of General Counsel, "The Edward M. Kennedy Serve America Act Summary," April 21, 2009.

35. Waldman, *The Bill: How Legislation Really Becomes Law*, p. 107.

36. Ibid., see pp. 111, 107, 117.

37. David Osbourne and Ted Gaebler, *Reinventing Government: How the Entrepreneurial Spirit Is Transforming the Public Sector* (New York: Plume, 1992).

38. Clinton, "Remarks on National Service at Rutgers University in New Brunswick," p. 227.

39. Armey, excerpts from House floor debate, July 13, 1993.

40. Clinton, "Remarks on National Service at Rutgers University in New Brunswick," p. 226.

41. Wofford quoted in Ethiel, *National Service: Getting It Right*, pp. 78–79.

42. Waldman, *The Bill: How Legislation Really Becomes Law*, p. 102.

43. Ibid.

44. Ibid., p. 103.

45. Robert Fechner, "Radio Address on the Columbia Broadcasting System," May 6, 1933. In Articles and Speeches, Box 1, CCC Division of Planning and Public Relations, National Archives Record Group 35.

46. Jeffrey Selingo, "AmeriCorps at 5 Years: A Success but Not in the Way Clinton Hoped," *Chronicle of Higher Education*, September 25, 1998, p. A38.

47. Ibid.

48. Ethiel, *National Service: Getting It Right*, pp. 15-16.

49. John McCain, "Putting the 'National' in National Service," *Washington Monthly*, October 2001.

50. Selingo, "AmeriCorps at 5 Years: A Success but Not in the Way Clinton Hoped," p. A38.

51. Ethiel, *National Service: Getting It Right*, p. 16. In addition, "Thirty-eight percent said they had a good impression of it, and 55 percent said they didn't have an impression one way or the other." AmeriCorps was described to the uninitiated respondents as "a program in which young people volunteer for a year of nonmilitary service. They are paid a minimum wage, and for each year of service they receive credits of $4,750 that can be applied to college or to vocational training. Twenty thousand young people participated this year [1995]."

52. Harris Wofford, "Letter to My Colleagues," Corporation for National and Community Service, January 19, 2001.

53. McCain, "Putting the 'National' in National Service."

54. Stephen Bates, *National Service: Getting Things Done?* Catigny Conference Series (Chicago: Robert R. McCormick Tribune Foundation, 1996), p. 30.

55. Suzanne Goldsmith Hirsch quoted in Ethiel, *National Service: Getting It Right*, p. 141.

56. Robert Gordon quoted in Ethiel, *National Service: Getting It Right*, pp. 49–50.

57. Harris Wofford and Steven Waldman, "AmeriCorps the Beautiful?" *Policy Review* 79 (September 1996), p. 29.

58. Leslie Lenkowsky and James L. Perry, "Reinventing Government: The Case of National Service," *Public Administration Review* 60, no. 4 (July 2000): 303.

59. David Broder, "A Service to the Country," *Washington Post*, October 7, 2001, p. B7.

60. Wofford quoted in Ethiel, *National Service: Getting It Right*, p. 100.

61. Clinton, "Remarks on National Service at Rutgers University in New Brunswick," p. 227.

62. Lenkowsky and Perry, "Reinventing Government: The Case of National Service," p. 303.

63. Ibid.

64. George W. Bush, "Executive Order 13331: National and Community Service Programs," February 27, 2004.

65. Howard Husock, "The AmeriCorps Budget Crisis of 2003: (A)," Kennedy School of Government Case Program, C15-04-1739.0 (Harvard University, 2004), p. 16.

66. McCain, "Putting the 'National' in National Service."

67. Adam Meyerson quoted in Ethiel, *National Service: Getting It Right*, p. 63.

68. The Rheedlen Center for Children and Families is now the Harlem Children's Zone.

69. Wofford quoted in Ethiel, *National Service: Getting It Right*, p. 101; for additional details, see Arianna Huffington, "AmeriCorps Comes under Dick Armey's Friendly Fire," AlterNet, February 11, 2002 (www.alternet.org/story/12388/).

70. McCain, "Putting the 'National' in National Service."

71. Pete Hoekstra, "Opening Statement," House Economic and Education Opportunities Subcommittee on Oversight and Investigations, National Service Oversight Hearing, October 17, 1995. Federal Document Clearing House, 1995.

72. Jon Van Til, "The Case of AmeriCorps: Conflict and Consensus in the Civil Society/Governance Relation," undated chapter outline (www.crab.rutgers.edu/~vantil/reports/AMERICORPS.HTML), p. 15.

73. Ibid.

74. Hoekstra, "Opening Statement."

75. Based on the author's review of testimony transcripts.

76. AmeriCorps Alums, "AmeriCorps Alums Policy Center" (www.americorpsalums.org/?page=TAPolicy Center).

77. Howard Husock, "The AmeriCorps Budget Crisis of 2003: (Sequel)," Kennedy School of Government Case Program, C15-04-1740.1 (Harvard University, 2004), p. 3.

78. Howard Husock, "The AmeriCorps Budget Crisis of 2003: (B)," Kennedy School of Government Case Program, C15-04-1740.0 (Harvard University, 2004), p. 6.

79. Alan Khazei, *Big Citizenship: How Pragmatic Idealism Can Bring Out the Best in America* (Cambridge, Mass.: PublicAffairs, 2010), pp. 154–56.

80. Ibid., p. 157.

81. Ibid., p. 161.

82. Lenkowsky quoted in Husock, "The AmeriCorps Budget Crisis of 2003: (Sequel)," p. 8.

83. Khazei, *Big Citizenship*, chap. 7.

84. Ibid., p. 201.

85. This included increasing the funds states would control and decreasing organizations' matching requirements. See Waldman, *The Bill: How Legislation Really Becomes Law*, pp. 115 and 117.

86. Ibid., p. 33.

87. Jodie Morse, "A Nice Guy Finishes—Well, Not Last," *National Journal* 29 no. 33 (August 16, 1997), p. 1647.

88. Waldman, *The Bill: How Legislation Really Becomes Law*, pp. 102–03.

89. Segal quoted in Morse, "A Nice Guy Finishes—Well, Not Last," p. 1647.

90. Waldman, *The Bill: How Legislation Really Becomes Law*, p. 104.

91. Segal's deputies, Shirley Sagawa and Jack Lew, deserve much credit for this.

92. Leslie Lenkowsky, interview with author, Chevy Chase, Md., September 4, 2003.

93. Santorum quoted in Sally Kalson, "You Sing, Rick; We're Busy Working," *Pittsburgh Post-Gazette*, October 17, 1994, p. C1.

94. Office of the Press Secretary, "President Names Harris Wofford as Chief Executive Officer and Eli Segal to the Board of the Corporation for National Service," July 18, 1995. Clinton Foundation Archives, Little Rock, Ark.

95. Wofford quoted in Senate Labor and Human Resources Committee, "Confirmation of Harris Wofford to Be CEO of the Corporation for National and Community Service," p. 7.

96. Ibid., pp. 36–37.

97. Ibid., p. 37.

98. Corporation for National and Community Service, "Bylaws," approved October 1996, p. 2.

99. Traditionally, outgoing presidents make one request of their successors. In 1993 President George H. W. Bush asked President Clinton to keep his Points of Light initiative going. In 2001 Clinton asked President George W. Bush to keep AmeriCorps going (Hillary Clinton quoted in Khazei, *Big Citizenship*, p. 164).

100. Lenkowsky interview.

101. Nick Bollman quoted in Ethiel, *National Service: Getting It Right*, p. 83.

102. Husock, "The AmeriCorps Budget Crisis of 2003: (A)."

103. CNCS CEOs who have served under President Obama (as of August 2012) are acting CEO Nicola Goren, Patrick Corvington (senior associate at the Annie E. Casey Foundation), and Wendy Spencer (appointed by Republican Governor Jeb Bush to head the Florida Governor's Commission on Volunteerism and by President George W. Bush to serve on the President's Council on Service and Civic Participation). Corvington's priorities included "strategically target resources toward addressing key national issues, better demonstrate impact, increase opportunities to serve, and embrace innovation" (Corporation for National and Community Service, "Corvington Addresses Staff, Outlines New Direction in First Days as CEO," Press Release, February 18, 2010). Similarly, Spencer's "strategies for strengthening national service and volunteering included empowering others, encouraging creativity, recognizing excellence, strengthening collaboration, ensuring accountability, and demonstrating impact" (Corporation for National and Community Service, "Wendy Spencer Takes Helm as CEO of Corporation for National and Community Service," Press Release, April 10, 2012).

104. See "Pro" articles, *Congressional Digest* 72, no. 10 (October 1993).

105. Quoted in Waldman, *The Bill: How Legislation Really Becomes Law*, p. 187.

106. Senator Nancy Kassebaum (R-Kan.) quoted in Waldman, *The Bill: How Legislation Really Becomes Law*, p. 182.

107. Senator Alfonse D'Amato (R-N.Y.) in ibid., p. 202.

108. See Waldman, *The Bill: How Legislation Really Becomes Law*, pp. 201 and 165.

109. Ibid., pp. 165 and 190.

110. Ibid., p. 167.

111. Ibid., pp. 167 and 207.

112. Ibid., pp. 227–28.

113. Ibid., p. 224.

114. Ibid., pp. 237–38.

115. Catherine S. Manegold, "Clinton's Favorite, AmeriCorps, Is Attacked by the Republicans," *New York Times*, March 31, 1995, p. A25.

116. Jerry Gray, "Senators Refuse to Save National Service Program," *New York Times*, September 27, 1995, p. A1; Gray, "House Cuts All Spending for Service Program," *New York Times*, June 27, 1996, p. B11; Tim Weiner, "GOP Tries to Fit Together Pieces of Spending Package," *New York Times*, September 10, 1999, p. A20; Hillary Rodham Clinton, "Talking It Over," October 4, 2000, Creators Syndicate Inc. (www.creators.com/opinion/hillary-clinton/talking-it-over-2000-10-04.html).

117. "House Passes Bills for Veterans and Housing," *New York Times*, September 17, 1997, p. B7.

118. John Gomperts quoted in Husock, "The AmeriCorps Budget Crisis of 2003: (A)," p. 12.

119. Ibid.

120. Lenkowsky and Perry, "Reinventing Government: The Case of National Service," p. 301.

121. Husock, "The AmeriCorps Budget Crisis of 2003: (A)," p. 13.

122. House Majority Leader Tom Delay (R-Texas) and others quoted in Husock, "The AmeriCorps Budget Crisis of 2003: (Sequel)," p. 9.

123. Manegold, "Clinton's Favorite, AmeriCorps, Is Attacked by the Republicans."

124. Grassley quoted in ibid.

125. Waldman, *The Bill: How Legislation Really Becomes Law*, p. 250.

126. Ibid.; David R. Sands, "Two Democrats Help Block Resurrection of Ameri-Corps," *Washington Times*, September 27, 1995, p. A3.

127. Grassley quoted in Manegold, "Clinton's Favorite, AmeriCorps, Is Attacked by the Republicans."

128. McCain, "Putting the 'National' in National Service."

129. Husock, "The AmeriCorps Budget Crisis of 2003: (B)," p. 6.

130. Corporation for National and Community Service, "President Bush Continues Support for National Service," Press Release, February 28, 2001.

131. Quoted in Juliet Eilperin, "Armey Blasts Bush's AmeriCorps Plan," *Washington Post*, February 6, 2002, p. A17.

132. Corporation for National and Community Service, "Bush Budget Continues and Expands National Service," Press Release, April 9, 2001.

133. Lenkowsky, e-mail correspondence with author, August 17, 2007.

134. Bush, "Executive Order 13331: National and Community Service Programs."

135. Corporation for National and Community Service, "AmeriCorps Applications Rise 50 Percent since President's State of the Union Address," Press Release, March 4, 2002.

136. Husock, "The AmeriCorps Budget Crisis of 2003: (B)," p. 3, quotes from pp. 4, 6.

137. Ibid., p. 9.

138. Ibid., p. 9; Husock, "The AmeriCorps Budget Crisis of 2003: (Sequel)," p. 2.

139. Husock, "The AmeriCorps Budget Crisis of 2003: (Sequel)," p. 7.

140. Ibid. In explaining the administration's decision, "Some speculated [this was] because [the administration] had promised the House leadership it would not seek additional funding after backing the supplemental appropriation for the National Service Trust in March."

141. Ibid., p. 8.

142. Corporation for National and Community Service, Office of General Counsel, "The Edward M. Kennedy Serve America Act Summary."

143. Corporation for National and Community Service, "American Recovery and Reinvestment Act of 2009, Agency Recovery Plan" (www.americorps.gov/pdf/09_0606_recovery_plan_cncs.pdf).

144. HR 1, passed on February 19, 2011, cut $60 billion from the FY11 budget, eliminating among other things the entire Corporation for National and Community Service and all of its programs (not just AmeriCorps). It was not passed by the Senate.

145. Author's calculation based on roll-call voting records: HR 1388 in 111 Cong. 1 sess. (national service bill) and HR 1 in 112 Cong. 1 sess. (House budget bill).

Chapter 11

1. Sagawa quoted in Steven Waldman, *The Bill: How Legislation Really Becomes Law: A Case Study of the National Service Bill* (New York: Penguin Books, 1995), p. 106.

2. Waldman, *The Bill: How Legislation Really Becomes Law*, pp. 104–05; quotes from pp. 115 and 118.

3. Sagawa quoted in Waldman, *The Bill: How Legislation Really Becomes Law*, pp. 103, 106.

4. All of the above: *Federal Register*, "Corporation for National and Community Service, Corporation Grant Programs and Support and Investment Activities," January 7, 1994, AmeriCorps Program Issues (I) (B) (1).

5. Stephen Bates quoted in Nancy Ethiel, *National Service: Getting It Right*, Catigny Conference Series (Chicago: Robert R. McCormick Tribune Foundation, 1997), p. 48.

6. *Federal Register*, "Corporation for National and Community Service, AmeriCorps Grant Regulations," July 9, 2002, Revised Sec. 2520.20 (b).

7. John M. Bridgeland, Stephen Goldsmith, and Leslie Lenkowsky, "Service and the Bush Administration's Civic Agenda," in *United We Serve: National Service and the Future of Citizenship*, edited by E. J. Dionne Jr., Kayla Meltzer Drogosz, and Robert E. Litan (Brookings, 2003), p. 56.

8. Ibid., pp. 56–57.

9. *Federal Register*, "Corporation for National and Community Service, Corporation Grant Programs and Support and Investment Activities," Sec. 2520.30. Also prohibited was work "performing religious activities" or "promoting or deterring union organizing" (ibid.). In 2009 abortion services and referrals were added (Corporation for National and Community Service, Office of General Counsel, "The Edward M. Kennedy Serve America Act Summary," April 21, 2009).

10. Jon Van Til quoted in Ethiel, *National Service: Getting It Right*, p. 115.

11. Anonymous program manager quoted in Ethiel, *National Service: Getting It Right*, p. 115.

12. Anonymous AmeriCorps member quoted in Ethiel, *National Service: Getting It Right*, p. 116.

13. Anonymous program manager quoted in Ethiel, *National Service: Getting It Right*, p. 115.

14. Harris Wofford, "Prepared Testimony of Harris Wofford, Chief Executive Officer, Regarding the Corporation for National Service Before the Senate Committee on Labor and Human Resources," Federal News Service, 1996, pp. 2–3; Leslie Lenkowsky, "Opening Plenary Remarks," National Conference on Community Volunteering and National Service, Salt Lake City, Utah, June 9, 2002.

15. Barack Obama, "A Call to Service," speech delivered in Mt. Vernon, Iowa, December 5, 2007.

16. Harris Wofford and Eli J. Segal, "Joint Testimony of Harris Wofford, CEO, and Eli Segal, Former CEO, of the Corporation for National Service before the Oversight and Investigations Subcommittee of the House Committee on Economic and Educational Opportunities," October 17, 1995. Federal Document Clearing House, 1995, pp. 2–3.

17. Aguirre International, *Making a Difference: Impact of AmeriCorps*State/National Direct on Members and Communities 1994–95 and 1995–96* (Washington: Corporation for National and Community Service, 1999), p. 36.

18. Ibid., p. 38.

19. Will Marshall and Marc Porter Magee, eds., *The AmeriCorps Experiment and the Future of National Service* (Washington: Progressive Policy Institute, 2005), p. 11.

20. Three to five community representatives were interviewed for each of sixty randomly selected projects. Interviewees included partner organization representatives, local officials and government employees, and project beneficiaries (Aguirre International, *Making a Difference*, appendix A).

21. Ibid., p. 84. Also see Ann Marie Thomson and James L. Perry, "Can AmeriCorps Build Communities?" *Nonprofit and Voluntary Sector Quarterly* 27, no. 4 (1998): 399–420.

22. Aguirre International, *Making a Difference*, p. 145. The study also found significant variation among the forty-four programs: 21 percent had a cost-benefit ratio above 2; 37 percent between 1 and 2; and 42 percent had ratios less than 1 (see p. 146 in *Making a Difference*).

23. Ibid., p. 145.

24. Marshall and Magee, *The AmeriCorps Experiment and the Future of National Service*, p. 19.

25. Abt Associates, *AmeriCorps Tutoring Outcomes Study* (Washington: Corporation for National and Community Service, 2001).

26. Harry P. Hatry, Elaine Morely, Martin Abravanel, and Martha Marshall, *Outcome Indicators and Outcome Management* (Washington: Urban Institute, 2002), p. i.

27. On critics, see, for example, Citizens against Government Waste, "AmeriCorps the Pitiful: A CAGW Special Report," Washington, 2000. On cost per member, see Aguirre International, *Making a Difference*, p. 145. As Waldman explains, some lawmakers then proceeded to "distort the distortion," as when Senator Rick Santorum complained that AmeriCorps members were "paid $30,000 a year" (Waldman, *The Bill: How Legislation Really Becomes Law*, p. 251).

28. Adam Herzog, "More Than a T-Shirt," in *Pass the Fire: Stories of Service* (Washington: Corporation for National and Community Service, 2005), p. 7.

29. Gary Walker quoted in Ethiel, *National Service: Getting It Right*, p. 42.

30. Along these same lines, one of Obama's rationales for creating issue-specific "corps" within AmeriCorps is "so that citizens see their efforts connected to a common purpose" (Obama, "A Call to Service").

31. Corporation for National and Community Service, *AmeriCorps' 1997 Annual Report to Congress* (Washington: 1997), pp. 9 and 15.

32. Abt Associates, *Assessment of Long-Term Impacts on Service Participants: A Profile of Members at Baseline* (Washington: Corporation for National and Community Service, 2001), p. 11; Corporation for National and Community Service, *AmeriCorps' 1997 Annual Report to Congress*, p. 15.

33. Eli J. Segal, "Press Briefing by the President and CEO for the Corporation for National and Community Service," September 8, 1994. White House Office of the Press Secretary, p. 2.

34. Milton quoted in Waldman, *The Bill: How Legislation Really Becomes Law*, p. 89.

35. Ibid., p. 92.

36. Ibid.

37. *Federal Register*, "Corporation for National and Community Service, Corporation Grant Programs and Support and Investment Activities," January 7, 1994, AmeriCorps Program Issues (I) (D) (2).

38. Corporation for National and Community Service, *AmeriCorps' 1997 Annual Report to Congress*, pp. 9, 15, and 25.

39. Macro International Inc., *Study of Race, Class, and Ethnicity in AmeriCorps Programs* (Washington: Corporation for National and Community Service, 1997), p. 5.

40. Abt Associates, *Serving Country and Community: A Longitudinal Study of Service in AmeriCorps, Early Findings* (Washington: Corporation for National and Community Service, 2004), p. K-3.

41. Macro International Inc., *Study of Race, Class, and Ethnicity in AmeriCorps Programs*, pp. 6, 55, and 58.

42. Other surveys have shown that significant numbers of Americans with incomes lower than $20,000 a year and higher than $150,000 a year self-identify as middle class. See, in particular, Pew Research Center, *Inside the Middle Class: Bad Times Hit the Good Life* (2008), p. 5.

43. State and National members were also older than their NCCC counterparts, so more likely to head their own, lower-income households and not live with more well-established parents.

44. Abt Associates, *Assessment of Long-Term Impacts on Service Participants*, pp. 11 and 14.

45. Clinton quoted in Waldman, *The Bill: How Legislation Really Becomes Law*, p. 6.

46. Abt Associates, *Assessment of Long-Term Impacts on Service Participants*, p. 15.

47. Sagawa quoted in Ethiel, *National Service: Getting It Right*, p. 38.

48. Suzanne Goldsmith Hirsch quoted in Ethiel, *National Service: Getting It Right*, p. 142.

49. Abt Associates, *Serving Country and Community*, pp. 20 and K-2.

50. Ibid., p. 21.

51. Eli J. Segal, "Testimony of Eli J. Segal, Chief Executive Officer of the Corporation for National and Community Service, before the House Appropriations Subcommittee

on VA, HUD, and Independent Agencies," March 15, 1994. Federal Document Clearing House, 1994, p. 12.

52. Fritz quoted in Corporation for National and Community Service, *Pass the Fire*, p. 8.

53. Cayce quoted in Waldman, *The Bill: How Legislation Really Becomes Law*, p. 253.

54. Emily Gantz McKay and others, "AmeriCorps Member Training Needs and Skills Assessment Form," in *Starting Strong: A Guide to Pre-Service Training* (Washington: Mosaica,1998), p. 167.

55. Abt Associates, *Serving Country and Community*, p. 21.

56. Ibid. As for how useful members found their training, the Abt researchers asked members how satisfied they were with regard to "participating in training, workshops, or educational programs." Fifty-one percent said that they were very satisfied and 31 percent were somewhat satisfied, with the unstated remainder (18 percent) presumably unsatisfied (see p. 30 in Abt Associates, *Serving Country and Community*).

57. Full disclosure: I was the principal writer for this curriculum.

58. Peter Govert and June Plecan, *A Facilitator's Guide for By the People* (Oak Park, Ill.: CHP International, 2001).

59. Constitutional Rights Foundation, *A Facilitator's Guide to Effective Citizenship through AmeriCorps* (Washington: Corporation for National and Community Service, 2001).

60. Constitutional Rights Foundation, *Citizenship Toolkit: Incorporating Citizenship into Your Member Development Plan*, undated (www.nationalserviceresources.org/citizenship-toolkit).

61. "Citizenship Requirements as Outlined in the 2003 AmeriCorps Guidelines," undated (www.nationalserviceresources.org/files/legacy/filemanager/download/ed_awards/Sect6-7.doc).

62. Constitutional Rights Foundation, *Citizenship Toolkit*, section 1 (www.nationalserviceresources.org/citizenship-toolkit-1).

63. Corporation for National and Community Service, "National Service Agency Launches 3 New Initiatives to Enhance Citizenship," Press Release, September 17, 2002.

64. Constitutional Rights Foundation, *Citizenship Toolkit*, section 3 (www.nationalserviceresources.org/citizenship-toolkit-3).

65. Elisa C. Diller, "Delivering Civic Engagement Training to National Service Programs" (Washington: Corporation for National and Community Service, 2001), p. 3; quote from p. 12.

66. Ibid., pp. 5 and 19.

67. Anonymous project director quoted in Jon Van Til, *Growing Civil Society* (Indiana University Press, 2000), p. 59.

68. Diller, "Delivering Civic Engagement Training to National Service Programs," p. 23.

69. William Strang and Adrienne von Glatz, "Evaluation of AmeriCorps Training Materials Implementation and Outcomes in AmeriCorps Programs," presentation to the International Conference on Civic Education Research, November 17, 2003. Prepared by WESTAT, pp. 5–6.

70. Other reasons offered included the fact that the survey measures were developed independently of the curricula and many members had already reached the scale ceilings at

the time of the pre-test, meaning that even if the curricula had an impact, it could not be measured (ibid., p. 11).

71. Ibid., p. 12

72. Diller, "Delivering Civic Engagement Training to National Service Programs," p. 11.

73. Aguirre International, *Making a Difference*; Abt Associates, *Serving Country and Community*; Abt Associates, *Still Serving: Measuring the Eight-Year Impact of AmeriCorps on Alumni* (Washington: Corporation for National and Community Service, 2008).

74. Aguirre International, *Making a Difference*, p. 97.

75. Ibid.

76. Ibid., p. 100.

77. Jon Van Til, "The Case of AmeriCorps: Conflict and Consensus in the Civil Society/Governance Relation," undated chapter outline (www.crab.rutgers.edu/~vantil/reports/AMERICORPS.HTML), p. 18.

78. Mandel quoted in Ethiel, *National Service: Getting It Right*, pp. 96–97.

79. Abt Associates, *Serving Country and Community*, p. 70; Abt Associates, *Still Serving*, pp. 11–12.

80. Abt Associates, *Serving Country and Community*, p. 40; Aguirre International, *Making a Difference*, p. 119.

81. Leslie Lenkowsky, "Statement by Leslie Lenkowsky, Chief Executive Officer, Corporation for National and Community Service, before the House Education and Workforce Committee, Select Education Subcommittee," April 1, 2003. Federal Document Clearing House, 2003.

82. Hirsch quoted in Ethiel, *National Service: Getting It Right*, pp. 139–40.

83. This may have resulted from different post-program survey timing (the last weeks of program participation for NCCC members versus several months after the program's end for most State and National members, giving the latter time to gain perspective (Abt Associates, *Serving Country and Community*, pp. 43–44); Abt Associates, *Still Serving*, pp. 16–32.

84. Abt Associates, *Assessment of Long-Term Impacts on Service Participants*, p. 10.

85. Van Til, *Growing Civil Society*, p. 53.

86. Anonymous quoted in ibid.

87. Abt Associates, *Serving Country and Community*, p. 45. Appreciation of cultural and ethnic diversity was defined as respondents' "opinion about the importance and desirability of relationships between people who do not share the same cultural and/or ethnic background" (ibid. p. 42).

88. Ibid., p. 45.

89. Abt Associates, *Still Serving*, p. 21.

90. Abt Associates, *Serving Country and Community*, p. 70; Abt Associates, *Still Serving*, p. 28.

91. Ibid., pp. 41–42, 45, and 70. Another study found that AmeriCorps increases the likelihood that a member who enters the program with a strong voting history but little other civic involvement will become more broadly civically engaged eight years later. See Andrea K. Finlay, Constance Flanagan, and Laura Wray-Lake, "The Impact of AmeriCorps on Voting," CIRCLE Fact Sheet, December 2011, p. 2.

92. Abt Associates, *Still Serving*, pp. 16–32.

93. Abt Associates, *Serving Country and Community*, pp. 42 and 70; Abt Associates, *Still Serving*, p. 33.

94. Abt Associates, *Serving Country and Community*, pp. 41 and 45; Abt Associates, *Still Serving*, pp. 24–27.

95. Finlay, Flanagan, and Wray-Lake, "The Impact of AmeriCorps on Voting," p. 2.

96. Abt Associates, *Serving Country and Community*, pp. 41 and 45; Abt Associates, *Still Serving*, pp. 24–27.

97. Wofford and Segal, "Joint Testimony of Harris Wofford, CEO, and Eli Segal, Former CEO, of the Corporation for National Service before the Oversight and Investigations Subcommittee of the House Committee on Economic and Educational Opportunities."

98. Segal quoted in Jeffrey Selingo, "AmeriCorps at 5 Years: A Success but Not in the Way Clinton Hoped," *Chronicle of Higher Education*, September 25, 1998.

99. Ibid.

100. Waldman, *The Bill: How Legislation Really Becomes Law*, p. 100.

101. Abt Associates, *Assessment of Long-Term Impacts on Service Participants*, p. 10; Abt Associates, *Serving Country and Community*, p. 37. Abt's follow-up survey in 2007 found that 66 percent of State and National and 57 percent of NCCC members stated that their AmeriCorps service helped them see the importance of education. Subgroup percentages within the State and National program were even higher: Hispanic Americans: 82 percent; African Americans: 72 percent; and members from disadvantaged circumstances: 74 percent (Abt Associates, *Still Serving*, p. 38).

102. Abt Associates, *Serving Country and Community*, p. 60; Corporation for National and Community Service, *Performance and Accountability Report: Fiscal Year 2004* (Washington: 2005), pp. A-29 and B-114.

103. Marshall and Magee, *The AmeriCorps Experiment and the Future of National Service*, p. 23. Data from the 1980s.

104. Wofford in Ethiel, *National Service: Getting It Right*, p. 91. The federal government also pays a small administrative fee to the sponsoring organizations.

105. Leslie Lenkowsky, "Principles and Reforms for a Citizen Service Act," Opening Statement of Leslie Lenkowsky, Chief Executive Officer, Corporation for National and Community Service, before the Senate Health, Education, Labor and Pensions Committee. April 9, 2002.

106. Corporation for National and Community Service, Office of General Counsel, "The Edward M. Kennedy Serve America Act Summary."

107. Abt Associates, *Still Serving*, p. 38.

108. Corporation for National and Community Service, *Performance and Accountability Report: Fiscal Year 2004*, p. A-29.

109. David Eisner, "National Press Club Newsmaker Luncheon with David Eisner, CEO, Corporation for National and Community Service. Topic: National Service at 10 Years—Lessons Learned and Future Directions," National Press Club, Washington, D.C., December 14, 2004. Federal News Service, 2004, p. 10.

110. Waldman, *The Bill: How Legislation Really Becomes Law*, p. 241.

111. Editorial Board, "One Pledge Fits All," *San Francisco Chronicle*, November 29, 2002, p. A28.

112. Christopher Marquis, "Revised Pledge for AmeriCorps Draws Critics," *New York Times*, November 21, 2002.

113. Spokesman for the House Education and Workforce Committee David Schnittger quoted in Marquis, "Revised Pledge for AmeriCorps Draws Critics."

114. Editorial Board, "One Pledge Fits All"; Executive Director of the AmeriCorps Alumni Association Michael J. Meneer quoted in Marquis, "Revised Pledge for AmeriCorps Draws Critics."

115. Mauk quoted in Marquis, "Revised Pledge for AmeriCorps Draws Critics."

116. Corporation for National and Community Service, *Performance and Accountability Report: Fiscal Year 2002* (Washington: 2003), p. 15.

117. Corporation for National and Community Service, *Performance and Accountability Report: Fiscal Year 2003* (Washington: 2004), p. 27; Corporation for National and Community Service, *Performance and Accountability Report: Fiscal Year 2002*, p. 15; Marshall and Magee, *The AmeriCorps Experiment and the Future of National Service*, p. 23.

118. Abt Associates, *Serving Community and Country*, pp. 32–33.

119. Corporation for National and Community Service, *Performance and Accountability Report: Fiscal Year 2003*, pp. 31, 37, and 41; Corporation for National and Community Service, *FY 2008 CNCS Annual Financial Report, National Service Trust* (Washington: 2008), p. 3. In some cases, I have calculated attrition rates from completion or education award earning percentages. Fiscal year 2003 is the last year that rates were broken down by subprogram in the CNCS Performance and Accountability Reports.

120. Van Til, *Growing Civil Society*, p. 61.

121. Ibid.

122. Senator Edward M. Kennedy (D-Mass.) quoted in Senate Labor and Human Resources Committee, "Confirmation of Harris Wofford to Be CEO of the Corporation for National and Community Service," September 7, 1995. Federal News Service, 1995, p. 3.

123. Bruce Chapman, "Politics and National Service: A Virus Attacks the Volunteer Sector," in *National Service: Pro and Con*, edited by Williamson M. Evers (Stanford, Calif.: Hoover Institution Press, 1990), p. 134.

124. Bridgeland, Goldsmith, and Lenkowsky, "Service and the Bush Administration's Civic Agenda," p. 56.

125. Anonymous quoted in Ethiel, *National Service: Getting It Right*, p. 120.

126. Ibid.

127. Malik quoted in Van Til, *Growing Civil Society*, p. 55.

128. Bollman quoted in Ethiel, *National Service: Getting It Right*, p. 87.

129. Anonymous quoted in Ethiel, *National Service: Getting It Right*, p. 120.

130. Van Til, "The Case of AmeriCorps: Conflict and Consensus in the Civil Society/Governance Relation," p. 21.

131. Ibid.

Chapter 12

1. Paul Pierson, "Increasing Returns, Path Dependence, and the Study of Politics," *American Political Science Review* 94, no. 2 (June 2000), pp. 251–67.

2. Steven Waldman, *The Bill: How Legislation Really Becomes Law: A Case Study of the National Service Bill* (New York: Penguin Books, 1995), p. 5.

3. Quoted in David Broder, "Hard-Line Hostility for a Volunteer Initiative," *Washington Post*, September 4, 2002, p. A21.

4. Curt Weldon, excerpts from House floor debate, July 13, 1993. Reprinted in *Congressional Digest* 72, no. 10 (October 1993): 251.

5. Quoted in William H. Crook and Ross Thomas, *Warriors for the Poor: The Story of VISTA, Volunteers in Service to America* (New York: William Morrow and Co., 1969), p. 36.

6. Waldman, *The Bill: How Legislation Really Becomes Law.*

7. William R. Anderson, "Memorandum for the Attorney General, re: National Service Corps Legislation," December 5, 1963. In Robert F. Kennedy's Attorney General Files, 1960–1964, Box 41, Kennedy Presidential Library, Boston, Mass., p. 3.

8. VISTA, obviously, was created under unique presidential circumstances: Proposed by Kennedy but passed under Johnson, it was not strongly identified with either. Given its early conflicts with Democratic mayors and southerners, it was also not intimately identified with the Democratic Party, although it became more so over time. However, more than president or party, VISTA has been identified as a program of the Great Society, and benefited or suffered accordingly.

9. "Reneging on AmeriCorps," *New York Times*, March 15, 1995, p. A24.

10. Waldman, *The Bill: How Legislation Really Becomes Law*, p. 250.

11. Robert Bauman, excerpt from a statement submitted to the Special Subcommittee on Labor, House of Representatives. Reprinted in *Congressional Digest* 43, no. 1 (January 1964): 31.

12. Marion K. Sanders, "The Case for a National Service Corps," *New York Times*, August 7, 1966.

13. John A. Salmond, *Civilian Conservation Corps, 1933–1942: A New Deal Case Study* (Duke University Press, 1967), pp. 177–78.

14. Jonathan Rauch, *Government's End* (New York: PublicAffairs, 1999).

15. Carmen Sirianni and Lewis Friedland, *Civic Innovation in America* (University of California Press, 2001).

16. Peter Frumkin and JoAnn Jastrzab, *Serving Country and Community: Who Benefits from National Service?* (Harvard University Press, 2010), p. 227.

17. Ibid.; see also Ann Marie Thomson and James L. Perry, "Can AmeriCorps Build Communities?" *Nonprofit and Voluntary Sector Quarterly* 27, no. 4 (1998): 407.

18. Thomson and Perry, "Can AmeriCorps Build Communities?" 407.

19. Frumkin and Jastrzab, *Serving Country and Community*, pp. 224–26.

20. Sagawa quoted in Waldman, *The Bill: How Legislation Really Becomes Law*, p. 106.

21. Frumkin and Jastrzab cite City Year's successful move from engaging in multiple areas of work to focusing on education as a model, neglecting to highlight the differences between a private nonprofit organization narrowing its work and a government agency, accountable to Congress and subject to interest group pressure, doing so.

22. See Carmen Sirianni, *Investing in Democracy: Engaging Citizens in Collaborative Governance* (Brookings, 2009).

23. Dana Goldstein, "The 'Asset Effect,'" *Washington Monthly*, July-August 2012, pp. 31–32.

24. Michael Brown and others, "A Call to National Service," *American Interest Magazine*, January-February 2008.

25. Ibid.

26. Ibid.

Index